THE OTHER SIDE

First published in South Africa in 2017 by Print Matters Heritage an imprint of
Publishing Print Matters (Pty) Ltd
6 Opal Way, San Michel, Noordhoek 7979
Western Cape, South Africa
www.printmatters.co.za
www.facebook.com/PublishingPrintMatters
info@printmatters.co.za

ISBN: 978-0-9870095-4-8

Publisher: Robin Stuart-Clark
Editorial Panel: Luke Arnold, Rob Meintjes, Vanessa Swanepoel, Harvey Tyson
Design: Publishing Print Matters (Pty) Ltd
Formatting: The Design Drawer

Printed and Bound by Novus Print Solutions

Harvey Tyson

THE OTHER SIDE

Behind the news 1

Other books by Harvey Tyson

Editors Under Fire, Random House 1993 (with end-of-book contributions from Nelson Mandela, Helen Suzman and Lord McGregor, chairman of International Press Institute). "Awesome reminder that nothing like the events in this balanced, chilling account should ever be allowed to happen again" William C. Faure, film producer, head of Combined Artists and founder of TV's *Carte Blanche.*

A Walk on the Wild Side, Struik's Zebra Press 1995, and *Itch of the Twitch,* Struik's Zebra Press 1996. "As South African as Oom Schalk but ... more polished. Harvey Tyson is rapidly becoming a national institution" Jennifer Crwys-Williams, leading literary critic.

Have Wings,Will Fly, Editors Inc 1998. "A natural history classic, like 'The Plains of Camdeboo'." *The Star.*

Birders of a Feather, Editors Inc 1998 "A magnificent book to have on one's shelf, to read and read again!" poet Tatumkhulu Afrika.

Laugh the Beloved Country, Double Storey Books. Juta. 2003, compiled, edited by James Clarke and Harvey Tyson. "I couldn't stop laughing ..." Archbishop Desmond Tutu.

Blood on the Path. A Saga of the founding of South Africa, Springbok Press 2009. "... it puts the story back into history ..." Dr Guy Willoughby, playwright and professor of history.

A glance at the "the other side".

WHEN YOU ARE TOLD every day "get out of the office, go!" in order to witness and record some exciting or significant event or some horrifying or hilarious incident, then life cannot be boring. By good fortune that was my compelling, sometimes discomforting, job for all my "working days" over most of the 20th century, except for a mere 20 years of sitting at a desk telling others what to do and trying to make sense of what was happening locally, nationally and on the world scene. Even that was never boring.

So I thought I might share a few of these experiences with you to remind your family of their own memories of fun and fury ... knowing that inevitably your view of events must be quite different. This is a reminder too that everybody's history always has at least two sides and that, to be closer to reality, we need to be aware of the directly differing views of others, especially of those of ethnic cultures different from our own.

However, there is no consensus on how to replace the one-sided national history imposed on a nation by an apartheid government for half a century – or how to replace the equally one-sided colonial history of the highly disputed 100 years before South Africa was created. We should all be aware that, for a national history to be valid, it needs to be accepted by all sections of society.

To reach that goal is a painful exercise, made easier if we step back and contemplate the widest of all pictures of our past.

If we are to make sense of all our versions of modern history, we also need to be aware that our shared "yesterdays" were fashioned by the tumultuous times of the "day-before-yesterday", that is, the 1800s which still haunt all of us, especially the people of many cultures still seeking equality and true democracy in South Africa. That is why my own story – and yours, wherever you are – should begin more than a century before we or our parents were born. For the context of our personal short-term histories, we need to begin by looking at that markedly disruptive 19th century.

Thus PART ONE of my life-story begins in 1820, when a young lad named Wood (the source of my middle name, I discovered late in life) decided to escape to a place he did not know, called Africa. His and his family's life-story is a lesson to all of us, of all races I suggest, for it begins, not with belief or culture, but with *starvation and death* versus *survival and growth*.

The rest of this five-part book is a personalised account of the "ups" and the laughter, as well as the "downs" and the drama, concerning the events of the 20th century and ongoing struggles to publish freely "the truth", then and right now.

Harvey Wood Tyson – September 2017

Contents

1

Looking both ways.

1800 – 1900

1.
The boy who ran away.

Hark! The huge vessel felt the thund'ring stroke
While whelming waves in sudden deluge broke;
The seas around for horrid vengeance rave
And every yawning gulf now seems a grave.

A Wilmot, on sailing to Africa, 1820.

n the desperate days before 1820, London's streets seemed filled with one-armed, one-eyed, one-legged young men and countless street beggars who knew no skill except warfare. They remembered little but their own battle-weary suffering and their admiration of their one-eyed idol, the late Admiral Nelson, and their victorious army leader the Duke of Wellington and his famous footwear ... which, it was rumoured, featured in Lady Wellington's London diary in an unforgettable entry that read: "M'Lord came home from the wars today and pleasured me twice in his top boots." Few other war veterans could afford a square meal, let alone top boots. (However, you will hear later in this story that the strongest, biggest, possibly most powerful chieftain in Africa in those days, once proudly wore Wellington boots.)

A little boy in Kent at that time would get no kick out of such tales. But he should have been thankful to be living in the post-Napoleonic War days in a smart home outside London, not far from the Thames. Yet his misery was beyond telling (partly, one suspects, because he talked so little). His loving father was dead; his mother was remarried to his new stepfather who bullied the child and kept him close by. Stepfather was soon working the boy mercilessly every day at his greengrocer's shop, and probably at home at the weekends. He refused to allow the child to spend any time in one of several good, close-by schools. Wee Georgie Wood might have been a character from a Charles Dickens' novel ... except that he was six years older than Dickens.

Finally George ran away from home, telling nobody except, at the last moment, his younger brother. His plan for the year 1820 was to join the people setting out for Africa and a new life. He did not know that only government-approved, volunteering, registered families, rich and poor, would be allowed to sail. Desperately he hung about the docks until he met a carpenter, Richard Smith, accompanied by his wife and two sons, about to board one of the small ships, the *Aurora*. Smith agreed to take

14-year-old George Wood as "an apprentice", and made him sign for seven years of unpaid servitude ... lasting until the day he might reach 21.

The beginning of the great emigrant adventure was not auspicious. One of the passengers described years later the emotional scenes of "brothers clasping hands or falling on the necks of sisters by those who were never to look into each other's eyes again". Much of this last-minute sorrow was premature, for the ships about to leave found themselves suddenly trapped for two days in thick ice on the Thames.

George's problems, once aboard ship, were different. Instead of receiving apprentice-training, he was at the beck and call of his employer, doing all the domestic chores his master was instructed to do for his family while at sea. The regulations were petty, but strict, as was necessary on a crowded vessel: cleaning quarters, fetching rations, moving all bedding on deck at dawn – provided there was no rain or flying spume.

One of the passengers recalls a first experience of storm at sea: "It came on to blow tremendously hard, the sea running mountains high ... breaking over us in all directions, boxes, plates and dishes, men and women and children all mixed together, tumbling and seasick .... The sea broke into our cabin windows, dashing glass and frame in. The things that were below rolling and sliding, took to swimming ... then fire broke out aboard."

Passengers on the *Nautilus* recalled that, having escaped "ice blocks in the sea" and fire aboard, the ship then struck on the dreaded Goodwin Sands, while its companion ship, the *Chapman,* was forced to sail by. Friends on both ships, when beyond shouting distance, waved forlornly at each other.

Great joy came when the two ships were able to reunite at La Palma, the dramatic volcanic island at the outer edge of the Canary archipelago. All passengers were drained of emotion and words. One wrote later of reuniting with her friend on the other sailing ship:

"... At four in the afternoon we spoke to her; all well. Only lost four children, had nine births," she recorded laconically.

Crowded on board the small vessel *Aurora,* relationships between the resentful apprentice, 14-year-old George, and Richard Smith and his two sons became increasingly strained. But Mrs Smith was kind to the boy and he responded warmly. When she fell ill he volunteered to work for nothing in the ship's galley in order to obtain pieces of meat he could boil down to broth and carry to her cabin. He probably mentioned this incident to his children only because he remembered it as one of those occasions when a passenger had laughed at him.

The long awaited arrival came months later. After rounding the long-awaited stormy Cape ("now the Cape of Good Hope," one passenger recorded hopefully) they finally anchored in Algoa Bay. The arrival was "anything but cheery" wrote one of the Londoners, John Centlivres Chase. He recalled: "From the deck we descried a coast lashed by a broad belt of angry breakers threatening, we feared, death for many aboard."

Beyond he saw barren sand hills, a series of "rugged and stony acclivities and, in the distance the dark and gloomy range of the Winterhoek mountains".

Settlers were lowered into "surf-boats" and pulled through the alarming bad-weather breakers into the shallow waters where they could wade ashore. Their wives and children followed, but were carried to the beach by waiting soldiers.

"And there they all stood, from the pages of a Jane Austen book," wrote May Bell, a near-blind 1820 descendant whose astonishing feats are described later.

She wrote that on the desolate southern African shore were "tight-trousered men and high-waisted women, excited little girls long-gowned and bonneted, little boys in long trousers fastened with big brass buttons to their jackets ..."

One child was murdered for those buttons, settlers remembered for years afterwards. But intimate, personal memories of that moment of landing remained far more vivid. A woman recalled, sitting with relief on land, contemplating a huge pile of dirty washing left over from her ship's cabin. At home, she was never allowed to wash anything. All used clothing was always removed by the staff. Who will do my washing now? She looked up at a penetrating blue sky and burst into tears.

But it wasn't the washing, was it? It was the cloying knowledge that she suddenly had no home, no roof over her head; no adequate protection for her children.

One small girl was soon bitten by a snake, a puff-adder, and died within days, despite the new arrivals' instant, ignorant, painful care. And on the first night in the dark, away from the fires, they heard wild, frightening noises.

Hearing the sounds of the wild on the first night ashore was the worst experience many families could recall later. One of the settlers,

HH Dugmore, remembered different circumstances when he was finally settled on his farm: "The shrill yell of the jackal and the hyena's howl were the regular nightly serenade ... by day the leopard's deep bass sounded for hours together among the krantzes, and there was the enormous responsive call of the wild dog, as the pack ranged ravenously."

Pleasant memories for a huntsman, but frightening first-night sounds and nightmares for mothers, cast ashore with babes in their arms.

Worse than all these travellers' memories continued to be the fear on land of silent, poisonous snakes, especially when mothers and children slept on open ground at night. One woman wore thick thigh-high stockings every night in the hopes this would "save" her. Their hired *boer* wagon drivers might have laughed at all the antics, but they had been in Africa since birth. And sitting beside a fire in the dark with a wagon and a gun was easier than being an "abandoned novice in the wild".

Colonel Jacob Glen Cuyler, who rode beside the massive wagon trains on their six-day ride to the allotted farms, pondered on what would become of these people, many of whom had never carried a spade or held a plough ... though even he could not have imagined the scene at Bathurst later, when two "farmers" were observed trying to round up the government-issue cattle granted to them, and which were nearly lost very soon to cattle thieves. The two farmers drove off the thieves, but were seen running about, extraordinarily dressed in coat-tails and baggy long-trousers, and seemingly helpless in driving home their cattle.

Another still unsettled settler needed to slaughter one of his sheep to feed his family. There was no one to look to for advice or help. Instead the settler and his sons took it in turns to try to obtain mutton, each of them running at the sheep shouting and hoping to end its misery and theirs with the wild stab of a knife.

Col Cuyler might shake his head over these fast-travelling stories, but thinking of more serious realities on the frontier, he realised that when he advised a party to carry a gun, he had not known that the alien innocents thought a gun was needed merely for protection from the nightly noises of the hyenas and an occasional leopard.

No wonder the settlers loved the resourceful, caring expertise of Piet Retief, living at the Winterhoek, above the shore on which they had first set foot in Africa. He assisted them wherever he saw them. How they would miss his capable experience of Africa when he and his fellow *boere* set off on their long trek away from the settlers and the Xhosa spears!

From their temporary new homesteads the settlers saw bush-covered or empty territory all around them. They firmly believed that they had been "given" their land, but it was offered with the unspoken and unforeseen risk of losing their property, their new homes and their lives. They had not "taken" the land, they honestly believed.

None of the 1820 newcomers facing unfamiliar or life-threatening problems would have appreciated that their fate was vaguely understood, and known *only* to the Colonial Office in London. The seemingly abandoned settlers' numbers amounted to a mere several hundred families and meant nothing to the general public or government in Britain, which saw 240000 countrymen settling abroad in that disruptive era. The 1820 Settlers contained a small but unusual number of teachers, preachers, doctors, lawyers and restless gentlemen – but never enough craftsmen, farmers or labourers who, in any case, had no intention whatever of serving the migrating gentry.

George Wood, at the end of his voyage a strongly built and tall 15-year-old, had worse things to worry about as they arrived in the hardly perceptible bay with its far, seemingly empty horizons. He had been told by "Master" Smith that he was about to be sent back to England in the same ship – on Smith's orders. George resolved to escape. He could confide in no one, nor seek advice, for fear of being reported to the captain; or Smith. He was suddenly alone in an unknown situation just a hundred dangerous yards from an unknown land. He could not have known how to swim for he had lived too far from the Thames' sometimes dangerous tidal waters to be able to walk there. His stepfather would never have given him time for such frivolities. The boy had learned to read and write, however; possibly taught by his mother clandestinely. His possessions were the clothes he wore or carried. He did not have a penny, not even a farthing. His childhood home "learning" was his only asset ... but it would not help him get to shore without official help. ☐

2.

When your best friend is killed.

A friend is worth all the hazards we can run.

Arthur Young 1741-1820

Only months later do we hear of George again, following his critical moment aboard the departing *Aurora*, when he stood half-hidden, perhaps, and watching other excited children and frightened mothers being transported ashore to rejoin their "brave" husbands. There is no mention anywhere of his escape from the ship, or how he followed the settlers being carried in wagons to their appointed farms, most of which seemed too small to render profitable in the southern climate.

All we know is that he appeared before a newly appointed magistrate in the new village of Graham's Town, months later in December of that fateful year. He was before the Law again, in order to be duly apprenticed once more. No doubt it was at his sole urging again, but this time to a wagon-maker named William Thackwray. This time his apprenticeship would be for six years.

Thackwray's son, John, was a kind-hearted lad and became George's closest friend. John may have come upon the stranded boy and brought him to his father for help. But this is speculation …. Later young Thackwray took to trading, and chances are that young Wood led Thackwray's oxen, and that an anxious father had released "an uncommunicative" or "difficult" apprentice so that his son might have a companion to help him on his hazardous trips to trade with the Xhosa people.

The trips were "hazardous" according to settler Henry Dugmore because they involved "the stealthy crossing of the border, the appointed meeting-place beyond it, the life-in-hand venture into the power of Xhosas, the danger of army patrols, risk of being waylaid" and so on.

The Colonial Government's ban on settlers trading with their neighbours was one of half a dozen curbs on the settlers' freedom which they deeply resented. In defiance, trading with eager Xhosa families became so common that finally the government formalised it by arranging trade fairs at far away Fort Wiltshire.

But John Thackwray had had enough, and set out to be an elephant hunter. George, an instinctive and attested "loner" apparently, sought no other friendships, and continued alone, trading with Xhosas on a greater scale. But, despite his habit of silence, he served his neighbours well, apparently. A man who had known George told his granddaughter that "wherever there was trouble, he would be called in to help; whenever there was a dangerous river to cross, Wood was the first man to cross it".

Marrying on the edge of manhood

George, at the age of 20 (not yet an adult and therefore, technically still in the final year of his London-registered or locally-registered apprenticeship) married a 15-year-old girl who – like him years before – suffered abuse from her stepfather. The youngsters were formally married by a preacher allegedly drunk at the time, and George was angry, probably beyond his customary few words.

In any event he changed, there and then, from the Anglican Church to the famous Reverend Barnabas Shaw's Methodist Church. (The plausible "other side" of the story here is that the Anglican preacher may have lectured the couple for marrying so young and that he performed the rites perhaps unceremoniously and with little grace .... In any event, the couple's first child was born after Wood became an officially recognised, independent adult and his wife Susan, a "Sweet Sixteen".)

The Wood family lived for several years in a small house in Graham's Town, but later he and Susan – who must have been exceedingly devoted – moved northwards, into the "wilds" with their two children. George sought out his friend. He also identified a promising site to create a new business with peaceful nearby Xhosa clans. This was the tiny settlement next to Fort Brown where George's only friend had become a professional elephant-hunter among the nearby mountain-ravines, far from Xhosa kraals and "civilisation". The Wood family thrived in their makeshift home in the small settlement around the fort. Soon George owned a very successful trading store. But John Thackwray was away often in the dense bush of the mountain ravines. And often he accompanied, as a guide, the explorer Andrew Steedman, who praised John's hunting skills – until the day Steedman came home and reported:

"We were on an elephant hunt. Making our way through the entangled forest we arrived at an eminence, when Thackwray exclaimed, 'There they are!' Descending a dark ravine to approach the elephants, unobserved, we were compelled to dismount and lead our horses over the roots of trees and branches that had been torn up and scattered by the animals in their progress. Thackwray and his assistant loaded their rifles."

The sun had set, and as the hunters crept through the dusk an elephant came straight towards them. At forty yards, both Thackwray and his equally expert Khoi assistant fired. The elephant fell and died. But "the report of the guns and the screams of the wounded animal had disturbed a whole herd, which rushed down the valley with tremendous violence, bending and crushing in their descent whatever opposed their progress."

Susan listened to these hunting stories with increasing unease. George would have viewed such adventures as foolhardy and insufficiently rewarding. Then, one day, the missionary John Ayliff reported from his Mission House across the frontier in Xhosaland:

"Two wagons were seen approaching the Mission House ... one of them contained the body of a young man named John Thackwray, a noted elephant shooter who was killed by an elephant yesterday afternoon .... It appears he had shot the elephant and it had fallen. When he and a Hottentot went up to it, suddenly it sprang up and the Hottentot escaped by the skin of his teeth by running under its body .... The elephant caught Thackwray, and the next thing the Hottentot saw was the creature in its agonies of death running away with the young man rolled up in his trunk. He was found soon after quite dead."

Death and human violence were increasing all along the frontier. George and his family were forced to retreat from Fort Brown to Graham's Town. It seemed calm in 1834, but in hindsight there was the ominous sign of border trouble when the random cattle-rustling of the Xhosa turned into organised horse-stealing.

At Christmas the *Graham's Town Journal* led its edition with:

"Reports of the most distressing kind keep pouring into town from various quarters."

Ensign Sparks and his small militia were attacked. Then on Christmas Eve, Xhosa warriors advanced on the town, mopping up homesteads as they came. One of the first incidents involved the Whitfields whose home was razed and stock stolen. (Sparks and Whitfield are among the names of editors of several top newspapers of the 20th century which supported equal rights for black and white in South Africa.)

Some of the Whitfield menfolk were murdered, but the older Whitfield boy was told,*"Hamba. Baleka."* (Go! Run!) He, his younger brother and two sisters ran into "the bush". Their treatment foreshadowed a war that would be both merciful – and treacherous. Mercy and treachery were confusingly exhibited by Xhosa parties bent on burning and looting all homesteads. In the village of Salem, for instance, Richard Gush, a Quaker, rode out to meet a terrifying horde of "running, leaping, shrieking" tribesmen. He removed his jacket and spread his upheld hands to indicate that he was unarmed. Two leaders emerged from the sudden stilled horde. Gush gave them token gifts of bread and tobacco and a lecture on the sinfulness of attacking peaceful people. Because of – or despite –his words, the Xhosa tribesmen decided not to attack Salem.(It is reported that, in all the years of warring which followed, only one white woman was murdered by Xhosas – and not one woman was raped. As in all wars, statistics are unreliable, but the culture of the Xhosas was that men fought wars, and women and children were to be left alone.)

On the other hand, no sooner did one band of warriors turn back from attacking a settler family, when two other settlers, Brown and Whittaker, in the fortified brewery at Clay Pits outside Graham's Town, were murdered. They had been promised safe conduct. When they came out, alone and showing they were unarmed, they were stoned to death.

IT WAS IN this civil emergency over the Christmas-New Year of 1834–5 that Sir Harry Smith, rejecting the delays of a sea-journey, rode about 540 miles (nearly 870km) from Cape Town to Graham's Town on relays of horses. It took him six days. One of his first actions when he reached the threatened town after meeting Colonel Henry Somerset, was to summon the Commandant of the Town Guard, George Wood who, aged 28, was now a respected and highly successful merchant, but ready to volunteer for any service.

George was gazetted Captain of a body of sharpshooters, but within a fortnight was promoted to Major, and deputed to lead a "Hottentot Corps". To everyone's surprise he immediately chose a Khoi leader as his senior officer and personal aide.

At this time he may have remembered a settler tale of the days when he landed in this wild country at the age of 15. A youngster of the Aylff family, about George's age, had gone looking for something to eat soon after they set foot on the shore of Africa. The boy had been given by a passing Dragoon, the local phrase for the question, *"Is this good to eat?"*

"As I went among the bushes I saw some beautiful black berries, and a Hottentot a little way off, so I called out pretty loudly to him: 'I say, Hottentot, is this berry *good for skof*?'" wrote Ayliff.

"He looked at me very hard. He said: 'What for you call me Hottentot?' I said, 'Well, you are, ain't you.' And he said. 'Ja, ik is, but we don't like to be called Hottentots.' He was angry and walked off. But seeing some little Hottentots, quite naked, I showed them the berries and asked, *'Good for skof?'* They looked at me, showing their beautiful white teeth, set up a hearty laugh at me, and off they darted into the bushes."

One day when Major Wood, with his Khoi troops, was among the hot, dry,and grim hills of Hell's Poort, a message came from the Xhosas that they had with them a white child and would give her to any white man who would ride out, alone and unarmed, to fetch her. It might be a ruse, as was the case with the men very recently stoned to death at the Clay Pits when told they were safe to approach. The major thought it over, and decided to go himself. He rode, openly unarmed and alone, to the appointed spot many miles from the town. A black man appeared on a horse, and silently handed him a little girl. She was only three and was "plainly terrified", for she flung her arms around George Wood's neck and clung tightly to him as he retreated from the open spot. He took the child home to Susan, and they cared for her with their own children, until he was able to trace the child's parents after the feverish times of war had been concluded. ☐

3.

When silence does not pay.

We do not quite forgive a giver.

Ralph Waldo Emerson. 1803-1882.

The peaceful era surrounding the 1850s signalled the arrival of settled conditions for the first time. "Farmers brought their produce to Graham's Town's Market Square and traders their far-fetched wares – ivory, ostrich feathers, rhinoceros horns, beautiful skin karrosses," wrote May Bell.

"The assemblage in the market square", wrote the Reverend Shaw "is likewise a kind of public exchange, where the merchants and dealers meet."

George Wood was now one of the merchants. By this time he was living in Port Elizabeth, "The Bay", and "thought nothing of riding on horseback through the night, and going off after breakfast to his usual hard day of work. By this time he had already made an immense fortune, chiefly out of wool," wrote Bell.

To commute between "The Bay" at Port Elizabeth to "the capital of GT" (not to be confused with Gin & Tonic in that disciplined, multi-church society) was no easy undertaking. Wood probably bought or hired horse stalls at, say, Sundays River crossing and the village of Salem, for his regular return journey of about 150 miles. Riding at night was the quickest method, but in his later years he would have used carriage horses to pull his light cart over the bumpy track across the long, empty landscape.

Wood seemed "not eager to make more" money than he had already done. At the same time he "was too shrewd to make bad bargains. He was impatient of fools, and cared nothing for anybody's opinion."

Put another way he seems to have been abrupt, unreceptive, and did not make friends. He seemed anything but a nice, easygoing fellow settler.

Two stories were told of him:

A man who was repaying him a large sum of money found he was "half-a-crown" short and said easily, "I expect you won't say anything about the half-crown," (a coin, the biggest in small-change, once worth 25cents).

"On the contrary, sir," said Wood grimly, "I want that half-crown if you please. It is men who are careful about half-crowns who are able to lend them to men like you."

They met on the market several times, but the debtor said nothing about the half-crown. One day Wood said, "Sir, you owe half-a-crown, and I will not release your bond until you pay me." It was paid then and there.

On the other hand, when a creditor wrote to remind Wood that a promissory note was about to fall due, he replied, "I have not forgotten." The creditor wrote to remind him again. Wood wrote out a cheque for the large amount due and sent it to the Commissariat, asking the Paymaster to oblige him by letting him have the sum in coppers. The creditor received the full amount in a wheelbarrow pushed by the gardener.

"It is not surprising that Wood had many enemies," wrote Bell. "He kept his charities as secret as his feelings. There was one particularly bitter enemy whose fortunes sank as Wood's rose. Bad luck seemed to increase the man's enmity; gradually he lost everything and would have been destitute but for a sum paid regularly by an unknown donor. By this time his hatred of Wood had become an obsession, and he lost no chance to vilify him. Only after Wood's death was it discovered that he had been his enemy's unknown benefactor.

The Reverend Walton said of Wood: "I know of some of his princely donations to charitable institutions, and of his private charities. If there was any case of real distress unrelieved (in this community) I will be bold to say that George Wood did not know of it."

Wood, it transpired, also subscribed regularly to overseas hospitals and orphanages, including always Dr Barnardo's Homes. His charitable spending continued for another generation, when Josie Wood set up the first Library for the Blind in South Africa and helped create and finance what was to become the National Council for the Blind after the birth of South Africa.

Yet with his complete indifference to what anyone thought of him, he was generally considered to be close-fisted.

May Bell wrote: "In his old age he took his family to Paris and while there visited an artists' gallery with his daughters. He was standing absorbed in some picture when one of the girls noticed that a stylish

Frenchwoman on the other side of the room was staring at him intently, even rudely. He was perhaps a noticeable figure, taller and broader than most men there, sunburnt, and not dressed quite as they were, but that did not justify the stare. His daughter, a little uncomfortable, was drawing her sisters' attention to it when suddenly the elegant lady ran across the room, flung her arms round his neck and to his surprise exclaimed: "Oh, my dear Mr Wood!" It was the little girl he had rescued after the Clay Pits massacre, now married to a Frenchman, and delighted to invite the Woods to meet her husband and see her happy home."

NEARLY HALF a century after May Bell's research provided Wood a properly documented place in the widely witnessed and recorded 1820 Settler history, he stood posthumously accused in the late 20th century of making his fortune by chicanery among the innocent Xhosa people while he was still a boy. As a youth he did defy the Colonial Government edict of "no trading with the natives". My own elders' version, however repudiates as a demonstrable lie both the gossip and a mention in re-written history's version, of his "chicanery". One side of the story is that, in his youth, instead of selling to those trusting souls the three-legged metal cooking pots they so eagerly wanted, he showed them a sample, but gave them only a strange seed to plant and took their wares with the promise that the proffered "seed" would grow the following year into the desired pot. It is assumed (an assumption originally based on envy, today based on one-sided "historical reappraisal of history") that, like the proverbial American travelling salesman of later times, he then vanished with the "cash".

A good story. It also fits a convenient mould of current prejudice. But the apparently true and original version – was the one which only George Wood himself was able to tell. He did so proudly, but only within the family.

One of his earliest ventures after teaming up with John Thackwray was to trade with black families beyond the Fish and Kei rivers (the "Ciskei"), bringing to Xhosa families the metal utensils they greatly desired and any other item they sought. Soon he had bartered enough to hire a wagon himself and take an entire load of three-legged pots across the frontier, where they caused, in modern parlance, a "sensation". When his wagon-load of stock was sold out, he told disappointed buyers in Xhosa:

"Trade with me, now, for this 'seed' (a bullet!) and plant it carefully, and next season I promise you will have a (metal) pot."

Whether this was taken literally by the Xhosa pastoralists, as some arrogant and educated whites tend to assume, or more probably symbolically as seems logical, we do not know. But George Wood built up a stable trade by returning often, earning a wide reputation in Xhosaland, and supplying as promised, a pot to every Xhosa man and woman who produced one of his paid bullet "deposits". It was a reputation that made the teenage "loner" both independent and – despite his silence – trusted on both sides of the Kei and Fish Rivers.

While he later led his community as an administrator, a soldier and political leader, his chief aim in life appeared to be no more than ensuring his own family possessed the security and relationships he himself had been cruelly denied. Thus his first two sons became the first two mayors of "the city of Graham's Town" and led the fight for equality of settlers' rights and possibly even separation from Cape Town government.

What seems to remain unchallenged in the "1820" history is the extraordinary fact that the settlers' enduring grievance was not against their black frontier neighbours but against their white rulers in Cape Town. They protested on the grounds that there were as many ex-British citizens in the East of the colony as in the Western Cape, and that the settlers were under-represented in the colony's new (white) Legislative Council, which was interested only in its own parochial affairs. They said that the civil service had no inkling of what services were justifiably required in would-be rivals Graham's Town and Port Elizabeth.

At last, in 1863, the new Governor of the Cape, Sir Philip Wodehouse, announced that, for the first time, the "Parliament" would assemble in the capital of the "Frontier Province". Its main town had been proclaimed a city, with a recognised city council, only the year previously. The community had only just appointed its first mayor, "young George Wood" (George the elder had retired from public life yet again). "Young George" was hurriedly elected a member of the "Eastern" party in the so-called Cape Parliament.

George Wood junior, by all accounts, was no speech-maker. He was described as "a plain man who says directly what he believes should be said, and only when it was deemed necessary to say it".

George's father, "famous throughout the land", according to his younger contemporaries, had journeyed for 20 years in his old age to

A scene from central Grahamstown in the early 1900s. The city was benefitting from the influx of scholars to its many educational establishments. It also prospered, like most towns in South Africa, from the opening of the Transvaal gold fields. Grahamstown soon became known, through its many different places of worship, as the 'City of Saints'.

attend the contentious Cape Town sessions. Getting there was a terrible experience, easily shrugged off by Cape Town members who refused to leave Cape Town. The start of the journey for George Wood Senior was described thus:

"Even strong men found it difficult to keep their seats for a day or two in the rough hilly drive over unmade roads from Bathurst to The Bay, after which (the elderly Wood) had to be carried on a man's back, rowed through the breakers, and pulled above the surging seas on a rope to get aboard the swaying ship. The stout wicker chair still exists, with thick ropes spliced to it in which he was tied and hauled up on deck. The performance was once watched, "heart-in mouth", by a witness to the "paralysed elder enduring the swaying, tossing exercise".

Governor Wodehouse ensured that the whole of the Cape Legislative Council had to endure the same long return journey by sea which the Western Cape's members had so casually dismissed as "irrelevant" in the past. Now the Parliament was in session in Graham's Town where the entire assembly was hosted to a banquet of welcome by the mayor, George Wood Junior. The visitors were then challenged in parliamentary debate next day by the same man wearing his newly acquired colonial Legislative Council gown.

"No", said Wood woodenly, as an opening bat at cricket might have to do.

"What do you mean, 'No'?" asked the Leader of the House. "I mean 'No'. This is rather too hasty draft legislation on too important a matter."

"Well, we shall have to refer it to a committee!" (A committee dominated by the Western visitors, impatient to go home.) The Speaker: "I must point out that the Second Reading of the Bill cannot be passed if there is an objection."

George junior stood up: "Then I object."

In so few words was the debate ended. There was no choice but to shelve the bill. George had made his point by outwitting "the system". He had frustrated an inevitable and constant majority-vote by the united Cape Towners. But the ambition of Wood Senior and Junior, to find support for an equally-ruled or separate province in the east, was never achieved, despite all their future efforts.

The Honourable George Wood Senior remained a truly astonishing man, and managed to escape history by being even more uncommunicative than his sons – who included the second son John Edwin Wood, second mayor of Graham's Town. The "Old Man's" chequered lifetime contained possibly the most remarkable achievements of any in southern Africa at that eventful time. Yet Wood was a misfit; not old enough to be a registered original settler, not belonging to any registered settler family, and operating hugely, yet silently in white politics. Mainly because of his extraordinary reticence, none of this was recorded for posterity ... until May Bell researched her family history and published it in the mid-20th century, just as apartheid history was about to be written and end all interest, possibly forever, in the plight of white 1820 Settlers disowned by their own forebears.

However, even George Wood's grandson, Joseph Wood, also became a mayor of their city – as well as a member of the Cape Legislative Council – and a voluntary, active soldier. His history is worth a glance for historical reasons unrelated to the settlers' Frontier Wars and their colonial disputes. ☐

4.
Joseph Wood's anger at the cross Rhodes.

Since man to man is so unjust
No man can tell what man to trust.

Anon.

Joseph Wood, like his grandfather long before him, became a leading figure in the settler community ... but though he also became a member of the Cape Legislative Council, he clashed with Cecil Rhodes in the legendary Tati Goldfields area beyond the Limpopo, and protested that Rhodes had exceeded Cape law in pressing his ambitions.

At a relatively young age Joseph – the only male of the family not a member of the company George Wood and Sons – was appointed colonel of a voluntary group of the Cape Mounted Yeomanry. When adventure beckoned, he lowered his army rank in order to be able to volunteer to go to the help of the late Chief Moshoeshoe's British-protected Basutoland. He found himself leading a group of volunteers in one of the unsuccessful sieges of the Moorosi rebels in the southern part of the Basotho kingdom.

It was only through Joseph's history that I ever heard of the little-known battle for Moorosi's Mountain. It was an epic which remains as dramatic and brave as any recorded military clash in southern Africa's history.

It involved three engagements of armed, hand-to-hand combat and months of sieges in 1879. It resulted in no less than three Victoria Crosses being awarded to British military volunteers involved in scaling a cliff-face on long ladders, under heavy rifle fire. It led to the brave death of a famous Phuthi chief and many of his warriors who defied the sons of Chief Moshoeshoe ... and the British army.

Accounts of this prolonged siege and battle are inclined to tread on the prejudices of South Africans of all colours. Yet very few are aware of these dramatic and historic clashes. They were fought, not by Wood's part-time volunteers, who were soon withdrawn in favour of British military experts to tackle Moorosi's long-prepared mountain-top fortress. The valour and skill displayed by both sides fighting on a mountain peak ranks (though not in the size of forces deployed) with the great Zulu battles of Isandlwana and Ulundi which were occurring in the same period.

Three times in the mountains of the baSotho, colonial troops, backed by tribesmen loyal to their late leader Chief Moshoeshoe, fought to capture Chief Moorosi and his baPhuthi gun-wielding renegades.

The renegades were hidden on a mountain-top surrounded on three sides by steep cliffs and on the fourth side by high walls with gun-slits for the well-armed, well provisioned fortress. The refuge had even been stocked over the years with a cattle kraal, in anticipation of an event such as this. A siege was easily withstood. Only direct attack could work — and that could be achieved only by single men scaling the cliffs on ladders.

Two soldiers came close to death in the attempt. Two soldiers were awarded the Victoria Cross. So was a military surgeon at the scene of the battles. It was the kind of military encounter from which legends are usually made.

Instead, history has almost forgotten the bloody battles that led to the death of Moorosi and many of his fighters. George McCall Theal's history, Eric Anderson Walker's history, Jeffrey B Peires's histories and several other South African history books have no word of it. (Monica Wilson and Leonard Thompson's *A History of South Africa to 1870* at least mentions his name ... but the dramatic battle did not occur until 1879).

Fortunately, South Africa's Military History Society has researched and recounted that eight-month confrontation involving the long siege and three battles on the mountain. It is an astonishingly detailed account, listing all the units; each operation; the commanders and even details such as which soldier shot Moorosi and what happened. Also the military recorded precise times such as: *At 12.30am an attempt was made* (after midnight!) *on the mountain by scaling up a fissure, which became known as Bourne's Crack ....*

Daring attempts, cunning defences, victory and tragedy are noted in neutral terms, with no sense of drama. The drama lives instead in the cold, detailed facts.

Deaths on Moorosi's side alone mounted to "some 200", while about "120 of his men escaped by jumping into the Orange River".

The full story was compiled by Hamish Paterson of the South African Military History Society – Johannesburg(Military History Journal, Vol 15 No 1 June 2010). It carries a depiction of Moorosi's Mountain, standing on a bend in the Orange River near the Lesotho border.

Later Colonel Joseph Wood served for nearly a decade in the

Cape Parliament. Instead of seeking the usual rewards of being a senior politician who was white and privileged, however, he set off with some friends in a wagon to seek adventure beyond the Limpopo River. He may have been lured by the legends of King Solomon, the Queen of Sheba, and the golden treasures of Ophir – but you have to really *want* to believe such romantic notions before you can entertain them, let alone believe them. Wood would not rush off to follow a fable. He may not really have been wildly enthusiastic even about joining in southern Africa's first recorded gold rush that began beyond the Limpopo two decades earlier, in the 1870s.

He did go to Tati, but the book Joseph Wood subsequently wrote about his trip was mainly about his ox wagon and the fabulous landscapes he and his companions discovered beyond the Limpopo.[1] He describes the constant encounters with African wildlife and his meetings with two of Africa's kings. He meets a San family out hunting, and admires their skills and style. The women seek unerringly for melons in the dry riverbeds, he notes. They and the children carry pointed sticks for their hunting tasks; the men carry bows and arrows ... walking miles and never losing their way. "There are places that are really wild, with an explorer reporting sixty lions in a single sighting." In this environment, Joseph Wood smokes dried Mopani tree leaves to experience what the locals do: "Tried and approved it," he writes.

But he did not approve of everything he learned in the months spent in the kraal of King Lobengula in "Buluwayo", including the great chief's taste for brutality and French champagne. "The King had no difficulty in accepting and carrying off all the champagne and biscuits in our possession." Lobengula drank it even while holding court from a box on his wagon, which was his home in preference to a traditional hut. "His dress was of the most restricted description, consisting merely of a band around his loins," but every word from the king was a command that had to be obeyed ... such as killing men and women who irritated him.

Lobengula had his favourite queens "always in attendance: each easily identified as royalty by the colour of her beads and by a small round ornament made of some sticky substance which is stuck on the back part of her head". Her hair remained in place but was shaved by using a piece of glass kept in the sticky substance at the back.

Another quirk identified in the king's life is that his "war doctor", perhaps the most powerful man in his kingdom is "strange to say a Fingoe from the Cape Colony where his people are regarded as mere slaves". The Fingo is instrumental in Wood's party being allowed to tour Mashonaland and the goldfields, where Mashona women are constantly "washing gold", using wooden dishes with a central hollow where the gold settles. Wood's party finds "no river where gold is not present". It is taken from the river beds and even from soil on the river banks, sorted by very vigorous hand-washing, and sold to Portuguese traders.

"The value of gold does not seem to be adequately known …. There is a strange superstition that if the occasional gold nugget is taken out of the river or its banks, no more gold will grow." Wood believed that if the white miners had only followed the Mashona way of extracting gold – instead of using an antiquated steam-driven stamping plant – they might have prospered at Tati.

The world may not have known much of all that Wood recorded of his impressions, were it not for Wood's compulsive need to "go public" with a book about his clash with Cecil Rhodes concerning the future of the disputed Tati Goldfields. (You can read the meticulous account online simply by calling up his full name: Joseph Garbett Wood.)

He published all available official documents and some scathing things about Rhodes's use of cavalry to ride north and "arrest a Member of the Legislative Council on the trumped up charge of stirring up trouble" between the two kings: Khama and the king of the powerful Matabele, who both claimed possession of the goldfield.

What Rhodes had done when he got wind of Wood's presence in the goldfield – which Rhodes wanted in his drive to connect Cape Town with Cairo –was to persuade the Cape authorities to detain Wood for "inciting unrest among the natives". Wood, like his grandfather George a man of very few words, was beyond speech with fury, especially when Rhodes followed Wood's footsteps back to Chief Lobengula and commandeered the mineral rights of all of Matabeleland.

One could write a book about the late 1800s goldrush to the ancient mine – with shafts dug deep in the past (and in the ground, to a depth of 50 feet, four stories down!). But many books have already been written and the best of them I believe you will find as a carefully researched general read is *The Baronet and the Savage King*[2] – offering no disputable "philosophical history" – but instead providing mainly the quotes of people "who were there", and whose words have withstood the test of time. None of these witnesses subscribed to the legends of former aliens in the area, or sought King Solomon's minions, or the Queen of Sheba's land of Ophir, or the legendary "She".

Author David Hilton-Barber's *The Savage King* provides long passages of vivid quotes from valuable historical, but unpublished documents (some of them come from his own Barber forebear). For instance, long meetings with Lobengula are described in two of those hitherto unpublished memoirs. The one is Dr DJ Cook's memoir in which he says the giant Lobengula (standing six-foot-ten and weighing more than an estimated 300 lbs) had a "great weakness" for drinking huge amounts of home-brewed beer – or French champagne – from a large basin.

Hilton-Barber's own great-great-uncle, whose memoirs also have not been published before, adds long descriptive passages of the scene in Bulawayo in that era. Fred Barber wrote: "We could not but admire his jaunty and dignified carriage, powerful build and massive limbs .... Around his waist was a great apron of cat and monkey tails, completely encircling his loins. But sunshine, a few ivory rings and brass armlets were his only attire. His hair was worked up to an apex, surrounded on the top by an oily shining ring, or *sekethla*. His face was pleasant in conversation, with a humorous twinkle in the eye. He was ready-witted and loved a joke, a grand savage, and every inch a king, a fit ruler."

But, wrote Barber, after witnessing Lobengula regaled in British costume, for the sake of his guests: "... he wore a pair of Wellington boots, and a spreading brown, wide-awake felt hat covered his sable brow. It was absurd, ridiculous. 'Loben' in European clothes was no longer a king, the dignity of his savage majesty was gone."

Here is Barber's memorable description of Lobengula reviewing and inspecting his army:

This was a magnificent sight. A great dusky phalanx of sable warriors, seven or eight thousand strong, each regiment under its own induna and distinguished by different coloured shields covered with bullock hide. Marking time with measured tread, they chanted solemn dirges and war songs, striking their shields with assegais, while distinguished warriors would bound from the ranks, spring into the air, stabbing and thrusting as if in desperate combat, each thrust signifying a man ... killed. Sometimes in his excitement a man would make too many stabs, and be greeted with howls and shouts of derision from his companions for lying, when he would retire crestfallen to the ranks."

Historical colour of this standard, provided without comment or "interpretation" is a privilege to behold. A form of history-reading in which you can make your own hindsight judgements of those of solid, contemporary witnesses. *The Baronet and Savage King* also deals deftly with the two highly disputed issues of 1820 history:

It reminds us that Lobengula was the son of the dreaded Zulu rebel, Mzilikazi, whose section of the tribe travelled like Vikings through several lands, plundering and killing. It also reminds us that Mzilikazi's best friend for life was the missionary Robert Moffat. He liked the missionary so much he insisted on giving his "father's name" to Moffat. The white missionary and the black marauder were "best friends" for the 30 years before Mzilikazi's death.

So far as Joseph Wood was concerned, after his meeting and help from Lobengula he was so angry at Rhodes and his audaciously illegal methods that he quit Parliament and was elected instead mayor of the frontier capital, Grahamstown, where he died years later in office. The local newspapers (though not *The Eastern Star,* which quit publishing in Grahamstown and would move its printing press by rail and ox-wagon to the mining camp of Johannesburg in 1886–87), reported a city council motion of condolences to Wood's widow at the death of one of the most upright and intelligent of its citizens.

Hem-hem, an upright colonialist!

His niece married my grandfather John Daughtrey Tyson who, as Commissioner of Food Supplies, also disagreed with Rhodes later, during the siege of Kimberley during the Anglo Boer War. It was only when I was a cadet reporter, posted to that city half-a-century later that I discovered a large portrait of JD Tyson hanging in the city hall. (His name in the 21st century is now justifiably and correctly reduced to one in a long list in a local history exhibit.) He had spoken as Kimberley's representative at the enthusiastic farewell banquet for the generally unpopular Lord Milner, apparently, on the eve of the founding of the nation of South Africa … and hosted the Duke (son of Queen Victoria) and Duchess of Connaught's visit to the Diamond City in 1906.

The fact that my grandfather had been Kimberley's leading citizen, hobnobbing with lofty *Engelse* retreating rulers, was embarrassing information which I tried to conceal as a cadet reporter in that city, for I was already aware of the unnatural and arrogant antipathy that journalists had for bureaucrats.

Missionary work, you will notice, is a subject I have emphasised at every available point so far. I have done so because of an astounding discovery I made while assembling this family history. It is directly relevant to my next tale. It involves another fruit off the family tree named William Tyson.

Unfortunately he chose the calling that a Scottish politician and several African writers have informed me was a lackey, a spy and a forerunner of white, racist colonialism. In two words: Christian missionary.

Now you realise why I can understand, even sympathise with the suspicion, if not the hate, in those sentiments. But I must stand by the facts of my kin in this case, rather than the emotions of some of my prejudiced friends.

Great-grandfather William Tyson was a dreamer and writer who, according to historical record, was not much fitted for regular work – in the same mould as some of his descendants such as I. At the age of 18 he was invited to preach in his local church on the Isle of Man. He did it sufficiently well to be ordained and sent as a 22-year-old Wesleyan missionary to Jamaica. There he joined up with John Daughtrey, the resident magistrate who was officially appointed to oversee the abolition of slavery and to introduce a workers' apprentice system.

William Tyson's near-lifetime mission was to secure for slaves, not only their release, but the means and skills for an alternative life in Jamaica. Later, he did similar, but much more arduous anti-slavery work in British Honduras. He had also done service in Africa, at the much more salubrious post of Grahamstown, and there he spent his last years. The Wesleyan Missionary Society said of him after his death,

"William Tyson, a true world missionary ... was an experienced, cultivated, and discerning minister ... who loved the people of God wherever he met them, and knew how to hold the balance amidst conflicting interests .... He had, for Christ's sake, braved the deadly yellow fever in Central America, and recovered from it as by a miracle, (He was) the faithful circuit minister, a close student of the Pauline Epistles and a trained theologian.

"During his life time he wrote two books and several articles for the *London Quarterly Review*. He was regarded by the Grahamstown Methodist 'Commemoration' Church as a freethinker who avidly read all views. Proof of this may be found in one of his books entitled *Imputed*

Righteousness, or the scriptural doctrine of justification: being lectures on the argumentative portion of St Paul's Epistle to the Romans."

My Go-oodness! A minor near-saint in the family – for Christ's sake! I became aware of this only while embarking on tracing this newspaper trail. Yet he had been superintendent of the Commemoration Church where I had, in the tradition of schoolboys three or four generations later, carved my name on a pew during sermons.

And to think that, at school, while fetching an errant cricket ball often hit into the old cemetery, I may have smoked a cigarette *stompie* unwittingly beside great-grandfather's grave.

Worse, I might have been tempted to recite a schoolboy favourite piece of soaring poetry, inappropriate yet unforgettable, about my other great-grandpa, the whereabouts of whose grave l knew not:

Here lies John Dunn
He was shot by a gun.
His name is not Dunn
– but Wood.
But Wood would not rhyme with gun
– but Dunn would.

Great-grandpa would have liked that, even if his name was not Wood but the family name of my other great-grandfather. Surely missionaries can't all have been colonial racists as some of my friends and most undemocratic communists believe?

YOU MAY DEDUCE from all of the above that the author and his antecedents belong to a bygone age; an era in which whites found questionable reasons for believing that the "Western culture" was superior to others; that their compatriots should be *seen* to embrace goodness and stuffiness; that it was a man's world in which each should marry a virgin and keep her at home for life; that the things that mattered most were good manners and good sportsmanship.

You belonged to this exclusive world only if you also displayed a sense of justice, honour and – if you could afford it – honesty, tolerance as well as *noblesse oblige.* It was all unquestioningly smug.

You may be right in some of these assumptions of this author's prejudiced pre-history – provided you have a sense of humour and remember that things like loyalty, love, and concern for others, are universal values which are themselves prejudiced by varying interpretations, standards and exceptions. All prejudices are innately false. Thus, history that is constantly re-written to suit the prejudices of successful later generations, seems to me to be often far less accurate than the newspapers recording events fleetingly as they occurred. And of course, recording their corrections as the river of time dictates.

At least you can gauge the proclaimed, or very obvious, prejudices of any newspaper and its limitations *on the day.* Histories written decades later usually assume omnipotence over contemporary experience that needs challenging far more often. Perhaps the free encyclopaedia, Wikipedia, which invites every opinion to challenge its versions of history, may grow one day into a better, increasingly stable route to accurate recording of humanity's activities. ☐

* Information of relevant family histories is taken from wider research done by Prof Graham Tyson, of the Charles Sturt University in Bathurst, Australia.

1. *Through Matabeleland: the record of a Ten Months' Trip in an Ox-waggon through Mashonaland and Matabeleland* by Joseph Garnett Wood, printed in London 1889; reprinted Bulawayo 1974.

2. *The Baronet and the Savage King* by David Hilton-Barber, published by 30 Degrees South, 2013.

5.

Battles fought in blood and ink.

When the white missionaries came to Africa
they had the Bible and we had the land.
They said "Let us pray". We closed our eyes.
When we opened them we had the Bible
and they had the land.

Archbishop Desmond Tutu (?)

The quote on this chapter's title page is a message on the Web which caught my eye online as I was about to write this chapter.

Is it true? I cannot tell, because I have not checked the context, which is the crucial test of truth. It may be a quip made by South Africa's finest Church leader and heroic political figure of great principles and apt quotations; or it may be part of something else that he may or may not have said or quoted. It may also be some politician's slogan. However, I'm using it deliberately without the normal "fact-check", as an online sample of Trump-invented "fake news". It is used here to point up "The Other Side" of the story that we all need to remember when we look at both general and personal history.

For instance:

Thomas Sheffield, a newcomer from England and his brother a printer, set up the *Eastern Star* in Grahamstown in mid-century; soon moving their press in the 1880s, partly by ox-wagon, to the new goldfields opening up in the Transvaal. Before he left the Eastern Cape Province, Thomas Sheffield wrote a brief history, *The Story of the Settlement*, published in 1884, beginning with the "Battle of Grahamstown". His words describing the first attempt to wipe out the proposed "capital" of the Eastern Frontier can be summarised thus:

Chief Makanna (sic), having assembled the Amakhosa host on the hilltop above Grahamstown, exhorted them "To battle! To battle!" His final cry was reported to be: "Drive the accursed white men into the ocean." The famous warrior chief launched his ferocious army of nearly 10,000 men determined upon death or victory. His massed warriors faced a mere 350 Europeans and Hottentots in the valley below. It was 2pm when Makanna launched his assegai-wielding warriors in an all but irresistible weight of men ... but the handful of Englishmen stood firm and undaunted. Using retreat and sudden resistance in tactics the Amakhosa had not yet seen, the unflinching defenders took up their defensive positions .... Grapeshot and canister arms belched forth upon the advancing horns of the assegai-wielding attackers. (After several more pages describing extreme, near-hand-to-hand warfare) the attackers turned and fled; their wounded seeking to hide in the Kowie rivulet.

The story of how the stream ran red with blood was later told in every nursery in Grahamstown, wrote Sheffield.

According to Sheffield, and much of the settler community, the settlers began to hate many of the missionaries who emerged from their own ranks, went to live in the Xhosa communities far across the frontier, and reported events from "the other side". Fortunately, as time passed, the disagreements, the bereavements, the wounds, the losses, and the anger of seven wars were gradually forgotten by settler descendants.

If they remember anything of their history, they vaguely recall tales of only the next major war in 1834–5 when Xhosa tribesmen – far from being inept – ran roughshod over the entire settlement to its furthest western reaches from the frontier. The victim's descendants today hardly remember their own families' experiences, in that "civil war", when farmers' wives and children fled in search of shelter and protection ... except in the village of Bathurst, where there are reminders of the women and children who hid behind the tall, stone walls of the village's newly-built church. Though Xhosa warriors did not normally attack women, in the heart of the village of Bathurst they hurled spears and fire harmlessly at the church's tall windows. Even that war, fortunately, is long forgotten by all sides. (Except by white historians, engaged today in furious battle among themselves with various versions in search of objective truth.)

But in Sheffield's time he was quick to print the settler community's version of the results of the 1834–5 war which had been estimated at the closure of the war to be: "3227 settler persons reduced to destitution (about 80% of the original 1820 party); 239 farm homesteads burnt down and 262 pillaged; 30140 cattle, 964 horses, and 55554 sheep stolen, to say nothing of the crops destroyed."

Neither he, nor any of his colleagues said, or appeared aware of, anything of the Xhosa causes for their cattle stealing and outright war.

Instead Sheffield's anger remained fixated on the Colonial Government. He describes Governor Lord Somerset as a "despot and a tyrant" and his successors in Colonial office as "inept or decrepit". He accuses them of seeking wars and failing to keep the peace or maintain treaties with the leading Xhosa chiefs. He says of the swashbuckling soldier-statesman Sir Harry Smith that his bullying tactics (making each chief kiss his foot or choose before witnesses a "war staff" or "peace staff") as ineffective and offensive. Sheffield dismisses a missionary's complaint that Harry Smith placed his boot on the neck of the great Chief Sandile, prostrated before Smith, as "false" .... But *if* it were true, Sheffield adds, the soldier should have pressed harder, thus preventing Sandile from waging his next war.

The newspaper editor (sounding a little like US President Donald Trump in his pre-election speeches two centuries later) also bemoans in his book the lack of support to settlers from both an uncaring, far away government and also a "too-caring" clergy. Colonial Government support was noticeably absent, for instance, after the settlers suffered the worst flood in memory. (The anecdote is told of the farmer who asked his neighbours during this memorable 19th century flood: "Did you perchance see my house float by?" That "dry" humour still existed, unconsciously in the Bathurst district a century later. A farmer told his companions in the Bathurst pub in the 1940s: "Man, *boet,* this drought has got so bad, and the winds so strong, all my ploughed land is now over on Henry's farm.")

Absence of help in bad times is one thing, but discriminatory injustice is intolerable. One discriminatory order which could never be forgotten by the settlers was that, when they arrived in Africa, each registered adult male was compelled to carry a pass, while neither the Dutch nor Khoi nor Xhosa within the settler lands were required to have one. It remains one of *four* never-to-be-forgotten injustices; a small historical irony, not to be lost when considering South Africa's modern history.

I have quoted Sheffield mainly because his blatantly partisan history appeared in his book published almost contemporaneously in Grahamstown in 1884. It was typical of the unfortunate views of many settlers of the time – yet the book has rarely been seen. Sheffield would have quoted from the early editions of the *Grahamstown Journal,* which was already publishing before he arrived on the scene. He had this to say about his elder editorial colleague:

> *First and foremost (of the settlers) is Robert Godlonton, then aged* 25 .... (Sheffield forgets he had already mentioned Thomas Pringle as among the "foremost" of these pioneers.) *With the establishment*

of the Grahamstown (sic) Journal and freedom of the press, Godlonton commenced a fine career, the outraged and unflinching champion of the settlers' rights, the bold exponent of the numerous wrongs to which for years they were subjected, and the unwearied defender of them from the foul aspersions cast upon them and the calumnies freely circulated against them in the colony and in the mother country, he obtained a hold upon the affections of the colonists which increased as he increased in years .... As these lines are being written, he is receiving congratulations from all parts on his 89th birthday. Feeble as a child, he is but seldom seen today beyond the privacy of his home."

While writing about Sheffield in *my* 89th year, I can but hope he was exaggerating. Both Godlonton and Sheffield reflected the partisan views of their readers, voicing only their side of the story. On the other hand, John Fairbairn (friend of Thomas Pringle who defied Lord Somerset's ban on the Cape press, and whom we shall meet later) voiced in his *Commercial Advertiser* the *very different* view of Cape Town's colonial establishment who resented all the settler troublemakers on the faraway frontier.

However, many believed Fairbairn to be "an enlightened liberal who entertained no view but his own and was too liberal with the facts". He accused the settlers of "exaggerating" their suffering, but when the official statistics were published he apologised and "forgives with his whole soul". Yet he still made no attempt to get more facts or reach within five hundred kilometres of the frontier. Instead he then violently attacked the frontier settlers on the dubious, but fiery notion that "their purpose is to kindle an unquenchable flame of hatred".

Thus there were already two views – both white, both palpably overheated, about the Frontier Wars. Unfortunately it was only Fairbairn's dangerously opinionated view that reached the outside world from Cape Town; never the more overheated, more emotionally prejudiced, yet more factually-oriented one from the frontier. So, based on Fairbairn's newspaper reports alone, the settlers as a tribe were angrily condemned in colonial Australia as well as in Britain.

Yet another 'other side' of the picture

In an attempt to balance these two unbalanced versions, today's historians offer "the other side", or rather different versions of those events of 200 years ago. For instance, in our time, Dr Peires, after years of dedicated research, produced his book *The House of Phalo*.[1]

His aim is deliberately designed to balance history with an interpretation opposed to the experience described by the settlers.

It is presented as a strictly fact-based, largely Xhosa view. Peires criticises the settler press:

> *Leading the pack was the redoubtable "Moral Bob" Godlington, editor of the Grahamstown Journal. From issue to issue he blasted the treaty system and called for a return to the good old days of the benevolent Sir Benjamin D'Urban. Godlington did not confine his politics to the editorials and the correspondence columns but they permeate the very news itself. Occasional cases of detectable misrepresentation seem to reveal only the tip of the iceberg. Through his energy and persistence, and through its ability to capitalise on the mistakes of its opponents, the Journal made a case of appealing sympathy: since the Xhosa not the Colonists were the thieves, the Xhosa not the Colonists were to blame. If the farmers could not observe the treaty, then it was the treaty not the farmers which had to go. Occasionally the Journal added a little cant to the effect that the D'Urban system was more effective in civilising the Xhosa. But the settlers' concern for the welfare of the Xhosa had not prevented them from applauding the good Sir Benjamin's attempts to throw the whole lot over the Kei.*

The Grahamstown Journal was not politically naive. It did not simply seek better protection for the farmer, it sought a return of Xhosa country between the Kei and Keiskamma Rivers.

Prof Guy Butler (right) and editor of The Star, at the opening of the Star-sponsored museum housing an old settler press.

Well said. Anyone paging through the overheated pages of the 200-year-old *Journal* today would sympathise with a heated reaction. Peires responses are generally true and provide imperative balance to a heated history. The research and balancing of history are also imperative to South Africa's future in the 21st century.

However, while Sheffield's version of history reeks of propaganda, some of Peires' own assumptions and generalisations – even in the single paragraph quoted above – are challengeable. We can try to absorb both versions, but what is missing in today's histories, and what I believe is required for true understanding of history is a *sense of the times*; the immoderate times of war in which both the mis-settled settlers and the Xhosa cattle farmers were the victims of senseless atrocities.

Intermittent battles, sometimes dealing in death through hand-to-hand combat, occurred in four wars (out of nine – only the early civil and civilian wars are considered here). As these four wars lasted through the "fighting life" of every father and son, it is hard to imagine what it did to the families on each side of the Fish River – especially those tales of warfare in the heavily wooded mountains inland.

Peires, rightly, in just a single paragraph, refers to the actions of unidentified witch doctors in Xhosaland who urge their warriors to rip open the stomachs of their killed enemies, lest the dead with their pent-up spirits wreak havoc on the slayers. Elsewhere, in the various histories, are equally brief, bleak references to the bitter battles in "the Bush" (densely wooded forest where even wild animals, except elephants, often fail to make paths). Those were the circumstances in which the silent thrust of the spear at close quarters was an instant match for the flintlock or later firearm, and death came suddenly, almost invisibly at close quarters in the daylight shadows. It was in those circumstances, that warriors were *again* told by witch doctors to rip out the heart and liver of their victims – and eat these in order to have strength and power over the enemy.

The British troops, and some farmer volunteers, must have retaliated with indescribable fear and fury, for they stopped taking prisoners, and left the bleeding corpses of every presumed "enemy fighter" hanging from trees where the thick bush allowed access.

Reports of such atrocities were seldom recorded at the time, even when quite widely known. Any thought of them would have created unspeakable rage and fear ... and in Xhosaland the rising belief in the "wisdom" of the witch doctors would have foreshadowed even more strongly the inexplicable power of a prophecy to kill all their own cattle in order to convince the Fates to drive the whites back into the sea.

But the latter conclusion is merely more speculation.

The attitude of the British Empire's soldier during war and peace in the 19th century also needs a mention. It still gets it, even today, in the four-letter language once exclusive to military men, such as:

"In the great days of the British Empire, a new commanding officer was sent to a South African bush outpost to relieve the retiring colonel. After welcoming his replacement and showing the usual courtesies (gin and tonic, cucumber sandwiches, etc.) which protocol decrees, the retiring colonel said, 'You must meet my Adjutant, Captain Smithers, he's my right-hand man and is really the strength of this office. His talent is simply boundless.'

"Smithers was summoned and introduced to the new CO, who was surprised to meet a hunchback, one eyed, toothless, hairless, scabbed and pockmarked specimen of humanity, a particularly unattractive man less than three feet tall.

"'Smithers, old man, tell your new CO about yourself.'

"'Well, sir, I graduated with honours from Sandhurst, joined the regiment and won the Military Cross and Bar after three expeditions behind enemy lines. I've represented Great Britain in equestrian events and won a Silver Medal in the middleweight division ....'

"At that point, the colonel interrupted, 'Yes, yes, never mind all that Smithers, he can find all that in your file. Tell him about the day you told the witch doctor to fuck off.'"

But fear of witch doctors and missionaries (and ignorant, swearing soldiers) as elements of continual warfare were over-estimated. What in reality would concern victims on both sides was the need for justice and truth — very scarce qualities in times of atrocities and endless warfare. And within colonial ranks there was little sign of balanced reporting, even in faraway Cape Town where newspaper editor John Fairbairn was campaigning on a programme of his own, in the safe knowledge that there is always "another side" to hard news and history — even "fake news". ☐

1. *The House of Phalo. A History of the Xhosa People in the Days of their Independence*, by JB Peires, published by Ravan Press, 1981.

6.
The war of '34'.

*Every man should let alone others' prejudices
and examine his own.*

John Locke 1632–1704.

War is the worst place to seek truth. And when the war is between men defending their kraals and their country against men, women and children trying to defend their homes in veld and bush, it becomes a dark pit.

The *sixth* of nine recognised wars broke out on Christmas Eve. It began as an uprising and protest at injustice in which almost all white farms in the settler country were plundered; their homesteads burned down or damaged; their stock stolen; and many farmers wounded or killed. But each of the Frontier Wars was unique in its circumstances, its militant tactics on both sides, and its issues. For a brief picture of the "other side" of this broad history, let us look at a summing up of a single incident: "the Xhosa war on the Fingoes (*sic*)".

It is an unusually documented version, which historians today seize on, for there can be many interpretations of "the facts". John Ayliff, who had for some time been in Chief Hintsa's territory, preaching to the "Fingoes", wrote that when Sir Benjamin D'Urban suddenly arrived on the scene:

> *Quite unexpectedly ... a large body of Xhosa horsemen were seen descending the side of the ridge towards the Governor's camp, and without any apparent concern, they rode straight past the piquets of advanced post and went into the camp .... Hintza (sic) requested to see the Governor who came out of his tent and saluted him.*
>
> *Hintza asked: "What is this fighting in my country?" Said the Governor: "Your men have invaded the Colony, killed many of the colonists, burnt down their farms, and carried off their cattle, and the traces of the cattle lead into your country .... We are following our cattle; and I ask, Hintza, why the Fingoes are being butchered at the rate they are, for this very morning 30 Fingoes have been killed close to my camp?"*
>
> *With contempt Hintza replied, "Fingoes! You talk about Fingoes!*

I fancy that a man can do what he likes with his own dogs. The Fingoes are my dogs, and I can do what I please with them."

D'Urban, unusually moved, said: "Hintza, you call the Fingoes dogs, I call them people, men and women, and I say that if you do not at once send out some of your attendants to put a stop to this carnage I will hang you upon this tree," and he pointed to the large Yellowwood under which they stood. (Hintza thought it wisest to send out messages, and he was kept in custody until the killing was stopped). Then Fingoes came flocking into the camp. The question was what to do with them. Finally the Governor allotted them unoccupied land in the Colony, Ayliff was put in charge, and he led 16 000 people out to freedom, he wrote.

"It was the great day of his life. The procession, nearly eight miles long, was a mile-and-a-half wide. It was raining softly, and they came down the steep hills in shifting mists, the women carrying all possessions on their heads and their babies on their backs, the men driving 22000 cattle in their midst, the boys looking after calves and goats.

"These saucy little fellows went along in high glee, singing in a kind of chorus ... in which the others sometimes joined. 'We are going, we are going to the land of the right, to good people ... We are free.'" John Ayliff, the well-known missionary from the Butterworth area of Xhosaland (one of several missionaries on "the other side" of the Frontier) led the Fingoes to "their promised land"; taught and converted them to Christianity. Even those not converted, it was said, came to the aid of the white settlers during all kinds of crises.

It sounds a simple, kindly story, though dismissed by at least one historian declaring that the missionary, Ayliff, "is an unsound witness". Whatever the facts may be, or its sequence, the death of Chief Hintsa, has bitter tastes for all sides.

On the one hand:

According to Bell's 50-year-old version, extracted from one of four sources of John Ayliff's published and unpublished documents of a hundred years earlier, the death of Hintsa was reported in the following manner:

Meanwhile, Hintza was asked for a hostage – and offered himself.

Harry Smith warned him that if he attempted to escape he would be shot: the Guides were in charge of him. He was courteously treated and had his meals with the Colonel, who thought him, but for his black skin, "The very image of poor dear George IV."

*Hintza gave pleasant words and promises, temporized, and one day – when it had been noticed that he was riding a very powerful horse – he dashed off and tried to escape. Smith caught him, avoided his jabbing assegai, and pulled him from his horse; in a moment the Chief was running down the steep, thickly-wooded hillside on the left, to where his followers hid in wait for him. Instantly Abel Hoole was off his horse, running to the edge of the slope and down through the trees, calling in Xhosa, "Hintza, come out of the bush! The Colonel says he will not hurt you!" But Hintsa scurried on. **George Southey** was nearer. He slid down a twenty-foot rock, scrambled through a tangle of undergrowth, the Colonel calling after him: "Fire! Fire at him." Then, from the bush, close to him, (the Chief's) head appeared with lifted assegai: like lightning, Southey fired – and found that it was Hintza he had killed ....*

There was a tremendous outcry in England .... Southey was accused of murdering Hintza, and of cutting off his ears, but a court of inquiry cleared him (according to Bell's research in the 1950s).

And on the other hand, according to entries in Wikipedia in 2017:

Hintsa was being guarded on the ride back over the Kei and the Fish by a corps of guides led by George Southey. Soon after breakfast, Hintsa asked Smith: "What have the cattle done that you want them? Why must I see my subjects deprived of them?" To which Smith replied, "That you know far better than I do."

Soon after that Hintsa spurred his horse forward and galloped away. Smith gave chase and twice tried to fire on the fleeing monarch. Twice his pistols malfunctioned but he caught Hintsa and pushed him off his horse. Hintsa got up and ran, still carrying his assegai.

"Shoot, George, and be damned to you," cried Smith to Southey ... "Mercy," cried the King. And again. "Mercy." But there was to be no mercy. Southey, whose Xhosa was fluent, fired, and hit Hintsa

in the head, killing him. Southey got to the body first and took off Hintsa's brass body ornaments for himself. Others grabbed for his beads and bracelets. Southey or his brother William cut off one of Hintsa's ears as a trophy and someone else cut off the other. A doctor travelling with them was seen trying to pull out some of Hintsa's teeth. Later, even Smith could no longer bear the barbarity he had caused and ordered Hintsa's body dropped from his horse and to be left in the bush for his followers to find. Wikipedia's website added:

His legacy:

Hintsa is considered a hero by many Xhosa. These days the Xhosa people know about him through poems and bedtime stories and he is often compared to Shaka ka Senzangakhona, commonly known as Shaka Zulu ....

South Africa institutionalized in 1999 the King Hintsa Bravery Award for leaders that live and act in the spirit of Hintsa kaKhawuta. It was awarded to Jacob Zuma in 2012. Earlier notorious earners of the award include Robert Mugabe from Zimbabwe. The award is being conferred by the ruling Xhosa king.

Historians today, here and abroad, continue to argue furiously with each other on much smaller issues and "facts", than those disturbing claims – 30 deaths of unprotected tribal family innocents versus the desecration after death of a truly regal Xhosa king. Usually it is the interpretation of such "facts", so thinly available and so far apart, that allow such stark contradictions in history. We can make our own judgements on the conflicting attitudes mirrored above. I believe the weight in this case, so far presented, should fall on the contemporaneous, documented board of inquiry, held in London by an administration hostile to the complaining settlers. It is reported that it exonerated Southey, but not the actions leading to Hintza's death. However I have not been able to read the London Commission's 19th century report.

Editor R. Godlonton's contemporaneous 3000-word analysis of official reports on Hintza's death, though unavoidably one-sided, cannot be ignored. It appears in the 600 pages of limited facsimile reprints available in Vol. X1 of the *Africana Collectanea Series* (Struik Cape Town, 1965).

Somehow South Africa has to come to terms on their history and reach agreement on its "interpretations". We can begin by always reminding ourselves of the wisdom of Marcus Aurelius quoted at the head of the next chapter. □

7.
The past – and the best road ahead.

There is only one thing here worth minding,
and that is to be true and just,
and to show charity,
even to the untruthful and the unjust.

Marcus Aurelius, (Bk.6,47) b.121 d.180.

The validity of history, we need to remind ourselves again, depends on how each culture views those of their neighbours and whether their differing views of history can be accommodated.

For instance the question of who "was here first" and the arcane allegations of who "stole our land" are of little relevance to the future. But even today, bitterness remains. For instance, the Khulumani Support Group states that the Cobuqua Khoisan were once forcibly removed before colonials came to five regions of the Eastern Cape around Mthata, Buffalo City, Matatiele, Aliwal North and Queenstown, and that Khoisan "freedom remains incomplete without the achievement of freedom for all".

The group seeks recognition of the rights of the Cobuqua people with reparations sought even as late as 1976.[1]

Whether or not this is credible or relevant, it does serve as a warning of how easily the concept of united nationhood can be infected by the bitterness of "cultural injustice", from any quarter.

In South Africa, with its 11 official languages and more than two dozen cultures, we should take special care in asserting our own cultural heritages. The so-called "coloured" people under apartheid for instance, range from the millennia-old origins of the Khoisan to "recent" royal princesses from Malaysia. Many of these citizens with their roots deep in Africa, also have European blood, as do many Africans and *vice versa*. Under the acute rule of apartheid, some of these were officially classified "white" – though most "whites" of mixed heritage were never questioned on the vital issue of racial privilege under apartheid.

People from India of different castes, cultures, regions, and religions have been in South Africa for several generations, but not even the early presence of Mahatma Gandhi, intervening through a preoccupied General Jan Smuts, could save them later from the direct depredations of property and justice under apartheid.

Whites include Dutch, French, German, Portuguese, Greek and other ethnic groups as well as four British nationalities, with their chronicled or documented histories going back 3000 years.

But by far the majority of the Bantu (meaning literally "the people") of South Africa are black, representing an array of cultures, each with its own "oral history" also stretching back from "yesterday" to the times before Christ when tribal legend suggested that they encountered the Phoenicians sailing up the Zambezi River! Some legends go back an estimated 5000 years.

Herein lies a test of our belief in oral history. It takes much effort for most educated people today to accept, as "factual" history, any version which is not "written" history. Thus we must pause again to remember the recent seminal and internationally acclaimed views of Jan Vansina, author of *Oral Tradition as History*.[2] And before questioning the sanctity of oral history, we should be aware of Vusamazulu Credo Mutwa's works, *Song of the Stars* and *Indaba my Children*[3] and read black writers such as Magema M Fuze[4] and Sol Plaatje's words on the past.

Credo Mutwa, a self-proclaimed spiritual *sangoma* of my day, has provided the answer to the challenge: "How can you compare written history with oral history?" He addressed an international audience of many hundreds in Tokyo in 1985, prompting the editor of one of his books, Stephen Larsen, to record: "In a spellbinding way he held his remarkably distinguished and erudite audience rapt with the breadth of his knowledge, his wisdom, and his humour."

In one of his books Credo Mutwa explains that the headmen of numbers of major tribes have over the ages carefully chosen "those with long memories who can repeat every word exactly as each is spoken" to carry the tribal message down the generations. The strange things they pass on have often "puzzled, disgusted, and shocked the world, without explanation", he wrote, and he went on in his book *Indaba, My Children*, published in London, to tell the legend of "the strange people with pink skins and hair like the manes of lions"; a legend that finally goes beyond all tribal credibility when relating that one of these aliens had "green eyes".

"The brat who witnessed these people and told us" of their manes like lions and "humanly impossible" green eyes, "had to be lying", the story-teller says ... yet the description of the invaders' ship is "proven to be" that of the ancient Phoenicians, and relics are found such as a broken sword and strangely patterned ceramics.

Make what you will of such stories, but read them first. (And be aware, in the current politically-stoked prejudice about Africa's past, that Mutwa is not suggesting the alien marauders came to teach Africans how to live – they came to plunder, as the Vikings had done in Britain.) Mutwa stresses that "all the legends are a strange mix of truth and nonsense". The traditional oral messages are filled with thinly disguised lust and blatant treachery; of strange beings and stranger adventures. They are exaggerations, as are the fables of all cultures, from the land of the Pharaohs to the lands of Araby and ancient Ireland.

Mutwa explains it thus: "African stories follow a standard pattern which dictates that the attention of the listeners must be held. One must play with the listeners' emotions as one would play with a toy doll. Make them laugh, make them cry, make them angry, thwart their expectations, puzzle them one moment, delight them or repel them, the next. And always leave them with wide open mouths, begging for more."

But, he added, the purpose of storytelling must not be forgotten by the sages. They must remember, word for word, the truths within the tales.

Oral history's demand for exceptional human memory was met by the white academic writer May Bell, whose book I have already quoted from many times. She was virtually blind when she came to research and write a popular book about her own ancestors. She not only had to find people to read to her from her selected sources; she lectured university students on the academic details of what had been read to her, *and wrote her book by dictating it from memory*. Her efforts should persuade sceptical European academics that oral history has a place in the culture of all races.

Western fiction, from the olden times of King Arthur's knights to America's *Gone with the Wind* by Margaret Mitchell, and today's epic war movies, follow a similar pattern of using legends in which literary truths are hard to identify.

May Bell's family history of the 1820s, however, was the opposite of legend. It was as precisely worded and contexted as it was possible to be after studying all the relevant, original, and contemporaneous *documented* material available, as well as her grandmothers' vivid oral memories, the works of Sir George Cory, and much unpublished material.

Though she had in the past contributed philosophical articles to various magazines, she would not produce a book, even a popular adventure-biography, without first going back to university to attain an MA degree. She studied all references to her ancestors, critical as well as laudatory, and included both sides. Her dedication to the study of documents must have increased the strain on her eyesight, which faded dramatically. Yet she would not give up her purpose.

She assimilated vast tracts of information which needed to be read to her, and she assembled it in her mind for her popular book *and* her academic lectures, delivered in her very different style and approach to history. She was acutely aware of her responsibilities as an academic, which could be met only through a remarkable achievement of dedicated memory.[5]

Whatever history we choose to believe, white historians studying South African history today have the even greater responsibility of reappraising the apartheid versions once taught in schools – and how those reappraisals affect a future communal society.

It is a tricky business ... as the ongoing historical debate about published versions illustrates. Popularly accepted are recently written versions by white academics and authors, such as Noël Mostert's sweeping epic, *Frontiers,*[6] or Dr JB Peires' deeply researched counter to traditional so-called settler history, *The House of Phalo* (see endnote 1, Chapter 5).

However, one is able to quarrel with almost every author who sets out to prove "facts" that will support his or her interpretation of any history. One remarkable example of this concerns the debate on the Mfecane and Chief Shaka's rule in the pre-1820s, and who was to blame for the upheaval of tribes affecting communities from KwaZulu to Zimbabwe to Lesotho, Swaziland, Xhosaland and elsewhere. Was it the magnificently trained Zulu warriors of Chief Shaka? Or the slave-traders on the Mozambique coast? Or other tribal clashes or natural disasters? It would appear sometimes that some historians are more interested in allotting blame (or credit) than on agreeing on the facts. *The Mfecane Aftermath, Reconstructive Debates in Southern African History,* superbly edited by Carolyn Hamilton,[7] is a riveting example of this.

In nearly 500 pages, 16 historians (all white) in South Africa and several from abroad, argue over the most minute details of the "who is to blame" debate. Even the word Mfecane is contested, because the term "Difaqane" had been used for decades, predating its use in 20th century liberal vs apartheid historiography. So was the word "Lifaqane"(wandering hordes), causing one historian to analyse "the battle of Dithakong and

'Mfecane' theory". So who is to blame for grabbing land and unsettling major tribes? And what are the consequences, and again, who can be blamed? Even liberal-minded historians, it seems, cannot agree even among themselves.

For outsiders and laymen like myself, enjoying the cut and thrust and the vast amount of knowledge – disputed of course – in the "Reconstructive debates" there appears to be an over-simple but excellent remedy to ongoing irresolvable disputes: "take a vote" and use the broadest interpretation of facts acceptable to the nation as a whole; recording all the while that there will always be another side to anyone's version.

Our greatest challenge

Yet even establishing a valid and credible southern African history and finding "the truth" is secondary to the sub-continent's greatest challenge. Far-sighted African scribes such as Mutwa and Sol Plaatje have reminded us, from different stages of the recent past – yet almost in the same words – of the first priority: It is the step which needs to be taken to bring all South Africans and their heritages together. Quite simply: "Through *education* of all 'the people'."

This has never happened. Instead, education has been an experimental plaything in South Africa. As a deliberate policy, education failed to bridge racial divides from the time of Alfred Milner and Jan Smuts to Nelson Mandela and Jacob Zuma. It went into reverse in the time of HF Verwoerd and PW Botha, and failed in Mandela's time – (through the over-ambition of President Mandela's new democratic government wishing to establish new forms of education – the failure of which I personally and sadly documented in advance for the new Department). Education certainly did not improve through the eras of President Thabo Mbeki and Zuma. The disastrous results are obvious and fully documented, yet their vital importance seems not to concern today's politicians sufficiently.

Let me spell it out in two sets of figures concerning child education, which I have culled from a university student's LLB thesis on the rights of children under international and SA law.[8]

Nearly two million children were without parental control in South Africa in 2017. They were "officially" in the hands of anonymous, though registered "caregivers" who drew monthly payments from the State. Many thousands of orphans were in State care institutions. Worst of all, there were nearly fifty thousand homeless "street children", many with HIV, some of them of both sexes made prostitutes in their pre-teens ... and all of them, including the near-two million homeless children under official "State care" were unlikely to receive any adequate education. There was no-one, apart from a careless or incompetent State, to take the blame. But surely every middle-class taxpayer of every hue might be persuaded to "adopt", through any currently registered "caregiver", the child in his/her care simply to ensure the "unseen" child is given adequate protection ... *and* education? Whatever the circumstances and their change, there should be a drive to persuade taxpayers to help – personally – the nation's unnaturally large proportion of orphaned or exposed children.

(Forgive this side-tracking ... it is my only "editor's opinion" that I intend to allow in this book on journalistic endeavour.)

IN ANY EVENT, the history of "The Other Side of the day-before-yesterday" becomes as fascinating as a mystery thriller. There are many books on it to explore.

However, this story's beginning is concerned only with a *family* history, one that links awareness of the memories of "the day-before-yesterday" with events of "yesterday and today", an era in which proof of events is readily available.

I am about to report to you on many latter-day stories that you may remember from your own, or your parents, lifetime. I trust that the probe into my family history will persuade you that my equanimity and qualifications for doing so are sufficient and not blindly prejudiced; "racist"; "colonialist" or worse.

Part One ends with a history of the 20th century portrayed mainly in real headlines. The entire century is reflected in a journalistic style so that it can be read in the time it takes to page through a serious daily newspaper. ☐

1. See https://cobuqua wordpress.com/2017/02/21/introducing the cobuqua/

2. *Oral Tradition as History*, by Jan Vansina, (James Currey Publishers, 1985), a book written originally in French, but published many times and still available. There is also free access to it on the Web, where you can find it by searching for his name. His work is a model of simple structure and absence of academic phraseology.

3. *Indaba my Children* by Vusamazulu Credo Mutwa, first published by Stanmore Press Ltd UK 1966, and *Song of the Stars, The Lore of a Zulu Shaman*, (Barrytown Ltd NY 1996).

4. *The Black People And Whence They Came* (Magema M Fuze, published by University of Natal Press 1982). Translation of a Zulu history written by the author, who knew Cetswayo and DinuZulu.

5. *They Came From a Far Land*, by May Bell MA and published by philanthropist Josie E Wood MA (Maskew Miller 1963).

6. *Frontiers, the Epic of South Africa's Creation and the Tragedy of the Xhosa People*, by Noël Mostert (Jonathan Cape, London, 1992).

7. The Mefecane Aftermath. Reconstructive Debates in Southern African History, edited by Carolyn Hamilton, published by Witwatersrand University Press 1995. One contributor argues that Ayliff was an unreliable witness because he contradicted himself and was mistaken in many of his articles.

8. The thesis was researched and presented by Samantha Yell, a final-year student at the University of Pretoria. It emphasises South Africa's constitutional imperative that demands the right of access to education of every child. It lists the many institutions involved, and their failure to guarantee that right to two million under-privileged or often unlisted orphaned children.

8.

A HUNDRED YEARS OF HEADLINES.

News from the 20th century.

very adult in the world today has had experience of the 20th century. Only our "millennials" have no personal sense of those recent times. But the rest of us have vivid memories of those days and they are worth re-assessing, comparing and preserving.

However, recounting any version of the history of the young South African nation since its formation in 1910 requires a little more time than an average chapter of this book. It will take as much as 40 minutes. But among the headlines here you will discover, or be reminded of, instant dramas, strange curiosities, world changing events, and human experiences.

It has always been my firm, if biased opinion, that the historical narrative is best told as history happens, and as the facts and judgements are reported, and corrected, along the majestic "River of Time".

But is that history?

How can a newspaper pretend to write it?

The answer to both questions should come, not from the press, but from recognised great historians:

"History," said Edward Gibbon, author of *The History of the Decline and Fall of the Roman Empire*, "is little more than the register of the crimes, follies and misfortunes of mankind".

"History," said Hendrik van Loon, "is the record of man in quest of his daily bread and butter."

"History," said Thomas Carlyle, "is a distillation of rumour."

"History," said Frederic Maitland, "is not what happened but what people thought or said about it."

And each of those views describes an element of news reporting. The fact that newspapers are not (or ought not to be) boring or pompous does not detract from their value as records of history.

"In analysing history," Ralph Waldo Emerson advised, "do not be too profound, for often the causes are quite superficial."

So are coincidences – and you should find some delightful ones here – such as the timing of the launch of television in this world – which *nearly* began in South Africa! But let us begin a survey of the 20th century with the beginning of a multicultural all-white governing structure recovering from a ruthless white-on-white war. The 20th century ends with a seemingly "perfect" free democracy as bright as a rainbow ... a rainbow that fades into the 21st century.

Bear in mind that these headlines of history reflect a largely white metropolitan readership of a newspaper dedicated to "the interests of all sections", but hampered by apartheid laws and fighting censorship to its death in 1990. Being essentially city-focussed the metro press has consistently failed to reflect adequately the huge issues of land rights and land possession. For that we are more indebted to the free African press of the early years of the 20th century.

These headlines begin with a description – in less than 160 words – of the origins of the South African multicultural State.

IN A FLASH –
HISTORY'S HEADLINES 1910–2020

Some of the events recorded here have had vast consequences in our lives, but small events too are important to us because even random recollections of little things may prove a true sense of time and perspectives.

***

1910 THE FOUNDING OF A NATION

**Provinces split on who should have vote
13 territories form four provinces
Confirmed: One nation. One flag**

The above headlines sum up the heavily debated fate of the following participants in a Union of South Africa:

1) Transvaal's South African Republic 2) Natal 3) Zululand 4) Orange Free State 5) Griqualand West 6) Griqualand East 7) the Crown-owned portion of Bechuanaland 8) The Border, including 9) Xhosaland and 10) Pondoland; 11) The Cape, including the 12) Northern and 13) Eastern Cape.

Mr J X Merriman, leader in The Cape, has insisted that the new Province will keep open its Voters' Roll for all qualified adult males of all races. Other Provinces will keep their current electoral systems which will be subject to the new State, not the Crown.

A 14th territory, now known as Rhodesia, has opted to remain outside the proposed Union, because of the failure to agree on a Federation with greater powers for each province (instead of the agreed centralised Union). It will therefore remain under the Crown.

Excluded from the proposed "South Africa" are Bechuanaland (but not the southern-most corner), Basutoland, and Swaziland which will remain as British Protectorates.

In 1913 the Native Land Act passed despite parliamentary opposition; recreating some mythical boundaries within South Africa. This Act prompted the coming together of African non-tribal leaders from the north-west national boundaries to the south-western Cape who, with support of some tribal chiefs, created the African National Congress.

The 1914–1918 War was badly reported in South African newspapers, partly because of blanket war-time censorship imposed from London. Only later was the significance and sacrifice of SA troops at **Delville Wood** on the Western Front in France appreciated.

And only decades later was honour adequately provided for the 648 mainly African volunteers aboard **SS Mendi** who met death, according to legend, in song. These men of the 5th Brigade, nearly all Africans recruited from all parts of South Africa, were heading for the French war front when their vessel collided with an allied ship in British waters. In facing death, their bravery was reminiscent of the fate of the soldiers who stood to attention and died aboard the Birkenhead off the Cape coast in the previous century when their courage in going down with their ship established the maritime rule "women and children first".

These two events will hopefully remain *shared* legends in South Africa throughout the 21st century.

***

THE 1920S AND ALL THAT JAZZ

Post-war blues and Black Friday
The above two headlines signalled the frantic end of one decade and the sad beginning of another.

Yet in the Western hemisphere, the 1920s was an era of exuberant, perhaps false, celebration; a time to forget politicking and the "World War to end all wars" and its global mourning of influenza and mass deaths. It was party time; a time to dance the Charleston, to shimmy, and all that jazz. It was a time for liberation – especially of educated women, even if most didn't get the vote until the 1930s or later. It was a time for civilisation to re-assess life and its values, after the horrible mass deaths of the First World War.

Generally it was the same pattern, in fact, as the post-war years of the next war in the 1940s.

As the following headlines indicate, "Progress" was literally in the air in the 1920s.

Aeroplane mails collide

APRIL 8, 1922. A British postal aeroplane from Croydon to Paris and a similar French aeroplane flying from Le Bourget to London collided in fog yesterday near Grand Villiers, crashing in flames and killing all six of both postal flying crews. The service, using four machines flying each way daily, was inaugurated only five days ago.

Deadly petrol

MAY 7, 1925. The Ethyl Gasoline Corporation of New York has suspended the sale of tetra-ethyl lead. Professor Henderson of Yale University asserts that the use of ethyl-leaded petrol would cause large numbers of the population to suffer from slow lead-poisoning ... through inhaling exhaust fumes.

Television invention for South Africa

MAY 2, 1928. Mr IW Schlesinger, the impresario who owns a radio contract in the Union of SA, is to have an interview with the directors of the Baird Company in London with a view to acquiring control of so-called television in that country. Mr John Logie Baird has established the world's first television broadcasting company, for which he has also invented the "televisor". His company, named 2TV, is sending out test pictures nightly to a receiving station several miles from his laboratory in Harrow (outside London).

Note: South Africa failed to be among the first in the world to have TV in the Twenties. Instead, television was rejected by the Union's new government after WW2 by the new Minister of Postal Services, Dr Albert Hertzog, on the grounds that it was a little black box broadcasting godless rubbish. His incontestable view was finally abandoned in 1976, years after the landing of a man on the moon, which had been televised to the rest of the world.

New traffic device

JUNE 13, 1929. An American traffic device is introducing an elaborate system of flash signals at a busy intersection in Johannesburg's city centre. More of these may be installed later.

Note: Traffic lights were called "Robots" during their first 50 years of operation in South Africa. A proliferation of more sophisticated robots encouraged the name change.

At this time there were lots of major issues in every sphere of life from technology to fashion, from ethics to art. Here is the reminder of just one event:

Sentenced to death

NOVEMBER 15, 1926. Herman Charles Bosman, a young school teacher, was sentenced to death today for the murder of his step-brother David Russell by shooting him with a rifle. The case was described as "a sad and pathetic one" resulting, not from a quarrel, but strained inter-family relationships.

Note: Bosman's sentence was commuted. He wrote a book about life in the death cell, and went on to write many humorous social satires that earned him a reputation as possibly South Africa's greatest writer – at the time – certainly the nation's best satirist.

***

A DEPRESSING 1930S

The Thirties were marked by two overwhelming events. The Great Depression, and the rise of the century's major demagogues: Joseph Stalin, Benito Mussolini, Adolf Hitler and Chou En Lai ... all of whom exploited the human sufferings of wars and global depression.

Krupps to sell cauliflowers

JANUARY 8, 1930. Having in the past supplied Germany with armaments, Krupps, the great steel firm at Essen, now proposes to supply the Ruhr with cauliflowers, other vegetables, fruit, and flowers. (Later, under Hitler, the ban on weapons-making was ignored.)

Sixpence for a kiss

JANUARY 13, 1930. A "kiss shop" opened in Glasgow yesterday morning, closed down for good last night owing to lack of business. Girl undergraduates in the shop were offering kisses, at 6d each, on behalf of several urgent charities, but the day's takings were only 1s 6d., paid for by two reporters and a man who misread "kisses" in the advertisement for "kittens".

Discovery of "missing link"

SEPTEMBER 3, 1936. Dr Robert Broom, a retired doctor, found at Sterkfontein caves near Krugersdorp, Transvaal, an adult Australopithecine jawbone. The discovery vindicated Professor Raymond Dart's momentous find in 1924 of a skull which he claimed was the "missing link" between man and ape. Dr Broom"s additional finding ended *scientific* rejection of a fiercely contested Darwinian theory. It also established that southern Africa, not Asia, was the likely "cradle of mankind".

Concentration camp releases

FEBRUARY 17 1934. Herr Hitler said last night tens of thousands of people sent to concentration camps had already been released. The prisoners had interfered with Germany's "restoration to political health". Those who abandoned their hostile attitudes to this were being released from the camps. Dr Joseph Goebbels declared that hostile citizens of Germany had been instrumental in persuading the English to denounce "our Nazi regime as a tyranny of blood terror. We have been (falsely) accused of all sorts of atrocities."

> **Note:** Nearly 80 years later, in the 2010s, a film-maker was banned from Monaco's Film Festival for jokingly claiming to be a "Nazi".

Nazis secretly making high explosives

SEPTEMBER 15, 1936. Germany is making large quantities of high explosives, despite the ban imposed by post-WW1's Treaty of Versailles. A Washington inquiry also heard allegations that Hitler's supporters were armed in 1933 with American-made weapons smuggled in through Holland.

Windsor change

DECEMBER 11, 1936. King Edward VIII has abdicated the throne. (He had reigned over the British Empire for 11 months, and quit to marry Mrs Wallis Simpson, an American divorcee. Everyone in the world relished the scandal, except the British, who weren't told about it until the last moment. Poor younger brother, Bertie, had to change his name from Albert to George, and take over the realm. As war clouds rolled in, George VI played his role magnificently, almost without a stutter. It was the time of "Knock Knock" jokes, and the best of them was:

"Knock, Knock."

"Who's there?"

"Windsor."

"Windsor who?"

"Windsor wife and loses the Crown."

Hindenberg disaster

MAY 8, 1937. The *Hindenberg* airship, that so impressed the world when it flew repeatedly over the packed Olympic Games Stadium at low altitude on opening day in Berlin last year, has crashed dramatically in flames after crossing the Atlantic and trying to land at Lakehurst in the US. The death roll in the disaster is officially announced to be 33 VIPs of various nations, the survivors numbering 66. Capt Max Pruss, commander of the Hindenberg, is in critical condition.

Allies open war front against Germany

MAY 4, 1939. The Royal Navy has taken up strategic stations to prevent invasion of Britain. On land, Britain, France, Holland, and Belgium are preparing to block Germany on its Siegfried Line. France's huge defences on its Maginot Line are fully manned.

Note: Hitler's Blitzkrieg soon raced around the static defences; invaded Germany's smallest neighbours, but failed to prevent most of the British Expeditionary Force from escaping on small craft, fishing boats and private yachts back to England. We kids had to stop singing the song of the year: *"We're going to hang out the washing on the Siegfried Line – have you any dirty washing mother dear?"* British troops fell back to be rescued by every small boat available sent to Dunkirk, but Churchill hailed the retreat as a victory. Of sorts. It was a moment of national courage and daring, and the

British Expeditionary Force survived to fight more battles, beginning in Africa and returning to Europe on two fronts later.

***

IN THE 1940S YOU COULD HEAR A BOMB DROP

During this decade, war affected most families across the planet, from Beijing to Buenos Aires; from Los Angeles to Hiroshima; from bombed London to obliterated Dresden. And of course it directly and heavily impinged on people from the ghettoes of Poland to the Jewish freedom fighters, later in the decade, struggling to develop their homeland in the Middle East.

Missing, presumed dead

CHRISTMAS EVE, 1943. Lt J Montagu Simpson of Benmore Farm, Sandown, Johannesburg, who served in the RDLI, in Intelligence, and in the SAAF, was previously reported missing. He is now presumed killed. He was in a bomber brought down last year. He was the only son of parents living in Johannesburg. He left bequests to his old school, and to his church.

> **Note:** Newspapers in the free world carried tens of thousands of single column head-and-shoulders photographs of uniformed airman, soldiers, and sailors decorated for valour or reported dead, wounded; missing in action, or, occasionally, back on leave and given great welcomes at home. General Smuts's Government enlisted only volunteers for war – and only "double volunteers" wearing the Orange Flash, to fight outside of southern Africa. Volunteers, over the age of 18, consisted of all races, both sexes, and all creeds or persuasions, from Jewish to Muslim, and from communist to ultra-conservative. Only the extreme right wing of Afrikaans *bittereinders* refused to join up to oppose Hitler. Darker-skinned South Africans were among the heroes, but they were seldom allowed to carry arms.

Local heroes

DECEMBER 2, 1942. Capt WJ van der Merwe, President Steyn Regiment, was killed in action in Egypt five weeks ago. He was on the magistrate's staff in Zastron before joining up. He leaves a widow and young son.

AUGUST 15, 1945. "I turned to one of the natives, Corporal Job Maseko, and asked what he had done. 'I blew up a steamer,' he replied. He told me how he had collected cartridges and removed the contents ...."

AUGUST 15, 1945. Proudly in uniform in this picture is Stretcher-bearer Lucas Majozi, the hero of El Alamein.

Note: There were so many internationally decorated heroes, even from a tiny section of small South Africa, that they seldom attracted attention unless they possessed top honours such as a VC or DFC and bar, or DSO and bar. South Africa's, too, came from almost every ethnic group and every creed in the country. However, when it came to sacrificed lives in WW2, it was the thin band of South African English-language schools that mourned the greatest losses. These lives were commemorated in roll-calls astonishingly out of proportion to their schools' numbers.

Flyers among the flowers

JUNE 18, 1943. Eight laughing men, all of the 21st Squadron SAAF, were photographed in a flower-carpeted field in Tunisia. All come from the same school in Johannesburg.

Atomic bomb kills nearly every living thing

AUGUST 8, 1945. The Atomic Bomb dropped on Hiroshima on Sunday wiped out more than 4square miles of Hiroshima, it has been estimated from reconnaissance photographs.

Note: War had already ended in Europe on V-E Day. V-J Day followed only after two A-Bombs were dropped on Japan. Wild celebrations in the Western world turned soon into global post-war disillusionment. The rest of the decade was a dreary time for everyone: austerity and food rationing in "victorious" Britain; survival in the rubble of Europe's upheaval, and populations everywhere else waiting for the new, bigger H-bomb to destroy the world.

Sentence passed at Nuremberg

OCTOBER 1, 1946. Twelve Nazi leaders on trial before the War Crimes Tribunal were this afternoon sentenced to death by hanging. They are: Goering, Ribbentrop, Keitel, Kaltenbrunner, Rosenberg, Frank, Frick, Streicher, Jodi, Seysss-Inquart and Bormann (sentenced in his absence). They were found guilty on some or all four indictments: 1) Conspiracy to wage aggressive war; 2) Crimes against peace; 3) War crimes; 4) Crimes against humanity. Hess was sentenced to life imprisonment on two counts. Raeder and Funk were also sent to prison.

Gandhi assassinated

JANUARY 30, 1948. While on his way to prayers here in New Delhi today, Mr Gandhi was shot and killed. He was fired at four times at close range. A young man was seized by the crowd. The slight, simply clad architect of Indian independence was the figurehead and spiritual leader of millions. He survived an attempt on his life just ten days ago.

Rise of "broederbond state" denounced

AUGUST 29, 1948. Smuts, who lost the general election this year, foresaw, under the Nationalist regime, an end of legitimate elections and of plans for an increasing franchise. He predicted that the new government would be run by an inner committee involving anonymous members of the Nationalist 'Brotherhood'.

(*Note:* Just a month before Smuts issued the warning, headlined above, apartheid came to South Africa as the *Nasionale Party* – to its own surprise and everyone else's astonishment – won the first post-war general election. It campaigned on hate, fear, and exclusive nationalism – often bitter enough to be reminiscent of Hitler's nationalist state. It won the vote of those *bittereinder* Afrikaners seeking an autocratic Republic of their own. It also won the vote of tens of thousands of white citizens tired of shortages of consumer goods and demanding white bread, which they were forced to do without even after the war years.)

***

THE CONFUSING FIFTIES

This was the period in which the United States spent billions on helping to re-build the Germany it had spent years bombing towards oblivion. The Marshal Plan inspired the policy of positive reconstruction – creating democracy in the western half of Germany while Russia's occupying forces were terrorizing and sacking the eastern half.

The world teetered on the brink of more wars, and much of mankind worried about the possibility of someone dropping another A-bomb – or worse, the new, many times bigger H-bomb. In South Africa, the African National Congress preached non-violence and democracy, while the

Nationalist Government condemned the ANC's peaceful protests.

At the same moment in the mid-1950s that the South African government was passing more laws and using police to enforce *segregation*, the United States government was using federal troops to enforce racial *integration*.

There were many other contradictory developments in this uneven decade.

Truman sacks MacArthur

APRIL 23, 1951. This headline, summed up correctly a dramatic personal battle of wills between "humble" President Truman and "arrogant" General Douglas MacArthur which signalled one of the great *political* stories in the Western democratic world in the 20th century.

ANC President Dr Moroka arrested

AUGUST 14, 1952. Dr JS Moroka, president of the ANC, was arrested today while attending to patients at his surgery. He was fingerprinted and charged under the vague and controversial Suppression of Communism Act. He was released on bail of one hundred pounds. He told *The Star:* "I want the African people to know of my arrest. I ask them to remain calm and to act with dignity."

SA airmen defend democracy in Korea

DECEMBER 5, 1952. Another batch of pilots left today to replace men serving with the famous Cheetah Squadron of the SAAF in aggressive, communist-controlled Korea. (Ironically) USA and UN have thanked the SA Squadron for serving and sacrificing lives in the cause of democracy. SA pilots were acknowledged in this war to be among the best-trained, most skilled in the world.

Big battle rages in Algeria

MARCH 12, 1952. French aircraft bombed strong insurgent positions in the Aurès Mountains in Eastern Algeria last night. A violent battle is in progress between French forces and a large insurgent band from Tunisia.

Total apartheid may take 100 years

JAN 20, 1954. (White) Farmers have been told that their need for labour will be met by "other means" when the races are fully segregated.

Total apartheid was in any case a long-term process, probably 100 years. Thereafter, farmers could rely on migrant labour, a solution recognized internationally, Nationalist spokesmen assured their supporters.

Troops sent to enforce integration

MAY 1954. Troops stand by to ensure that the Governor of Arkansas does not stop black children attending the Central High School at Little Rock, as the Supreme Court has ruled that segregation is unconstitutional.

"Black spots" in "white area"

MAY 1954. Newclare and Sophiatown are declared "black spots" in a white area. All freehold rights and leases are cancelled for black people who are being moved to Meadowlands, Orlando, and other townships being created in the veld in the South Western area. Police are on standby to ensure orderliness for families being removed.

Freedom charter signed

JUNE 26, 1955. Political leaders representing Black, Indian, "Coloured" and White factions gathered under the aegis of ANC President JS Moroka at Kliptown, southwest of Johannesburg to sign the Freedom Charter – a policy document adopted by the ANC. The words were designed to resemble the US democratic Constitution.

"Whites only" in Sophiatown now official

OCTOBER 9, 1958. "Rubble wasteland fills the suburb where once thousands lived," writes a *Star* reporter ... Meanwhile the removal of 57800 Natives from Johannesburg's western areas might take five to ten years, at an enormous cost of millions of pounds.

***

THE SENSATIONAL SIXTIES

The 1960s brought so many sensational headlines that they began to cancel each other out. Assassinations of internationally-known leaders became almost a habit. Flower-power lost the scent. Cults turned vicious or violent. But the Sixties were by no means all bad.

Good news for the planet

At the beginning of the decade Russia put the first man, Yuri Gagarin, in Space, and his safe return in 1961was hailed as the greatest deed of mankind. That applied until 1969, when Neil Armstrong became the first man to land on the moon.

There was also good news for the world in 1967, when young Professor Chris Barnard achieved the world's first heart transplant at Groote Schuur Hospital in Cape Town, and Louis Washkansky became the first man on Earth to carry another's heart in his breast.

During this decade young hippies smoking marijuana and scattering flowers, went to a giant Rock Concert at Woodstock to celebrate love and goodwill … sexual love, that is, and goodwill towards other feely-fellow, flower-power people.

'No problem' became, almost overnight, an over-used phrase to describe life in general.

Women take world leadership

In 1960 the world's first woman Prime Minister, Mrs Sirimavo Bandaranaike, took control of Ceylon. The second was Mrs Indira Gandhi of India in 1966, and Mrs Golda Meir of Israel in 1969.

Pop stars rule

The biggest pop stars of the decade were the Beatles, four young men who peddled music, not violence nor drugs nor sex. Beatles music was sometimes compared with Bach. The Beatlemania outdid and outlasted all the self-regarding rock stars of the decade and beyond, except for Sergeant Elvis Presley, who was acclaimed "sensational" even before he came out of the army in 1960.

Skirts go *up*

The mini-skirt emerged from London's Carnaby Street, hardly covering the thighs of model Lesley Hornby (skinny "Twiggy") and was greeted as the decade's greatest matter of interest. "Surely no fashion has ever caused such a sensation nor so aptly epitomized the mood of our times," raved one caption picturing legs, mainly. Some churchmen blamed the mini for causing droughts, floods, and bad thoughts. Bad thoughts caused the banning of another sensation, the itsy, bitsy bikini, from public swimming pools. (Private swimming pools were still the preserve of the very rich at the time).

Democracy takes hold

Democracy was bursting out all over Africa during the decade, but proving less democratic, and less enduring, than democracy in the new Israel after the Jewish state scattered its combined enemies in the Six-Day War. The Israelis were so confident and argumentative after 1967, it was said that if you put three in the same room they would end the debate by launching five new political parties. I met a deputation returning from a meeting with premier Golda Meir, who had asked a press photographer to stop flashing his camera while delegates were talking. The photographer retorted: "Mrs Meir, you do your job. I'll do mine." And so it was to be; for some years.

Democracy retreats

But the editors of Israel's more thoughtful newspapers were becoming concerned. At a time that Israel was changing its leadership, an editor in Tel Aviv told me: "We built this nation on an ideal of liberal equality. That is changing. We are starting to use bad law and the old British enemy's "Emergency Regulations" to silence dissent. If we're not careful, the balance will swing towards doctrinaire religion and nationalism." A Palestinian editor in Jerusalem told me: "The balance changed long ago. We are oppressed, censored and imprisoned without fair trial." Down in South Africa, under anti-Semitic Verwoerd's rule, there seemed to be no balance at all.

In the USA, things went crazy. Three top leaders President Jack Kennedy, Dr Luther King, and Senator Robert Kennedy campaigning for the presidency, were assassinated in broad daylight in front of crowds and TV cameras. (See below. An attempt on the life of President Reagan occurred later.)

"Soweto" is the name

JAN 1960. From this date and for three more years, people argued over a name for the South-Western Townships of Johannesburg, destined, through forced removals of family homes, to become SA's biggest all-black city. One white letter-writer suggested the name "Verwoerdstan" to honour the founding by the government of separate racial "Bantustans". An African reader suggested "New Zimbabwe" – at a time when Zimbabwe referred only to the past glory of the famed Zimbabwe Ruins. "New Zimbabwe could well signify a glory that is to be ... another New Harlem" wrote W Mbokodo. Instead, from 20 August 1963, the geographical acronym "Soweto" was formally accepted by most of its residents because it favoured no tribal language. Soweto was also popular no doubt because it was not acceptable either to the Place Names Commission nor the National Party. Negative reasoning seemed to be emblematic of South Africa in that time.

Republican referendum

JANUARY 1960. Prime Minister Verwoerd announced his proposed referendum for (white) South Africans to vote on cutting ties with the British Crown. Later he walked out of the Commonwealth as well, because it was too "black", his party reasoned.

Let me be very frank says UK Premier

FEBRUARY 1960. "We cannot support your racial policies," Mr Macmillan told Dr Verwoerd and the assembled members of both Houses of Parliament today. He warned of a "Wind of Change sweeping through Africa". (His speech signalled the transformation of a series of African colonies about to gain national independence.)

Prime Minister Verwoerd shot

APRIL 16, 1960. Dr Verwoerd was shot twice in the face today while attending the Rand Easter Show in Johannesburg, but spectators in the grandstand overcame the alleged assassin, a middle-aged European man who was arrested. The Prime Minister was rushed to hospital where his condition is reported as stable. Verwoerd made a remarkable recovery and his iron rule lasted until his assassination in Parliament six years later.

D-day dawns for decimalisation in SA

FEBRUARY 12, 1961. Today you must convert the familiar "tickey" (a coin for three pennies also known as "thruppence") into two cents plus half a cent. (A tickey would buy more sweets than R3 might in 2016) A pound becomes two rand, and "ten bob" converts to one rand. And a shilling is not 12 pennies or cents any more. You cannot say "shilling"; you must only say "ten cents". And don't ever talk of the weight of anything again. You *must* say, "John's mass is 500kg" – depending on whatever mass a kilogram is supposed to have. Find out by checking a handy conversion table – and also check your petrol bill for rands per litre not shillings a gallon. You may still use the word "ounces" – but only in international terms, such as: "Gold is 35 dollars an oz."

Saying "it's miles away" is forbidden. Instead say "kilometres", which is a longer word for a shorter distance.

Final warning: watch out for the comma. It's about to appear – and disappear – in the oddest manner. You can no longer say "ten point one". It is now "ten comma one". This is going to be tough for a while. Sort it out, and get used to it.

Horror scenes at Sharpeville

MARCH 21, 1960. A frail fence collapsed. On one side were 130 white and 77 black police, nervously guarding a municipal office. On the other side an estimated 20000 people trying to hand back to the local authority the passes they had been forced to carry at all times and everywhere outside the "Native Areas". The crowds of men, women, and some youngsters surged forwards. The police opened fire, without waiting for orders. And kept firing. The result was a wild scene of carnage: 249 people lay strewn across the ground – 69 of them dead or dying, many of them shot in the back as they attempted to flee the hail of bullets.

Nobel peace prize for Chief Albert Luthuli

In **1961** the president-general of the African National Congress receives South Africa's first Nobel Peace Prize. He was recognised by most communities as a man of honour and integrity, not in favour of political violence.

Mandela still escapes police net

NOVEMBER 1961. Police have not been able to trace Mr Nelson Mandela, secretary of the continuation committee of the All-in African National Action Council and organiser of its demonstrations. Police searched his home in Orlando last night. He is still at large. (But about 18 months later, Security Police raided the home of Arthur Goldreich in Rivonia near Johannesburg, and arrested 17 top ANC leaders, including Walter Sisulu. The betrayal of these men led to the Rivonia Trial – followed by the dramatically staged Treason Trial after Nelson Mandela was caught.)

Death sentence for Mandela?

Facing the death penalty, Nelson Mandela made his historic speech, in which he declared that he would rather die than live under oppression. It resulted in the punishment of an indefinite life sentence on Robben Island. (It lasted 27 years).

President John F Kennedy assassinated in Dallas

On **NOVEMBER 22, 1963,** all the world (except South Africa) watched the inexplicable drama played out on TV. And re-played and re-played, even today. America was still in shock when, days later, the headlines went round the world:

President's assassin is assassinated "on tv"

The murderer who walked up to Kennedy's assassin and shot him at point blank range while the prisoner was handcuffed and under escort, has been detained and questioned. His victim's role as an assassin remains a mystery, but he was known for his Soviet sympathies, according to reports.

SA Prime Minister assassinated

SEPTEMBER 6, 1966. Prime Minister Verwoerd died of stab wounds inflicted on him this afternoon by a man wearing a parliamentary uniform. (The headline was read on city streets across South Africa within minutes of the assassination. His murderer, Dimitri Tsafendas, was an accredited messenger in Parliament; a Portuguese citizen of South Africa who proved to be mentally disturbed).

Martin Luther King assassinated

APRIL 5, 1968. Violence erupted across America today as gangs of Negroes, infuriated by the assassination of Dr Luther King last night, went on the rampage in many towns and cities. Almost inexplicable violence raged in other areas of America – in the Manson killings, gang wars and cult murders.

Senator Robert Kennedy assassinated

JUNE 5, 1968. A huge grieving crowd gathered outside the Good Samaritan Hospital in Los Angeles today as a team of neurosurgeons fought to save the life of Senator Robert Kennedy, who was gunned down before horrified supporters at his campaign headquarters. (He died shortly after this report).

***

THE SAD 'SEVENTIES'

The mini-skirt could go no higher. Instead, in the 1970s, hems came down below the knee. Apartheid in South Africa also had to deal with reality. Commonsense defeated racism several times in this decade. Sadly, however, hate, bad law, and oppression would fly unchallenged in the colours of apartheid for another twenty years.

Manipulation of segregation, in attempting to live a normal life, became an art. Violence followed. By the end of the decade official apartheid was already crumbling at the edges.

Six die in rioting. 10 000 on rampage in Soweto, rioting continues. Toll now 23 dead, 250 hurt, taut uneasy calm. Police wait, ready to shoot.

These were some of the headlines in *The Star* on **JUNE 16, 1976** and for the two following days. But for an afternoon newspaper, publishing special editions every hour as events on our doorstep occurred, there were many other front page headlines updating, each hour, news of Soweto students' uprising. It was the most difficult and best covered event in my personal experience. The headlines were so fresh that people going to Soweto after work could decide from published reports an hour earlier, which way to go home and by what means. Motorists learned from a special edition not to take the main highway to Pretoria, which was barricaded by rioters.

In times of chaos and government censorship rumour normally flourishes. This time it didn't. Society had to face the facts, despite the absence of TV and the bias of government-only radio news. Accuracy and balanced reporting were essential as tension ran like a lit fuse through the streets and suburbs and townships of the city.

Government removes some race barriers

DECEMBER 10, 1979. Owners of drive-in cinemas, clubs, hospitals, libraries, theatres, halls, circuses, cafes and restaurants, and organisers of receptions, fetes and exhibitions, can be given open exemptions from enforced separation, according to the Minister ... (The catch was that organisers could apply for once-only permits. It meant that normality and commonsense might rule by special exemption, if properly applied for on every occasion. The Government was attempting to apply cosmetics to the decaying face of apartheid.)

info scandal – Vorster quits

The "Info Scandal" began with a government-supporting English-language newspaper destroying much of its print-runs or "returns", in order falsely to claim a higher circulation. It ended with the downfall of Prime Minister BJ Vorster.

The "Infogate" investigation was sparked by the *Rand Daily Mail* finding evidence about the upstart *Citizen*'s illicit attempts to grab *The Mail*'s morning newspaper market. *Mail* reporters not only uncovered their rival's fraudulent attempts to misstate its circulation figures – but also exposed *The Citizen*'s pretence of being "politically independent". They went on to investigate the source of *The Citizen's* funding, and in doing so unearthed a "Deep Throat" source who would guide them into the inner recesses of government. What they found was an illicit party propaganda fund, made up of public money that was unaccounted for; hidden from Parliament, and illegally spent – not only to start an apartheid-supporting newspaper.

Further investigation, led by the *Rand Daily Mail* and chased by most of the English-language press, ultimately brought down Dr Eschel Rhoodie, Head of the Information Department, his Minister, and the Prime Minister. It was a great triumph – especially for PW Botha, who used the scandal and ensuing commission of inquiry to get rid of Vorster and take his place. Then "PW" moved political power into the President's office – and took that title from Vorster as well.

A news story of such proportions takes a thousand headlines to complete. Here are just a few of *The Star's* street poster headlines during the resulting commission of inquiry.

Info man chased woman

Info woman chased boss

Eschel used 'jap spider' on staff

Citizen man accused of theft

Big profits for the Rhoodies

Yet, despite all that scandal and all that effort, there were other headlines in this decade which caused deeper harm to the country and which made news around the world.

Kruger – Biko death exploited

On **14 SEPTEMBER 1977,** the Minister of Police, Jimmy Kruger, was trying to prove himself to his National Party Congress. He tried to justify his apathy and defuse the international "fuss" over news reports concerning the death in custody of Black Consciousness leader Steve Biko after they had beaten him up in the police cells. Kruger hit out at the media, saying they were exploiting the situation. He told his party congress that he was not pleased – but he was not sorry. "It [Biko's death] leaves me cold."

Those five words, in the shocking situation of the time, were possibly the most chilling ever uttered in public in the apartheid era. However, Kruger – except in terms of the power he held – was not a chilling personality. He was frightened, and he was inept, which made him one of the most dangerous of men in a would-be police state.

Kruger closes world newspaper

On **19 OCTOBER 1977** he not only closed the Argus Co newspaper *The World* and arrested the editor, he banned 18 organisations which he deemed were causing the State trouble. The threat to free speech and the injustice of it were palpable, but the folly of his actions was impossible to understand. Closing down Percy Qoboza's "black" newspaper might have done more to disparage South Africa abroad than all the critics of apartheid together. The irony was that The Minister of Police's announcement came as visiting editors from overseas were about to speak at a conference in Pretoria on the "Image of South Africa". I too was a speaker. In the car taking me to the conference I threw away my prepared opposition-debating points (as did my overseas colleagues) and scribbled one of *The Star*'s earliest *front-page* leaders castigating the Minister of Police under the heading BITTER SIGN OF FAILURE. The conference was also a deserved failure, but was heading that way in any event.

***

THE FATEFUL 1980S

This decade ushered in computers that could be used outside of government and international corporations. The computers were made more cheaply – and much smaller – so that a few privileged people could use them in their homes. World communications were beginning to change for the first time in 300 years.

But the decade was dominated by the Superpowers, and the Cold War which froze political change across the world in a balance of nuclear terror. However, in 1989 …

The Berlin wall falls

Its collapse signalled the collapse of Russian tyranny – and liberated or created more than 40new nations. It ended an undeclared ideological war. Almost overnight, communism, in practical terms, was dead, and the spirit of freedom was rousingly rampant.

The fall came just in time to save South Africa from potential civil war. The white Nationalist government had been engaged throughout the decade in under-cover strikes against its African neighbours. It had done so in the guise of a champion of anti-communism, and it had successfully become an independent arms producer with a self-sufficient economy, in spite of – or rather inspired by – international sanctions. In the face of the threats from the banned ANC, and the increasingly brave and active United Democratic Front at home, the government assumed more and more war-time powers – all to meet a so-called communist threat. And now there was no communism … the apartheid State was suddenly bereft of its only moral excuse ("opposing communistic dictatorship and colonisation"). With the collapse of communism, the apartheid government was not only morally disarmed, but physically vulnerable. The decade ended while Nelson Mandela's release was being negotiated.

Here are some headlines of that fateful decade:

SA to make its own fuel

AUGUST 2, 1980. The parastatal Sasol, will soon be refining oil from coal! But only for local use. (*Note.* Another parastatal, Armscor, was producing not only rifles and ammunition, but one of the most advanced heavy, long-range guns in the world, for export, and for use inside Angola).

South Africa's atomic programme, assisted by international interests despite boycott, thrived under total secrecy and tight security law.

Angola battles

JULY 2, 1980. South African forces struck across the Kunene River today, to enter Angola and soon withdrew. They claimed capture of 30 storage depots; 300 enemy dead, and they flew out 250 tons of Soviet and Eastern bloc military hardware, including Sam-7 rockets. They drove out of Angola numbers of captured vehicles, including a Russian-made armoured car.

> **Note:** SA invaded Angola as early as 1976, but government claimed at first that these troops were mercenaries – which prompted some of us to circumvent military censorship by reporting on an "unofficial invasion of Angola" using South African forces.

New unrest in black townships

JULY 12, 1980. Violence has caused one death so far in unrest in Johannesburg following the fourth anniversary of the 1976 Soweto Riots. Police are promising a tough response from now on.

United States President shot

MARCH 31, 1981. Emerging from a building into an open street where some supporters waited, President Ronald Reagan was hit by a bullet fired at fairly close range yesterday. His courage and his humour minimized his apparent injuries.

Bomb in SA capital. 19 dead

MAY 20, 1983. A large car bomb killed 19 and injured 219 civilians of all races when it exploded at lunchtime outside air force headquarters in Church Street, Pretoria. You have to witness the results of a "car bombing" to understand – and wince – every time you see this headline still constantly repeating itself in various parts of the world three decades later.

East Cape rises up in rebellion

SEPTEMBER 1984. Frustrated black youths stormed through the townships seeking out "collaborators" and "necklacing" suspects. Government buildings were set alight and crowds watched as individual victims were burned to death as a ring of fire enveloped their heads and shoulders. Enforced boycotts were made against shops. Township mothers were forced to eat their grocery purchases on the spot; including soap. The immediate causes of the riots are unemployment and lack of a political voice.

France in new bid to isolate SA

JULY 27, 1985. France is spearheading a world-wide campaign aimed at the total isolation of South Africa until it abandons apartheid.

10 ECC countries recall envoys

AUGUST 1, 1985.

> **Note:** The two above headlines might have been far more effective had the intention been followed through 10 or 20 or 30 years earlier.

PM Baulks at crossing the Rubicon

AUGUST 15, 1985. PW Botha's expected "Rubicon" speech on reform and benefits for excluded races failed to take place. Instead, while the world awaited his much heralded announcement of massive reforms, he offered a damp squib. The rand currency has plunged.

New state of emergency

JUNE 12, 1986. Sweeping powers, effective from midnight last night, have once again been given to security forces to detain and arrest people without a warrant.

> **Note:** This was the second of several increasingly harsh measures. Despite nearly 100 laws inhibiting freedom of speech, strict "emergency" censorship was suddenly imposed on the press three times! In the first stage, *The Star* carried empty spaces to indicate censored stories. Its front page, with ominous empty spaces scattered across it, was reproduced around the world. When empty spaces were banned(!), it carried a notice reading: "CENSORED. This newspaper may have been censored. We are not permitted to say where, or how, or to what extent." Under the third stage of three years of this military-style rule, the newspaper – instead of risking means of evading the restrictions – actively and repeatedly broke the new laws and Emergency Regulations.

Machel dies in crash

OCTOBER 19, 1986. President Samora Machel of Mozambique is killed in an air crash in South African territory. Few details are ever made public, and no credible sources of information are available.

Police try to seize the Star

MARCH 10, 1987. The newspaper took a calculated risk in publishing a statement by the Parents Detainees Committee. The newspaper was saved from closure by a Supreme Court injunction.

> **Note:** A reminder that in at least two institutions in the apartheid era some still retained their independence.

Transport chaos as trains set alight

APRIL 16, 1987. Two more trains were attacked today as a wave of arson and assaults against SA Transport Services moved into the fourth day.

Chorus grows for Mandela's release

DECEMBER 5, 1989. Newly released political prisoner Mr Govan Mbeki thinks Nelson Mandela will be released soon. So does Mandela's daughter Zenani. But the government remains silent.

San Francisco quake disaster

OCTOBER 17, 1989. Motorists have been crushed on twisted highways and there are countless fires. More than 60 people have been killed in the quake. The death toll is expected to rise.

THE DARING, MIRACULOUS NINETIES

The 1990s brought peace and democracy to South Africa. The courage, the statesmanship, the patience and far-sightedness of the active leaders of two bitterly divided, undefeated groups banished from our minds the risks that were involved.

Govt bombshell – "we want full democracy"

FEBRUARY 6, 1990. Pres de Klerk has announced that the government is ready to accept a democratically elected interim power-sharing government which will negotiate a new constitution.

Mandela walks free

FEBRUARY 12, 1990. Seventy-one-year-old Nelson Mandela,

accompanied by his wife and ANC leaders, walked free from prison yesterday, and addressed a huge crowd from the balcony of Cape Town's City Hall. Few people had seen his face, or pictures of him, in nearly three decades.

Government and ANC take first step to peace

MAY 5, 1990. The African National Congress and the government reached an historic peace accord in a dramatic breakthrough in Cape Town yesterday. The armed struggle has been halted in return for concessions.

"God help us all"

SEPTEMBER 8, 1992. This was the banner headline following front-page leads over earlier reports that year stating:

Massacre of mourners

Revenge fury after gang attacks ANC in Sebokeng.

34 slaughtered by Impis

Terrified women and children were among those hacked to death when Zulu impis went on the rampage in a Boipatong squatter camp in the Vaal Triangle late last night.

Koevoet link to massacre

The government, still in shock at the breakdown in constitutional discussions is facing a new crisis sparked by claims that former Koevoet members took part in the Boipateng massacre. (*Note.* Koevoet was a notorious police counter-insurgency unit. It acted as violently and illegally as the Civil Cooperation Bureau, a military security unit seconded to city councils to crush opposition within SA municipal areas in the late 1980s.)

Chris Hani assassinated at front door

APRIL 10, 1993. The head of the SA Communist Party and former MK leader was shot dead outside his home today. It is believed that right-wingers are involved in the murder of the popular ANC figure. The plan is to destabilise all proposals for a non-racial constitution, and a democratic election.

The battle for Jo'burg

MARCH 28, 1994. A month before the crucial national election, there were armed riots and killings in central Johannesburg. For the second successive day the staff of *The Star* looked down from their windows and saw 10000 Zulu marchers, armed with kerries and many in traditional battle dress, shuffle-dancing down Sauer Street when suddenly shots were fired among them from nearby rooftops. By the end of the day several of the Zulu supporters of Chief Mangosuthu Buthelezi's IFP (anti-ANC) party had been shot in various parts of the city, including eight killed by nervous guards at ANC headquarters. Others appeared to have been shot by *agents provocateur*.

Star photographer among slain

APRIL 18, 1994. Running gun battles continued as National Peacekeeping troops and Zulu men from immigrant workers' hostels clashed in Thokoza township, East Rand. *The Star*'s award-winning photographer Ken Oosterbroek was shot and killed in the street while covering the action.

The murders and public violence; the plotting, pretences, and crises inflicted on us by extremists, mainly in the "killing fields" of KwaZulu are forgotten as if they were merely a bad dream.

We remember only the goodwill – and the joy of sharing in long queues on a long day, the act of democracy that brought us together at the polling booths in 1994. It didn't happen automatically. The planning, the bargaining, the making of the Constitution, and the organising of constituencies and mobilising of millions of voters – millions of whom had never voted before, and many of whom were illiterate – required time, effort, and some sacrifices from thousands of volunteers to make it happen.

Peaceful election among scenes of joy

APRIL 27, 1994. South Africans of all races, for the first time in 300 years of recorded history, queued up to vote together. They watch misty-eyed, the colourful new South African "interim" flag snapping in the autumn breeze. (It was due to be replaced in 1999, but everybody accepted the original "temporary" design.)

The rainbow covenant

MAY 11, 1994. Before huge crowds, under an Air Force fly-past, President Nelson Mandela was sworn into office yesterday with a covenant that reads: "We shall build a society in which all South Africans, both black and white, will be able to walk tall, without any fear in their hearts, assured of their inalienable right to human dignity -- a rainbow nation at peace with itself and the world."

Nkosi Sikelel' lafrika – forever

DECEMBER 11, 1996. Mandela calls on citizens to realise the vision and grasp the opportunities of the Constitution he signed into law yesterday.

The 1990s saw many more world events – the death of Princess Diana, for example; the rise of HIV; the cloning of a sheep named Dolly, raising many ethical issues. But – apart from winning rugby's World Cup – South Africans focused only on political freedom. The 21st century would bring different priorities.

***

2020 VISION – YOUR OWN FUTURE BOGGLES THE MIND

You are bound to remember more about the 21st century news story than I do, so I shall be brief on detail in order to peer momentarily at the future. This is scientifically possible because the first decade of the 21st century gave us – for the first time in mankind's brief, million year existence – a general, scientific awareness of what to expect.

Millenium countdown: apocalyptic possibilities

JANUARY 1, 2000. Computers – and the millennium – got off to a nervous start, as the world waited for "apocalyptic possibilities" on the first day. A bug named 2YK was due to wipe out millions of computers across the world. It didn't happen – either because 'IT' people were too smart, or because everyone was so dumb they didn't recognise a hoax when they saw it. The mere possibility, though, of a global wipe-out of electronic digital systems seemed as frightening as the possibility of some silly predictions of 'End of the World' coming true in 2001.

Instead, on Sept 11, 2001 the headline of the year was:

Hijacked aircraft destroy NY World Trade Centre

The tragedy, the horror, the implications of that event were replayed over and over during the decade. Clearing the rubble of seven buildings began within two weeks; rebuilding soon afterwards. Before the end of the first decade of the 21st century, the No.1 Tower on "Ground Zero" had already reached 48 storeys of a 104-storey, 541m tall new building. The triumph of its completion was over-shadowed by warfare in the Middle East, and the spread of terrorism across the world.

Computers change our world

AUGUST 2001. Computer strength and growth could be *witnessed* jumping exponentially from that year onwards – a growth rate equivalent to changing from first gear into the speed of sound. First it was Napster, pirating music to the tune of three billion files in this single month so that you could file a thousand music tracks and play 30 of them day and night.

By the end of the decade, social networking in the guise of YouTube and Facebook had blanketed the world. Twittering took off in the next decade, and everyone became a potential instant recorder of history, just by clicking their cell phone cameras at the critical moment ... another instant phenomenon. Twitter became a weapon that sometimes fired backwards, harming the thoughtless or prejudiced sender. In India cell-phone ownership grew from 2m in 2000, to nearly 550 million hand-sets in 2010, thus empowering tens of millions of the rural poor. During the decade the iPod and iPad down-sized computers. Computer animation changed imagery in cinemas and in documentary television. Indeed, computers began to change how things would work in future on this planet. Extraordinary "inventions" of new materials and new methods of making and doing things were so numerous that their future influences were hardly measured.

Invasion of Iraq

MARCH 20, 2003. The Iraq War began with a flourish as the world watched US forces on television, advancing across the desert at 40km per hour to reach Baghdad. The foolish "instant victory" was about to unleash a thousand demons.

Iraqi citizens tear down Saddam's statue

APRIL 9, 2003. The toppling of President Saddam Hussein's statue by his own people signals the end of the war after only 20 days. (In fact, the invasion of Iraq and the vanquishing of Saddam's forces was quicker than that ... they seemed to vanish in the morning mist. Then began the guerrilla war – and the internecine civil wars between three tribal forces. Seven years later "terrorists" and suicide bombers were killing more people than Saddam's army did in 2003.)

China rising to be world's biggest economy?

MARCH 2004. I witnessed first-hand, after years-apart visits, the astonishing growth, not only in China but in India, Malaysia, Vietnam, Thailand, South Vietnam, and the Philippines. I had visited China in the 1990s, shortly after the massacre on Tiananmen Square. Then, after a return visit about ten years later, I wrote an article headed "China Wow!" describing the reactions of American businessmen and professionals arriving in Shanghai to view their skyscrapers, their bullet-trains, their giant dockyards and flying freeway bridges, and Beijing's new airport – the biggest in the world. It is inevitable. China's billions of citizens will re-shape the world, just as they are shaping the lives of a third of the world's population with their computerised industrial and transport revolution ... but the scale of domestic poverty will surely postpone the day. After 2020 perhaps?

Financial crash on Wall Street

SEPTEMBER 15, 2008. At 1.45 am today the 164-year-old investment bank, Lehman Brothers filed for bankruptcy in the Southern District of New York. American financial houses immediately fell like dominoes, starting the worst financial depression since Black Friday in 1929. All the economies of the First World soon collapsed, but the 21st century economic crash was carefully called "a recession"; grudgingly upgraded later to "The Recession". By the end of 2010, US unemployment was doubling each year. Three nations of the EU were on the brink of collapse. By 2016 a nervous world was observing sagging investment amid hopeful signs of increased trade.

A giant migration following terrorist wars in the Middle East brought fear of further social change. The changes are due to outstrip the fears; in time.

***

THE FUTURE: A 2020-PLUS VISION

By mid-21st century, super-intelligent computers – much smarter than any human being – will be small enough to be placed inside bodies and brains to improve the health and skills and wits of men and women, said digital guru Ray Kurzweil in an interview back in 2010. Miniature computers will monitor our brain cells and the digital world, then process automatically and without search-engines the relevant accumulated knowledge of mankind (and of computers) and make decisions for human beings based on that knowledge.

HEALTH: People will reprogram their biology to ensure that they are healthier.

FOOD, TO FEED BILLIONS MORE PEOPLE: Computer-invented technology will grow vitro-cloned meats in computerised factories run by artificial intelligence. They will provide the food for which we now slaughter animals.

DANGERS: Technology remains a double-edged sword and can destroy. There will be a need for computers to develop rapid response systems to cope with new dangers like "bio-terrorism". However, some scientists believe that if computers become more intelligent than people – they might decide to dispense with people, or re-invent them.

The mind boggles. This century is going to out-compete science fiction. (This is a subject planned for the next book, *End of the Deadline*, dealing with the future of the free media.)

The only guaranteed-correct vision of this reporter is that he won't be here to witness the exciting explosion of change in mankind's lifestyles. ☐

2

Too early for the news.

1920 – 1945

9.
Confessions of a desperate newsman.

As strange as it may seem my life is based on a true story.

Patrick Conway.

Rashly, and with great reluctance, I agreed to talk about a newspaperman's life to an apparently equally reluctant audience. That was a dozen years after my official retirement, when I had gone back to being a "roving reporter". Now I was "retired" yet again, facing this audience and wishing my days had ended as an infant in the Jazz Age, at the time of even greater incipient depression.

"Ladies and gentlemen," I greeted the palpably bored tea party in a local church hall: "When I enquired about a theme for this talk, I was advised: 'Talk about *anything or nothing,* it's your choice.' So I've decided to talk to you about nothing. And as the nearest thing to nothing is some other good-for-nothing's ego, I shall tell you, very briefly, about a few of this particular ego's experiences.

"What on earth can I say that is of the least interest?"

They didn't seem able to find an answer.

I ploughed on:

"I confess that I've been in a jail ... though that's pretty common these days. In fact I have boasted a longish criminal record. But seldom have I admitted that I slept with a nun. Some people show considerable interest and scepticism when I do confess it. Yet it is a fact. More than once a young and beautiful nun invited me into her bed which I shared with her through each night in her own nunnery.

"Once I shared – briefly in pitch darkness – a canoe with a caiman more than 2 000 miles up the Amazon. It happened in the legendary Black Lake with the pink dolphins. But that's unlikely to interest you.

"What else?

"As a young newspaper reporter, I became, for some inexplicable reason, the momentary confidant of one of the heroes of the Boer War, the Great War, and the Second World War – who is better remembered as an author of the founding documents of the League of Nations and, 25 years later, of the United Nations – the only person in the world to sign both treaties.

I speak of General JC Smuts. That is a small memory which I treasure, as is the finer and greater honour of conversing with that greatest of statesmen, Nelson Mandela, on private and public matters before he was everybody's leader as president of South Africa and understandably the friend of every person in the world by the time of his death.

"Of considerably lesser interest for you should be the peculiar fact that I happened to meet all of South Africa's prime ministers and presidents of the past 60 years, from Drs DF Malan, HF Verwoerd and 'Lion of the North' JG Strijdom, to BJ Vorster, PW Botha, FW de Klerk and Thabo Mbeki, as well as Roy Welensky, Hastings Banda, Ian Smith, Kenneth Kaunda, Robert Mugabe and other leaders of nations south of the Sahara. But that's because it's merely part of what I did for a living. This entire list may not be worth one discussion you might have been privileged to share with a true friend and incandescent freedom fighter, Helen Suzman.

"While deliberately name-dropping I suppose I should mention that I also met one of the nicest of US presidents, one of the wittiest of

A first close-up meeting with a caiman persuades you it is not a peaceful thing, like a sloth. It is a crocodile's cousin with a less appealing face. I hope to tell you of an encounter with one in a canoe up the Amazon in a planned third book: Vanishing Places.

British prime ministers, as well as most of the polite crowned heads of Europe from Sweden to Spain and many boring heads of state from Italy to Istanbul.

"What else?

"The only other experiences with which I can try to catch your interest are some of my moments of terror:

Facing the drawn guns of East Germany's *Vopos,* the people's police, behind the Iron Curtain.

Being totally lost without papers or money or any form of verbal communication in Red China shortly after the Tiananmen Square crackdown.

Being stranded in Belgrade in similar circumstances on the edge of war in Bosnia.

Staring at death in the eyes of the long-horned "lion-killer".

Or staring into the scorpion pit of a Sultan's prison beyond the road to Samarkand.

Or staring at Jesus, in a moment of bewilderment, in a house of ill repute.

"Those are just some of the things I have to tell which may seem to you to be stranger than fiction. Yet each is cold, unassailable fact. The distortion is that they are *out of context.*

"It is the point I want to emphasise today. Whatever you are told by or about somebody; whatever you read in a newspaper or a biography or an autobiography; whatever you see with your own eyes – is not the reality, or the truth, unless it is seen in its full, correct and hopefully precise context. None of us should ever make assumptions about anything until we have the broad, properly sourced evidence. I have only to mention the word 'gossip' to remind you of how one-sided and dangerous facts can be; or refer to 'the heavens' to remind you of how inadequate our understanding of reality is.

"To illustrate my point let me put my experiences just described in context for you."

Which is what I then set out, carefully, to do. And will do so again in the following pages, or where relevant in the second book about the global media and their future, which I hope to complete.

The need for proper context, which is truth's crucible, is the reason why I'm now going to venture into the dangerous territory of memoirs, where I often promised myself never to wander. ☐

10.
Dancing through the Roaring Twenties.

I learned a "pome" at school today:
"Hairy Mary Mother of Cheeses."

Elder brother, informing us of his first day in kindergarten.

In 1920 Johannesburg was losing its early "wild west" mining-camp spirit and gaining some of the equally vigorous yet more desperate sophistication of the Western world's "Roaring Twenties".

Gold seekers, seen as "English", but still arriving in Johannesburg from many parts of the world, far outnumbered Afrikaners, Tswanas, Zulus, Xhosas and other black and brown visitors of every origin. The city was little more than three decades old. It was founded above a gold reef on a bleak, high plain 6000 feet above sea level and two days by wagon to the nearest reliable flow of water. In the early days drinking water was sometimes sold at a greater price than whisky. It may be the only large city that has ever grown in such greedy and precariously unnatural circumstances.

Yet it has never stopped growing.

By the 1920s, theatres, ballrooms, clubs, cocktail lounges and *Thé Dansant* restaurants abounded. Numbers of English language newspapers competed in catering exclusively to the interests of the gold-diggers, who were the prospering *Uitlanders* in a former Boer *Republiek*.

But the champagne went pop! It then dribbled away on that Black Friday when Wall Street crashed in 1929.

Ragtime was the rage with Tiger Rag the dizzy best. But there were the clever tunes of Cole Porter coming along, and the sophisticated stuff from George Gershwin. He had hurriedly composed *Rhapsody in Blue* for a New York concert featuring Paul Whiteman's orchestra. And there was the lyrical stuff, such as Irving Berlin's *Blue Skies*, released in 1926 and soon played in all the cosmopolitan places on earth, including the boisterous new town of Johannesburg.

It was to tunes such as these that my mother and her younger sister had come from Cape Town to open a dance studio in Jo'burg. (Every man, woman and child in Western society was expected to be taught how to dance intricate steps in the 1920s.)

The 1920s – age of zest. A time of cloche hats and swinging beads, of quicksteps and foxtrotting, of jazz bands and ivory cigarette holders, and lots of champagne while oblivious to the looming Depression and a second world war.

Later my mother married and retired to produce a family in Forest Town, a leafy Johannesburg suburb which was then on the outskirts of the brawling city, on the sunny side of the lightning-prone ridge.

It was proper that the small print of the births column in the classified section of Africa's biggest daily newspaper failed to carry what I personally would believe to be the most important event of its day. My mother had bigger news to worry about and was probably saving the money for the announcement of my fate in the smallest print in the deaths column.

The doctors told her after my birth that I was going to die before I was three weeks old. Why?

Starvation, they said. I was tangled up with *pyloricstenosis*, for which Africa at that time had no name, let alone a cure.

"*Pyloricstenosis,*" laughed my brother, though he wouldn't have used that precise term. For him it wasn't all bad news. At two-and-a half years old he didn't care much for the new crybaby. He would have been intrigued by the fact that they had found a volunteer to slit my body from chest to groin in an effort to access and untangle my innards, but he probably felt that the operation would soon end happily-ever-after for me … and improve life for him.

He was a sharp kid, my elder brother. But he died young: Early in his 70s, and that was a long time ago.

The first sounds I ever heard were not the roar of Transvaal thunderstorms, but the roar of African lions, just a hundred yards away. It was a romantic start to life, spoilt by the fact that the noble creatures were in the Johannesburg zoo, close to the cage of the lonely polar bear.

My interest in life began a few years later, when I discovered that I had a birthmate; a cheerful and funny friend. He was world famous! His name was Mickey Mouse, and we were both born in 1928. Mickey Mouse was not as interesting as a troubled character named Goofy, or as lovable as Donald Duck. But Mickey was among the first celluloid animated film characters in the history of the world. Betty Boop with the goo-goo eyes was, I think, an afterthought among the earliest of animated characters – a sexy little animation, without the adjective, which had not yet been invented. What her significance was, I cannot say for certain as I was not the least interested in girls at the time. Mickey was my man. More so than a later character called Popeye the Sailor Man, whose weekly cinematic cartoon, in which he always beat up the bully was, to my suspicious mind, nothing but propaganda to persuade one to eat spinach.

The sudden spread of silent movies and comics introduced Mickey, without need of language, to people across the globe, from Patagonia to Persia and from Peking to Poland. He has changed over the years, and in his late 80s, he was being rejuvenated and being given a less earnest, more mischievous and more childish personality.

I met Mickey in a "bioscope", but only after we had moved to the village of Strand on South Africa's Cape Coast in 1933. We were by then both about five years old (which is old for a mouse – though when we reached 50 years of age, he was younger than ever and had developed lithe, techno-synchronised movements). Back then, I sat saucer-eyed as he moved too jerkily on a screen that was filled with downward-moving diagonal lines.

"Why's Mickey always in the rain?" I asked.

Mickey in Steamboat Willie, *his first movie, made by Walt Disney in 1928.*

"That's not rain. That's a technical ... that's just an optical illu ... a ... a film thing ... that's the way it is," I was informed.

"Shush now."

Later I was taken to the big city, Cape Town, where the bioscope (movie house) was The Alhambra – a magic place with Aladdin's lamps and King Arthur's castles; with trees on the ramparts and stars shining in the roof while it was daylight outside. Looking up at the moving wisps of artificial clouds above the artificial turrets, I asked:

"What if it rains on us, as well as on Mickey Mouse?"

"If it rains, put your cap on. And shush."

We got snappy advice in those halcyon days, and learned not to trust anything we saw, let alone what we were told. But I learned that lesson only when I was much older, and had already mastered the art of smoking, which was before my eighth birthday.

The first thing I remember clearly of my childhood was in another world before I met Mickey Mouse. It happened in about 1931, when my mother asked my nearly five-year-old older brother what he had learned that day at the convent kindergarten. We were then living at Springs Mines, in near-isolation at the far end of the East Rand gold reef.

"We learned a pome," said Daughtrey. (That was his name which he changed when he was six and called himself Jack.) He was much smarter than I was ... except that he didn't know that his real first name was a badge of his clan; the name of a hero who had led black people out of slavery in the West Indies, something I didn't find out until after his death nearly 70 years later. Nor was I aware that the hidden piece of "wood", signified by the initial "W" separating my two names, also had relevance for our entire branch of an unknown tribe.

"What poem did the sister teach you?"

"Hairy Mary, Mother of 'Cheeses'," he said.

My mother, after a shocked silence, started to laugh. So we kids also laughed.

"Did you recite that to Mother Superior?" my mother asked.

"Yes."

"What did she say?"

"She asked me what church I belonged to," answered my brother.

"What did you say?"

"I said I would ask you, so Mother Superior said, 'well do that *today*'."

My mother decided: "Tell her you are a Bush Baptist."

The next day my brother came home, put down the vitally important lunch satchel which I envied, and said proudly: "When I told Sister, some others in our class put up their hands and said they thought they were Bush Baptists too."

The only significance of that memory is that I consider it my first amusing experience, childishly retold within the family, until I understood it. It initiated my lifetime luck of encountering laughter everywhere thereafter.

But it didn't begin that way. □

11.
When our mother left home.

*At the Christmas party I was able to comfort myself
with the knowledge that I was the first among my
peers to detect that Santa Claus was a fraud.
I knew then that you couldn't trust anybody,
even your own perceptions in finding the truth.*

The day my mother left home "forever" is one I cannot remember. I have no sense of her saying goodbye or driving off in our gleaming Erskine car. I learned later that, after her divorce, she took *her* mother to change punctured tyres on the long journey to reach us kids, who had later been moved to the East Coast by train.

On the roads, granny had to open the gates and lift her long skirts and wade the drifts, even along the main roads, which were often dusty with upgraded cart tracks. Granny would have to check whether the rivers were low enough for them to plunge into with the Erskine, so that they could continue their journey to the Eastern Cape. She also had to get out and push when the car got stuck in the mud.

Few women drove cars in those days, let alone out of town. But there were some spectacular exceptions. From the start the early Automobile Age created sensations and records almost every month in Africa. In 1905, for instance, a wager by a visiting Austrian nobleman, Count de Revertera, that he could drive from the Highveld to Cape Town in less than a fortnight, seemed too ridiculous to take seriously. Yet he managed it in 11 days, driving 12 hours a day. When all signs of roads petered out, he persevered by keeping the throttle open and driving his motor-machine in cautious circles until he found a wagon track.

By 1924 the route had improved so much that a Hupmobile driven by HE Rose accomplished the journey in 38 hours 38 minutes – motoring day and night, plus another day and an evening. Despite his emergency stops being held to the minimum, the train got there hours before he did. Not long after my brother was born, a man named Gerry Bouwer drove a Chrysler Six from Cape Town to Johannesburg and beat the train by four hours after he raced non-stop for a day and a night. It was about this time that the Cape Town to Johannesburg official road speed record was challenged on the grounds that hundreds of gates along the route had been manned by farm labourers who were paid to open them as the car approached. This was deemed to be both a direct and a devious advantage.

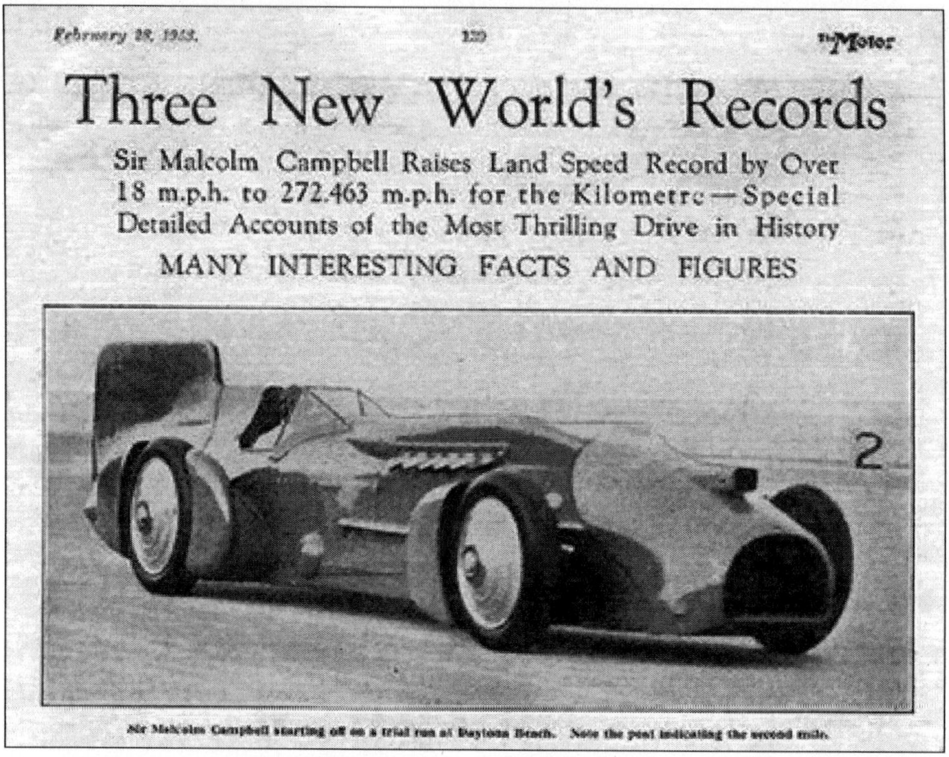

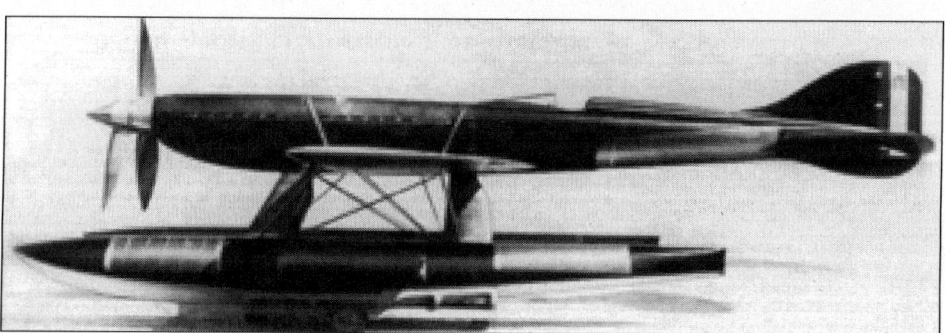

February 28, 1933. The Motor

Three New World's Records

Sir Malcolm Campbell Raises Land Speed Record by Over 18 m.p.h. to 272.463 m.p.h. for the Kilometre—Special Detailed Accounts of the Most Thrilling Drive in History

MANY INTERESTING FACTS AND FIGURES

Sir Malcolm Campbell starting off on a trial run at Daytona Beach. Note the post indicating the second mile.

Sir Donald Campbell starting off on a trial run at Daytona Beach. Note the post indicating the second mile.

Soon long-distance record attempts by cars on public roads were prohibited because too many animals and pedestrians were being injured. This did not affect motoring journalist Malcolm Campbell. In 1929 he used the Verneuk salt pan in the dry and desolate Northern Cape in his failed bid to set up a new world land speed record in his streamlined Bluebird.

Erskine Model 51 Sedan in 1928. Note the trunk (large suitcase) on the rear luggage rack. The Erskine was a brand of Studebaker Corporation of Indiana USA, from 1926 to 1930.

At the same time children of the Western world were collecting miniature models of the 1931 **Schneider Cup winner, Supermarine S.6B seaplane**, the world air speed record holder with a streamlined shape we little boys would never forget, especially as it transformed, years later, into the RAF Spitfire.

While my mother's journey in a three-year-old 1928 Erskine may have been a minor pioneering effort for amateur women drivers in Africa, it paled into insignificance beside the power and excitement of the Morris Oxford driven by two Girl Guide officials, Misses EC Budgell and ML Belcher in 1930. These two women drove from Rondebosch in Cape Town to Oxford in the UK on an untimed journey of 14500 kms across Africa. However they enjoyed an unusual advantage in central and northern Africa (as my non-competitive mother was too modest to point out) in that they never had to worry about snow.

My mother would have agreed that Africa was less hazardous for motorists in those early days of mechanical transport than it is today. However, the occasion of two women, mother and grandmother, travelling alone across South Africa was considered more than foolhardy. It was seen as dangerous. And her abandonment of the marital home and her independence were a sensation and a scandal.

Journeys 80 years ago in Africa were often measured as two-, four- or six-puncture daily drives. It took my mother and grandmother six days to travel only 800 miles (about 1300km) to Grahamstown. There were no tarred roads between towns and in bad weather some major routes far from towns were often muddy tracks, and not always wide enough for cars to pass easily. There were very few bridges.

However it was not the punctures, the mechanical breakdowns, the opening and closing of farm gates on the corrugated highway, nor the waiting at muddy drifts for flooded rivers to subside, which caused most delay. It was the banks of snow on the Amatola Mountains at Hogsback which trapped them.

My wonderful little aunt (and future foster-mother) much admired her sister-in-law's courage and volunteered to look after her children, down on the farm near the old Xhosa frontier.

When I was finally reunited with mom after her divorce, I didn't remember her. I ran instead to the vaguely familiar figure of granny. I recall vividly that mom cried, and I hoped vainly that it was the last time, because I realised much later without being told, that she was very brave.

She was a glamorous dancing teacher when she married, and the divorce changed her into a desperately hard-working woman, sacrificing all for her children. She had become the victim of all those man-made laws of the world's free, democratic nations.

My mother left us when I was about three I suppose. She suddenly disappeared from our home on a goldmine on the East Rand. My father had been transferred from Johannesburg head office to the secretariat of a goldmine in the veld near Springs on the East Rand. He had been a very young volunteer fighting on the Western Front in World War One – hardly 18, I suspect – though he must have grown up overnight when a bullet broke his jaw as it blasted right through his face.

He was invalided out of the trenches to a military hospital in London and patched up. He returned to the same hospital later. This was after he'd been sent back to France where he was hit with shrapnel during nearly four awful years of those muddy, bloody trenches.

For the rest of his life there were periods when he had to have his broken jaw fixed, but except for jokes about "bits of shrapnel moving around in here somewhere in my leg", he never ever spoke about the war.

It was only at his death, and when I grew older than my father that I began fully to appreciate what men (and boys like dad) suffered in the trenches on the Somme and other battlegrounds in World War One. Even

100

early post-war descriptions of the 1914–1918 conditions did not match the reality of its madness. Imagine being shipped out of those trenches as a youth, hospitalised in Blighty and then patched up and sent back as a grown man into that nightmare – twice more.

Much younger Harry Oppenheimer, head of Anglo American Corporation, revealed many decades later: "So Harry Tyson was your father? He was a great favourite at Anglo, you know."

He needed to be, apparently, and Anglo had to keep finding him different jobs. He was a handsome, charming chap. Amusing, I know, for I later watched his amateur-theatre audiences laughing at his antics. But I think he carried mental as well as half-healed physical wounds ever since the war, and he also suffered from a peculiar, quick chemical reaction to booze. His occasional erratic, often tragic, but sometimes hilarious and brief alcoholic bouts offended too many people too often, it seems.

IN MY MOTHER'S ABSENCE from our mining house on the Reef, my earliest memories revolved around two people: My temporarily sober, no-nonsense father, who introduced me to fairies, and Polly, who demonstrated her love ... and fed me our favourites: banana-custard and polly-crackers.

My father and I were resting one Sunday on real green grass beside a dam, the only stretch of open water to be seen in our area on the ash-dry winter Highveld. The water was pumped from the cooling plant beside Springs Mines No 2 shaft gold-pour sheds. It was glorious water, gushing in steaming fountains. I stared at the hot, leaping founts in wonder and looked away only when my father pointed at something. There, suddenly, appeared biscuits – ginger biscuits – growing in the grass.

"Fairies," said father, answering the obvious questions about source, ownership, and donor of these miraculous gifts in his usual amused, cool way.

And I never forgot the "reality" of it. I would have sworn that those biscuits had actually popped out of the ground on grass stalks. It took me a long time to accept that what I had seen was not real. I had been fooled by my own perceptions, and while I was soon ashamed of this, I still treasure the delight of that magic moment. And of that demonstration of a father's love, not easily expressed. It was only six decades later, when I came across a letter he had written to his sister, my "foster mother", about the early death of a friend of hers that I realised what a caring guy he was.

Years later I was able to comfort myself with the knowledge – on another occasion far away – that I was the first among my peers, and among even the older children attending a Christmas party, to detect that Santa Claus was a fraud. I knew by then that you couldn't trust anybody, even your own perceptions in finding the truth.

Proof is needed. And proof on this occasion was in the shoes visible below Santa's red robe. I'd seen them on the feet of some unknown "uncle" an hour earlier … and he was still in them, now behind a whiskery ho-ho-ho.

My other earliest memory is of Polly, in the good old times back at the mines. Polly was twice my mother's size. It seemed that I could hardly touch both sides of her with my arms spreadeagled. She was warm. She was jolly, and, after mom disappeared, she made our favourite weekly banana-custard dish almost every day. Sometimes I would sneak into her room at the back and get her to read to me, which she did badly and with much struggling. But always willingly. I loved her, and I know she loved me, even though she had her own, grown-up children far away.

Polly had a huge smile along with a tear or two, and she had a much richer, darker skin than any of us, or the blanketed African recruits we saw marching down from the railway station to the goldmine's compound. They walked in groups through our mining township's back lanes, the alley which existed as access for the horse-drawn cart of the Indian vegetable "sammy" and the horse-drawn carts that came after dark to empty the shit bins. (Indoor, water-born sewerage was a rarity everywhere in South Africa then.) The red-blanketed mine recruits seemed even jollier than Polly, with their shouting and loud laughter and waving knobkerries.

Much later in life, when I was home for the school holidays at the age of eight, brother Jack and I would walk alone at night to the Number Two Shaft compound, where all the migrant mineworkers stayed for about six months, (contracts for six months, then transported home for six months for farming or harvesting, before coming forward to recruiting stations near their homes to sign more six-month contracts). We would sit on the film projection roof and watch the open-air "bioscope" screened in the arena for hundreds of men on contract work.

They were bored with heroic but unmotivated celluloid lovers like Ronald Coleman and Errol Flynn. They roared for "Cowboy Jack", including Buck Jones on a white horse. We also shouted for Buck Jones. Almost inevitably a Cowboy Jack would be rolled out after Mickey Mouse.

The mineworkers, strangely to our way of thinking, found Mickey Mouse to be only mildly amusing. They hardly laughed at the slapstick of Charlie Chaplin or the Keystone Cops, and not much more at Laurel and Hardy later. It never occurred to us that we were living in separate universes with separate legends and different senses of reality and values. The mine recruits lived proud, tribal lives separate even from Polly. It never occurred to us that those laughing men had never seen a film before, and might never do again, unless they volunteered for more time in the mines.

My little world gravitated later in that decade of the 1930s towards a shining Hollywood hero. He was a devil-may-care, debonair Errol Flynn, who embodied all other rollicking roistering heroes from Robin Hood and Captain Blood, to the leader of the Charge of the Light Brigade. With the charisma of the ace pilot who won World War One, he was the love-light of all beautiful film heroines.

Like everyone else, I was unable to discern at the time that in real life he was a chauvinistic bully who assaulted women. The all-male world press failed to report adequately the truth about Hollywood. The media were too respectful of Hollywood's celluloid empire in those days. But I knew nothing of this at the time, and wasn't even aware of Tarzan and the Apes.

I was still learning to climb a tree. ☐

12.
Growing up in a gwenya tree.

What is childhood but a series of happy delusions.

Sydney Smith, circa 1820.

t was when my mother hurriedly left home without me – and Polly was feeling a strain on her health trying to cope with my father, my brother, and me – that we two kids were transferred to the care of my beloved, and, we considered, scatterbrained aunt's family. They lived on a farm near a Crown reserve of dense bush in the Eastern Cape. Our father must have taken us or put us on the train to Grahamstown, on the understanding that my mother would fetch us when she was in a position to do so. Our move to the farm began in trauma, but the extended family – and mGwenya – "salved" that.

Lucky the little child whose life is centred on a tree. If allowed to, a tree will stimulate a child's imagination and grant adult memories that go beyond literal truth. A mother tree may provide not only one's first roots, but a private place of shelter and an exclusive world hidden from grown-ups and filled with solo games and dreams. Many kids had tree houses, the best of them built by themselves and without interference from adults. We – that is my new farm-family consisting of my cousins Alison and Nancy and my brother and I – had *two* homes in trees: our First Tree the mGwenya (*sic*) in the garden, and later, a second treehouse standing high in the thick Eastern Cape bush.

But the treehouse in the bush was not a great success. It was too high and too modern. This was in the sense that it had its

*Jeffrey Farnol's second of about 40 books;
an unlikely social satire concerning the
19th century adventures of a Regency buck
(see end of chapter). We kids understood only
the adventures and only those not involving
his women.*

The mGwenya or 'Wild Plum, (Harpephyllum caffrum) originated in the riverine forests of the Eastern Cape. But when it is domesticated it grows to a height of 15 metres and provides easy climbing for little people. Some kids fall off the lower branches of mother Harpephyllum caffrum occasionally, without being able to blame her – because the mGwenya embraces these diminutive inhabitants and provides them with tree homes ... despite the fact that children never wait for mGwenya's plums to ripen into sweetness, but gobble them up while they are still green and bitter.

own 'lift' (elevator), where none other existed except in what we believed to be the big city far away in Algoa Bay.

Brother Jack was the engineer who installed our lift. With the help of some friendly Africans he organised for an abandoned differential sump from an old truck to be hauled up by rope to the house in the tree top. Then Nancy, youngest and smallest of us, was nominated as the first ground-to-house elevator-passenger and ordered to step into the lift. "The lift" comprised a small square of planks, attached horizontally to the rope and she was instructed to hang on when the rope was released.

The result was more spectacular than any of us could have imagined. She shot up into the upper foliage and reached the rickety veranda in one short scream. The sump at the other end of the suspended rope came hurtling down, smashing branches in the trees and shaking the earth. It was a success! Except Nancy wouldn't stop screaming for help and it took hours to coax her down.

106

However, our true mother tree which shaped private individual lives was a many-branched, evergreen, giant mGwenya living just outside the kitchen. It cast its blessing and its shade over much of the homestead. It was especially inviting because its broad branches were within reach of small people, enveloping them in their embrace. In its folds you could escape grown-ups calling from just below. You could escape from our cook, or anyone telling us supper or our bath was ready, or when the hunting dogs wanted to play a silly game. You could escape from anything when hidden in the folds of the mGwenya tree.

Our mGwenya seemed to spread peace, not only below and between its great limbs, but across the barnyard outside the gate, where we risked our lives in a tin boat on the dam while playing pirates. Once mGwenya seemed to provide necessary comfort after an awful accident when we found a wounded man, lying blood-soaked in a ploughed furrow close to the house. He had been gored on the horns of an ox which had suddenly gone crazy. Aunt May, without any training whatever, was as usual called in — not merely to administer her daily ration of pills and other *muti* — but to render major medical aid. So we were shushed-off back to mGwenya.

Aunt May was full of antics and laughter most of the time, pretending to be scatterbrained. Yet she attended to every family and human crisis on the farm and many of the domestic emergencies in the district. When things went really bad — when Uncle Ross was far from home and training volunteer Xhosa troops in the war years, or when he was home, blasting-and-damning at his loudest, her giggle assured us that everything would soon be right again.

She showed her quality one Sunday as we set out in the ancient, open sedan for the little church far away. A rat suddenly emerged below her feet. As the rat and Uncle Ross's boots did battle on the floorboards of the moving car, Aunt Maisie simply lifted the skirts of her Sabbath dress and leapt out of the roofless, moving car onto a flat embankment that was level with the top of her locked car door. She didn't even lose her hat, and stood there clutching her bonnet laughing. Asked how she had managed it, she laughed again: "I just lost my commonsense." mGwenya brought benign calm to our ceremony of witnessing the execution each weekend of a rooster for Sunday dinner. We watched in pretended trepidation as its head was chopped off, then we analysed and calmly rated its headless performance as its corpse danced around scattering blood. Our mGwenya spread her huge limbs and hid us, during this ceremony, from the view of the household's grown-ups.

All I've said rises from the mists of fallacious memory. Our first experience of the pitfalls of memory came to us kids when Uncle Ross agreed to tell us one of his bedtime stories. He came with a confidential warning: "Don't tell that story again of the cowboy who could put a bullet in an Ace of Spades at twenty paces. The children are getting the wrong ideas. Tell them a Bible story."

"Once upon a time," said Uncle Ross, my surrogate father – who was compelled by settler custom to attend our tiny country church across the valley *every* Sunday – "there was a little baby found in the bullrushes whose name was Jesus."

"No! No!" we chided him, as Sunday school experts. "That was Moses."

Momentarily Uncle Ross looked nonplussed, surprised at his memory blank. But he was never one to admit a mistake. Uncle was known, from Grahamstown to Port Alfred, as the man who never ever made a mistake.

"Yes, that Moses story is a different tale," he improvised. "This is one about the cowboy who was found as a babe beside a river on the Western prairie on Christmas Day – so they named him Billy Jesus Kid. As soon as he was old enough he made his middle name a secret."

We agreed that all smart kids did that. And we revelled in the latest news that Billy the Kid could not only hit the ace of spades at thirty paces, he could, with just four quick shots from his trusty six-shooter, entirely eliminate the ace from the card. Imagine what he could do to the rotten hearts of a posse of rustlers!

Don't Go Back

I returned many times to the old farm, and later for long holidays in my teenage school years, to a brand new homestead on another hill, but until quite recently, I never consciously came upon another mGwenya tree during all my thirty-thousand- plus days.

Instead I treasured in my memory our mGwenya's strength, gentle beauty, and her protective powers – only to find disillusion from young Nancy before her 75th birthday. She warned of our farm memories: "Don't ever go back there. The ruins of the house are now scattered and mGwenya looks half the size. The family outhouse (a latrine, filled with spiders and an occasional visiting snake, and hidden at the bottom of a path deep in the bush) isn't as far away as we used to think it was on dark nights – and the dam we played in was always just a square hole of about ten by ten metres. Our remaining Xhosa playmates are old. Maboet has missing teeth!"

Nancy has since those days of childhood and later years of child-rearing, volunteered much of her life to teaching Xhosa adults to read and write, both in their own language and in English.

We had lived our past in two worlds, separated not between black and white, but between young and old.

Throughout my childhood in the 1930s black and white and brown children played together in the *veld* near the mine properties and of course on the farms. We were all best friends; as close as children can get; until we white kids were packed off to schools where we momentarily envied the black children who hardly went to school at all. They of course envied us, for we appeared to them exceedingly rich, even in those desperate days of the Great Depression when "privileged English" kids like us had just one pair of khaki trousers, a pair of shoes if we were lucky, and shaven heads to deter ringworm.

Many Afrikaans kids were worse off. Some far worse off. Their fathers and families had lost everything they owned back in the South African (Anglo-Boer) war. They were farm children with no farms. These second-generation victims of Kitchener's war had no shoes but most had ringworm.

Many were without homes and lived on neighbours' farms as *bywoners* with very little education, just like black kids, except they felt less secure. Some white parents no longer owned oxen so they had at one stage to pull the plough themselves. The Afrikaans kids, whom we were not to know until near adulthood, had good reason to feel much more bitter about their historical fate. Years later, apartheid drew us apart from nationalistic Afrikanerdom – deliberately at first under early nationalistic politics.

It was not until apartheid was finally overcome – by active white opponents in South Africa as well as African National Congress forces and supporters – that some of us were able to comprehend more fully Afrikaner nationalist extremism and its aggressive actions against, not only the black races, but against all other "outsiders", including "die Engelse" and even the better educated, moderate and ("*sies*") liberal Afrikaans traditionalists.

The other side of the story

The Poor White Problem dominated the nation in the period between the two World Wars, but most Afrikaners were too proud to recognise the reality, let alone talk openly about it. For every 50 articles you may read on the poverty of black people in the last century, you will probably find only one referring to the plight of the Afrikaner in the first half of that century.

The poverty in the farming community wasn't even their fault – a fact quickly seized upon by Nationalists who remembered what shocking victimisation the *Engelse Oorlog* had caused *Die Volk*. The aftermath of the so-called Boer War (as the *Engelse* dubbed it) saw farms destroyed, concentration camp victims returning to razed homes, and the displacement of countless Voortrekker descendants.

Their bitterness, and much of their Church, did not help them recover from their plight. Who can forget the stories of half-starved, unskilled *bywoners* squatting on Transvaal and Free State farmlands they might once have owned? Or accounts of the farmer and his wife cultivating their land on their own, with her holding the plough and her man pulling it, in the absence of an ox or any farm stock ... let alone farm labour.

The only asset these people of the *platteland* had, in the first era of the new nation, was the vote ... as Jan Christiaan Smuts well knew.

As I was reminiscing during the writing of this chapter on my childhood, two loose photostat pages fell from the covers of a book off my shelves that I was re-reading. The photostat reflected some other book written in the late 1930s under the chapter heading "South Africa's Difficult Problem. Page 223". It reminded me that "the white slum problem is breeding fast" (as it is today, desperately among black youth and, on an infinitely smaller scale, among whites of every origin).

The *arme blankes* problem was dealt with in Carnegie Commission Reports of 1929 and 1931. In 1930 it was not only a Great Depression phenomenon – or altogether a post-Anglo-Boer War problem. As the photostat reminded me, there was an "Indigency Commission in 1906" report written by Philip Kerr (later the Marquess of Lothian) advocating the formation of agricultural labour colonies to cope with unskilled, unemployed whites.

After the Wall Street Crash 22 years later, the Carnegie Corporation of New York, in conjunction with the Dutch Reformed Church, instituted an inquiry in 1931 into the *arme blanke* situation, and found that about

300 000 people in the Union of South Africa might be described as destitute "poor whites".

That's a small figure in today's terms, but it was the equivalent of **one-sixth** *of the 1 850 000 white earners in South Africa* according to government statistics at the time. The figure incorporated between a quarter and probably half of the Afrikaans population! Almost all of the destitute were unskilled rural whites "who pay no taxes and spend practically nothing".

Nor could these destitute families expect any grant from government or recognised charity. They lived off their landlords' land, and they were lucky if they were relatives of other victims of the Anglo-Boer War and its aftermath ... or at least sympathetic landlords constantly concerned about the war victims' plight.

At the same time, the government was doing practically nothing to help "the poor whites", let alone dealing with the political "Native Question", because by 1934 the national debt was 273 000 000 pound sterling ... which signalled amounts for South African taxpayers that they simply could not afford to pay. The South African State was broke. And it was during a time of very sparse voluntary donations from overseas, with virtually no official international hand-outs.

Some sociologists – and indeed most politicians and many historians who should know better – ignore, or are ignorant of such circumstances. But even a kid in my day knew how serious and ubiquitous poverty was among whites in the Great Depression. There were no handouts, even if you were a starving invalid claiming to be a member of the British peerage living in a farm in the Cape.

Fortunately the new science of "social history" is filling in the gaps in our selective histories of those days. Many "poor whites" lived at starvation level – but they had the vote, and in the North, beyond the Cape Province, it was a racially exclusive vote, mostly a rural one. This weighed heavily in favour of white Afrikaner Nationalism, which was able by 1948 to take over government even though it held a minimum of the national white vote. The Nationalists supported the farming communities and their indigent *bywoners* and exploited the extra-value rural vote. The "Nats" campaigned on the ubiquitous fear of *die Swart Gevaar* ("Black Danger") and the easily aroused hate of British colonialism. They called for Afrikaner "patriotism" (exclusive racism) and a return to Voortrekker independence.

It was powerful medicine among the poor and it spread through the Church to Afrikaner middle classes as well. It spread as fast as fascism or totalitarian communism was spreading in Russia, Italy, and Nazi Germany at that time. At the same time Smuts's supporters could focus on no other threat, even though they should have been slowly advancing their policy of equal opportunity to all races.

"Politics is the art of the possible," was an absolute in that period. The coalition governments of the Smuts era could do little to help the Poor Whites in the Great Depression decade, and no white-elected party would even notice a "Poor Black" problem. Rural life among blacks was not directly disturbed by global economics in that era.

Once in power in the post-war boom, the "Nats" solved – *quickly and very efficiently* – the "poor white problem". But the apartheid government did so for its own narrow, ideological purposes.

The obvious lesson today from this must be that voters of all parties should demand an end to mass corruption and insist on *efficient* administration. The whole nation, not merely some get-rich-quick sectional leaders, should focus on uplifting the very poor. It's a classic government socio-economic problem – not a political one, nor as President Jacob Zuma claimed, a "white capital" threat.

Back in my childhood at the height of the Great Depression in the early 1930s, we assumed that black and brown people preferred the way they lived, preferred visiting the farm trading store to the town shop,

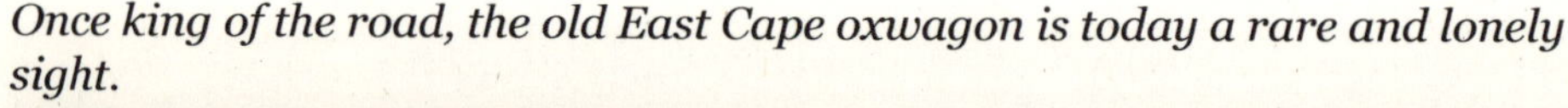

Once king of the road, the old East Cape oxwagon is today a rare and lonely sight.

as we did; that they preferred *not* going to our tiny countryside frontier church, as we were compelled to do. The Xhosa families, all of whom we knew well, seemed satisfied – often happier than us – and never said or acted otherwise.

We spent time in their warm, rounded mud-walled homes and loved their stories and their *putu* (mielie meal porridge). We grew up together that way, oblivious to any existing social or political strains during the prolonged depression before "The World War", and even during those strange years of the early 1940s our white household on the farm would pack up before Christmas and head for a distant camp on a lagoon at the coast.

In the absence of Uncle Ross (selected by the military as an "expert" Xhosa-speaker to train Xhosa volunteer troops) Aunt May would leave the front and backdoors of the homestead unlocked, as well as the dairy, the shed stacked with crops, and the lorry (truck) keys. The land and the fruit trees and the animals were all in the care of the staff and in the trust of the family kraals (village homes) in the surrounding valleys and hills. Dense, almost impenetrable coastal bush still surrounded most of the farmlands that had been hewed out by our settler ancestors.

We kids were stunningly privileged once, to ride for a while with the farm workers on the ox-wagon that took two or three days to reach the sea, about thirty miles away where our tin shanties on stilts stood above a calm lagoon beside the pounding surf. The wagon was loaded with supplies, including chickens in crates, and fishing tackle that would provide us with food for two months.

We sometimes rode shorter distances, into the deep bush of the Crown lands, and sat above the wagon's brakes or on the *disselboom,* or walked with the whipman and beside the cow-in-milk. This halcyon era ended when the lorry could be used for the seaside trip, and milk and even eggs could be purchased from a farmer a few miles from our lagoon-side shacks.

During WW2, white mothers and children lived confidently in isolated farm homesteads while their husbands were "Up North" in the Libyan Desert, or fighting the war elsewhere, for years. The wives were miles from their nearest white neighbours but surrounded by kind folk who were descendants of the African warriors of the Frontier Wars.

The doors and windows of the settler homesteads on the hilltops, looking into darkness on every far horizon, were often open at night, and never barred or locked. None of us ever saw a policeman – except the one who patrolled on a horse, and always arrived, once a month, just in time for lunch.

This inn, one of the oldest existing licensed premises in Africa, is more popular and better known to its black and white community than both of Bathurst's historic churches, together. The churches' roles as places of refuge for terrified women and children in the Frontier Wars is virtually forgotten ... and has been for 50 years.

This mutually trusted feudalism in the white-occupied areas sounds incredible today looking back wisely from our "free and open" democracy. Yet, in growing up we felt no guilt about our unperceived privileges or about our insensitive ignorance.

We loved the big, bare-breasted maidens who came from the tribal lands in our holidays, shouting, singing, and laughing as they picked fruit in the orchard under the eagle eye of our African foreman. It was only when segregation was spelt out in the blatantly inhuman laws of apartheid

The Pig and Whistle.

that nearly half of white South Africa began to wake up, and some of them to march or protest, at last.

Many English-speaking whites of course, were protesting on racial grounds – that is, anti-Afrikaans historical prejudice – and fear and anger at the domination over them of Afrikaner nationalism. But apartheid, failing in its attempt to separate white *vreemde Engelse* from *ware Afrikaner*, then drew instead an unbending line between white and "non-white". Finally whites had to cross that colour line into discomfort and danger to be against racism. Apathy, fear, and prejudice held back hundreds of thousands of whites of both languages who ought, by then, to have known better than to remain silent.

Those who stood up to fight apartheid included many Afrikaners. Those who accepted apartheid, including large numbers, probably a majority of English-speaking whites justifiably fearful of brutal Stalinist Communism, forget all about it today.

But you couldn't, could you, if you raised your head an inch above the sand and began to witness the constant injustice, cruelty, and humiliation? The sufferings, which were almost unknown on the farm in the tribalised East Cape bush, would later become cruelly prevalent and inhuman.

The change would plague all our lives.

Indeed, even before apartheid became official, there could no longer be illusions about the world we were living in at home. Though we couldn't read the headlines, we soon became aware of white strangers bringing hate by turning normal English and isiXhosa words into insults. And we ought to have known that those suspiciously sophisticated Africans (the ones carrying briefcases, which no white farmer had ever owned before) and who brought news about injustice and bitterness, were in no way twisting the truth.

MY MOTHER was still trying to find work and a home for us down in the Western Cape at the far end of the country. She and gallant granny finally made a return trip over the winding 800-mile road from Cape Town back to Grahamstown to fetch brother Jack and me. The dirt roads were even narrower, much muddier than those on mom's original trek down from the Transvaal.

The coastal road from Eastern to Western Cape meandered through forests and formidable passes around The Wilderness, where the two women with two small children and their Erskine sedan had to be dragged up the slippery roads of the steepest inclines by timber-loaded trucks, or occasionally spans of oxen, before they finally reached False Bay below the mountains where one descended the winding, sandy, Sir Lowry's Pass.

My mother, during her years before marriage, danced ballet and taught tap-dancing, fox-trotting, quick-step, the waltz and the fashionable tango in a studio in Johannesburg with her equally vivacious younger sister. But the Depression had ended all that 1920-style frivolity. Now, in the early 1930s, she rented a cottage in little Gordon's Bay next to her sister's husband's fishery, and she found work as a fish hawker – the only white woman fishhawker in Africa, probably.

She drove a small van over Sir Lowry's Pass – a precipitous dirt road that delayed many overheated and steaming vehicles on the outward journey in those days – to hawk fresh fish to farmers without fridges.

My brother and I loved the old cottage that she had found on the edge of the sea. We discovered a great pool between the rocks – almost a miniature lagoon – with smaller pools housing our pet octopus and other interesting denizens. We caught eight-legged "catfish" and stood on the main road to sell them as fishermen's bait to passing anglers – until my mother on her way home one day in her van found us hawking our wares, and simply stopped in the road and, for some reason, just cried. The second and only time, I'm sure, because she was resolute.

However, I had to leave home again. To start school, as there was none in Gordon's Bay. So, at about the age of five, I found myself confined in a strict, strange and sacrosanct place. It was filled with *g-i-r-ls!* (yes, girls). My big brother had vanished into a bigger, better, boys' school nearly a thousand miles away by train, and I was mystified, lonely, lost in an unknown world.

What I missed most, I suspect, was granny reading to us of King Arthur's tales of chivalry and the exploits in 18th century England of romantic characters invented by her favourite, then famous author, Jeffery Farnol whose 40-or-more old-fashioned romantic novels covered the swashbuckling era of Olde England's regency.

During our pre-school childhood my brother and I used to prod, sometimes even pinch, granny to keep her awake so that she could read aloud her current favourite Farnol on hot, sleepy Cape afternoons. Her reading of Farnol and of the exploits of the deceptively languid Scarlet Pimpernel invented by Baroness Orczy for her French Revolution yarns, ruled my imagination, and my young life.

But that happy make-believe was to end abruptly. □

13.
'The happiest days of your life'.

It is the supreme art of the teacher to awaken joy in creative expression and knowledge.

Albert Einstein.

I owe a lot to my teachers and mean to pay them back some day.

Professor, humorist Stephen Leacock.

n 1937 after being a "home owner" in the *Harpephyllum caffrum* (mGwenya) tree on the farm, and a boarder at the convent school at False Bay near Cape Town, I went at last, at the age of eight, to my second boarding school. For most boys, boarding school *did* provide the best days of their lives. They had the privilege during their schooldays of coming closer to life's realities than any other period in the biblically allotted three score years and 10-plus. At what other stage on life's journey can one live so intensely?

A new world awaits your entry, and you are placed on intimate terms, right away, with realities of such things as bullying, personal

This sketch by Robin Jacobson of School House is taken from the cover of "Still Upon a Frontier", a history of Kingswood College 1892–1993, by Howard and Joyce Kirby.

insults, teasing, or physical challenge on the one hand, and on the other, comradeship, loyalty, adventure, and a true experience of life's best qualities. For brother Jack and me, these were not only our happy days, but lucky ones, for we were at Kingswood College, back in the Eastern Cape.

Jack, having endured and enjoyed his initiations long before, stood ready to protect me. He was ready to fight anyone. It wasn't necessary because, despite his unusually small size, he was well respected, having shed no tears during his first days at school after being wrapped inside a blanket and bumped down two flights of wooden stairs. He was among those who introduced me to the truly great schoolboy values of honour and justice.

On Honour

In Jacques House Prep at Kingswood College in the Dark Ages, we were often allowed, in our early pre-teens, the honour, after Lights Out of visiting the prefects' room, between first and second dormitory. The invitation was in the form of a casual cry: "Come through, all those talking."

In those quaint old days, it was a point of honour that you should "own up", regardless of the circumstances, if you were guilty of the crime of whispering after Lights Out. Obviously you did not simply walk through to the prefects' room, uninvited. You did so only at the moment a prefect uttered, as "whispering" grew too loud, the traditional and repetitious call: "Come through

You and your fellow eight-to-10-year-old felons would then troop through to the prefects' room, bend over in your thin pyjamas, receive two cuts with a cane (or, occasionally and illegally, a cricket bat, which actually hurts less) then walk slowly in the dark to your bed with your hands casually at your sides – *never* rubbing the hot sting from your buttocks. To signal pain just might bring two more cuts – certainly the mocking laughter of your peers and fellow victims. If you were invited twice a night to "come through" for talking, you tried to avoid the extras attached to repeated performances. (You might be given "bad marks" which could lead to a non-physical form of imprisonment known as "gating" – but everyone preferred a caning to the deathly boredom and deprivation of being gated.)

Fortunately, schoolboys are cunning little creatures, and it took our dormitory age-group only about two years to work out that honour would be satisfied if the boy talking the *loudest* should be the only one to accept responsibility for the crime. Unfortunately, deciding who this might be often led to strong, sometimes physical debate. In the latter case, half the dormitory would finally be invited to the prefects' room, and each boy given three cuts instead of two.

On Justice

Or rather injustice, for nothing is remembered so well as an injustice at a good school like Kingswood College, Grahamstown, where justice is king.

One day I was in the act of collecting in the queue two Thruppenny coins (tiny silver 'tickeys') of weekly pocket money when housemaster Jack Slater said, almost as an afterthought:

"Oh, Tyson, see me afterwards."

"See Me Afterwards" were the three most dreaded words in the English language in our days in the Prep. They signalled the long walk up the sloping passage from the Jacques House dining room to the housemaster's study, where Jack Slater, heroically-built ex-Springbok wing, would carefully select a suitable rod, and administer justice. You were never allowed to rear up in pain, so it was necessary to know in advance how much justice was being dispensed.

"Four cuts," the housemaster intoned.

I had taken only two of them when I did the unforgivable. I stood up. The cane paused above the housemaster's huge frame as I asked:

"Sir, why *four* cuts?"

"For breaking that paling on the fence and bunking out. You know it's always four for being out of bounds. And you know I caught you. You saw me wave at you from my car.

"Not me, Sir."

Mr Slater's expression changed from irritation to puzzlement, and then I do believe I detected amusement more than remorse as he exclaimed:

"You're quite right! It was your elder brother. Send Tickey Tyson in here right away, there's a good chap."

It was with enthusiasm as well as alacrity that I summoned Jack, and harried him all the way to within 20 yards of the housemaster's sanctum, reminding my brother repeatedly to accept only two cuts, because he owed me the balance, which I'd already received. I saw this as a half-restitution of justice.

However, my life is still marred by the injustice that followed. Big Jack Slater did administer only two cuts to my 'big' brother, Little Jack Tyson. I counted the swish-thwack twice, from a safe place in the flowerbed outside the housemaster's office. But my brother refused to take the next *"See Me Afterwards"* which came my way – as it seemed to me he was honourably bound to do. And my tentative proposal to Mr Slater that he let me off my next hiding was too easily brushed aside. It is difficult to plead a case strongly when you have already obeyed an instruction to touch your toes.

On Learning

The excitement of discovery, of exploration, of erudition – these were especially stimulating in our little world, so filled with forbidden fruit. The Prep (lower school) in Jacques House in those days was governed by a strict set of Calvinistic commandments handed down by the still-living Reverend Jacques.

These included: No organised sport on the Sabbath (not even an "unorganised" plunge in the swimming pool on a scorching Sunday afternoon).

No bioscopes ever, except perhaps educational films, and those not less than five weeks apart. No meeting with girls – ever – for all your days at school.

The no-girls rule created an obsessive interest in the forbidden subject. Questioning classmates who had sisters somehow increased the mystery. The only two available models for exploration were two relatively mature "ladies", quite 15 or 16 years old, who wore low-cut dresses instead of gym slips. They teased the horde of little boys through the fence, and made jokes we tried to work out afterwards. Far from being aloof and alluring, they were known to us (utterly inaccurately) as Bubble Guts and One Eye, and were the subject of endless, intimate, and hopelessly inaccurate speculation.

That's what Rev Jacques's arcane rules gave us.

The no bioscope rule led most of us to bunk out to the moving-picture house regularly. It was an unrivalled, daring, and much-loved adventure. The route involved walking around or through the cemetery, then a long walk to town within a concrete-lined canal, and a gallop up a side street and swift swerve into the film theatre foyer. Then straight up the stairs to the projection box where you could pay the entrance fee undetected and find an illicit seat in the tiny gallery where only illicit watchers were allowed. It was almost impossible to get caught, except if you were Saul Solomon or me. Saul had a jaw the shape of the bottom of a garage swing door. I had one shaped like an ice pick, and it was these physical protrusions which were our undoing.

Rushing out of the dazzling sunlight into the blacked-out gallery, Saul and I groped for our seats, making the major mistake of passing in front of the projector with our heads thrust forward. The privileged prefects below, and the illegal Kingswood boys, studied our profiles on-screen then roared with laughter.

"*See me afterwards,*" said a prefect at supper that evening.

"What for?" we asked.

"You bunked to bioscope today."

"How do you know? How do you know it was us?"

The prefect just laughed. "You ought to be film villains," he said.

We discussed the unfairness of such a "cop", to no avail.

Kingswood today has become a recognised leader in educational transformation. Though a Church School, I think it caters for black, white, brown, and Chinese pupils; boy Buddhists and Muslim girls, Jewish adherents and Rosicrucians and even "foreigners".

There are girls' dormitories all over the place.

Instead of the cane, there is erudite self-analysis and discussion.

It's extraordinary.

In fact Kingswood, founded in the 19th century, has for a hundred years seen itself as "a transforming influence"; a "church school" that has embraced pupils of all races; ever since the eras of anti-Semitism; the 'twixt war years of anti-boer; and the late apartheid years of colour prejudice.

Thus it was among the first boys' private schools anywhere to abolish another concept – that of males-only dominance.

On justice justified

Two school lessons on the all-importance and sensitivity of justice and loyalty in our lives have stayed with me forever.

The first lesson occurred when I entered Upper School and found myself in woodwork class. For me it was a disgraceful waste of decent wood as I failed to complete all but one of the items we had to carpenter from our woodwork master's model.

We would follow his example, step by step, from reproducing his drawing of a 3D design, to carving and polishing the finished product.

My sole existing evidence, from a Brownie Box camera, of happy school holidays in the early 1940s.

My only success occurred when I made a breadboard. It is true that breadboards do not have multiple parts and dovetail joints and things, and hardly require three-dimensional drawings, but as a display of near-perfect carpentry a properly flat breadboard is a thing of wonder.

Unfortunately, at whim and impulsively as I was about to hand in my beautifully completed work for marking, I swapped it for the woodwork master's model, expertly bevelled and oval, on the bench beside us.

Perhaps I did this on the spur of the moment because he had never given me more than three out of 10 for any of my considerable efforts. Clearly he was a man full of technical prejudices.

"Thick as two planks," my classmates agreed.

He gazed at his own work, grunted with surprise, said, "Tyson, you're improving!" – and wrote down 6/10.

Six out of 10 for the perfect model! It just showed how I was being discriminated against. I opened my mouth to protest ... but instead of biting like a piranha I stood there gulping like a fish out of water. The problem was, I realised at the critical moment, that if I sought justice I risked being falsely accused of theft of his work and cheating. It wasn't fair. And it wasn't right. He must have known all along that justice was on his side. Justice was served.

I developed a genuine and intense regard for justice at school. Especially as we were about to experience as adults a half century of blatant and increasing institutional abuse of it.

A much later lesson in life was that the chivalric values of honour, loyalty, and justice were to be found everywhere in human society, not only in environments of privileged society and good education, but also in vicious criminal gangs at times ... yet not necessarily throughout democratic parliaments and high-minded universities or in holy orders.

I live bitterly still with the memory of a celebrated martyr to the cause of African freedom, an Anglican priest from Britain, who refused to come forward and admit he was the source of a newspaper story – a report innocent enough, but illegal under apartheid law– which might have given him a technical, but honourable criminal record and a small fine. Instead he chose to let the reporter rot in jail with a life-searing *indefinite* jail sentence.

"Let him be a martyr to the cause," the reverend gentleman said, smugly.

So the reporter stood by our creed of never revealing the name of a confidential source, whatever the circumstances. (It is hard to remember a worse torture than knowing you may be jailed "forever" – but can be instantly free by betraying your own code. Numbers of journalists risked that imprisonment and long-term mental torture.) Our man suffered badly. For many months. He would not reveal his source even though, if revealed, the good man of the church would never have been in any danger – even of reputation.

That is why I hate would-be-but-never-quite martyrs, and realise that I'll need to live another 50 years before I shall understand their convoluted value systems. Instead I passionately honour Nelson Mandela for not acting as a martyr – yet offering his life for his beliefs. And Helen Suzman, who grieved and fought for the victims of injustice; who risked her freedom and abandoned her comfort – yet laughed at threats and never backed down.

But I go too far ahead in this story of freedom of the press. Back at school there was no inkling of the issues our country had to face. Instead we lived with the headlines of big bad Hitler, and speculated about the daring "ace" fighter pilots who would destroy his Reich one day. Then we heard of two of our seniors who, after leaving school had volunteered for warfare training at an army camp where the one accidentally shot dead his best friend. That made "us boys" think twice for a while about the glories of war. ☐

14.
The war?
What war?

*The little boats listed drunkenly with the
weight of men ... And always down the dunes
came new hordes of soldiers, new columns,
new line ... the red background, the red of Dunkirk
burning; the abandoned ambulances ...
Red, too, were the shell-bursts, the flash of guns,
the fountains of tracer bullets ...
The scream of falling bombs.*

War correspondent AD Devine, 1940.

WAR DECLARED screamed headlines across Europe and the British Empire on 3 September 1939 ... except in newspapers in South Africa. Instead, *The Star's* unprecedented headline spanned the entire front page and read:

GRAVE CRISIS IN SOUTH AFRICA.

The unspecific banner headline covered *two* front-page leads. One announced that the Allies had "opened war on Germany". But the main story, on the left of the page, announced that Prime Minister JBM Hertzog opposed declaring war against Hitler and advocated "benevolent neutrality" with Nazi Germany. A sub-headline announced:

COMPLETE SPLIT IN CABINET.

While Prime Minister Hertzog called for a vote of confidence, General Jan Smuts, as a partner in government, demanded that the country sever relations with The Reich. On 4 September, Smuts quickly found a majority of supporters in the Cabinet. The newspaper reported:

HERTZOG RESIGNS: SMUTS NOW PREMIER.

On 5 September, the country was told:

GENERAL SMUTS FORMS HIS CABINET.

It was a new Cabinet uniting Afrikaans and English-speaking South Africans willing to join the free world in fighting tyranny. General Smuts would be Premier *and* Minister of Defence. Young Dr Jan Hofmeyr would later become an extraordinary Minister of Finance and act as Prime Minister during Smuts's many trips to the theatres of war. On the night of 6 September, backed by a majority of only 13 in Parliament, Smuts issued a proclamation, which enabled the earliest editions of *The Cape Times* of 7 September to carry — at last — the banner:

SOUTH AFRICA DECLARES WAR ON GERMANY.

Smuts's proclamation, however, made it clear that: "the Union of South Africa ... takes a stand for the defence of freedom, and the destruction of Hitlerism and all it implies, but has no quarrel with the people of Germany as such."

This showed a wise sensitivity, but was prompted mainly by the need for a balance in national politics. The reasons for this are cloudy today, partly because the "social history" of life in South Africa in the war years 1939–1945 has never been recorded adequately or sufficiently. This is only partly due to the influence of war's blanket censorship. It has been insufficiently recorded also because of the secret "civil war" waged by a very small band of pro-Hitler activists seeking to get rid of what they saw as British domination and creating an exclusively Afrikaner Republic.

The majority of Afrikanerdom, however, like the other cultures in white, brown, and black South Africa, appears to have had no sympathy with Nazism. Despite a natural yearning for an independent republic, Afrikaans-speaking voters largely supported "England's" war against Hitler. Under the Smuts war-time government the nation was encouraged to think about nothing else except "The War Effort"; to remember "Our Boys up North"; and to support them in battles moving from Abyssinia to Libya to Sicily and Italy. And much of the early public war-time discussion included the fate of South African volunteers risking or losing their lives at sea in the Royal Navy, in the air in the "Battle of Britain" and on land from Dunkirk to the Berlin border.

While British Commonwealth countries such as Canada, Australia, and India contributed larger numbers to the world's war effort, South Africans actually experienced "The War" itself in their own country. The ports were blacked out at times when raiders were detected in South African waters and for some time submarines were sinking ships more often here than anywhere else except the North Atlantic. For five years South Africans lived on an almost exclusive diet of news of naval battles across the world; of defeats and occasional victories on land and in the air. Almost daily the newspapers and radio reported "casualties" among "our boys": youngsters and married men with families who were Afrikaners and English-speaking, and occasionally isiXhosa, Zulu, Indian, Malay or other tribal language groups.

We lived on a diet of life-and-death news all those years – even though the news was hugely distorted by censorship and our own side's propaganda.

South Africans gave material support (even school pocket money) to all kinds of war funds. They cheered South African-made armoured convoys that paraded through the towns, emphasising yet again the country's War Effort.

They stood in silence at school, honouring their war dead (and the dreaded "missing") reported each week. Countless families had cause to weep. South African English-speaking senior schools suffered roll calls of war dead (all volunteers) that rivalled in proportion any similar institutions anywhere in the world.

All of this was almost taken for granted as the way of life.

What added to tension in this land, however, were the core and the corps of pro-Hitler activists, and their spreading, smouldering sense of nationalism and grievance. With five years of "War Effort" and its unquestioning propaganda on the one hand, and, on the other hand, the passive as well as active underground support for "the Aryan enemy", political life among the country's voters became extreme. Afrikaans secret societies propagated the view that Hitler was their friend and would win the war. But these secret societies were unable to become broadly volatile, and were heatedly rejected by most Afrikaners.

When peace came and world markets opened again for a strained South African economy, political volatility returned, and Afrikaner nationalism exploded.

It may be unfair then to accuse General (later British Field Marshal) Smuts of being remiss in failing to bring radical change to black-white race politics in the latter part of his era of administration.

The great racially-based political division was not seen then as black vs white. In stark practice it was a white power struggle between the *Natte* and the *Sappe:* the Nationalist Party and the South African Party. Theirs was the only race war occurring in the Union of SA ... and it contained heated emotions that dominated all active politics.

World War brought to a head that inevitable *racist* struggle between two white groups. Peace provided an extreme political swing which turned the clock back. The election of a National Party government, representing a minority even in an all-white parliament, precluded South Africa's chances of progressive political reform towards independence and broader racial equality.

It also isolated South Africa from the world's post-war boom. This country not only missed – but rejected – the explosive global growth and skills shift out of war-torn Europe. In turning itself inwards, South Africa's government deprived the country of the rich, economic and humanitarian benefits that were welcomed by all other Commonwealth members around the world in the 1950s.

Most of this went over my head at the time, for my memory of the start of the "Second World War to End all Wars", was watching the grown-ups' faces as we huddled round a radio in our little cottage by the beach at The Strand, where our mother now earned enough to live on. She did so by inviting local residents to earn money by baking, sewing, soldering, carving and making goods for her co-op shop named *The Helping Hand*. She chose to establish her shop right on the seafront, partly it seemed, in order to spoil us with fun times on the beach during boarding-school holidays.

Chamberlain and Hitler agree on "peace in our time". Hitler reneges and Neville Chamberlain gets a bad press and a bad name in judgemental history. However, he believed he had won priceless time for Britain to start rebuilding its fighting forces.

Her co-operative project ended not long after we had watched her and granny listening to Neville Chamberlain announcing in subdued triumph that he had visited Herr Hitler in Munich and had returned to London to assure Britain there would be "peace in our time".

Yet in a very short space of time we again heard Chamberlain, on this occasion speaking in a hushed, flat, tired voice, telling us that "we are at war with Germany". My mother looked serious, but not worried. We instinctively knew that she was aware that the war would give her a new life. But granny looked very sad.

Yet while "we" might be at war with "Mr Herr Hitler"; and while General Smuts's party might be volunteering for war, General Hertzog's party was dead against it. Tension rose in our village of The Strand. In the bioscope, when they played *God Save the King* (*net in Engels* – only in English) at the end of the main film, half the audience would try to walk out, and the other half tried vainly to stand at attention while simultaneously trying to wrestle the departing protesters to a standstill.

War on our home front was proving as difficult to manage as was the aim of the popular song advising us to "hang out your washing on (Hitler's) Ziegfried line" – while the very opposite was happening: his blitzkrieg was about to bypass, then wring the stuffing out of, the French's "invincible" Maginot Line.

Much of the war had to be fought at home in South Africa, in the way we had witnessed it being fought by "adults" in the aisles of the bioscope.

The war was at all times a great puzzle to me.

A new hero, Winston Churchill, was heard on radio, taunting "Mr" Herr Hitler. Yet moments later, it seemed,

Winston Churchill tells Adolph Hitler and the world "we shall never surrender".

"Winnie" was helplessly outnumbered when the Russian communists joined the Nazis in destroying Poland. I remember studying with some anxiety a British cartoon depicting a great Russian Bear, with blood dripping from its claws and fangs as it ravaged the little soldiers of tiny Finland.

And again, in a cartoon only moments later, it seemed, the raging Russian Bear transformed into beaming "Uncle Joe" Stalin – having suddenly switched sides to become democracy's best friend; closer to us even than Hollywood.

While mom rose to senior rank in the Women's Auxiliary Air Force (WAAF), to her disgust she was never allowed to fly. She had followed with intense interest the exploits of Amy Mollison and the handful of famous women pilots. Inspired by the news of the female few, she had spent nearly two years of her spare time before the war doing voluntary basic training in the hopes of becoming a trainee pilot.

Her elder son Jack matriculated in time to join the army. He was too young to join up – just as my mother was too old to be an SAAF pilot – but unlike mom, he was able to break the rules. This despite being so small that he looked like a 14-year-old. I assumed brother "Tickey" Tyson had been taken along by the burly Sappers as a mascot. Instead, he came swaggering home, filled with tales of battle, wine, and women (having been seduced enthusiastically by some professional ladies in Rome). He tried to impress us all with his deep experience and knowledge of Italian. I assumed he was speaking halting Latin.

My own war experiences were filled with disillusion. One memory was witnessing wild Aussie troops – the brave and loyal ANZACs

(Australian and New Zealand Army Corps) – swarm off the "biggest troopship in the world". They had jumped overboard from the giant *Queen Mary* and swum to the Adderley Street pier to riot in Cape Town streets.

Another memory was being a confident 12-year-old on holiday *without* adults in Durban, suddenly losing both confidence and directions in the unexpected nightly blackout – a total, groping blackout – in a big, strange city.

My very worst experience of war, however, occurred at boarding school where we carried out an evacuation exercise in peaceful little Grahamstown. When the sirens went, we gleefully rushed out of class and threw ourselves into a carefully designated ditch. I landed on a pile of dog shit. The horror of it clung to me for years.

WAR DID strange things to people. It was not something sociologists could measure or newspapers could report, yet it affected every child; every bystander, every worker and every family touched by physical, social or psychological dislocation caused by mass warfare and constant, unpredictable death of young people.

Even so, few seemed the least aware that World War Two caused an estimated 55 million deaths; Communist Russia suffering nearly 30 million; China 10 million, and Germany and Poland seven million deaths each. The size of battle can be measured by the fact that on every average *day* of America's active role in WW2, the victorious US lost 270 aircraft and thousands of men. It was a daily loss of more aircraft and airmen than exist in an entire air force of many nations today.

The end of the WW2 was, for me, as puzzling as its beginning. We 16-year-olds and our older mates were big boys by now, matriculants and prefects, some of us having *definitely* given up smoking for the second or fourth time. We followed the D-Day operations avidly and held our breath in the hopes that war would not end before we had a chance to join in – or rather "join up", as non-enrolling patriots and self-regarding democrats enjoined all their neighbours to do.

As we embarked on our two-day train journey back to school, we realised that peace might break out at any moment. By the time the train reached De Aar rail junction in the middle of the empty Karoo, we felt the war in Europe must be over. We jumped onto the platform before the train stopped (it was our usual habit) and collared the first railway porter who, like all of them in those days, was a white, middle-aged or elderly man.

"Is the war over?" we chorused. "*Watter oorlog (*What war*)?*" the man asked in genuine bewilderment.

"What war?" indeed. South Africa had had so many of its own. But you'd think he might have heard of it, if only to anticipate a *dop brandewyn* (a shot of brandy) in celebration of whoever won on V-E Day (Victory in Europe). Anyway, the Allies still had to drop the A-Bomb on the Japs. Finally V-J Day (Victory over Japan) arrived. What a party!

But no liquor was to cross my lips until some time after I left school. Ah, school days! In much later years I used to tell pupils at school prize givings: "These are the best days of your life. Remember that. They're the very best you'll ever have ... until you leave school. Then it gets better. *You* must ensure that every decade gets better."

That is the real value of education. I learned another personal lesson late in my school life. It was that my mother had agreed not to accept alimony from our occasionally errant father – on the grounds that he had undertaken, despite supporting two later wives on a mine secretary's salary, to keep my brother and me at a top boarding school and ensure we experienced a good education. It was a great sacrifice on his part, and made obvious the fact that his later cash-starved women – both delightfully witty company – did not marry him in quick succession for his money.

All my life I cherished his gift to me of a good education. Mine was so good that I failed to pass matric. Or so it seemed. My name appeared on no lists, and I assumed I'd crashed in several subjects. I knew that my failure resulted from the fact that I had managed to bunk the maths classes of an ineffectual part-time substitute teacher for several months. (This seems to require an explanation: two of us impulsively bunked the first few classes of this fourth temporary, emergency, war-time maths master in just 18 months. It was an interesting challenge until it dawned on us that, in a separate class of involuntary Latin scholars numbering only 14, we could never go back until he departed. He left only at year-end. Thus, running for cover for the maths periods every day, and hiding from all eyes of Upper School, became a nightmare.)

Instead of failing, however, my papers were re-marked and I was lucky enough to receive, belatedly, a first-class pass with sufficient distinction to elicit a scholarship to university.

I've been lucky all my life.

However, I had always expected luck to help me. I had adopted an adolescent philosophy. It was based, I suppose, on reading about schoolboy heroes such as The Scarlet Pimpernel, who pretended to be a languid, non-caring English Gentleman of Leisure. Yet he suddenly leapt into action in the disguise of a beggar in the French Revolution in Paris or somewhere, to save damsels in distress. Or reading about some other elegant stock hero, usually a fighter ace of WW1, who lazily finished smoking his cigarette before taking to the air to challenge and beat Germany's notorious Red Baron.

"Style" in my book, meant not to practise at sport, not to do extra study, not to be seen to care, but especially not to appear eager.

Whatever the influences behind this concept of a lifestyle were, they led me to believe that in life one should not be seen striving, let alone grabbing competitively and greedily for an advantage or an upgrade. These would come to those who wait if one showed no undue interest in any opportunity of self-advancement. It is a weird philosophy, but it seemed to ensure against failure. Just wait for something to turn up, which it appears to do, often, all through life.

The trick is to recognise it when it arrives.

Sometimes we confuse luck with "justice", thinking that our so-called achievements are justified through our own qualities and efforts.

An example of this fallacy might be found in an essay written in my last year at school. To my extreme embarrassment the essay was marked "30/20". Thirty marks out of twenty! The entire class was in shock. They looked at me as if I had treacherously informed on every one of them.

"Sir? Sir? Sir!" they protested. Attempts at hiding my change of feelings from embarrassment to over-stuffed pride almost failed as the headmaster explained. "Unfortunately, I marked that one last. It was so much better than the rest of yours that I would have had to reduce your marks to under half – or give him 150 percent. Which do you want?"

Suddenly I became about as popular as a piranha in the communal bath. Did I deserve such punishment?

Where was the justice in it?

The answer came 18 months later when the "30 out of 20" helped me get a job. I used it (instead of anything written in first-year English at Rhodes University) as the "example required of the applicant's writing ability".

The editor of *The Star* told my mother: "Your son's work is academic, fictional and immature. He'll have to develop." But I got the job – mainly because my mother was beside me, in the full-dress senior officer's uniform of the WAAF, in which she had served for six years including the whole of WWII. The newspaper company's policy after the war was to engage no one but senior returning ex-servicemen. My mother claimed the same rights (but for "my young breadwinner, my son".) No one could be a breadwinner on the salary of a cub reporter – but I was accepted.

WHY WOULD ONE WANT TO BE A JOURNALIST? The quick answer was obvious in my case: "Because I'd like to write and I'm no good at anything else." But there was a more subtle influence at work. It was the name carved – among hundreds of others – on the back of the benches in the Kingswood College gallery of Grahamstown's Commemoration Church. As a matter of ritual, all of us had carved names or initials there, but the name AD Devine, so apt in church, was one of those carved in deep capital letters as high as your hand. He must have executed it during a full year of church services as long sermons drifting up from the preacher's pulpit to where we sat (or lay hidden, to execute our immortal craft) in the three- or four-deck wooden gallery that swept around three sides of the church's interior.

Devine, obviously a champion carver, was a generation ahead of us but known to current schoolboys because he had written books – a couple of thrillers, we believed. And he was a Fleet Street journalist! He became the unspoken, unacknowledged inspiration for this kid at school early in the war. But it wasn't until 70 years later, while I was seeking examples of great journalism that I came across anything Devine had written. Here is a sample of it, which appeared in the *Readers Digest*, way back in December 1940:

> *... You remember the old quotation about the miracle that crushed the Spanish Armada "God sent a wind"? This time "God held the wind". Had we had one on-shore breeze of any strength at all, in the first days, we would have lost a hundred thousand men.*

Devine was summing up his earlier dispatches to Kemsley Newspapers of his eyewitness account of the battle and retreat at Dunkirk which he had experienced months before.

"*.... And always down the dunes and across the beach came new hordes of men, new columns, new lines ...*" *while the rescuers watch the skies expecting an onslaught.*

Later they celebrate. By some "miracle" hundreds of thousands of soldiers have been plucked from under the guns of the Nazi's all-conquering Blitzkrieg. Devine reported:

The whole thing from first to last was covered with that strange feeling of something supernatural. We muddled, we quarrelled, everybody swore, everybody was bad-tempered ... And yet out of all that mess we beat the experts, we defied the law and the prophets, and where the government and Board of the Admiralty had hoped to bring away 30 000 men, we brought away 330 000. If it was not a miracle, there are no miracles left ... I was given a motorboat about as long as my drawing room at home, thirty feet. It had one cabin forward and the rest was open, but she had twin engines and was fairly fast. For crew we had one sub-lieutenant, one stoker and one gunner. For armament we had two Bren guns – one my particular pet which I had stolen – and rifles. In command of our boat we had a real live Admiral – Taylor, who was in charge of "small boats" ... These included a car ferry, surely on its first trip in the open sea. There were yachts; one the Skylark – what a name for such a mission! There were dockyard tugs, towing barges. There were sloops, mine sweepers, trawlers, destroyers. There were Thames fire-floats, Belgian drifters, lifeboats from all around the coast, lifeboats from sunken ships. I saw the boats of the old Dunbar Castle, sunk eight months before. Rolling and pitching in a cloud of spray were open speedboats, wholly unsuited for the Channel chop ...There was never such a fleet went to war before, I think. As I went round the harbour passing out orders, it brought my heart into my throat to watch them leave. They were so small! When this armada of oddments was under way, we followed with the faster boats – Royal Air Force rescue launches ... and kerosene-powered landing craft used at Gallipoli 20 years before ... It was the queerest, most nondescript flotilla that ever was; manned by every kind of Englishman ... bankers and dentists, taxi drivers and yachtsmen, longshoremen, boys, engineers, fishermen and civil servants and bright-faced Sea Scouts; one or two to each boat ... The little boats that ferried from (Dunkirk's) beach to the big ships in deep water listed drunkenly with the weight of men .... And always down the dunes and across the beach came new hordes of men, new columns, new lines ... the red background, the red of Dunkirk burning; the abandoned ambulances ... Red, too, were the shell-bursts, the flash of guns, the fountains of tracer bullets .... To the whistle of shells overhead was added the scream of falling bombs. Even the sky was full of noise – anti-aircraft shells, machine gun fire, the snarl of falling planes, the angry noise of dive bombers ....”

Devine's immediate despatches to his newspaper office helped set the tone for Britain's belief in the "miracle". Many more miracles were needed as Japan and Germany marched across the world, and Britain's war in Europe against Hitler suddenly turned into Hitler's war on England. Winston Churchill intoned: "We shall fight them on the beaches ... we shall never surrender." It is good to know that a schoolboy hero, Devine, had been among the very last to retreat from Dunkirk; finally rescuing French soldiers who feared his boat could never reach the English coast.

A schoolboy would never question that he did what a war correspondent was not supposed to do: get involved.

MY LIFE AS A JOURNALIST would begin in a decidedly different world, with different values as well as different priorities. I had left university after only one year for several reasons. Rhodes University, in the City of Saints, appeared to be trying to accommodate half the armed forces returning from WWII as I entered it straight from school on a last-minute scholarship in 1946.

The ex-servicemen came with state-sponsored university fees plus spending money for three years of academic study. Sponsored academic study turned out to mean, for most new entries, chasing girls, playing poker and indulging in dirty weekends – but only for some of the returning heroes, unfortunately.

The queues to be interviewed by the Board of Studies on the opening days were so long that an ex-Royal Navy sailor next to me changed his mind about taking a BA and crossed to the shorter BSc queue. Then he moved to the BCom queue. He was persuaded in his changing choice by how fast each queue was moving. A more patient air force type stuck to his decision to "enlist" for a BSc, only to cause disillusion among studious civilians when, half a year later, he climbed out of one of the army trucks we used as varsity ferries from the aerodrome, to ask: "Anyone know where the science block is?"

The ex-servicemen (and I, because I arrived at university beyond the academic deadline as a lowly first-year "ink") were housed in the WAAF aerodrome barracks, which the women's auxiliary air force had wisely evacuated. The ex-servicemen, and five belated "inks", were ferried, day and night, into the distant town in army trucks in which the ex-soldiers, sailors and airmen sang countless verses of dirty songs that were an education for any new 17-year-old.

The ex-servicemen sometimes hired trucks for "long weekends" carrying off the best female students to the seaside. Deep bass voices would be heard, singing in the women's beach hotel bathrooms. These much admired baritones soon disappeared, or were "sent down" in their first year. It was fun, in a way, but hard for a first-year "ink" to compete. The inkettes seemed to cope well enough, I noticed, even if those going to the seaside for the weekend missed their daily bath.

For me it seemed a pleasant, but wasted year. I had passed all my subjects with much luck, but greatly distracted effort, and knew that none of it justified the money being spent on my bursary, family donations and eking out my long-term bank loan.

Instead, to join a newspaper (by grace of my mother's war service), I had to attend a shorthand and typing class in Johannesburg attended in those days only by giggling girls. ☐

15.
Sexual and other explanations.

*Writers of confessions, from Augustine onwards,
are men who are still a little in love with their sins.*

Anatole France, 1920.

Those names, and places, and dramas and adventures confessed in a speech in a church hall, which I reported at the start of Part II of this chronicle, are all true of course. I wish I had photographs to prove them, but the cell phone camera wasn't invented then, and I still don't have one now.

Yes, there was an angry alligator (caiman) in our canoe in the Amazon, beyond "the drug triangle" above Brazil. It's worth a mention.

Yes there was a beautiful nun in my life.

Yes, I was a fly on the wall when a Third World War nearly did flare out of control in Berlin.

Yes, I did find problems in Samarkand, Beijing, Belgrade and other places where newsworthy tensions were simmering at various times.

But, as I said in that address: "What I've tried to do is to illustrate how very easily – sometimes enthusiastically – people jump to the wrong conclusions without bothering to ensure the facts they gather are in the correct context."

Now let's look at the correct context of some of those personal revelations.

Firstly my statement about being *stranded in Belgrade* without identification papers on the eve of the outbreak of the horrifying, undeclared civil war:

Well, it's a long story, but only about a serious *personal* drama. It involved a tricky night-ride in a time of extreme political tension, from Prague to Belgrade in an emergency bus in which I could communicate with only two passengers who spoke English. One was an undercover Iranian arms dealer, the other a desperate woman from Manchester. Each of us had different reasons for sneaking into Yugoslavia via the back door at a bad time. The woman was in search of her husband, lost in chaotic Eastern Europe. The arms dealer was on unspoken business, and I was an inquisitive, 64-year-old semi-retired freelancer with an ex-reporter's notebook in search of information.

It was after midnight before we drove into Belgrade. Threat of war had caused instant cancellation of flights from Prague and Vienna, stalling my simple plan to arrive by plane and take a taxi to a hotel. Instead I had spent 16 non-stop hours on this disorganised emergency road trip. Now, in the taut, dark hours before war, the streets of Belgrade were deserted … which means not a soul, not a solitary beggar or patrolman was to be seen. I could discern no sign of life as I stood in the drizzle in one of the city's main streets where no name was visible. I was acutely aware I had no contacts. I was without a map in a city I had never seen before. I had no knowledge of the Serbian language, and nowhere to stay.

I felt somewhat lonely as I waved goodbye to my fellow seekers – the last two friendly people with a smattering of English whom I was likely to meet in Eastern Europe during that major crisis.

But instead of the bus disappearing down the dimly lit street, I saw its brake lights blink red in a cloak of spray. The Iranian passenger leapt out and hurried back to me. He had in his hand my wallet, my passport and my air ticket to Rome and Johannesburg – and the notebook with all the information I had gathered while journeying through East Europe as it broke free of the Kremlin.

"Here," he said. "Your wallet. Your papers. You showed them for me." (I had shown my validated "New South African" papers to the border Police in trying to help the Iranian through). "They were on your empty bus seat," the arms trader shouted before running back to the bus bound for Budapest or Istanbul in another world.

So you see, I had been utterly and desperately stranded – but without comprehending it, and only for a few brief minutes. It was no big deal, just the usual kind of momentary crisis for me.

Followed by the usual luck. I'm always losing things. However, I confess that I can still feel that prickly memory of being penniless, alone and highly vulnerable in Belgrade on the eve of civil war.

Fortunately I stumbled on a still brightly lit Macdonald's; the first burger site I ever visited. (The tale of the death of Yugoslavia, and of the horror and evil that followed, may be examined among the travels depicted in the planned work entitled *Vanishing Places*.)

AT THE BEGINNING of this account, I also told you that I was lost in inland China – once more without papers. It was soon after the Tiananmen Square crisis, but I was a writer merely being inquisitive again in my retirement, not investigating the dangerous plot that had shaken the world shortly before we were allowed to enter the country.("A first", again, because New South Africa passports were suddenly, though momentarily, trusted instantly across all sides of the politicised world.) Yes, I was lost in the hostile communist state. *But* the context is that I was merely a tourist, going for a spur-of-the-moment early-morning bike ride, exploring a city near Guilin. I started to worry because every time I turned a corner, the next street-block filled with featureless five-storey apartment buildings, looked precisely like the last. I was trapped in a vast, moving bicycle jam of about 20 cyclists abreast and stretching down the barrack-like boulevards as far as the eye could see. I was surrounded by thousands of pedalling Chinese on their way to work, not one of whom I hoped to recognise.

Obviously none spoke English, and I could not understand a word of any Chinese language, nor write Mandarin.

Cycling in a city in China sometimes requires more skill, luck, endurance and patience than many of us can find.

But it didn't matter anyway because it was impossible to ask directions even in plain English as I had no idea of the name or address of the place I was staying at on the outskirts of the city. I couldn't, in a moment of near-panic, remember the name of this city I was in. All I had with me, besides my borrowed bike and underpants, were a shirt, a pair of sand shoes, and a pair of shorts with empty pockets.

Anyway, after seeming hours of wrong turns and increasing worry-lines, I managed by trial and error to find my way out of the city and to my lodgings where I was reunited with my wallet, my identity papers and other suddenly beloved belongings.

It provided a lesson for the future which I failed to learn: When in the Orient, get someone to write down in Chinese, Japanese, "whatever", the name and address of your hotel — and paste it on your forehead if necessary.

My misadventure in mid-China however is of little interest. My minor miracle is of no consequence to anyone but absentminded me.

As for the presidents and prime ministers I've interviewed ... well, I happened to meet Gerald Ford once at a golf function, and further investigation persuaded me that he seemed to be one of the more honestly sincere politicians I'd met in the world, and quite unlike the man, unsuccessfully trying to chew gum and think at the same time, as depicted in a hostile American press.

Gerald Ford.

History is unlikely to be kind to **Gerald Ford**. Yet it is worth considering that he should be revered, by his countrymen at least, as being one of the least ambitious, most punctiliously honest and kindest leaders in the big cruel world of national and international politics.

In politics, sincerity will get you nowhere.

I say that purely on the evidence he has provided, "under oath" as it were. The only possibility that this evidence is skewed might be that he carefully omitted to provide some of it. But that is unlikely in view of his basic approach to admitting his human fallibilities and mistakes, and with his awareness, especially after the Nixon scandal, that any deviousness was doomed to exposure.

Ford's personal history in being propelled reluctantly into the US Presidency, is chronicled by himself under a well considered title *A Time to Heal*.[1] And it was in this very mode that he made himself highly unpopular by officially pardoning President Richard Nixon, who had rightly been forced out of office.

Ford's rating in the popularity polls plummeted from a highly favourable 71 percent all the way down to 49. He was wounded by accusations that he had allowed conflict of interest as a "financial benefactor" to sway his judgement in pardoning "his lifelong friend".

Nothing was further from the truth. Nixon was not his friend, and "never gave me a dime" at any time, Ford said quietly.

What is revealing about this is that Ford writes of the accusation: "I had all I could do to keep my temper under control," and decided the slur was partly his own fault for failing to "get his story across" on this issue of healing.

That "turning of the cheek" should be enough to make his popularity go down a few more points ... but he had already turned his attention to another problem. Americans, he believed in this Nixon period of mistrust and political dishonour, were losing faith in themselves and their nation. Ford saw "a self-destruct attitude" that wounded the country and tore at his own convictions.

"We didn't need newer goals or nobler ones. What we did need was a renewed sense of purpose and a strengthening of our national will to pursue those goals."

So he promptly announced – as a *Republican* President! – a program for the return to society of Vietnam-era draft evaders and deserters. He announced the establishment of a Presidential Clemency Board to assist Vietnam War draft dodgers.

Brave healing indeed. And he did it in the same manner as he wrote his book: understanding the rights of those who opposed his view, and presenting his own story in refreshingly unpretentious yet vivid style.

He was unwilling to knife his political enemies. And he had nothing to hide. So, unlike Nixon, he appeared to have no sure place in history.

BUT ... fortunately the American nation is rich in freedom of opinion with many of its expressed – and voluntarily suppressed – prejudices always open for review. And now, decades after his brief political leadership, President Gerald Ford's re-assessed role is being spectacularly celebrated. In late 2017, the US Navy was ready to launch a few super-class aircraft carriers, and would name the first vessel the *USS Gerald R Ford*, placing his name back in the forefront of naval history.

What a fine gesture. And what an irony!

Gerald Ford, the man of peace, will be remembered now because the biggest navy in the world will send his name across the globe on the prow of the most powerful warship built so far.

Even without the ship, I feel so chuffed at having spent a few hours with the gentle, honourable, honest Gerald Ford.

Harold Macmillan, most stylish of world leaders, with good humour as well.

However, except for the grandly stylish **Harold Macmillan**, who made the timeous Wind of Change speech in Verwoerd's parliament, I cannot remember anything of any importance he or any of the VIPs said when I found myself shaking hands with them ceremoniously or privately while "working" in various parts of the world.

Oh yes, there was PW Botha, who impressed me with the words: "Tyson, I don't like you. And I don't like your face."

I've quoted that, in its proper context, in another book which makes clear that while it said a lot about the prime minister, it was of little significance. It concerned no major political issue ... although our newspaper exposé of him using taxpayers' money and defence force facilities to go helicopter-hunting rare and protected black-faced impala, I find revealing about both the man and his government. These kind of presidential political scandals have become so common that the lesser ones hardly make news today.

In the apartheid era I had personal "run-ins" with every government leader after Prime Minister Malan, and the newspaper I edited had private and public quarrels and boycotts involving every commissioner of police. It's the kind of stuff worth forgetting about.

As anecdotes of interest, I would single out – from the random, superficial, deliberately out-of-context samples featured in my earlier "confessions" here, my experience of "revolutionary plots" in two manifestly settled and staid democracies. Yet the only serious and sensational point in these events is that I, as a newsman, actually became involved with the plotters when my profession demanded that I should act as a neutral observer. *Fie on me!*

Fortunately, in their proper context, you will see that my experiences allowed no question of holding back real news, or any conflict with the journalistic ethic of disinterest (using its unambiguously correct, prime meaning).

For instance, I witnessed a plot in Britain to break into Westminster Abbey to steal a priceless item. I was working temporarily on *The Scotsman*, Edinburgh's elite newspaper, and when the day's work was ending – at about two in the morning – the subeditors would adjourn to the neighbouring pub. Scottish pubs closed alarmingly early, but in our case we were smuggled into the "closed" private bar and allowed to buy wee rounds of whisky while five of my colleagues entertained themselves by endlessly discussing a plan to steal the Stone of Scone – a symbol of Scotland's ancient independence – from its symbolic 700-year-resting place under the Queen's throne in Westminster Abbey. It was great fun for me, an outsider, to be a witness to the game. But perhaps it wasn't a game, I discovered later.

The "Stone of Destiny", which rightfully belonged to the place where rebellious Robert the Bruce was crowned King of Scotland in the year 1306, had been taken by King Edward I of England in 1296 ... and not formally returned until 1996.

A piece of old sandstone named "The Stone of Scone" was used for centuries at the crowning of Scottish kings until 1296 when King Edward of England invaded and carried off the legendary 66cm x 41 cm rectangle of dirt to put under this throne in London. On Christmas morning 1950 the stone was stolen from Westminster Abbey by Scottish nationalists who took it back to Scotland. Four months later it was recovered and restored to the abbey. In 1996 the British government returned the stone to Scotland.

However some students had already pinched it on Christmas Day, 1950 and left it in a church in Scotland, which returned it as "stolen property" the following year. Now these adult Scottish nationalists were talking of stealing it again. The real problem was what to do with a scratched, damaged piece of red sandstone, once these delightful, dreamy, Scottish nationalists had got hold of it. Yes, it had to be mere pub talk I believed, until much later and far away, I read that some unnamed citizens of Edinburgh had been questioned about such an alleged plot. Whether it was "my" little secret band of barroom nationalist Scots colleagues, I never tried to find out.

On another occasion, while exploring the back streets of Brussels one night, I stopped to question a barman in a deserted pub, in the way journalists often do. When he discovered I could, through Afrikaans, almost understand Flemish he was quite receptive to my questioning. We were interrupted by a trapdoor which suddenly flung up from the floor and a dozen young women and men popped out from underground in search of refreshments. After introductions between the mutually surprised parties, he assured them I was quite harmless and would never say a word. So they continued discussing in Flemish, ways of destroying the government which they believed was unfairly influenced by French-speaking Belgians.

I went back to the trapdoor pub next night, out of sheer curiosity, to join them in the hidden cellar – but they had fled. I suspected again that they were merely romantic nationalists, though was not so certain following a mysterious bomb explosion reported in Brussels after I left that week.

My third encounter with underground political plotters was in that relaxed and lively land of law-abiding citizens, New Zealand. Our bus driver explained that there were far more sheep in New Zealand than people. "And if they ever get the vote," he said, "We are done for." As we drove round a corner we saw a large flock of sheep huddled together, sheltering their heads from the sun. "There they are!" cried the driver, tooting his horn. "Break it up! Break it up!" he shouted at the sheep, then turned to us with a wink and said: "They're always putting their heads together .... That's ominous in a non-voting majority."

So revolutionary plots are not always what they seem, as we've discovered often in my own country, and their context is easily distorted in the chase for political power.

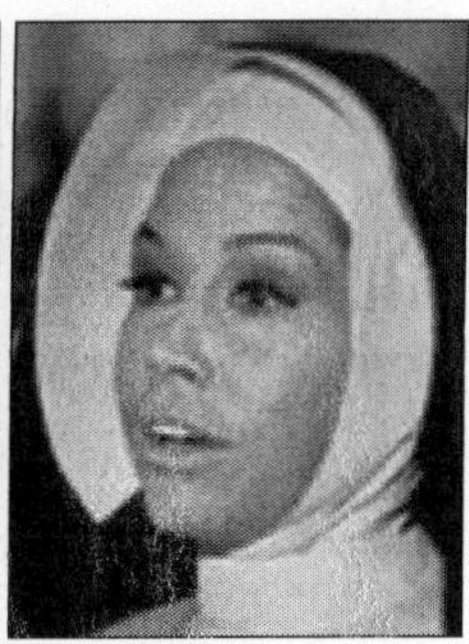

Which one is mine? None of these. Mine was a real nun. Not a film star like these poseurs (from left): Julie Andrews, Audrey Hepburn, Ingrid Bergman and Mary Tyler Moore. Ingrid Bergman, third from the left, is closest to my memories of Sister Margaret – not her real name.

ALL THAT REMAINS to be explained about the claims in my little speech in the local church hall are: How I came to be invited into the bed of a beautiful nun.

Even when an explanation is not sought, it is definitely required. It is my best example of why truth demands that history, news reports, and all non-fictional anecdotes need to be placed in their proper context.

Guess which nun was mine.

My encounter with a nun is the only item on my life-list that seems, without fail, to grab a listener's attention, on those exceedingly rare and rash occasions when the delicately private subject is mentioned. The interest is in the details – kept secret by modesty and shame for most of my life – of why we shared a bed. And why she took the initiative.

It happened when I was young, innocent, and still had a lot to learn about women and sex. My very first lesson had occurred one evening long ago when the youngest of three sisters, about my age, cornered me behind a door and said – probably in those very words – "If you show me yours, I'll show you mine."

With no sisters, one had to be very incurious in those secretive times not to accept such an offer. But the memory of the five-year-old pushing forward her bared pelvis remains only because it seemed such a negative sight. I expected her to have a different kind of "dinghy" from those my brother and I had (named after the little vessels appended to trawlers and yachts that we saw in Gordon's Bay). She had no kind of dangling dinghy or Afrikaans *dinges*; she

149

appeared to have less than nothing to show, and I felt cheated. But perhaps she felt the same.

This begins to put in proper context the facts about my nights with Sister Margaret (true name withheld). I adored her. She invited me into her bed because I was inconsolable and very lonely, and I had no one to play with at the convent because nearly all the convent boarders were these silly girls. I think Sister Margaret, young and soft-hearted, didn't like to hear me crying in the night.

I shall never forget her.

How times change relationships! How context alters illusions!

And when I mention my undying love for a nun how quickly people jump to the wrong conclusions without bothering to obtain the facts.

It is as misleading as history when it is written in hindsight by academics who learn so much yet fail to comprehend and record what the actual situation, comprehension, precise timing of conjoining events and social contexts were when events occurred in previous eras.

It is the same with those introductory casual references of mine a moment ago to "communist police holding us hostage behind the Berlin Wall", which will be explained later. Earlier references to things like "pink dolphins in a black lake"; to caimans in my canoe and to the snake pit on Ghengis Khan's Silk Route across Asia, and some other strange events will belong in personal travellers' tales appearing later, I hope, in their proper context. They have nothing to do with this story of journalism. □

1. *A Time to Heal* by Gerald Ford, published by WH Allen, 1979.

3

Learning the ropes

1945 – 1950s

16.

Green monster seen in the 'Big Hole'.

Scepticism is the chastity of the intellect.

George Santayana, 1940s.

The headline above might be taken as a signal of sorts; a sign that the warring world had already returned to the trivialities of peace only 18 months after World War II. This was the case in most of pre-apartheid South Africa – but not in Europe and much of the planet, which faced turmoil and unremitting, almost incomprehensible socio-political change.

Here at home, however, the biggest worry among the white electorate seemed to be the total lack of white bread and the shortage of nylon stockings. Voters thought shortages of luxuries were a political scandal. Non-voters, the vast, silent majority, wondered hopefully about a new, more democratic age.

Tall buildings on the skyline give emphasis to the scale of Kimberley's man-made "Big Hole" – but the modest skyscrapers did not exist in the 1940s when the diamond city's streets were little changed from their hey-day in the late-nineteenth century. (Source: David Brossard).

Life was back to pre-war "normal".

What had changed was the size and subject of the headline announcing the presence of a monster in the historic derelict mine; a report which seemed to be attempting a peacetime sensation in place of news of war and death. The headline was splashed across a page of a Johannesburg Sunday paper in 1947, only 18 months after V-J Day ended World War II. The "Green Monster" report was bylined "Kimberley Correspondent" and datelined "Kimberley, Saturday".

While some readers might have smiled wryly or shaken their heads in disbelief at such "sensationalism", for hundreds of thousands of readers it truly was a sensation. For me, an 18-year-old cadet reporter of three months who was about to enjoy the third day off of his brief working life, it was alarming, challenging, and a call to arms.

The "Monster-in-the-Hole" story sent me rushing to the never-closed offices of the *Diamond Fields Advertiser* (known as "the DFA") to see what could be done. I found a lone subeditor, a veteran of war and copy-editing, upstairs at midday on the Sabbath. He paused to knock his ash-filled pipe against his shoe. "Nothing," he smiled.

"Nothing? We won't even check it out? We won't publish that it's a lie; that we weren't scooped?"

I was newly aware that only the other three reporters on our daily morning paper, and now I as well, were responsible to Argus Newspapers and to the SA Press Association —and to the world! — for all news coverage throughout Griqualand West and the Northern Cape. And now some anonymous "local correspondent" in the Diamond City was in our territory beating us with a world Loch Ness-type scoop. Worse. It was a big lie!

"It may not be a lie," said the subeditor. "If I'd been drunk on Friday night, I might have seen a green monster too."

"And it'd make headlines?"

"It depends on which newspaper you choose to read," he shrugged.

(No weird or nanny governments demanded control of the press in those halcyon days. If you didn't like or disbelieved the paper you read, you stopped buying it. The principle behind this involved at least two forms of "freedom", fought for in two world wars.)

We left it at that. But I learned something about truth in ten minutes that day, which a year of Philosophy One at Rhodes University and two years of extramural study of Ethics and Philosophy at the University of South Africa failed to explain.

Back in the 1940s there was never time in newspapers for schools of journalism, and there was contempt for academic degrees in our craft. As for objective truth, subjective truth, relative truth, the whole truth and the rest, most newspaper editors brushed aside such shades of relevance as they would brush aside the concept of "differing realities". They demanded facts and plain honesty; "things which every man, woman and child understands ... and if *you* don't understand, you're fired".

However, such simplicity soon faded. With the acceptance of the reality – if there is a uniformly recognized reality – that there can be no objective truth, the rising "tabloid" press (soon confused with the "popular" press) pandered to the naiveté and superstitions of a vast, newly literate generation, and provided "the kind of stories they want". Some tabloids, many of them published as "broadsheet", appeared to think people want to read about little green men appearing from outer space to rape our ever-decreasing stock of 18-year-old virgins.

You can always find witnesses who really believe this happens. In the following decade, when the world was avidly discovering and tracking flying saucers, I listened in 1954 to a widely-respected middle-aged woman who stood up at a very earnest and well supported public meeting in Durban, and told a huge audience that she had once travelled in a flying saucer with some kind green gentleman who had returned her to Earth after a fascinating intercourse (inter-connection might have been a better word). She believed that was a reality and that she was speaking the truth, in the cause of science. I reported her speech, without any comment whatever of course, recording only the subdued, almost silent response of other amateur flying saucer fans. No one referred my report to a press council. (These weren't invented until authoritative and trusted newspapers had to create them in order to fend off government attempts at control in most countries, except America.)

Aside from the effects of the invasion of the tabloid press, public opinion has also steadily become more liberated – meaning more liberal with the truth; more liberal with the rigid idea of simple honesty. It is noticeable that politicians in democratic states where they were once excoriated when caught out in a public lie, find today that they can often lie their way out of it quite blatantly.

The new trick in public life is to deny flatly the truth for as long as possible and, when finally cornered, merely to "apologise sincerely".

Then carry on as before. Tolerance is a great virtue; dishonesty becomes relative, and lying to the public is no big deal any more.

But that may be too simple a summing up of a deterioration of established standards. Later we shall look at "truth" again. Suffice here to quote Alfred North Whitehead, mathematician, logician, educator, and philosopher, whose staggering complexity of thought, coupled with the extraordinary literary quality of his writing, made him one of the most quoted men of my younger days.

"There are no whole truths," he said, surprisingly as co-author of *PrincipiaMathematica*. "All truths are half-truths. It is trying to treat them as whole truths that plays the devil."

In practice, half-truths were reality for us, and untruths were avoided where possible by those newspapers striving to uphold standards in a still uncensored society.

Before the academic proposal became conveniently popular that "we are all subject to our cultures and our prejudices – so there can be no such thing as objective news reporting", we insisted on "*trying* to be objective"; on giving two sides on every issue where possible, but qualified unfortunately by adding: "if relevant". (But this unbiased attitude never applied to apartheid, when it was officially accepted and christened, and which we righteously condemned in the comment pages. In news reports we reported ministerial statements in the words they were uttered, and reserved analysis and judgements for the comment pages. However, our news pages highlighted news that illustrated apartheid's cruelty and illogicality; its greed and its corruption, and they challenged the claim of any "benefits for the Bantu", as toted by the government.)

Famous philosopher Alfred North Whitehead, was talking of reality, not "fake news", when he reminded the world half a century ago that "... all truths are half truths ...".

"Truth" in those days wasn't the problem for the "accountable" press that existed at local, provincial and national level in Western democracies. What had to be constantly guarded against were inaccuracies. Even in this regard standards have changed. The erosion of traditional standards can be traced and measured.

Traditionally across the Western World a few decades ago, in order to prepare any report fit for publishing, you had to identify all sources of information and provide the initials, names, and full addresses of every individual quoted. That tested both the source and the truth. But within two decades of WW2, and with the explosion of urbanization and communication networks, the strict rule of publishing full *addresses* of people in the news disappeared. Within another decade, first names or initials were allowed to slip out of newsprint and broadcasts. Thus two cardinal points of authentication disappeared.

"If you haven't got the man's address, let alone his initials, how can he be made accountable for his facts?" I can hear a veteran down-table sub asking.

Fortunately the ubiquitous cell phone camera has emerged as a sword of truth of unfolding events. Unfortunately it cannot fight the flood of fake news, opinionated tweeting, and the "alternative facts" that emerged in 2017 elections in the free world.

In the 1980s in South Africa, when editors and journalists regularly faced jail for refusing to reveal the names of informants – and when those sources who were traced by the authorities were arrested or tortured – we were forced to conceal their identities, and faced the possibility of prison for refusing to reveal such sources. But at least the fact that we were publishing truth while hiding its source forced us to work exceptionally hard to possess, in place of witnesses, other evidence. For example, discarded police cartridge shells at the scene of a shooting which police claimed was the work of "terrorists". Or unofficially sneaked photos or relevant documentation – with which to defend ourselves if the newspaper were accused of "publishing false and damaging reports".

Fortunately those bad times are gone … though never forgotten.

And never far away.

In sum, truth is *not* the problem for those media trying to uphold it in normal times. Inaccuracy is the double cross they bear. A mantra of journalism is: "Doctors bury their mistakes. We print ours on the front page."

Violence and dispute between workers' unions were a precursor to the massacre at Marikana. (Source: Greg Marinovich).

Another mantra I used often at cadet schools is a misquote of famed US journalist Herbert Swope telling a new generation of reporters: "You need seek only three goals as a news reporter: 1. Accuracy. 2. Clarity. 3. Accuracy. And if you press me for a fourth quality, I would add: 4. Accuracy."

(There is yet another journalistic saying quoted by Swope which I have never before repeated. It says: "In every new journalist there lies hope; in every editor disappointment.")

Lesson from Marikana

A news reporter of a new generation covering the events of 16 August 2012, when dozens of people were mowed down by the police in full view of television cameras near Marikana, complained, in digital text on the Web's *Daily Maverick* about his training. What he learned during the bloody violence in the platinum mining belt was that there were things about journalism about which no journalism school gave warning.

"There are many things you have no idea how to handle ...." wrote Sipho Hlongwane. "But the death of one man I encountered through Lonmin has changed the way I operate. It has changed how I perceive things ...."

In fact, he broke down and cried. He did so because, though relatively young, Hlongwane is a very talented and perceptive journalist.

The man who taught him about one of the supreme limits of journalism was Daluvuyo Bongo, the National Union of Mineworkers' secretary at Lonmin. Mr Bongo sounded absolutely petrified on the phone; repeating again and again, "I just don't know what to do anymore."

He said he was in hiding because people wanted to kill him. When the reporter next heard of Mr Bongo he was dead; murdered in one of Lonmin's hostels. What could – what should – the reporter have done? He did not know. He did not even know what Mr Bongo looked like; whether or not the man had left behind a helpless widow and children ... what should a reporter have done after making that phone call?

And then a miner came to Hlongwane and told the journalist: "My child is sick. She breathed in the teargas yesterday. The police were firing teargas and rubber bullets just anywhere. It didn't matter that there were women and children in the shacks. Many children got the gas."

All Sipho Hlongwane could do was drive the miner to a clinic to get medication, while he thought about the people of Marikana, desperately wanting to be heard.

"They know that we the press showed up in Marikana only when people started dying. We know that they know .... What a horrible bloody mess."

Most journalists never allow themselves to feel that pain. Others get hardened to it. But one lesson we reporters should never forget is the strictly limited function we have in society. We are there to report the facts, well enough so that they are noticed. I believe we are not on the scene to run the show or try to tell everyone else what to do, let alone what to think. That's where too many reporters "mess things up".

A graphic experience

The first time I ever messed things up occurred the first time I was sent to court to cover "a very important court case".

"Done courts before?" asked the news editor.

"No sir. Never been in a courtroom."

He looked at me for a long time. "Well, this is an emergency. Just listen carefully to what is said, and write it like any other news story."

Cadet journalists on daily newspapers almost everywhere at that time were apprenticed to senior reporters who taught them the job – usually on a local paper where they were able to learn in practice the skills required as well as every aspect of ethics and reporting in order to become jacks-of-all-trades. (Jills-of-all-trades were still a rarity. They were usually restricted to Arts and Women's Pages … areas where I also worked on the *Diamond Fields Advertiser* as an emergency fill-in. Creating fashion pages and reporting the fashions and rites displayed at local weddings were repugnant duties for any young male in those days, but the experience taught me a great deal more than I realised.)

Most cadets wanted to be crime reporters, and they learned – or should have learned –that melding in with the woodwork was usually far more effective than being a foot-in-the-door journalist. The regrettably common technique of brashness is always best reserved for special circumstances.

An early experience I had of the latter, on a larger daily paper than the DFA, was a dramatic one, literally. I was sent to interview the stars of a theatre production's full dress rehearsal before an audience of charity donors. To my astonishment, our senior photographer arrived during the first act, bent on getting a good "snap" and getting out.

He stopped the show, literally.

"Get closer together. Stand in the light. Smile," he told a speechless cast.

Then he flashed his Speed Graphic a couple of times, jumped back into the audience, and walked up the isle to the exit. After the final curtain and the bouquets and the plaudits, and the opportunities for interviews, I allowed an impression to arise that I might be a critic from some other newspaper. I was a shy, most reluctant foot-in-the-door journalist.

We learned instead, how to handle murder witnesses. We learned to read the kinds of grief or shock that blurred many faces. We learned that when we were required to approach a widow while ambulancemen were removing the bloodstained corpse of her murdered husband, the reporter should refuse to impinge on her privacy. It was probable that this would lead to her finding the comfort she sought by turning to a silent journalist nearby, eager to tell all she could about her terrifying experience. The most competent senior reporters would teach their apprentices to become fairly sensitive judges of human nature – and to be careful how they reported the versions given by neighbours.

Cadets learned through practice things academics of journalism had never experienced: how to handle the authorities; how to treat informers; how to gain — and justify — the trust of people whom they sought to use as essential regular contacts.

They learned to check and then re-check their information; and of course when *not* to take notes.

That was why South Africa's biggest daily, *The Star*, had transferred me to its smallest sister, the daily *Diamond Fields Advertiser*, to learn, I assumed.

More likely, they just wanted to jettison the new kid who had been foisted on the city newsroom.

And now I was to be thrown in the deepend to report this "very important court case" in Kimberley. It was obviously an emergency move. No one had ever heard of a cub being set free in a court house without a trainer. □

17.
Accusing a man of the wrong crime.

Differing judgements serve but to declare
That truth lies somewhere if we knew but where.

William Cowper 1731–1800.

B lissfully ignorant of all the legal traps, I found my way to Kimberley's Supreme and Magistrates' Courts complex.

"Just tell the story," I repeated in my head, comforting myself with the knowledge that I was equipped with a compulsory certificate asserting I could write shorthand at 120 words per minute – which is faster than almost everyone speaks in court; thrice as fast as court evidence was recorded in those days.

I found my way to the empty press box – it was empty, I assumed, because there was no other newspaper represented, no other court reporters within a hundred miles. But the seating I had selected turned out to be the vacant jury box. South Africa still had juries in those days. They were cherished in Kimberley, where it was said that no "honest jury" would ever convict anyone of illicit diamond buying (IDB) because the people of Kimberley did not accept that the gemstones belonged to De Beers, but belonged to anyone smart enough to find one and slip it into his pocket.

And where would the law stand if – just once – one of the thousands of residents who walked everywhere with eyes downcast watching for a glint in the dust, actually found a diamond in a road excavation, or somewhere?

Jurymen were strongly on the side of freedom on the diamond fields.

However, the notion that the gradual abolition of the jury system in South Africa signified "a shocking distortion of justice" – was false. HH Morris KC, in one of his famous, and true, legal anecdotes published in 1950,[1] illustrated the fault of Euro-American justice in Africa with a powerfully shocking story.

The Law Examiner had set the following question: "A farmer caught a boy stealing apples. The farmer pursued him and called on him to stop. The boy did not stop. The farmer then shot him dead. What crime, if any, did the farmer commit?

IN and
OUT
OF COURT
by H. H. MORRIS K.C.

Answer: "The farmer has committed no crime."

When challenged, the student amended his answer. It now read:

"This is a cold-blooded murder. When I first read the question I thought it referred to a native boy."

HH Morris offered another example of the flaws of the jury system:

A farmer doing jury duty swapped places with his son on alternate days during the hearing. When found out, he explained: "Well, we had to get the ploughing done."

I too, when later covering the Kimberley Circuit Court, witnessed a vivid example of why jurymen might be suspect. Women on juries would have improved matters, but they were forbidden to serve in court on the grounds probably that they needed protection from interestingly impolite things that happened in rapes and murder trials, and from dirty deals on the diamond diggings, and even from their husbands' little fraudulent escapades. On the occasion that I watched one of these worldly-wise male juries at work the issue was murder. A dramatic and violent one.

When proceedings resumed on the fourth day after a long lunch break in a refreshment house across the road in Kimberley's 100 degrees C heat, a voice in court shouted: "You've got the man; you've got the bloody axe – what are we waiting for?"

Today – my first day in any court – the forum where a verdict and possible sentence were to be heard, oozed with silent decorum and passive anticipation. I quickly moved out of the empty jury box to the obvious row of seats right below the judicial bench, but was told in no uncertain whispers by a court orderly that it belonged to absent Supreme Court clerks.

Studiously avoiding the dock, I finally left the well of the normal higher court, and retreated into the public gallery where I proceeded to record every word of the chief magistrate's verdict and sentence, except for a couple of sentences at the start and the end which he delivered in a whisper in what I thought to be an unbecoming deferential air, while the accused sat at ease, not in the dock, but in the well of the court with his battery of defence lawyers.

The nightmare details have long been banished from my mind, but the gist of it is that the magistrate reluctantly found guilty the eminent person figuratively in the dock – one of the executives of De Beers Diamond Corporation probably, for these men ruled the city.

The upholder of the law informed the eminent accused of the court's abhorrence of drunken driving and of its deserved harsh penalties, which included suspension of driving licence and three months in jail in an extreme case such as his.

I rushed back to the newsroom and wrote an almost verbatim account. Despite my immortal words being heavily cut in subediting, I was proud of the report that appeared in the paper next morning. However, the tiny editorial floor that day felt like a funeral parlour.

Lots of sad whispering was going on in its corners. Soon the eminent person's bevy of lawyers was telling the chief sub (in the absence of the ever-absent editor) that their client intended suing the socks off the local rag. Their eminent client was not a jailbird, as the irresponsible reporter had recklessly alleged. The wrongfully accused man was an utterly free citizen who had merely been reprimanded with a suspended fine for his trifling error.

It transpired that my notes were entirely accurate ... but for the trifling mistake that I had not heard the chief magistrate's opening whispered words in giving sentence: *"I have a good mind to* (... suspend your licence, etc)." Nor had I heard him when he dropped his voice to deliver, in the guise of an afterthought, the words: *"Instead you are fined fifty pounds – and the sentence is suspended for six months."*

I don't know what lesson I could have learned from my nightmare, except that it should have ended my journalistic career almost before it began. I still don't know why I wasn't fired. What I found out earlier than most is that all court cases offer huge lessons in life, and greater lessons in truth.

Even in perfect circumstances, truth is an eternally elusive thing.

You can test it yourself with this example:

A competent and clearly independent court wishes to establish blame for a collision between two cars in a broad street in daylight. Numbers of people have a clear view of the accident. The selected witnesses are neutral to the parties involved. They are passersby, palpably disinterested – but not uninterested – in what they have seen. The plaintiff and the defendant are each able to locate two of these witnesses. For the purposes of this example, we can assume none of the witnesses has been 'briefed' in advance; that they are solemnly under oath, and that they are asked, for example, the following basic questions:

Where were you, precisely, as the collision occurred?

What time of day (what was visibility like) when the accident happened?

Did 'A' collide with 'B' in this car smash? Even photographic evidence is usually insufficient proof of who collided with whom. Newspapers, to avoid anticipating court decisions, used to report that A and B 'were in collision'. No such niceties of the law are observed in the media today.

At what speed was each of the cars travelling?

Did either vehicle swerve? Or both?

No need to inquire about the colour, model or licence numbers of the vehicles – you will already have half a dozen – or as many as 16 – *different* answers from the four selected witnesses responding to the four questions. If you don't believe me, try the test on your friends, without alerting them to the motive for stopping to watch some event together. After considering their witnessed versions of the event, you may appreciate why newspapers carry so many inaccuracies ... and the need to take care in apportioning blame.

In my day (*ugh!*) when reporting on crashes, we used clumsy phrases such as "two cars came into collision". That avoids, before the facts are fully established, accusing A of "colliding with" B. However, today such niceties are ignored. It seems that anything goes. I heard a newscaster report recently: "Both cars were chasing each other"!

The fact is that even when there are only two witnesses telling, without bias "the truth, the whole truth and nothing but the truth" it is likely that their attempts at sincerely truthful accounts will, in *fact,* carry inaccuracies or contradictions. We were always aware that the sources of every report were "only human". This is true of scientific reports, official documents and statistical analyses as well as politicians' claims, public speeches, tip-offs, and excited eye-witness accounts. Every origin of news (and source of truth), even a forensic laboratory test, is subject to human error.

Ergo: Always quote your sources.

The general practice today is that much detail goes unnoticed in the constant competitive rush and clamour of competing news distributors in print, radio, TV and exploding digital media. In general, I believe standards of accuracy have markedly declined.

However, nothing can rival the full freedom of information enjoyed in South Africa for instance after 1994 and until recently. The past cannot rival today's proliferation of news sources that are now available at an instant computer or international TV click.

There are also, of course, many and marvellous exceptions to the often thin reporting in today's print media, and there is much more and better comment from outside "experts" in the news these days. Some recent investigative reporting has been brilliant. The *Cape Times* was reflecting before its change in ownership in 2013 – the naiveté of some of its leader comment notwithstanding – all the nuances of politics, finance, arts, crime, social and environmental issues with an intellectual quality its mass readership hardly deserved.

One of the best investigative reports I've ever seen, in terms simply of reporting details that are checked and precisely sourced and put into context, was a report in the *Mail & Guardian* some years ago (March 2010).

The original investigation dealt with the normally private, closely guarded and always sensitive information about a family's economic activity. In this case it concerned President Zuma's myriad family, both in wedlock and out, and it dealt with the sudden spectacular rise in all their business assets and interests since he came to power. The series of simultaneously published reports, backed with precise, accountable data in every case, managed to avoid treading anywhere near coded infringements on privacy and decency.

In any case, its voluminous and telling series of reports, expertly documented, and topped with carefully bounded comments on "individual persons", were relative to public interest. (Remembering, of course, that the "public interest" or "the people's interest" is very different to the "popular interest" or the public's interest in the private affairs of other people.)

The *Mail & Guardian*'s investigative series reminds one what a joy it is to possess such in-depth reporting; of how important it is, and how responsible and relevant the reporters' exposure of malfeasance should always be.

City Press did a follow-up on the Zuma clan's business profits in July 2014. By then the scandal had become so repetitive that the public no longer regarded alleged corruption in government as "news".

In 2017 the *Sunday Times* in South Africa had completed a long series of weekly exposures of government corruption which made allegations of financial "State Capture" by the President and outside forces common knowledge.

Without that newspaper's constant campaigning, the startling often "incredible" corruption in many State enterprises might never have become a major national issue.

Our problem is that the organs of State and the electorate fail too often to act on abuse of justice, on exposed corruption and to threats to democracy. And that, I know, is describing the threat to freedom far too lightly.

But let us return to the good old bad times .... ☐

---

1. *In and Out of Court* by HH Morris KC (Central News Agency 1950).

18.
When I broke the rules of ethical reporting.

Rules are made to be broken.

An old proverb, proven here.

As a cub reporter and strictly neutral observer I confess to twice breaking the rules by becoming actively involved in events I was sent to report and should have been dispassionately observing.

Riding a war-wounded Royal Enfield 350cc motorcycle between the slippery, unused tram tracks of the Diamond City near midnight, six nights a week, is my abiding memory of Kimberley back in 1947.

Work on the newspaper began at 10am six days a week, while work began much later on the seventh day, Sunday. On weekdays, work did not finish until you had returned to the office at about midnight to make the "final calls" to police stations, hospitals, and fire brigade.

This onerous duty for the *Diamond Field Advertiser*'s only cub reporter produced an occasional paragraph for next morning's paper, but hardly ever a front-page story. Yet late-night calls were compulsory and vital, even if you died doing them ... which I once nearly did.

In the late 1940s, a start on a newspaper also provided lessons never taught in today's journalism schools. My first problem, for instance, was that the only phone in all Griqualand West that was accessible to me was the one tied to my desk. And how could I get out there to cover events at first-hand if there was no public transport in the sprawling Diamond City? In its heyday Kimberley boasted luxury horse-drawn coaches and later "world-first" illuminated electric trams. But as its fortune-makers started moving to the City of Gold, they appeared to take with them everything the City of Diamonds owned, except its buildings, its Big Holes and its tram tracks.

"How do I get to Beaconsfield?" I asked.

"You walk," they said, and advised me not to stop even briefly at the Halfway House pub miles down the road. After a month or two of this I used all my childhood savings in the post office bank to buy an ex-army

Next to the Jeep, some believed this to be the most efficient transport of its time — at a fraction of the popular Jeep's cost. It was the British army's Royal Enfield 350 Matchless. Without its effete bags and saddle covers, this one looks just like mine did … habitually leaning to the left,though the pictured bike clearly hasn't been dropped from a dizzy height.

issue motorcycle. I'd never ridden a motorbike before, and immediately fell off it. The general dealer who recommended this purchase confessed: "That bike was dropped by parachute in the Libyan Desert in The War, that's why it's slightly bent," he explained. "But it was never used. And it's a Royal Enfield, so it's perfectly sound. You only have to lean slightly to the right to go straight."

It worked. The technique worked so well I was soon able to ride the slightly wounded army bike without having to press down hard on the right handlebar. The hand throttle was inclined to stick, but this was a bonus, and soon I could ride (with a hard lean to the right) without even touching the handlebars. This seemed necessary because Kimberley's weather is extreme, moving from 100 degrees C in summer to *minus* several degrees in mid-winter. And so it was that one bitterly cold winter night, I was riding home from late-night emergency calls, with my hands in my pockets and easily avoiding the tramlines when suddenly a cat ran across my path. I sat bolt upright to grab the hand-grips as the heavy motorcycle swerved sharp left, but couldn't get my hands out of my tightly folded pockets in time.

Next thing I knew I was in Heaven. I woke up, flat on my back and opened my eyes to see that I was surrounded by giant penguins, with what looked like the edifice of a cathedral looming above them. I thought for some while for the right thing to say, and then asked:

"Where am I?"

The penguins paid no attention and kept jabbering away at each other.

It transpired that they were Free Masons in starched white shirts and formal dinner jackets who had emerged from the Masonic Hall when I crashed onto the pavement at their front door. I remember nothing else, but became aware that they were very kind to me, took me back to my boarding house and ensured that my bike was safe and not much more bent than usual. I fetched it to ride to work next day.

That motorbike gave me my first lesson in basic journalistic ethics.

I'd been sent one Saturday (my occasional day off) to cover officially the opening of Kimberley's first racing dirt track, just beyond the golf course (with its unique putting "greens" made of thin jet-black gravel containing thousands of glittering garnets).

After the third race a call went out for members of the public with motorbikes to join in the fun. There were very few acceptances. Then the licence plate number on my parked Royal Enfield was broadcast with an "order" to the owner to come forward and support the cause.

I explained to the officials that "I'm not a member of the public. I'm from the press. I cannot take part." That caused a few guffaws as someone wheeled my bike onto the track.

We were to take part in an egg-and-spoon race, and my partner would be the senior journalist who had come with me that day "for the ride", so to speak. But not literally, and certainly not at this public function, I objected, because I was covering the event for the *DFA*.

Yes, you'll ride, said bystanders, and my senior, with too much after-lunch amiability, agreed. He was a war veteran, a war hero indeed, who now did two things constantly: smoke his pipe, and drink brandy. He lurched onto the back of my bike and the bystanders arranged us both for the race: me (leaning to the right) and Mac sitting behind and facing *backwards*. He was instructed to hold on with one hand, and balance an egg in a spoon with the other.

I rode cautiously, allowing the bent Royal Enfield to take its natural course to the left around a short circuit. After the second lap, to my astonishment, I found we were far in the lead.

"Have you still got the egg and spoon?" I shouted over my shoulder.

"Yes," he assured me, his teeth still clamped to his pipe, obviously. "Is the egg still okay?"

"Look!" he said, letting go of his grip on the bike for an instant, and thrusting his left arm back for an instant. That was why we were leading by so far, and why the spectators were laughing. He had been riding with the spoon in one hand, the egg in the other, and both hands clinging to the bike. I turned to remonstrate, but he turned as well, and the bike flew off the track into the fence. When we were finally disentangled with the help of too many hands, there was no sign of the egg or the spoon, but I seem to remember that Mac, miraculously, still had his pipe in his mouth. We went home with considerable regrets and considerable bruising. I was seriously disturbed by allowing myself to become part of the spectacle and thus not able to report it with the required disengaged neutrality of an ethical (cub) journalist.

Worse than this blemish, was the fact that I repeated the same error within months, and displayed even more dubious aspects of a disreputable reporter. It started in all innocence and great beauty, because South Africa was entering the beauty-queen era by choosing its first (I think) Wool Queen. Griqualand West had assembled several beauties and our "province" had to choose one for the national finals. To protect the young ladies from wolf whistles, the event was staged in a side-room in a local hotel, with someone from the Agricultural Union and a local businessman as judges.

The rules said three independent judges were needed. There was no third candidate at the meeting for this judicious role. The organisers, the officials, and the two judges ... and the girls ... all looked at me, for I was the only other independent presence in the room.

"No. No," I protested, but "no" was not accepted, and after an embarrassing period of stalemate I finally agreed to place an X on a third slip of paper – provided anonymity was assured, and the names of the judges not recorded.

"Well, *you*'re doing the news report," they said.

They could see no ethical problem whatever.

The beauty queen officials could see only stubborn selfishness and

THEN AND NOW. The choice for a 1940s illustration would be the beauty queen on the left. The difference in beauty queens in the past 60 years is not in people or beauty. It is in style, and attitude and clothing (and its amount).

– worse – immaturity on my part. It was, however, not only an ethical issue for me, it was also an intimate social problem.

I knew one of the candidates. I would have to vote against her – which I seriously wished to do, for I'd never see her again if she were to be transformed into a glamorous Miss Wool princess. On the other hand there was a stunning stranger who deserved to be queen ... and I might be in good stead if I were able to tell her afterwards what the critical third judge's opinion (my genuine vote of course) had been. Kimberley had few pretty girls who were not well known and well appreciated, but "the stranger" duly won.

I have to admit that, in small temporary ways, I did benefit socially from my unethical behaviour, but in maturity as a "journo" I have obsessively avoided joining or participating in any organisation or public promotion. Except corporate golf days, where I participated as a guest and don't remember ever winning a worthy prize.

In 1947, however, my political bias and personal prejudice increased, unfortunately, in the run-up to the critical and infamous 1948 General Election, due the following year. It grew in reaction to the racism and extremism of the National Party's candidates. We few – very few – DFA *Engelse* reporters enthusiastically favoured the United Party candidate.

"Our" candidate was a shoo-in, even if he had chanced to be a lame duck with two left feet who received no publicity ... but he happened to be Harry Oppenheimer, crown prince at the time of the world's diamond industry. Although none of us ever met him at the time, my instructions were to report his speeches assiduously. Kimberley's only daily press virtually ignored the Nationalist candidate.

The only other politician covered in Griqualand West during that disastrous election was the United Party's leader, General JC Smuts, who came to support Kimberley's favourite candidate and whose one-night stand filled the main rugby stadium. I confess I took down in my still-new shorthand *every word* he said.

This was a great mistake because he spoke at considerable length.

By acting as a stenographer instead of a reporter, I failed to analyse what he was saying. Instead, after spending precious hours transcribing my shorthand, I discovered he had said little of significance and had repeated himself at length many times.

It took most of the rest of *his* life for me to learn that he had little respect for crowds, and always spoke down to them; with little forethought. He was patronising in such situations, yet he spoke with dedicated attention and intense illumination to any audience he respected such as assembled soldiers, or scientists, philosophers, and always to young people if he thought they were listening.

The great length of my version of Smuts's speech on the front page of the *DFA,* I decided afterwards, was a shameful display of prejudice as well as one-sided reporting. Yet neutrality in election reporting was almost non-existent as the battle for control of SA continued. It was "Nationalism versus the unheeding majority" of exclusively white voters.

Within a year, however, I was transferred from Kimberley to the administrative capital of South Africa, Pretoria, where all the political action was occurring.

The first mistake I made there, at the start of my very first day, occurred as I drove my motorcycle up onto the broad pavement at the entrance to the *Pretoria News* building ... and banged into the opening door of a car. It was the manager's car. Not much damage, really. No one was actually hurt, physically. But the incident attracted unjustified attention, especially on the raucous editorial floor above us.

The *Pretoria News* seemed vast to me – five times the size of the *DFA* – but it was in fact a small, though fast-moving little afternoon newspaper. What it lacked in size it made up for in professionalism, for it had to compete on its specialist homeground in that sophisticated, highly politicised era with no less than *five* other dailies on sale in the capital city, as well as against the political news-gathering of the international press. In retrospect I realised that, for any reporter anywhere, this was Big Time. □

19.
Inside the newsroom on deadline.

In the case of news, we should always wait for the sacrament of confirmation.

Voltaire 1750s.

Back in the late 1940s when I arrived on *The Pretoria News*, as a junior reporter still in my teens, I found things very different from the dear old *DFA* with its ancient flatbed press that slowly clicked out copies of the newspaper before dawn, with a sedate, Victorian sense of pace and propriety. By contrast, the all-male mainly ex-servicemen's *Pretoria News* newsroom in its brand-new post-war building, with a brand-new rotary press, had a marvellously charged atmosphere ... taut with the kind of frenetic energy to be found only on afternoon newspapers with "instant deadlines" at the height of the day. The descriptions for that newsroom which spring to mind are: Smoke-stacked. Edgy. Uncomprehendingly noisy.

The men back from war in Europe were tired of taking orders. I remember veteran reporter Gerhi Strauss being an hour late for work each day for a week. At first he blamed his "overload of investigative night-work". By the end of the week he was blaming the red robots (traffic lights).

"But you walk to work," the news editor reminded him in amazement.

"Ja ... but now the traffic police have stopped us jay-walking," he said.

"You spent an hour waiting for robots?"

Gehri shrugged, so we merely glanced at the Diary and went back to our desks.

Every newsroom in the world has a Diary, in one form or another. *That's* what makes a newsroom work. In the "old days" the Diary – as big as a Dickensian ledger and bound with sturdy covers – would start filling up a year in advance with formal, annual news events; then adding more monthly, weekly, and hourly entries until today's deadline. The Diary would anticipate events, inquiries, follow-ups and ideas for stories ranging from renewal of a long-remanded court trial to an instant investigative piece or a potential "sob story". Finally, the very latest news possibilities, as well as the ideas discussed in that morning's early News Conference would be added to the Diary. Then reporters' names, including those on each of the regular "beats", would be apportioned: *Jones – Check why three deaths lately in that hospital.* Or *VanZyl – Try Town Clerk again on city corruption*, or merely *Smith – police calls, (and don't skimp on the other emergency calls, dammit.*

The Diary would be kept in the office of the news editor, his deputy and assistants or, as in the *Pretoria News*'s case, on an alter-like shelf in the newsroom where one could genuflect. It was a mysterious privilege to be "off the diary" and "on assignment".

The Reporters' Room desks in *Pretoria News* were as new as its brand new post-war building, and stood in three or four open rows, like a platoon on parade, all facing the door of the subeditors' room. That was the maw through which our stories went – into the hands of senior journalists who had seen it all and suffered disillusionment through handling so much badly written copy by self-opinionated or untutored scribes.

Subeditors ensured that the news system functioned; that news pages were collated and designed in fresh ways daily; and that newspapers created a personality and rapport with their readers.

We hated the subs.

They always mauled our immortal words. They despised us for what we wrote. It was a relationship that has worked wonders for a couple of hundred years.

In South Africa, where multicultural, multilingual, multi-gender reporters have gloriously refreshed the scope of news-gathering, the Subs Bench has shrunk pitifully in the great cause of publishers' profit. This, in my opinion, has caused an outrageous diminution of standards of concise, clear, accurate and dispassionate reporting in newspapers of all languages.

With the ease provided by electronic editing, it is clear that sufficient, trained subeditors might have improved all the carefully protected standards of the past. The self-serving "law of maximum profit", has dictated otherwise. The problem remains a worldwide one – if it *is* a relevant problem these days when speed is more important than precise accuracy of language; when constant repetition and misquotes fly by unchecked.

At deadline on an afternoon newspaper like the *Pretoria News* "in the good old days", the copy editors would "sub" a story precisely and at almost second-reading speed; cut it to fit its designated place in a page lay-out; compose "just the right" headline, and send it to The Works, where it would be set in type, copy-read, then returned within minutes on printed galley-proofs corrected and ready for publishing. The original typed stories, known as "copy", were dispatched in carbon-paper triplicate; one to the news editor or directly in haste to the subs; the second to a Branch editor for possible dispatch to our sister papers around the sub-continent; the third, edited down and delayed slightly, for Sapa, the nationally-shared news agency, linked to their world counterparts. All copy – with sub-editing instructions – and all reporters' shorthand notebooks, were meant to be stored in case there were future queries, or legal issues.

In those days it was so noisy in the hectic newsroom near edition times that you couldn't hear the typewriters banging away. This was normal – so that if you *did* hear those hefty typewriters clacking, then something untoward must be going on.

There was so much smoke; you saw everything in a different light. You spurned air-conditioning (if there was any) and kept all the windows open ... not because you objected to the smoke. Everyone smoked. You were either a pipe smoker, a chain smoker, or learning to be one or the other and reading all those classic essays describing the joys of tobacco, or how to tamp your pipe properly at three different textures so that you could savour the sound of nicotine bubbling. But perhaps I indulge in nostalgic exaggeration.

Let me therefore relate a specific incident, unusual enough to stick clearly in one's memory.

I was sweating at my newsroom desk situated half-way down the row by the open windows. This was my position which others avoided because of the torrid Transvaal sun beating down on it from noon. I was sweating because of the deadline crisis that had arisen on an empty day. It had been suddenly decided that the only possible local mainlead for the paper that day was a story from the boring meeting I'd been attending.

Turning my account of it into a front-page lead was like turning an insignificant bore into a heroic lover in a romantic drama. *That's* why I sweated. I felt that the entire edifice of the front page would depend on the wording of my first sentence. Crumpled sheets of aborted copy filled my wastepaper basket (every desk had one).

A linotype machine was the best-loved instrument in printing from the late 1800s to the 1970s. The 'artistry' of setting hot lead in columns of words died with the advent of lithographic printing and computer typesetting. Years after the long-armed. mobile machines became obsolete, they were exhibited in the front windows of many newspapers across the world.

Now I completed a new opening sentence in the appropriate style ... and was about to add the full stop when a hand came down, and ripped the copy-paper from my machine.

The hand belonged to The Editor, no less. He read what I hadn't been given time to read; *humphed*, and passed it to a waiting messenger. Now I had to type a second paragraph, without being sure of how my oft-attempted first one was finally worded. And The Editor stood there, waiting. Perhaps I would have frozen in that heat – were it not for Philip Stohr, erudite senior writer and ex-serviceman sitting just behind me, where the sun didn't shine. He drove the editor away.

The paragraphs began to flow, until I needed to pause to light a cigarette. To my horror, I found I had one, already lit, in my mouth. And another burning in the ashtray. I threw the third one into my waste-basket and resolved never to smoke again. Then I heard Philip's voice behind me:

"I say, old man ...." Nice be called "old man" when you're still a second-year junior. "I say! Better do something about that waste-basket. It's smoking."

That sounded to me like a joke ... until it burst into flames reaching up to my elbow, and we both jumped up and threw the fireball out the window.

It was not an easily forgettable experience. I hadn't had time, while writing the last two "takes" of the, *ahem,* mainlead to see what happened to my flaming waste-basket as it dropped two storeys into the side alley. Did the fire spread? Was anyone hurt?

Philip assured me there was nothing to worry about. Shortly before I arrived on the newspaper, he said, a chap called Willy had leapt up with a roar of rage and hurled an ultra-heavy Underwood typewriter out of that same window. No one had been injured.

That's alright then, I felt; until I began to wonder what would happen if we were ever to work in an air-conditioned office with sealed windows.

The thought was enough to force me to give up my new non-smoking vows ... though I'm proud to say that by taking to Ernest Hemingway-type cigarillos (shorter and thinner than Cuban cigars) I was able to kick the habit quite easily on my 15th attempt two decades later. Those things taste like ash in your mouth, so I recommended them once to a fellow sufferer also trying to give up ... only to find, when he gave me a lift to work at 6am that he was on his second cigarillo already, and was chain-smoking that rubbish. Once he finally left the newspaper, however, he gave up smoking reasonably quickly.

Looking back, I realise now that I was just a kid reporter in the nation's capital at the time – though all junior reporters had onerous duties in those days.

We might report political rallies on one night, and crime the next. And sport every weekend. Saturday was a full working day, but you spent afternoons at the "House of Rugby", reporting major league matches at Loftus Versveld.

It was not fun, because you had to write three running reports simultaneously. One for the last deadline of your own afternoon newspaper and another, slightly shorter one for the same final deadline of the big sister, *The Star.* Then a third for the urgent deadline of the national news agency, the SA Press Agency (Sapa).

This was accomplished by scribbling, as the rugby match progressed, a running report on a thick pad with two carbon copies ... sometimes while you were standing on the sideline, sometimes squatting, to write. Then, as the final whistle blew, you "upfronted" the score, "subbed down" the carbon copies and wrote three different intros.

When these running reports had been dispatched as fast as it was

*The famous photo of the raised police baton at the first Cato Manor riots.
The photo went round the world many times and featured as communist
propaganda for 40 years – without credit to or permission of the
photographer, Laurie Bloomfield of The Daily News, Durban.*

possible, you returned to the office and wrote a fourth version, the review
in hindsight, for Monday's *Pretoria News*.

Of course you were paid extra for all these simultaneous versions
of the same event. I remember framing an annual cheque from Sapa for
two shillings and sixpence (25 cents in today's twenty-times devalued
currency – though in 1948 it would have bought two beers). It was
explained to me that this was my share of the newspaper's annual grant
from Sapa for our services. Being a junior reporter meant I was at the end
of the food chain ... even though most of the seniors had never written an
exclusive intro for Sapa in their lives.

Nevertheless, as a junior journo one was privileged to witness
great events. One did not do so by simply staring from a front seat of the
theatre of life; one also immersed oneself in great events such as parties
for the chorus girls of touring world productions of enthralling shows like
Oklahoma!

One was able to become the temporary escort around town, for
instance of a glamorous, foreign, older girl – 24 years old! – with long legs

and a face like Rita Hayworth. It was worth a lot more than two shillings and sixpence. So was the experience one gained as a newsman.

However, the most memorable for me at that time – the most shocking – was seeing a man's brains oozing from his head as he died on a shop pavement. Three journalists (war veterans Gerry Reilly of the *Rand Daily Mail* and Philip Stohr of the *Pretoria News,* and I, as an afterthought) used up a precious long-weekend-off by driving the slow, winding road to Durban to witness for ourselves the first of the notorious Cato Manor riots, described exaggeratedly by some as a Zulu pogrom of the Durban Indian community. The uprisings came in the form a series of racial riots, started according to most, by an Indian shopkeeper – a general target of poverty-stricken Zulu shoppers – who slapped a Zulu child for stealing fruit off his stand.

About 50 miles before our destination we encountered the first signs of violence in Pietermaritzburg, where looting was in spate among the closed shops in the city centre. Fleeing figures and running police were everywhere. Gerry's veteran Austin Princess (an elderly but capacious and elegant automobile capable of carrying a small party to a dance) now crawled through chaos, and rolled to a stop next to a fallen man. I got out of the backseat to help the poor guy – but instead stood still and just stared motionless at his spilled brains at my feet. The man, still holding the knobkerrie he'd used to smash a shop window, was indubitably dead.

Rita Hayworth was the western world's pin-up girl for most of the 1940s and 1950s. Her smile and her long legs were known wherever cinemas existed. She was the star of the 1950's global musical stage hit: Oklahoma, and shared the screen with top names such as James Cagney, Cary Grant and Fred Astaire. Her mother, from Spain, had been a dancer with the Ziegfield Follies, but Rita soon dominated the entertainment world with a new screen-name and a flaming red hair-style.She was too good to be true, but no-one cared.

There was nothing we could do, but drive on … carefully through an abortive riot in the wrong city. The image, which never left me, was shored up by another image of a similar man, very much alive, smashing another shop window in Durban during later Zulu-vs-Indian Cato Manor riots. The image this time was a close-up picture, taken by news photographer Stan Bunn at the very instant that the looter's knobkerrie shattered a jeweller's window. It showed the man grimacing in the split second that the bulging, broken glass began to fall. The picture won a world award.

However, for me, it looked nauseatingly like a photo of a man who was about to have his brains scrambled on the pavement. It was an augury of much violence we would have to witness.

I still had a lot to learn.

Scooping the 'Africa Pack'

Pretoria was home to many overseas newspaper correspondents in the early days of apartheid – before some were expelled by the new Nationalist government. The capital was also a gathering place for several of Fleet Street's pack of Africa correspondents under the leadership of humorist Don Wise and others covering the continent's news-breaks and wars.

They emulated the adventures first described in Evelyn Waugh's satirical novel *Scoop*. The satire encouraged them to adopt an equally legendary lighthearted attitude to the travails and brushes with death they unexpectedly faced. I think it was Don who famously

Ruth Williams, a London typist, and Prince Seretse Khama of Bechuanaland. They staged a royal marriage in 1949 that was the most controversial – and romantic – in many decades. It created an international scoop for one down-to-earth local reporter competing against the world's media.

opened his dispatch on war in West Africa with a first line on the theme: *Sitting on the airport verandah waiting for war to break out, a bullet-hitbody nearly fell into my gin.*

His communiqué concerned the plummeting body of a jilted lover, perhaps, who had committed suicide and toppled from the upper gallery of the airport onto the restaurant area below. He explained that it had nothing to do with the civil war he had come to report, but was typical of the taut atmosphere.

Every ace in the Africa pack wanted an insouciant intro or a dateline like that. Hence *Banana Sunday*, written by Chris Munnion of the London *Daily Telegraph*, a marvellous collection of date-lined stories by "Africa hands". Their legends still had to be experienced however when, at least a decade earlier, the first of the African Pack had come alive for us back in the 1940s as the telex chattered out a query from Fleet Street to a foreign correspondent temporally based in a Pretoria bureau.

According to a local reporter who was tending his branch-office telex-machine at that moment, the query concerned the Fleet Street correspondent's expenses for the previous month.

"He requested expenses, without explanation, involving a sum several times my monthly salary!" exclaimed the local reporter, lost in admiration of the casual reply sent by the old Africa hand. "Then the Fleet Street man answered London's query with a four-liner explaining that he had to hire a taxi to take him to Bechuanaland in time for the Seretse Khama wedding ... and he had to phone Pretoria for another taxi to bring him back five days later with his urgent coverage ... a double taxi trip of, what? About 500 miles?"

The marriage of the beloved Bechuanaland king to a London secretary-typist named Ruth was one of the biggest, most politically-charged and romantic weddings of the decade. The couple were banned from Africa for several years, until Seretse returned in triumph as King of Botswana.

His marriage was also the making of, not only the desperate taxi-passenger journalist, but more so of an untravelled and inexperienced reporter on *The Star* in Johannesburg.

Ernest Shirley had joined *The Star* after the war at about the same time as I applied for a job. But he was a much older fellow who had once worked on the railways and he probably came directly from the army into the ranks of journalism as a "senior" reporter.

He set off, sensibly and without undue flare, by train to cover the Seretse Khama royal wedding in Gaborone. However, as an ex-railwayman and signals and communications expert, the first thing he did was to ply the staff at Gaborone railway station with small gifts of whisky and chocolates in return for his *exclusive* private use of the Bechuanaland capital's only available telex line. He also took the trouble, before the ceremonies began, to contract every vehicle of the town's few transport operators for his exclusive use over the next 24 hours.

These preparatory arrangements afforded him a fine scoop and a proof of the journalistic adage of that era: "Your story is only as good as your ability to communicate it to the outside world."

His story hit the streets hours before the international press could file their reports.

In the days of cablese

Two of my favourite oft-quoted replies in word-saving "cablese" to queries from editors far away included this one:

> *London Office: "How old Welensky?"* (Sir 'Roy' Welensky was in his later years, the last prime minister of the "Central African Federation".) *Foreign Correspondent: "Old Welensky fine. How are you?"*

Another irritated correspondent, left almost forgotten in Nationalist China's islands of Quemoy as its guns shelled the Communist mainland every morning and communist forces returned fire at drinks' time every evening, filed the story repeatedly, then gave up. He never

Sir Roy Welensky, Prime Minister of Rhodesia meets Prime Minister Harold Macmillan of Great Britain (right) wearing his new "African" hat. Macmillan was visiting much of the continent in 1960, ending up in Cape Town where he addressed Prime Minister Hendrik Verwoerd and both Houses of Parliament . Macmillan warned them not to ignore "the winds of change" blowing through Africa at that time.

received a reply for weeks until he woke up his foreign editor in London with a cable:

"*Boo!*"

After a day or two of dignified silence came the query:

London office*: "When outbreak war likely?"*

Foreign Correspondent. *"Know not. Balls not made of crystal."*

It was said that he was nearly fired for causing the "telex girls" almost to faint.

Meanwhile I was doing a fair amount of cablese reporting myself. I had scooped up an extra job; that of Pretoria "stringer" to the official African correspondent of *United Press International*. His name is one name I have never forgotten. It was Mr Schoup, and I set out in search of a series of news scoops for him. It was damned hard part-time work, but I didn't mind ... until I received my first cheque for use of my very first scoop.

It was no more than my Sapa annual remuneration that I had been so bitter about after so much "after-hours" weekend work: a cheque for not much more than 2s 6d – and nothing for my expenses.

In high dudgeon, I quit serving UPI, and was delighted when a passing UPI Big Shot from overseas called to ask me why. He couldn't believe that even a second-stringer could be so badly paid. Even so, there was no joy for any of us when, about four decades later, United Press International died. The cause was reported as: "a paucity of funding". Any kid reporter could have warned them of that 40 years previously.

In fact I did, didn't I? □

20.

A baby's laugh o'er the general's coffin.

Fame has no present; popularity no future.

Anon.

I n September 1950, this chapter's headline seemed to reflect, through the eyes of a new generation, the end of a grand era of which total war had been only a part. The headline appeared (in similar words) across the front page of the *Pretoria News*. Below the headline was a photo of a woman weeping as she watched the silent march of the military funeral of (British) Field Marshall, General Dr Jan Christiaan Smuts.

But the picture in my memory is one viewed from where I stood on a balcony of Pretoria's old Raadsaal. It looked down on a coffin, dwarfed in size by the huge, horse-drawn gun carriage carrying it. Cavalry officers riding equally magnificent black or white horses led the procession of troops and armoured columns around Pretoria's Church Square.

General J C Smuts. He was hailed as the greatest man of his time by leaders and intellectuals across much of the world after the two world wars ... but not in his own homeland. (Source: Yousuf Karsh).

After all these years I can still "hear" with intense clarity a toddler's peal of laughter floating across the silence – literally the deathly silence – of the crowds massed in the square and strung out over the great length of Church Street that day.

The unexpected sound of laughter was the "angle" on my report, different from the news agencies' coverage. Different from all the coverage of all the local, national and foreign media on this day and for days on end between the time of his death and his burial. Yet the intro to the report on his funeral was not designed as an angle. I wasn't looking for angles. The Oubaas's death had already been mourned, and his life re-examined many times worldwide, in the few days since his passing on September 11 that year.

What his funeral brought home to me was an acute and unfamiliar sense of personal loss, because I had been fortunate enough to be near him often recently; sometimes alone with him in his last days. The baby's laugh at his funeral I saw as the essence – or rather the poignant contrast that etched the essence – of a break in time and a split in the continuity of a nation's history.

It was a laugh utterly innocent of irony, joy, or awareness-of-the-moment. And nobody knew how much that moment would mean for millions of us.

The *Pretoria News* was brave to use my unprecedented reporting style and that ambiguous, off-beat banner headline in a city in mourning – yet so hotly and tensely divided.

The political darkness of apartheid was already blanketing the land. It was woven from a concept that became so narrow, so racist, so cruel, that its shadow was to become internationally notorious within the decade, exaggeratingly placed on a par with words invented only two decades previously, such as fascist and Nazi.

Yet, at mid-century, apartheid still had to be explained to many enthusiastic supporters of Afrikaner nationalism. It was being sold in its original crude colours of *die vrou in die kombuis en die kaffer op sy plek.* "The (white) woman/wife in the kitchen, and the black man in his place (politely translated)." Later it became even more racist: *Die kaffer in sy plek en die koelie uit die land.* (The even more polite translation is: the black man in his place and the Asiatic out of the country.)

At the same time Nationalism also still demanded the separation too of *Die Engelse* from *Die Volk.* Extremists still targeted *Die Engelse* as a race apart.

The majority of South Africa's whites-only electorate – and it was a large, clear majority – had voted for Smuts and against apartheid's slogans. But the weighted, almost "double-vote", thinly spread across the *platteland* slipped the Nationalists into power. The United Party, which had failed to correct the imbalance in rural voting rights, believed it would triumph again soon; that the National Party's victory was an unfortunate aberration. Even the Nats feared they would be defeated after their first term in power. The voting majority of English and Afrikaans white citizens was reasonably confident that the official race segregation would then be abolished ... or preferably, they vainly hoped, reduced to meet "commonsense and respectability".

When the new government bent the law to keep power, it was soon greeted by ex-soldiers carrying burning, blazing torches in rallies protesting unconstitutional cheating. It was a brave period when the Pretoria champion of the United Party, Blaar Coetzee, staggered and fell in exaggerated exhaustion while leading a continuous day-and-night stand in the Transvaal Provincial Council to defeat the concept of *Christelike Onderwys*. This new ideological policy demanded separate Transvaal schools – and a separate style of education! – officially dividing Afrikaans and English-speaking children; including millions with two home languages.

The element of "apartheid" to be enforced on white children "of separate races" was opposed by the United (all-white opposition) Party with every legal and constitutional device available to the small strata of still-free people. The Nationalists held their supporters by hastily de-emphasising educational apartheid between whites in the Transvaal, and emphasising their fight against British colonialism.

Overnight, it seemed, the great white opposition faltered. The Torch Commandos stopped marching. Also, like many other Afrikaners, Blaar Coetzee changed sides – so effectively, he later became the "Nat" minister responsible for forcing the brown people of soon-to-be infamous District Six out of Cape Town and offering their poor homes – and rich property sites – to whites.

The weakness and prejudices among Smuts's successors leading the parliamentary opposition soon caused a split. Disintegration within the opposition as well as within the nation rendered the UP ineffectual for the rest of its political life.

Smuts's death really did mark the end of an era. Yes, an end to British colonialism, but also an end to some old-fashioned values in public life, such as courtesy, honour, *noblesse oblige* and carefully nourished respect in providing an efficient civil service. (Fifty years later, deposed politician Helen Zille might have had something relevant to say about this.)

Smuts, "the world leader", retired to spend his last years in a corrugated iron farmhouse, reached by visiting dignitaries driving to the end of a corrugated dirt road.

His brilliant Minister of Finance, **JH Hofmeyr,** was blamed for throwing away the election by being too liberal; too sympathetic to "the

Hofmeyer, a far-sighted genius.

non-whites". The young deputy party leader disappeared at that point from politics, but remains among the youngest in the democratic world ever to occupy such a high national post.

He believed firmly in racial equality and saw his public financial post as a duty owed to all people of all races.

Hofmeyr was a genius who gained an honours degree at Cape Town University and a Rhodes Scholarship to Oxford at the age of 15. He died prematurely in his mid-40s, just six months after the apartheid he abhorred came to his country in 1948.

He was visibly uncomfortable with the trappings of state. I remember once, after reporting one of his erudite and impeccable speeches, helping to push the finance minister's private, elderly little Baby Morris motorcar which we found in the street, unable to restart after the meeting that night.

"Mr Minister, where's your chauffeur and Cadillac?" we asked.

"I use those only on official State occasions, not for public meetings," he piped.

We asked him to keep his little Morris in first gear, his foot on the clutch and, soon, his foot on the accelerator.

Then three journalists manhandled Finance Minister Hofmeyr's old car down the dark, empty street.

At his funeral soon afterwards, 10000 people mourned his spectacular life and the loss of his unbending ethics.

Now both great men were removed from the political scene. When Smuts died soon after his deputy leader, young Hofmeyr, I came to associate the baby's laugh at Smuts's funeral as a turning point in many forms. It seemed to signal the beginning of the end of Rule of Law. But no one could possibly have imagined that the baby who laughed so innocently would be 46-years-old before apartheid could finally be destroyed.

Jan Smuts continues to be castigated by his critics for failing to address the "Native Issue" of his time, and thus failing to prevent apartheid. His critics formed the majority of South Africans and they ranged from deprived Africans and most ANC leaders to white liberals and whites-only trade unionists. He was attacked viciously, and occasionally physically, by Afrikaner Nationalists. He was abused by their rightwing extremists who occasionally fired shots, and who cursed him as "a traitor".

He was adored by the troops he led into three wars – one against Britain and two against Germany.

Outside of South Africa – and across the rest of the world – he was seen as a hero or a genius. He was afforded a ticker-tape welcome in the streets of New York. The Chancellor of Cambridge University ranked Smuts's status with the university's finest representatives: Milton and Charles Darwin.

Smuts was invited to give the main address at the 100th anniversary meeting in London of the Association for the Advancement of Science. He surveyed subjects from mathematics and physics to biology and astronomy and from physiology to philosophy ... and then, on one particular day gave 13 lectures on different scientific and general issues. He could quote pages from books he had read years previously.

As a military leader he was compared by some enthusiasts with Napoleon.

Winston Churchill admired Smuts as the finest world leader he knew.

And the world recognized him as the man who shaped, partly wrote and became the only person to sign the founding documents of the League of Nations and United Nations.

Some teachers of philosophy compared Smuts with Einstein! Botanists hailed him for his work in classifying and encouraging the study of grasses.

I WAS OF COURSE a relatively inexperienced kid reporter at the time of my interviews with General Smuts and my reports on his speeches in the immediate post WWII years. Yet, he inexplicably invited me to sit at his bedside during his last days before his death.

During the life of that extraordinary, complex and imperfect human being's lifespan, I had read his early biographies. And soon half a dozen more were on my bookshelf. Yet only recently did Richard Steyn's finely researched biography *Jan Smuts, Unafraid of Greatness*[1] recapture for me some of the essence of that world leader. The new book rejuvenates old memories.

It reminded me that my final meetings with General Smuts had involved awe and embarrassment. Awe in his private presence, embarrassment at not mastering or fully understanding, often, what he was reminiscing about; whether to interrupt or ask questions or to leave quietly when he fell into deep silence.

This is what happened 66 years ago ... so far as I can recall the details and surroundings leading to an encounter I could never forget:

The whole literate world knew that he was dying. A group of newsmen waiting outside the homestead of Doornkop for firsthand information of General Smuts hourly condition, was given a health bulletin and some noncommittal answers to their questions. As they were about to leave, a member of the household approached *Pretoria News* political correspondent Harry Colley and me (a junior assistant) and to my astonishment and embarrassment said that the Oubaas would like to see me.

After questioning the message, the English-speaking and Afrikaans political correspondents departed, and a puzzled Harry left with our newspaper's driver, who was instructed to come back to the farm, near Irene, and pick me up.

I was directed to the open door of a small room looking onto the garden. There, on a high, made-up bed on the left of the doorway was the international leader; the field marshal and ex-prime minister; the distinguished scientist and philosopher. He rested on the pillow fully dressed, but without his tie or his usual walking boots. His eyes were closed.

I remember sitting down silently on a wooden chair placed near the centre of the sparsely furnished little room. I waited there, not knowing what to expect and looking back through the open door on one side and, on the other, the open window which reflected some of the early afternoon freshness of the Highveld's spring. My daily newspaper's deadline was gone, I reminded myself, with relief.

Finally the Oubaas opened his eyes, greeted me ... and closed them again. After a brief and, for me, uneasy silence, he started to speak. No small talk whatever, though he intimated he just wanted to chat. I remember my flush of pride when he said he knew he could trust me. I remember little of what was said, but he spoke mostly in English and certainly didn't use the word "chat".

I believe that, in his enforced passive state, he wanted for his own satisfaction to frame in precise words some of the thoughts in his head. Our conversations leading to this end were irrelevant.

What was instantly precise at the start of our first "interview" was a reminder that of course nothing said in this room would go out of it. My pride at being his chosen confidant changed to transparent disappointment ... then to relief when he launched into a number of subjects, none of them about current affairs or politics or wars or personal reminiscences, but mainly and philosophically about academic and esoteric issues ... a few of them expressed in technologically arcane and academic Afrikaans.

Now I know I should have at least attempted to take down in shorthand every word, whether it be about Holism, or ecology, or theology or agronomy, philosophy or cosmology. I desperately wished to question him about his astonishing, seemingly ruthless, almost instantaneous decisions involving lives and deaths of friend and foe in times of military crisis and violence. I'd have wished to question him about *all* his thoughts when he faced death in several different circumstances as a soldier – and when he pronounced, or declined to order, the death of others.

(How, for instance, had he successfully contrived to escape his own death early in the Anglo-Boer War, by dismounting from his horse – and walking it – in front of the enemy?

Was it cunning or compassion which decided him, almost instantly, not to derail or strafe with fire an enemy troop train which crawled uphill in the night, rattling past his guerrilla volunteers, all determined on destroying it?

Why did he order the instant death of a self-confessed spy among his men, when there was still time during his retreat to hold some kind of review of his sentence on the well-known, fellow Afrikaner?

Why, when his car ran a gauntlet of gunfire in Johannesburg during the violent miners' strikes, did he sit and watch while his two loyal companions joined in rapid-fire against their attackers? For once, Smuts had felt he owed an explanation. As they drove on he told them: "There was no target. Now your guns are empty. I still have my ammunition."

As he lay now on his deathbed, there were other questions – never hostile in these circumstances but worth asking – about his policies usually involving angry whites and angry blacks.

But the subjects of our discourse did not include anything about his actions in his life, nor about his personal matters. And it was not the time for questioning a patient who had his own agenda during those few long intimate hours that I was bidden to spend in three sessions with that interesting, formidable man. Instead he spoke aloud his esoteric thoughts and arcane, jumbled memories, without me trying to take advantage of his condition. His thoughts were, in any event, private and off-the-record. They were spoken to some young man he felt he could trust. They would never have been uttered to anyone holding a pencil and notebook.

Apartheid's baptism

Apartheid was itself a baby at mid-century. It was first opposed in the heart of Afrikanerdom by Smuts and Hofmeyr. Apartheid had been adopted and christened in this self-same Church Square, little more than two years before his funeral, when the election result for Smuts's neglected United Party seat, Standerton, was announced.

That late-night announcement from the "platteland" hinged on the news of Smuts's personal political downfall. It was greeted by the gleeful blare of taxi hooters parked around Pretoria's central square. The arena was not yet dominated by President Paul Kruger's statue. Instead the central motif was a fountain and shallow pool, beside which the *Rand Daily Mail* had set up a notice board and a tall barometer to track election results. A few journalists had come to watch, fully expecting to see recorded the election victories of Smuts and his United Party, a war-forged party combining old SA Party Afrikaners and new English-speaking supporters who admired Smuts, the internationally respected Boer War leader.

The Standerton election result signalled otherwise, and the Nats of the ethnically and racially exclusive National Party whooped with joy and wrestled the *Rand Daily Mail*'s staff – and one or two other journalists, including me – into the fountain.

"Nou is julle Nat!" ("Now you are wet"), they punned, raucously.

This baptism under apartheid marked the end of the power Smuts had wielded in southern Africa; SouthWest Africa; East Africa; in Westminster; in Europe; and in helping to forge both the League of Nations in the 1920s and its successor the United Nations in the late 1940s.

Smuts was many things, besides soldier, statesman and scientist. While still a teenager, he had written an essay in which he declared "the Person" (the Soul) to be the highest manifestation of life. Later, in his introduction to holism and evolution, he explained how he had come "to realise that personality was only a special case of a much more universal phenomenon, namely the existence of wholes and the tendency towards wholes and wholeness in all of nature".

Now Smuts was dead. His passing emphasized the emptiness that a million of his supporters felt at the prospect of a "nation" going mad. They were already appalled at a minority government (a minority of the minority whites-only electorate) which was filled with former supporters of Nazism who were now engineering a massive prostitution of:

- **The Constitution**,

- **The Senate** and its "inflated" Senators, accused by *The Star* of being personally corrupt for going to Parliament for the sole cause of ensuring a two-thirds majority vote in joint session to abolish "Native" and "Coloured" voters from the Common Roll. (*The Star*, when sued *en masse*, happily paid, but without apology, each "enlarged" Senator a token sum, when ordered to do so by:

- **The Supreme Court** and

- **The press**, whose right to publish information freely would finally be curbed but not crushed after 45 years and many press commissions and hundreds of court battles.

All these, and other crimes of apartheid, are dealt with in about 1600 books, including one of mine, on the subject. ☐

1. *Jan Smuts, Unafraid of Greatness*, Richard Steyn (Jonathan Ball 2015).

21.
The three Malans.

Ah, but a man's reach should exceed his grasp,
Or what's heaven for?

Robert Browning in the 1880s.

n the beginning of formal apartheid – during the all-white, politically tense post-Smuts era – two extraordinary men pitched themselves into the very heart of the battle over white-man's power in South Africa. They were both Malans.

One was "Sailor" Malan, the fighter pilot ace who became a hero of the Free World facing Hitler; the other **DF Malan**, the reverend who led his flock mistakenly down an evil road.

Dr D F Malan, church leader, newspaper editor, head of the Afrikaner Nasionale Party.

Fate decreed that he should officially introduce to South Africa the official policy of apartheid. It left him unsmiling. His fanatically nationalistic party also expected him to introduce a new constitution – limited to "like-minded people only" (i.e. Nat Party supporters.) Fortunately he failed.

The Reverend Dr Daniel F Malan was an ardent Christian who ushered in the birth of official apartheid. He was not among the many extremists who had hoped Hitler would win World War 2. He was born in Riebeeck West in the Western Cape where, ironically, he was taught at Sunday School by a young, global-visioned neighbour named Jan Christiaan Smuts who was leading in the opposite direction.

Malan grew up to be a *dominee* in the Dutch Reform Church and unfortunately for the press, he became, like Hendrik Verwoerd later, a newspaper editor after joining the Afrikaner National Party. Dr Malan resigned as editor of *Die Burger*, the party's official mouthpiece for many years, to lead the Nats and become the first prime minister of the National Party in 1948.

The Rev Malan epitomised all the basic ills, and the hates, fears, and aspirations of exclusive independence embodied in Afrikaner nationalism. Yet he was not an ardent extremist of racist passions. Extremism followed inevitably and quickly in his wake.

The bespectacled figure of Prime Minister Malan was at the height of his power as we watched him at the dramatic unveiling of the inner sanctum of the Voortrekker Monument. The ceremony was on the hill near the military headquarters of Roberts Heights – quickly renamed Voortrekkerhoogte, and the official dedication of the monument was timed for precisely noon, Central Africa Time (then known as SA Time), when the sun's rays on that chosen day would send a beam of light through the central aperture of the new monument to rest on the Voortrekker holy shrine below.

Ten years earlier, as a child on holiday in the Western Cape, sitting on the stone wall of the old bridge at the end of the main road of Somerset West, I had witnessed the start of the 1937 symbolic re-enactment of the *Groot Trek*. Families in wagons and newly bearded horsemen dressed in nineteenth-century corduroy, travelled from various cities (where each main road was immediately renamed Voortrekkerstraat) and converged on Pretoria for the laying of the foundations of the Voortrekker Monument.

Organisers of this fervently exclusive trek had encouraged only *ware* ("true or pure") Afrikaners to build large families "for the sake of *die Volk*"(the People).

You could already hear echoes from across the world of Hitler, who was still new to power in the 1930s. Numbers of "pure Afrikaner" adherents copied some of Hitler's (anti-British) ideas and in their growing fanaticism were prepared to sacrifice their Calvinist principles by discarding their *faux*-Voortrekker trousers and *kappies* to start families in private laying-ceremonies on the monument's foundations.

Now, nearly ten much calmer years later, in November 1947, the monument stood at its full, solidly-braced height; visible it seemed from 30km in every direction. On the slopes surrounding it had arisen a vast tent-city, complete with canvas-roofed dining saloons, ablution blocks, worship places and a press village. Though few mentioned it, it is truly conceivable that many puritan couples were again seeking to start families, legitimate or otherwise, at the monument's portals during this week-long celebration.

This time, not just *ware Nasionaliste*, but all Afrikaners were invited to attend the politicised religious celebrations, as were outside observers. The wicked *Engelse Pers* were there – I shared a tent with two other journalists – but we *persmanne* were made to feel like unwelcome *vreemdelinge* (strangers) in our own land. The famous generosity and courtesy of Afrikanerdom was suddenly wiped out by ideological fervour.

The nights, for working male *vreemdelinge* at least, were long and uncomfortable, until Dedication Day dawned and the media gathered in the main press tent. They waited impatiently for news while seeking descriptions of the politically holy event. I remember wandering over to the typewriter of "Sapa" Jones, a wizard with words, who was supplying them every hour, as news agencies are required to do. His first intro was clacking out on the teleprinter under the canvas not long after dawn, to be seen or heard later in the day by audiences across the land. "Little cotton-balls of cloud cover the sky," he wrote, or something like it. "Tens of thousands of corduroy-clad men, and ladies in their Voortrekker bonnets are staring upwards, trying to judge when the sun will reach its zenith

This scene was captured by famous photographer Margaret Bourke-White for Life magazine on her first assignment in Africa. She captured it on that historic day in 1949 when nearly 200 000 people gathered before noon to witness the sun's rays falling inside the monument at precisely the correct moment during the opening ceremony.

and send rays into the heart of the Voortrekker Monument today ....” Hot damn! Little cotton balls of cloud ... I wondered if I would ever be able to write like that.

At 7am the cloud-cover was already disappearing. “Sapa” Jones would have to produce at least four more updates before the Great Monument’s Great Moment arrived. Over breakfast I nervously began to compose my own irrevocable intro. But it wouldn’t shape up. In the light of the drama about to break, this was fortunate, for my deadline wasn’t till 12.30pm when the ceremony would be in full swing. By then – like the sun – the dedication would be past its zenith at that “holy” place.

By 9am the hillside below the monument’s steps was filling with spectators, forming the greatest assembly yet “counted” and recorded on the subcontinent of Africa. There was not a black or brown face visible in that multitude. And no one remarked on this fact.

There were prayers and there were hymns. There were sunshades, crying kids, and ice creams everywhere. The sun was shining like billy-o, as it was meant to do. Sometime before noon, with some harmless cloud, but – not a cotton-wool blob now to be seen – the prime minister and his party stepped onto a giant platform that faced the masses seated in an arc covering the steep sides of the hill.

From the furthest seats, at the foot of the looming monument above, the speakers far down the hill looked no bigger than midgets. Fortunately we newsmen had seats close to the “action”.

And action there was.

The Leader rose to speak. He was a rotund figure in a style of “morning suit” and he wore a large, tight, white collar. His chubby yet always stern and determined visage was spanned by heavy spectacle frames that made him look deceptively owlish. As the prime minister began his address to the crowds of semi-worshippers, he was interrupted by a wild cry. It came from somewhere on the furthest reaches of the open-air aisle on Dr Malan’s left.

The Reverend Prime Minister paused for only a moment, then continued to address his adoring and silent audience who were intent on small shadows at their feet that might trace the sun’s path over the vast sepulchre. But there was another cry. And another, as a figure came leaping wildly down the broad aisle that had been cut into the hill. Everything froze – except for one advancing flapping frame. The figure was onto the platform and dashing towards Dr Malan before the astonished police jumped into action – only a moment before the intruder could reach him.

My eyes were riveted by now, not on the intruder, but on Dr Malan. He never retreated, he never even blanched. He stood there, his mouth, slightly ajar, staring in amazement at this ultra-madman: this terrorist, perhaps, standing, almost touching him, but who was finally caught in the belated restraining arms of policemen.

The intruder was clearly a religious fanatic. He let himself be meekly led away after being prevented from thrusting some Bible text into the prime minister's hand. And the prime minister, his voice, stance and demeanour quite unchanged, continued his long sermon to "his People".

I would never have thought this clerkly, inward-looking sermonizer with his bleak Old Testament messages, would have such physical courage. He did. You had to admire it. His giant audience, strangely enough, seemed to take that for granted.

Flight Lieutenant A G "Sailor" Malan, leader of 'A' Flight, No. 74 Squadron RAF.

'Sailor' Malan duels in the sun and leads by torchlight

Adolph "Sailor" Malan, first great hero of the Battle of Britain, led the fight in the skies to prevent Hitler's invasion. After the war he returned to South Africa to lead the torch commandos in protest against an apartheid government.

"Sailor' Malan was among the bravest and most colourful figures of his time; the most revered by his supporters; the most feared by his enemies; and probably the most quickly forgotten figure in SA politics. He was the very model of an international all-time hero, but quickly forgotten for sad reasons which soon became obvious.

Adolph "Sailor" Malan, was christened in 1910 before the world outside Austria had ever heard of Adolf Hitler. Malan was born in Wellington in the Cape, close to the birthplace of General Smuts and Sailor's relative, Daniel F Malan. At 15, Adolph Malan joined the Mercantile Marine in Cape Town where he earned his Sailor nickname. At 26 he was a fighter pilot, trained in South Africa and ready for the

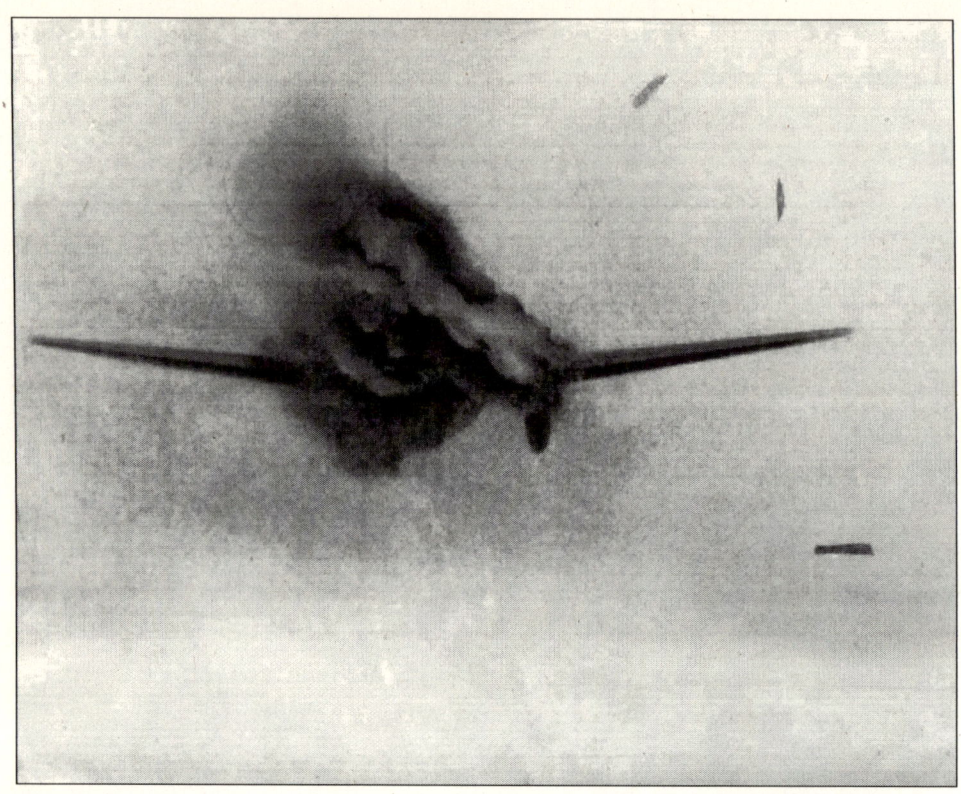

This dramatic shot of a Heinkel He 111 disintegrating over Dunkirk was taken by a gun camera in Malan's aircraft recording his first aerial victory. Although debris and billowing smoke can be seen, and the film recorded the loss of the Heinkel's starboard undercarriage, his claim was categorised as 'unconfirmed' because he had not watched the aircraft's total destruction. By the end of July 1941, however, Malan had achieved 27 confirmed victories and shared in others to become the highest scoring pilot of the war in Fighter Command.

impending World War against Hitler. At 29 he flew his first sortie against Hitler's Luftwaffe as a flight lieutenant in the Royal Air Force's famous 74 Squadron.

His group of pilots was dubbed "the Tigers" because of their fierce fighting record and their badge: a tiger's face above the motto "I Fear No Man".

In a very short time he was wing commander of this elite Royal Air Force squadron, and as early as 1941, after surviving and helping to win the Battle of Britain, he was regarded as the RAF's first great fighter pilot in the 1939–45 war. During that famous Battle of Britain in the skies over the Channel in 1940–41 he shot down – with no regard for his own life – 32 enemy aircraft. It was a record number not surpassed until the last stages of WWII.

"But he was much more than an individual performer," according to his biographer squadron leader Douglas Tidy in his book *Fear No Man*.[1]

"Sailor Malan had assimilated the fierce and fanatical 'tiger spirit', and this spirit he inspired in others so that he carried the squadron to great deeds with him."

He did more than that.

Malan developed a set of simple actions for fighter pilots to follow in the heat of battle. Soon his ten commandments were being followed throughout RAF Fighter Command. His succinct, almost instinctive "rules", were passed on to succeeding generations of trainee fighter pilots around the world. His advice read:

Wait until you see the whites of his eyes. Fire short bursts of one to two seconds only when your sights are definitely "ON".

Whilst shooting, think of nothing else. Brace the whole of your body.

Have both hands on the stick. Concentrate on your ring sight.

Always keep a sharp lookout. "Keep your finger out."

Height gives you the initiative.

Always turn and face the attack.

Make your decisions promptly. It is better to act quickly even though your tactics are not the best.

Never fly straight and level for more than 30 seconds in the combat area.

When diving to attack always leave a proportion of your formation above to act as a top guard.

INITIATIVE, AGGRESSION, AIR DISCIPLINE, and TEAMWORK are words that MEAN something in Air Fighting.

Go in quickly – Punch hard – Get out!

The "rules", sadly, failed to save his younger brother, George, who was killed while flying as a Spitfire pilot with the RAF's No. 72 Squadron in Tunisia in early 1943.

"Sailor" Malan had already introduced, two years earlier, a new formation of RAF fighter-attack during the air defence of Britain. Fighter-pilots' aircraft, always meticulously identified by colour and number, flew at first in the famous "Vic" formation, like an arrow-head aimed at invading German bombers. But by the time the Battle of Britain began the Luftwaffe were able to operate from airfields in France, enabling German fighters to escort their bombers all the way to England. So when the RAF and Luftwaffe met in the skies above England and the English Channel the ineffectiveness of the three-fighter "Vic" formation tactic was quickly exposed.

The two aircraft close behind their leader in the "V" were open to surprise attack from the rear, while only the leader was able to keep look-out for the enemy. Sailor Malan quickly adopted another tactic, one evolved from the German pattern in the Spanish War in 1939, which required a four-aircraft *Schwarm*. Famous ace Douglas Bader tested a new version which was adopted by "Sailor" Malan's senior pilots and dubbed the *Finger-four*. It involved two pairs of fighters in each flight, with the Flight Leader in front(representing the tip of the tallest "middle-finger". The element leader on his right as the third finger, with the element wingman further right (positioned as tip of the little finger). And, on the far left, flew the flight wingman (in "index finger position).

Which all goes to show how sophisticated air duels had become since WW1. Leaders like "Sailor" Malan continued to be hugely successful individual aces, but preferred to count their victories as a team effort.

In 1940, on a single day at the height of the battle for the skies – a day known to the RAF as "Sailor's August the Eleventh" – the squadron fought, landed, refuelled, and fought again – *four times*.

When the young, surviving pilots, covered in oil and sweat and shaking with fatigue finally returned to base, a single flying unit – the Tigers – had destroyed an astounding 38 enemy aircraft *in a single day*. In a two-week scramble in 1941, Malan's wing destroyed 42 hostile aircraft, with 15 more "probables" plus 11 more German planes damaged.

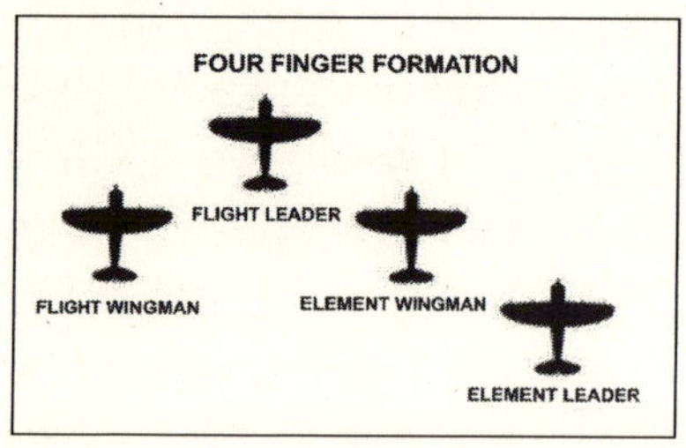

Sailor Malan was presented by the king with the DFC, then DSO, then Bar. He was also awarded by Britain's Allies the Belgian Croix de Guerre with bronze Palm; the Czechoslovakian Military Cross; the French Legion of Honour and the French Croix de Guerre. He is little known to later generations here and across the world only because he was citizen of a country soon besmirched by apartheid.

The dark-haired, handsome, Afrikaans-speaking hero returned to his homeland in 1946, months after the war, with his English bride. He did not attract great attention for he was a quiet, calm character who could not tolerate "fuss". But he was appalled with what he saw happening to his homeland, and in the early 1950s, he quietly helped rally all the ex-servicemen he could persuade to become members of his Torch Commando. It was said that a quarter of a million men joined the cause. At a rally in Durban of 28000 torch-burning "troops", he told them: "The strength of this gathering is evidence that the men and women who fought in the war for freedom ... are determined not to be denied the fruits of that victory."

The Torch Commando was the spearhead of a national campaign against the Nationalist government's plans to ensure its tenuous grip on power by removing coloured voters from the common roll. The colour franchise in the Cape was protected by the Act of Union of 1910 through an entrenched clause stating there could be no change without a two-thirds majority of both houses of Parliament sitting together.

The Nationalist government, with unparalleled cynicism, soon managed to pass its High Court of Parliament Act, effectively removing the autonomy of the judiciary; and thus enable itself "legally" to pack the Senate with its nominated and unelected NP sympathisers. The enlarged senate provided enough votes to enable the government, with a temporary, unelected and false two-thirds majority, to disenfranchise the "coloured" electorate. Later the same artificially enlarged Senate allowed the government to get rid of the last African representation in Parliament, which had been an independently black-elected and strategically placed group of MPs – just four white "guardians".

For five long, tense years, however, tens of thousands of ex-wartime volunteers carried the flame of freedom, instilling fear into government and its many party organisers who ran the country.

The Torch Commando finally flickered and died partly because it began to appear to most of Sailor Malan's ex-servicemen followers that their cause was lost or – sadly – considered by whites to have become irrelevant. But the main reason for the demise of the great protest movement of anti-apartheid whites was the quarrelling among its sub-leaders. The broad aims of "freedom" were in conflict with their personal political interests. The leadership split irreparably into doubting conservatives, vacillating liberals, and a small and active minority of over-enthusiastic, undemocratic, postwar Stalinists. (The spectre of totalitarian communism was a huge aid to the fascist Nationalism in South Africa throughout its long life.)

The broadly based Torch Commando movement realised too late that its fatal flaw was its failure to recruit enough brown and black ex-servicemen supporters.

However, the Torch Commando was the father of a much more determined and courageous daughter: The Black Sash, an all-women urban organisation that defied apartheid and outlasted its 48-year rule. The Torch Commando also inspired a tiny little brother, an underground Natal group of "growing-older" ex-servicemen who called themselves "the Horticultural Society". They travelled to both pro- and anti- republication and apartheid rallies in convoys of cars to combat violence at robust all-white meetings quarrelling over the merits of abandoning Crown and Commonwealth.

Sailor Malan was suffering from Parkinson's Disease and died at the early age of 52. He was buried in Kimberley in 1963, but he had observed, after the Sharpeville massacre, the rise of militant black opposition to apartheid within his country.

Like Smuts, who had also voluntarily and physically risked his life many times, "he feared no man".

A third, less magnanimous, Malan

Another of the Malan clan, General Magnus Malan, Minister of Defence, is the third Malan figuring in South Africa's apartheid history, but would not be worth a mention if, at his death in July 2011, he had not suddenly been seen by some scribes as the éminence *grise* behind President PW Botha.

For anyone who witnessed Magnus in action in the 1980s this theory was hard to accept and probably apocryphal. He appeared to be a typical bully, one who knows how to abuse power when unchallenged, and when to be meek in the presence of stronger men. The generals under him who prosecuted war in Africa disliked more than feared him. He was their *bête*

General Magnus Malan, a follower who followed President PW Botha's "Total Onslaught" policy so enthusiastically that his undisciplined 'underground' men committed torture and murder to defend apartheid.

noir (why is it the French have the best phrases to describe him?) but only because he – and PW of course – frustrated the top army officers' broader more civilised vision of how to "save South Africa". "Only political reform, not warfare, can solve South Africa's problems," said the generals. Their top commander, Malan, voiced this view … but followed instead his unbending prime minister.

Magnus Malan was no evil genius. He reminded some of us of the third stooge of the comedy team *The Three Stooges* which we saw on the bioscope in our boyhood … except that he wasn't funny. He was one of the few Nationalist politicians who actually enjoyed the company of his boss, PW Botha who, when he promoted himself to president, appointed the general as his token minister of defence. The general didn't appear to mind that the president himself had enjoyed that post and still ruled it.

Instead General Malan created a secret little unit with no accountability to anyone but himself. Perhaps he saw himself as the military equivalent of General Hendrik van den Bergh, ex-head of the police. But unlike van den Bergh he was unable to control his men – who committed torture and murder in a vain attempt to stop anti-apartheid protest. ☐

1. *Fear No Man*, The history of No. 74 Squadron, Royal Air Force. First published 1972, available online.

22.
'Knock twice and ask for Jesus'.

*A 20th century working ship –
ferrying purposeful passengers to adventure,
fortunes, new lives and old loves
– make today's luxury liners feel like hearses …
and aircraft seem like flying prisons.*

THE WINCHESTER CASTLE, launched in 1930, served as a "migrant" ship sailing to and fro between Southampton and Cape Town after World War 2. In 1949 the stately lady joined the Union Castle's regular mailship service. Union Castle ships sailed from both ports at 4pm every Thursday.

The first memorable quote I picked up during my first glimpse of a foreign country was: "Knock twice and ask for Jesus." It was a translation of the advice offered in beautiful Spanish Madeira, and it seemed to hint at Opportunity, Hope, Faith and the promise of rewarding travel. But the words were taken out of context, and the promise was something very different ... something small, sad, and tawdry, as you will discover.

I'd set out to see the world as soon as I was a legal adult. I had completed more than three years of employment, and when I was refunded my contribution to my puny pension, a sum of less than *fifty* pounds (the rand note, when introduced many years later, was worth two to the pound), I calculated I had enough to buy a one-way steerage class berth on an old ship to Europe.

From Pretoria I hitchhiked over dusty, corrugated main roads to Grahamstown to see my girlfriend, then hitchhiked to Cape Town to see my mum and get aboard the *Winchester Castle*. I was thrilled with my cabin, even though it had six bunks stacked closely together, a sealed porthole — though with funnelled air from the top deck, but no artificial "air conditioning", a term unfamiliar to most of us.

Our berth, I seem to remember, was below the waves and close to the ship's propeller. I was experiencing a personal economic crisis. The cost of my ticket left me with little more than £10 to explore the world. I would need every penny to tide me over until I found the adventure and the glimpse of fame that I sought with such naïve optimism.

Fortunately I and my hitherto unknown cabin mates had very little cabin luggage for the 14-day voyage (and together we had very little baggage in Storage, it transpired). When the steamship's engines started up, and the screws began to turn, our cabin began to shake. It shook, rattled, and rolled for the next two weeks. We became so used to it that we found the silence quite eerie in harbour at Madeira and at dockside later in Southampton.

Sailing so soon after the war meant ships were packed with first-time voyagers, mostly young men and women setting out to see the old, free world. (The return journeys were filled mainly with new migrants to Africa, seeking a new, free world.)

My cabin mates and I had the least money to spare, and bemoaned the strange custom of having to tip a steward to get a beer or packet of cigarettes. To cover some of our expenditure we devised a plan to make money on the ship's competitions, concentrating all our efforts on the Fillies Stakes, in which young women were encouraged to enter the race and win cash prizes by cutting a thin roll of linen tape down the middle for several yards.

We persuaded a pretty nurse, one of our soon-gathering group of seekers after adventure, to compete as a favourite in the main event. To win, she had to practise every day for several days beforehand. I desperately wagered nearly a third of my remaining capital on her at even-money. Three whole pounds. During Race Night our crowd was delirious with joy. Our highly-trained nurse cut tape with tiny scissors on the open, rolling deck at such speed she was soon five lengths ahead, and unbeatable.

She looked up and gave us a victory smile ... Her unmonitored hand slipped. The scissors cut sideways for a split second. The ribbon fell from her grasp and we were out of the race. Her smile turned to tears, but those didn't help. Fortunately I did not own a wallet, for there was now even less than little to keep in it.

Our sorrows were diverted days later when we tumbled into lighters and were ferried ashore at Madeira as dusk fell. The bougainvillea-bedecked island was as exotic as I had hoped: the steep cobbled streets, the flowers, the music; the picturesque grilled Spanish windows. In our own country we hadn't even heard of burglar bars in those days. I explored the port's city on my own and was delightfully lost when a self-appointed guide attached himself to me and led me to the door of an impressive house.

"Knock twice and ask for Jesus," he explained in the only complete English sentence he seemed to possess.

"Jesus?"

"House of him."

It didn't look a bit like a church to me. Intrigued, I knocked twice, was immediately welcomed in ... to behold a crowded room of familiar faces. It was standing room only for what seemed like half the male company of our ship.

"The girls are very busy. You have to stand in the queue," I was informed.

Jesus was the man upstairs, literally. He was busy counting money apparently. Fortunately I didn't have sufficient desire or spare cash for the rushed peak-hour services offered by his hardworking all-women staff. Most fortunate, because one of the boys in our cabin thought he had caught some genital disease in Jesus's place, and caused minor panic aboard ship. It was a false alarm.

We were all very innocent and uninformed in that era.

We reluctantly tipped our bar steward on our last night outside Southampton. On the dockside the next day he gave us a wave — and stepped into a *motorcar!* Would I ever be so rich?

Size does not matter

The excitement of a first visit to Britain took a long time to grow. My first impression had been from the boat train travelling from Southampton to London. Everything in rural England looked miniature, yet strangely familiar. Then I realised that I was recognising scenes out of popular books and English films – but mainly meadows full of farm animals, sheep, and cattle so unlike ours, which were the imported toy models many of us had played with as children.

England itself looked to me remarkably like a toy model. But it was somewhat depressing to see London suburbia from the elevated railway track. One saw nothing but a mass of chimneys across acres of roofs, spreading to every horizon.

Not a single building higher than Johannesburg's skyscraping Eskom House, which was soon to be a national landmark at home.

My disillusion increased on seeing Trafalgar Square, Piccadilly Circus, and other places, ill-lit, drab from war-and-tears, and seeming to my African eye to be disappointingly tiny. Even the room in our Earls Court lodgings felt cramped, but that was because there was only one bed, and three of us were sleeping on the floor. Darkness fell at 4pm. Pubs weren't open even by 6pm!

We fanned out, looking for work. The most successful in our ship's motley crew was a fellow who boasted of a job he'd found in Regent Street. We were overwhelmed by the splendour of the electric lamp shop where he was employed. We scanned the premises, but failed to see him ... until a shop assistant in a crisp, formal morning suit clicked his fingers, and our man ran out, carrying a stepladder, which he climbed like a monkey to reach a chandelier which he brought down and handed to the formally attired assistant to present to his customers.

Our friend eventually ended our mockery by reminding us that he was the only member of our ship's gang who *regularly* earned beer money. We were going to have to climb a lot of steps to pay our landlady, we realised.

Fleet Street regains its fame

Journalists moved between office and nearest pub during traffic hours. At dead of night, newspaper vans jammed the area.

In 1949, Fleet Street was not the least bit interested in the past few hundred years of its history; it was on its toes staring at the next five minutes.

History would soon pass it by as Britain, badly wounded after its WWII victory, gradually lost its precarious place at the centre of world

Fleet Street towards the end of its 'Good old days'.

communications ... a place it had earned long ago by laying most of the world's vital international cables – an undersea spider's web of global communications, centred exclusively on London.

Post-war Fleet Street was still admired for its skills and its dash even by newsmen on the greatest newspapers of America.

Britain, among its bomb-shelled ruins, its weary warriors and its broken industries, still saw itself as the leader of a great empire. It still possessed, momentarily, the biggest navy in the world. And newspapermen, particularly Australian, New Zealand, and South African journalists, followed a well-trodden path to Fleet Street's doors to become a significant part of their spring-coiled, over-exploited editorial staffs.

The "colonial" journalists were forced when entering Britain to join, as "temporary migrants", the newly-roused post-war labour unions. The "colonials" ignored British trade union rules and strikes and sabotage. But all journalists watched the unions' tactics quickly bring down Britain's great export industries and threaten its pre-war markets for bicycles, motorbikes, cars, blankets and other exports desperately wanted in India, China, and other then third-world countries.

I remember, when going back to Britain a decade later, gaining an exclusive interview with perhaps the most powerful man in Britain, Vic Feather, leader of the Trade Union Congress. The TUC's power was still throttling the British press, with its demand for splitting jobs and unsustainable overstaffing, when I was able to ask him:

"In hindsight, don't you feel that trade union demands for extreme postwar change seriously damaged the nation; killing its giant ship-building industry; forbidding 'containerisation' and preventing technological advances?"

"We-ell," said Vic Feather, a man renowned for his wit, and the very opposite of the Tory's view of radical red workers, "I don't think we are ever unreasonable. Take the case of cybernetics that you cite. Yes, we were opposed to it at first ... but finally, when we found out what cybernetics meant, we supported it."

Who could match that riposte? Who could argue against such candour?

The curse of austerity

In 1949, however, the dust of war debris and demolition still covered the land. Pre-fab buildings arose everywhere like tatty cardboard cut-outs to meet an emergency in

Traditionally, since the time of Samuel Johnson, lunch-'hour' was one of the most productively creative periods for scribes.

accommodating families and public life. These structures, and the awful minimalist austerity architecture of new or restored buildings, became permanent and depressing monuments to drab austerity.

A quip attributed to Churchill said at the time: "An empty taxi pulled up at Westminster yesterday, and (Prime Minister) Clem Atlee got out."

It said a great deal about Britain's disillusionment immediately after victory in war.

The British people never thought, as they struggled to rebuild their cities, that they would need to start digging new and deeper bomb shelters to meet a greater threat than they had ever experienced before.

Instead, they tried to deny it ... despite reminders from one of the world's oldest and most famous philosophers.

The A-Bomb was a constant horror threatening the world. It was a real threat that most people have forgotten, but which may yet return, in the shape of an even bigger H-bomb, to haunt or terrorise the wider global village within a century of the atomic bomb's birth.

When I had amassed sufficient capital in London to be able to buy a beer or two, I would spend some time in The *Daily Mirror*'s favourite pub – not El Vino wine bar, but the historic British pub across the road near Fetter Lane. It was livelier than the favourite haunts of other Fleet Street papers, and made the famous Press Club look drab and sad, with its regular soaks sitting about in quiet corners hoping for someone to buy them a drink.

The *Mirror*'s pub was a piece of the heart of London, but beat twice as fast as the rest of that great organ. There I bumped into a British journalist I'd known who had been working for a while as a subeditor in Pretoria after war service.

"I'm back on the news beat," said Tony Hose. "I'll be working this Sunday. Why not come along and see the peaceniks?"

I leapt at the invitation.

The world was gathering for a Peace Conference – not another mass Demo for Peace, but a gathering of eminent international figures who would be seeking ways to avoid the mortal danger the world had found itself in after two massive, death-dealing, war-time atomic bomb attacks ... and constant new A-bomb tests.

The immediate postwar years were dominated by a reckless arms race to find even bigger nuclear deterrents. Nuclear weapons were being exploded above ground, below ground, and beneath the sea by half a dozen nations with such abandon and results so awesome that the consequences could not be publicly faced.

The subject was reduced to satires such as the famous review *Beyond the Fringe* which kept London sane and rolling in the aisles for years.

A serious anti-nuclear demo would draw merely a small, hardy group of placard-wielding demonstrators.

Thus the press, at this greatest of all International Anti-nuclear Conventions, appeared to outnumber the audience as well as the eminent speakers.

Press facilities for this event were grander than veteran reporters of that era had seen before. There were long lines of telephones, temporarily supplied in a land desperate for new phonelinks. There were stacks of handouts – erudite papers and popular backgrounders on every aspect of the issue. And the eminent speakers were being lined up to tell the world, through the press, how serious – how dangerous – was the threat of nuclear war. The times suddenly felt exceedingly hot, even though the Cold War had hardly begun!

With a mixture of pity and awe I turned to my host, the man from the *Mirror*. "Tony, how on earth are you going to cover all this in half a column?"

(A tabloid page, with giant headlines and a pix splash, meant that the equivalent of half a tabloid page would be the *Mirror*'s "max".)

"Oh, they only want a para, old son," said Tony blithely. "I'll find it soon enough."

He fought his way through a huddle of reporters to reach a slight, silver-haired man whose visage was familiar. His words were riveting, and I was even allowed to prompt him for more. Later Tony let me read his scribbled text of what the *Mirror*'s coverage of the great Ban the Bomb event would be next day.

It went something like this: **Bertrand Russell**, winner of the Nobel Prize for Literature, famous philosopher and political thinker, spent his 78th birthday on a bicycle, pedalling from his home and back, a distance of several miles, to attend the World Peace gathering in London yesterday. "Why am I here? I think it worthwhile trying to help save perhaps a million lives in this country," he said.

Whatever the precise words were, they seemed to say it all.

Bertrand Russell.

But I knew then that, even though it was not remotely possible, I didn't really want to work on the world's best product of tabloid journalism. Fleet Street's unrivalled experience, expertise, variety, and competitiveness however, made the *Mirror* a huge challenge and wonderful school for any journalist.

I thought long about this while waiting for a job somewhere – anywhere – in "The Street". And I wished, naively, to enter it independently, without using contacts, if it were possible to foster them, or even to use the letter of introduction Laurie Gandar had written for me back in Pretoria.

Instead I found myself taking shorthand notes in some legal office, working as a packer in mid-winter in Harrods' cold basement, yearning for a temporary job above-ground, or enough money to pay for the required uniform and transport to work at some pedestrian post in the then glamorous Heathrow International Airport. Unless one could find a newspaper job, or find joy in standing in long queues, day and night, it seemed to me that life here could hardly be greyer. □

23.
Crashes and shambles – and Europe in ruins.

They talk about who won and who lost.
Human reason won. Mankind won.

Nicolai Kruschev (before his USSR collapsed).

German cities that were special targets of Allied bombers in the closing years of war were reduced to rubble. I walked down a main street of Mainz years after the war – and saw only one occupant – a cat. (See – Appalling damage in Europe" below.)

The aftermath of war was heavy upon its victor, Britain, as well as on vanquished Germany, for at least half a decade.

The damage in Europe was too big for any individual to comprehend, but on a miniscule scale I was certainly aware of the enforced austerity in London. It forced me, for about the tenth time, to give up smoking! I survived at first by selling to shady characters on the street ("spivs"), the precious hoard of duty-free cigarettes I'd invested in aboard ship.

Finally, for want of any response whatever from a beleaguered Fleet Street, I swallowed my pride and carried my precious letter of introduction to Kemsley Newspapers. It was soon clear that Laurie Gandar (assistant editor of the *Pretoria News,* later the first great campaigning editor of the *Rand Daily Mail*) had been held in high regard by the top brass of Kemsley's, for they offered me a choice of a post in Sheffield or York, and the promise that if I progressed I could apply, if I ever reached the serious age of 25, for a post on their Fleet Street papers.

"You are forced to be a member of the journalists' union, unfortunately, if you wish to work on our nationals. And you have to be over 25 years of age to work in Fleet Street," they explained.

The Serious Provincial Press

"Goodbye Fleet Street," I told myself ... a term that became literally true because the newspapers themselves departed downriver shortly before I returned there a decade later.

It was a reluctant leave-taking, but I soon became aware that Britain's spread of great provincial newspapers is its backbone of a free, accountable press. Some of those papers are as erudite and exclusive as *The Times* once was.

Surprisingly few journalists of the provincial newspapers seek jobs in Fleet Street. An exception of course was the personnel of the *Manchester Guardian,* which itself moved to London, changed its name to *The Guardian*, but cherished the values of its most famous editor, CP Scott, and remains today, in the view of many of us, one of the best dailies in the world.

My choice was between the *Sheffield Telegraph,* a fine morning newspaper, and the *Yorkshire Evening Press.* I was advised to choose York, a beautiful, historic city and one of the few in range of wartime Germany's bombers which had not been badly hit.

In fact York's centre was already a shambles – **The Shambles**, an intact butchers' row of medieval shops that constituted one of the more picturesque places in Europe. I chose to go there – not because of beauty or history, but because I preferred the buzz of an afternoon/evening paper, and its title sounded rather like another of "Britain's best" ... the prodigiously "upmarket" *Yorkshire Post.*

My salary would be five pounds a week.

However I quickly earned a fair amount of income by writing

features on The Shambles, on York Minster, and on other famous landmarks of medieval England. My highly taxed wage failed to match the first income I had ever earned in Kimberley. But at this stage it felt to me like King George VI's salary — and life was moving from 10pt lower case newspaper type to 20pt headlines.

The Shambles in York, a medieval butchers' market place whose quaint, 500-year-old buildings missed the German bombing (Source: Keith Laverack).

BEWHISKERED LADY ROBS SWEET YOUTH
She's a "luvvy", says victim

My first permanent English landlady was a luvly old duck in York with a mischievous eye and heavy grey whiskers on her chin. She immediately appropriated my (compulsory post-wartime) food ration book. She lived in a two-bedroomed tenement beside the River Ouse close to the walls of the city of York. The lodgings were within walking distance of York Minster and The Shambles, and of the offices of the *Yorkshire Evening Press.*

The furthest walk seemed to be to the public bath-house. My luvvy — in her sixties and three times my age — did not own a bathroom. But she did own — or rather she appropriated — my British sweet ration coupons as well as my food ration book. I saw neither sweets nor coupons again.

She fed me well and called me "luv" — which startled me until I realised she called everyone "luv", from the postman to the county sheriff. She was a kind and lovable character. We became real friends, though I could not get used to her northern habit of serving High Tea (replacing supper) in broad summer's daylight. I would have loved her even more if only she'd been young and Spanish and served a full dinner at 10pm each sultry night.

LONDON-EDINBURGH EXPRESS CRASHES
Death numbers still not confirmed

Hanging out of the side of a small plane as it dives is a sensation one can cling to. It happened to me in York, above the railway line that carried the Flying Scotsman's lookalike from London to Edinburgh. However, this particular passenger express wasn't flying. Its wrecked coaches were lying in a crumpled zigzag, marking one of the worst rail accidents in British history. Half of Fleet Street appeared to be rushing to the scene, two hundred miles between the steam express's starting point and destination.

My job, as a mere local reporter, was to provide captions to aerial photographs – what else could you do up there in the sky? Well, one thing you were supposed to do in these circumstances, was to cherish – in very specific order – all the photographic plates the veteran snapper took out of his new 1949 model Speed Graphic and handed back to you, carefully, one by one, in the wind.

Afterwards I was gratified to receive a note from the news editor, in appreciation of the fast-written captions. But I was puzzled that the chief photographer wanted me fired. He was still furious at the out-of-sequence jumble of photographic plates I had returned to him.

COURT MARTIAL KILLS ITS FILM IMAGE
The verdict makes deadline

A rare experience and one I still treasure was to report a military court martial at the famous Strensall Barracks of a major British Army training centre in Yorkshire. It taught me many things – about competing with Fleet Street, about British law, and about stereotyping.

Yes, Counsel for the Defence demonstrated a brusque and unsympathetic air, signalling the fact that he had been officially appointed, against his will, to defend the silent, fearful soldier accused of some heinous crime, sensational enough to attract Fleet Street.

Yes, the junior officer did not hide his reluctance, or his contempt of the downcast, fearful private soldier in the box. And the Prosecutor was another relatively junior officer, casual and confident and apparently enjoying his well-briefed role.

On the Bench were senior officers, ready to pass sentence and judgement (possibly in that order) on a disloyal soldier. The entire court and its assisting staff apparently knew each other. The only foreign body was the accused soldier.

So far, so expectedly stereotyped.

But the two senior army officers who acted as "assessors to the judge" who sat between them, seemed to be asking the accused all the sympathetic questions his young defence counsel should have asked ... and breaking all civil court procedure by suggesting good answers. Well, you can't report that in your own words, can you? How do you portray the atmosphere – as well as the evidence and findings – in 400 words?

"Is that the last 'take'?" asked the voice in the receiver.

"Yes," I said, putting down the phone and absentmindedly shaking the outstretched hand that wanted to grab the heavy telephone handle to phone *The Daily Express*.

I could not remember what I had dictated, and could only hope that I had made it clear – but not in comment – that the court martial sentence was sensationally wise and lenient. Almost an anti-climax in fact.

A press car had been sent to bring me back to York. When I walked reluctantly into the newsroom the news editor nodded his head.

"Made deadline," he said, (the utter priority of every report in a panting afternoon newspaper). "Your story took a novel approach," he added.

Nothing more, thank heavens. I was told later that this was real praise. But what I remember was that I had been forced to learn how to dictate, for printing, a report on the instant it reached its unpredictable climax.

All I know is that the experience allowed me – years later and with unjustified confidence – to deal instantly with such things as an hour-long national budget speech handed to me by an official messenger in

A typical scene in the postwar years 1945-60s. Telephone lines, at home as well as in these public cubicles, could hardly cope with the growth of demand in most countries. Here are British newsmen, hanging on the lines to get their stories through to their news-desks.

Cape Town's parliamentary gallery just as my phone connected to Durban for a "special", post-deadline, extra-time-restricted telephone call to the news-desk.

"Hang on a moment," I told an equally anxious voice, and began dictating a summing up of the national budget the moment I frantically found its tax proposals intermittently spread between pages 35 and 42. The Natal *Daily News* main pm edition was being held back for those 200 or 250 words, which happened to trump the headlines of the morning papers next day.

It is satisfying to find this small if dubious speed-skill develop without one being aware of it.

I mention this incident in the knowledge that today The Budget Speech is available for analysis in advance behind closed doors – and that telephone "trunk calls" do not have to be especially reserved days in advance. Today you might click your phone camera and transfer your words or document images across the world in seconds. What must be missing today, amid all the "i-" and "e-" equipment relaying instant words and pictures and providing the voice of a nagging news editor in your ear, is the sense of isolation mixed with the surge of adrenaline that we used to feel when we got our story through.

It tasted better than a blue-labelled Scotch.

ESCAPE FROM ARREST FOR MURDER
Bloodstained suspect flees

York was a great place to enjoy, but my itchy feet got the better of me, and I resigned on impulse and hitchhiked to Harwich in order to explore Europe, which was still reeling from World War 2's mass-bombings.

On the ferry I met two girl cyclists from Cambridge, and I hired a bike in Rotterdam after we agreed to cycle together, exploring the Netherlands. It sounded a little risqué. We were too shy or naïve to utter even the word "breast", for in the mores of the time it was a sexy forbidden item that one affected not to notice in public. The word "sexy" did not exist.

When a Dutch traffic cop stopped to admonish us, he warned me in English: "Do not ride on the breast side. Ride on the backside."

It was one of our true, innocent jokes.

However, the girls had to go home to Cambridge, and I set off alone to hike eastwards as far as my emptying pocket would take me. While the girls had been with me, there had been no trouble getting lifts, even for three, when not riding bikes. Suddenly it was very different.

I finally hitched a lift to the German border in the car of a hunter who was going on a rabbit shoot, but the trail went dead after that, and failure to progress lasted so long that I joined up with a dark-haired, disconsolate Spaniard experiencing the same problem.

He spoke five languages, I gathered, but the ignorant fellow failed to understand a smattering of English, Afrikaans or even a word of isiXhosa. So we communicated only in sign language. To add to our woes, his nose started to bleed and – like the passing traffic – it wouldn't stop.

After what seemed like half a day's wait, two Danish journalists pulled up in a small car and started asking us questions in easy English. They were interested in my fellow hitchhiker's bloodstains, and amused at the fact that – with seven-and-a-bit languages between the two of us – we couldn't speak a word to each other. They explained that there was a major manhunt going on all round us. Police in three countries were looking for two young men wanted for a brutal murder.

It took a long time to get the message across in sign language to my new Spanish friend, but I decided that he understood the problem when he waved goodbye. The two of us probably had the same (inexpressible) thought about each other: "*You,* my foreign friend, could be a cold-blooded murderer."

My misunderstanding with the girl I favoured from Cambridge was more tragic. We had agreed to meet under the clock at London's Charing Cross station at noon in a month's time. I waited two hours, then left in fury. It transpired that she had waited under the clock at Charing Cross station too, for a couple of hours. She had waited under the clock on the Metro line. I was just above her, under the clock on the main line. She was beautiful, and we tried to keep in touch, but we never saw each other again.

There were no mobile phones in those days.

APPALLING DAMAGE IN EUROPE
More rubbish than people

Though it was now nearly five years after the second world-war-to-end-all-wars, there were very few travellers, let alone tourists in Europe in 1949–50. It seemed an ideal and an extraordinarily cheap time to visit Paris, Florence, the Alps, and the Rhine. But the journey presented only sad vignettes.

Mainz railway station, for instance stood in a pile of bomb rubble. Standing on the damaged station's steps in broad daylight, I could see no sign of life whatever – not a vehicle, pedestrian, no street names or direction signs; no road markings. Nothing but rubble. Even on the direct walk at midday from railway station down to the faraway river front there was no sign of life except a scurrying cat.

Was this all there was left of Mainz? Not a soul on a busy weekday?

No. A river-boat arrived, loaded with passengers, looking quite normal. On board I ordered a cup of ersatz coffee, probably made of acorns. I was just beginning to relax when I got the bill. It was the black market equivalent of my budget for dinner-and-bed at some hostelry down river.

Cologne seemed to be in a similar state as Mainz. I was assured it was not. Even though it was getting dark I walked to view the famous cathedral nearby. You could see it standing starkly alone against the sky. It was a miracle, people said. And you would wish to believe it, for everything surrounding the cathedral had turned into rubble.

Hamburg was a city I visited later with optimism. I had interviewed the post-war mayor of Hamburg – a liberal who had visited Pretoria; had expressed enthusiastic support for our newspapers' opposition to apartheid, and who had showered us with visiting cards and invitations to call on him at City Hall, Hamburg.

This I hoped to do. But I arrived late, and the buildings were in total darkness. I found very few surrounding buildings that showed any lights. I walked in the semi-dark until I found a hotel. The city was also dead, it seemed, for I knew without looking that the docks and surrounds had been flattened by bombing.

Cologne's ancient cathedral "miraculously" withstands all bombing raids, though the centre-city and parts of the railways remain in ruins for several years after WW II.

"What's there to do?"

"You can go down to the Reeperbahn," said the pretty receptionist, "that's where the nightlife is."

It was the Red Light District; a street crowded earlier with wide-eyed pedestrians. But the tawdry place was quickly emptying, so that when I arrived I saw a young girl, 16 perhaps, standing alone in a deserted square, seeking to solicit someone.

"How old are you? What is a young girl like you doing in a place like this?" (Perhaps I even used those words!) She obviously didn't understand.

"I got nice tits. You want?" she parroted, and was vocally angry when I walked away, unable to express my sadness at this common result of total war.

ALL THE MORE REASON, then, to wonder at the German miracle that followed. With the help of the commitment and genius of America's Marshall Plan, the threat and occupation of East Germany was nullified, and a new, morally transformed half-nation arose in West Germany. Out of the rubble and ruins rose a shining new democracy, created almost within a decade. Another miracle was in the fact that Germany, flattened and suffering more damage than the rest of Europe and the UK together, recovered twice as fast as Britain and quickly grew into the biggest economy in Europe. The victors in the British Isles suffered their lesser losses the longest.

When I visited Detroit in America many years later I was reminded of the question: "Why does a booming Detroit of 1945 look in the 21st century like it has been bombed ... and a bombed-out Berlin of 1945 is now booming?"

It's not about miracles. It must have something to do with care and despair; determination and depression. Whatever it is, it leaves democracy as well as dictatorships with a highly complex, paradoxical problem affecting helpless humans as well as ideological economic issues.

MINOR MIRACLE IN ANTWERP
A drop of cheer-up

When I finally reached Antwerp, I spent my last coin on another cup of ersatz coffee. It left nothing in my pockets except my passport and a return portion of a cross-Channel ferry ticket. Sitting outside a dismal dockside café in the early-morning drizzle, I tried to work out how I could get from Harwich to London, and find lodgings.

The least I needed was a coin to open a luggage storage locker in Central London, so that I might grab the bag containing all my other possessions, and scour the city on foot. Food and lodging – or just a sandwich in the next two days – would be a bonus. As I pondered, the café owner came out and, before I could stop him, poured a large tot of brandy into my half-empty coffee cup.

"No problem. No problem. You look too sad. This cheer-up is free."

The sun came out in Amsterdam. The problem vanished. I crossed the Channel and hitchhiked to London; and, without claiming my luggage, walked several miles to a place where I'd once stayed; found within days a very temporary job, and set out again to find work in Fleet Street.

SERIOUS UNEMPLOYMENT IN LONDON
Immigrants emigrating?

It may have been during this stint of mine in London that Giles – Britain's best cartoonist at the time, illustrated the current economic crisis with a drawing of two dark figures with rolled-up trouser-legs tip-toeing into the sea off Brighton, where an observant policeman tells another watching copper: "The economy's so bad, even the *illegal* Pakis are leaving."

Nevertheless, I persevered in my search for a Fleet Street post (without mentioning my age) and for my efforts received but one response. It came from a small Australian news service which recognised my colonial problem and responded lugubriously with:

"There are only two of us here ... if one of us dies suddenly, the other may be in touch with you."

After retreating to the *Kentish Times* (where local correspondents could make more money and achieve more space in the Fleet Street papers than many of their fulltime staff) I felt it time to go home to South Africa, where life was real and life under apartheid was earnest. ☐

4

(Source: Greg Marinovich).

From our correspondent.

1950 – 1990

24.
Romance, legionnaires and some tall tails.

When rows of corpses in cupboards become a routine experience, they very soon lose any capacity for pity, horror, sympathy, repugnance or tragic despair. Except the undiminishing despair of being forced to hear the same joke in the morgue every Monday.

Durban reminds me of true-life murder dramas; of broader human tragedies, and of some of the happiest days of my life ... the life of a "roving" general reporter. The best job in the business; each day choosing the story one wishes to cover.

Late in 1951, as winter fell on London, I returned from Britain to Natal on the warm Indian Ocean shoreline, to join the province's *Daily News*, as a junior general reporter. It is an afternoon paper, once in the Argus Company chain. It was more cosmopolitan and less "colonial" than the independent, family-owned morning *Natal Mercury* of those days. Each assignment, for me as a stranger in town, was an adventure.

Tails and Tales

Two early experiences included gingerly touching the tails and the hidden tales of other new arrivals in the city.

The tails belonged to seven or eight of the largest African pythons so far captured for the Fitzsimmons Snake Park. They had been caught

First known picture of a Python Nataliensis, one of the biggest snakes in the world, painted in 1840 by explorer scientist Sir Andrew Smith, father of South African geology. His snake appears to be digesting its dinner. When a python is slim and hungry, it might be persuaded to lie with its full length stretching in your bedroom from door to window, ensuring privacy if not security. [See following caption.]

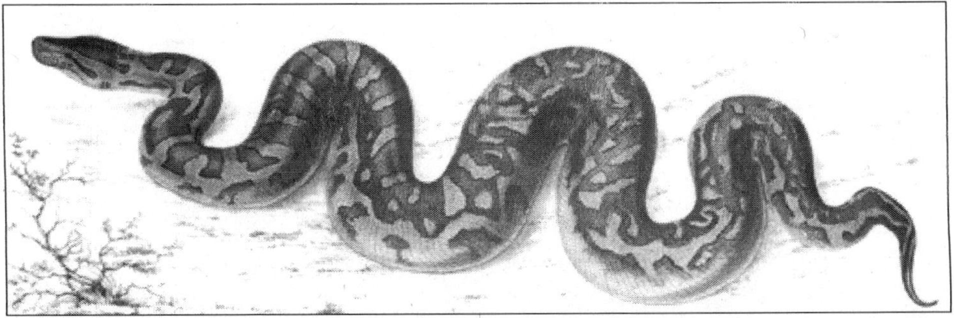

in Pongola in northern Natal where cane rats provided food for huge entanglements of snakes.

The African Rock Python is one of the biggest snakes on Earth and I was holding one as thick as a rugby forward's thigh, and the length of three people if laid end-to-end for its dinner. Instead, three people were needed to hold it down for measuring. As the reluctant third, I nevertheless moved fast ... to grab the tail-end.

Diana Dors, forerunner of Marilyn Monroe as the world's cinematic "sex symbol". If she had filled your bedroom, it would not have ensured either privacy or safety.

The second newsworthy visitor was Diana Dors, a famously voluptuous blonde film star, whom my cameraman colleague, Laurie Bloomfield, and I were called upon to photograph and interview.

I learned nothing from Miss Dors, and was not required to hold her down so that we could measure her. But Laurie, while looking around her room for something to photograph, discovered one of her stunning sequined dresses. He found two built-in *wooden* platforms in its bra.

This hard, titillating news about a world famous film star was never published. It was the kind of private, unwritten, and secret knowledge we privileged newsmen were exclusively privy to. Today, her excessive boobs and their timber support and dress design would make the front page.

Of course there was much to be done in reporting courts and crime.

This involved mysterious murders and unspeakable tragedy, as well as a daily call at the mortuary where the friendly sergeant used to greet us on Mondays with "Check for yourself what's come in. I've a helluva headache. Kicked by a horse. A White Horse (whisky)," he'd laugh.

No one would have thought, in those days, that he might have needed counselling about his job. For him, and for us, that would indeed have been a laughing matter. When rows of corpses in cupboards become a routine experience, they very soon lose any capacity for pity, horror, sympathy, repugnance or tragic despair. Except the undiminishing despair of being forced to hear the same joke every Monday.

However, if you could wangle yourself the "off-Diary" job of

Roving Reporter by promising to bring in a news story every day, then there was a vast oyster bed of stuff out there – especially on the beach, where people were trying to drown themselves and pretty girls stood, all in a row, waiting to get their pictures in the papers.

***For instance*: the case of a "monster".**
"The monster" turned out to be a jealous lover who murdered a beautiful blonde whose missing corpse has been discovered, allegedly through "the vision" of a spiritualist, in a culvert on the Natal South Coast 100km from her home.

"Yes, of course the Crime Beat should handle it, but I can bring you a colour piece or an interview with the spiritualist, quite separate from the manhunt. Yes, I'm certain of it ...."

And so, off you'd go to join in the biggest story there is. (Though in this particular case, it was the news editor himself who left his desk to take up the chase – and over-enthusiastically jumped on the fleeing killer during a police manhunt.)

In any event, we would stay off the routine diary in search of bigger, and better news, or something that might seem unusual and interesting to our European readers; our avid Asian readers, and our few English-literate African readers whose majority favoured the Natal Zulu paper.

***For instance*: Picking the brains of the world's top specialists.**
It was great to have the space to interview at length and write "in-depth profiles" of the top brains of the world's brain surgery business, gathered from the Western world for congress in Durban.

Or learning from a smart criminal how to wire and steal a car without anyone noticing.

***For instance*: Questioning a plan to sjambok jailed prisoners.**
A smiling Minister of Justice was happy to "justify", on the record, such a plan.

***For instance*: Interviewing a parrot.**
The bird had frightened off a burglar by shouting in the dark: "Hullo! Hullo! Who's a pretty boy, then?" We needed to highlight the parrot's acumen ... by checking the rest of its vocabulary.

***For instance:* the tale of the giant headline about a horse's tail.**
Every journalist has a hundred tales arising out of his work. My most
fondly remembered story was one told by the Racing Correspondent of
the *Natal Daily News.* Some punter had shot the favourite which was
about to run in The July Handicap!

"The July" was considered in South Africa an even bigger event
in those days than any kind of Olympics or World Cup or the election of
a new prime minister. Indeed, shooting a "July" horse in the rump with
a shotgun might be considered, by the Durban public at least, to be even
more serious than assassinating the Prime Minister, depending of course
on the comparative personalities of the horse and of the PM.

Yet, at this dramatic moment in Turf history, The *Daily News*
Racing Correspondent was not to be found at home or anywhere else when
the "July Favourite" racehorse was fired on from the rear while exercising
near the beach at dawn. In the absence of "the man on the racing beat",
the news editor dispatched every reporter he could find, perhaps even the
fashion editor, to get the story of the attempted murder of a racehorse.

However, our intrepid Racing Man, Pat Aguilar, happened to have
been tipped off even before the news editor or any of his acolytes came
to work. Pat told us later: "I was first on the scene. I then rushed into the
office, but before I could open my mouth the news editor screamed at me:
'You've missed the story! Where have you been!!?'

"He didn't even notice that I was holding a fistful of written notes,
and standing there smelling of gunpowder and horseshit."

A romantic port filled with stories

Durban in the early 1950s, with its palm-fringed waters and green-
hilled hinterland, still had a faint aura of adventure. Colonial domes and
colonnades still dominated its streets. Haunting evidence still lingered
of the old Zulu kingdom, with its memories of battles and ancient forests
and wild elephant trails down to the bay.

The harbour was filled with ships, sailors, promenading
prostitutes, and passengers on exotic voyages between West and East. (In
more cynical times, it was said that Point Road, leading to the harbour
mouth and docks should be renamed Rowboat Road "because it has 'ores
down both sides".)

As one of the busier ports in those days of Suez Canal closure
and oil crises, exotic shipping news was easily found. I remember my

French Foreign Legionnaires – in full dress and living a legend.

very belated schoolboy thrill at encountering contingents of the French Foreign Legion arriving aboard a troopship on its way back to Marseilles with survivors of one of the great battles -- and defeats -- in modern Western history.

With the battle of Dien Bien Phu in French Indochina (Vietnam) in mind, I managed to talk my way aboard the visiting troopship and found myself escorted, though unofficially, to the stripped-down eating area where the Legionnaires were drinking beer. They were forbidden to land, though a number had jumped overboard and some were missing, presumed drowned. I joined a crowded table in its beer-drinking preoccupation, desperately wanting to hear about the exploits of these tough-looking crewcut men in boots, camouflage trousers, and vests.

Had any of these been among the thousand Legionnaires at the battle of Dien Bien Phu?

No answer. I couldn't tell whether this was because they might still be obeying at least one order: don't talk. Or because of our multilingual language problems. Or because none had been in that chilling battle that signalled the long-forthcoming end to Western colonialism in South East Asia.

It was many years before I found an in-depth record of the story of Dien Bien Phu, which had come to us at the time only in staccato reports and rumours of horrors and heroes and valour and sacrifice in the proportions, it seemed, of the ancient Battle of Marathon. The battle of Dien Bien Phu was described much later in a book aptly titled *Hell in a Very Small Place* by Bernard B Fall, perhaps the greatest civilian expert on the war in Vietnam. Fall wrote:

On May 7, 1954, as the last excruciatingly long battle in the drawn-out struggle for control of Indochina was at its height, a French colonel saw from a slit trench near his command post, a small white flag, probably a handkerchief, appear on top of a rifle hardly 50 feet away from him, followed by the flat-helmeted head of a Viet Minh soldier. This was final proof that the enemy had tunnelled their way under and into the heavily barricaded hilltop fortress.

"You're not going to shoot anymore?" said the Viet Minh in French.

"No, I'm not going to shoot anymore," said the colonel.

"C'est fini?" said the Viet Minh.

"Oui, c'est fini," said the colonel.

And all around them, as on some gruesome Judgement Day, soldiers, French and enemy alike, began to crawl out of their trenches and stand erect for the first time in 54 days and nights, as firing ceased everywhere.

The defenders had spent nearly two sleepless months in a tiny underground hell on an exposed hilltop. Enemy casualties around this small hill had reached *twenty-five thousand* as Chinese and Vietnamese troops pressed forward from all sides. They crushed the above-ground battlefield to the size of a soccer field. The sudden silence at the moment of French surrender seemed deafening. In vain, 82926 French parachutes had been dropped to supply the defending fortress. The forlorn 'chutes covered the area like freshly fallen snow. Or like thousands of burial shrouds.

General Vo Nguyen Giap had taken Dien Bien Phu by an extremely efficient mixture of 19th-century siege techniques (sinking TNT-laden mineshafts under French bunkers, for example) and modern artillery patterns plus human-wave attacks. He had pounded the French-held hilltop with 200 artillery pieces and a new weapon, supplied during the last week of the siege: Russian Katyusha multiple rocket launchers.

The critical battle in the valley of Dien Bien Phu was over. Close to 10 000 captured troops were to begin the grim death march to the Viet Minh prison camps 300 miles to the east. Few would survive. About 2 000 lay dead on the battlefield in graves left unmarked to this day. Only 73 made good their escape. Ultimately, 90 percent of the entire garrison – ten thousand men – had sacrificed their lives, in defeat, for France.

None of those veteran French Foreign Legionnaires who refused to answer my questions in their returning troopship in Durban harbour would forget those days ... whether they were in that famous battle or some other bloody fight in Vietnam. They would see themselves, instead, as the last of the lost legendary and romantic Foreign Legion. Only the Americans seemed to forget the lessons that the Legionnaires had learnt in South East Asia.

Into the drink in a Russian ship

A second strange and exotic encounter I had with a ship involved a Russian freighter, arriving unbidden in Durban docks during the taut, early days of the global Cold War.

South African Security Police lurked in their cars when I and the *Mercury* shipping correspondent – ignoring the police surveillance – talked our way onto the small cargo vessel. We were conducted immediately to the captain's cabin, and left there for seeming hours. Suddenly the surprisingly small cabin was filled with the captain and two officers.

"Right," said the captain, thrusting aside a pile of harbour and ship's papers. "All 'pepers' and t'ings finished. Now we trink toast."

The vodka appeared like magic. Before we could ask a question we were into the second toast:

"Your country!" he said as we downed the white lightning "... and now to mine!" he added as we drank another. Then followed a toast to "your wives". And another to "the officers' wives".

I forget what the next toast was for, but another bottle of vodka was on the table. My colleague from the *Mercury*, Steve Harper, was normally a passive teetotaller. When the ship's captain had a brainwave and proposed the toast of the first son of the first officer (who we learned had four other amazing children), Steve in mumbled politeness opted out.

I think I managed slightly slurred sips for most of the children, but in the end we newsmen acknowledged defeat and were helped down the gangplank by two crewmen ... with no answer to any of our questions about the reason for the mysterious visit of a suspicious Russian cargo ship.

The Special Branch police ("Secret Police" we usually called them) were still waiting on the dockside.

"What's going on? What did you learn?" they asked.

"I learned that the chief offisher has five children," I told them. "The resht you can learn from reading our newspapers."

The end of this story varies due to the long waiting in a foreign ship's cabin; the ingestion of atmosphere, domestic information and other substances; the lack of notes and failure of our joint efforts in interrogation. But I do remember that I persuaded Steve not to get into his car in sight of the non-intelligent agents, and I think we went back to our newspapers in a taxi, much wiser and determined never to touch ship's vodka again unless we felt forced to do so in pursuit of knowledge.

Stolen Gold in the Hold

Another great dockside story broke when tons of stolen gold were discovered, hidden below deck in the sedate Union Castle mailship, no less, as it was about to sail for Europe. The news editor himself rushed aboard to confirm the scoop he'd extracted from his carefully cultivated harbour HQ contacts. The gold was worth millions, making it "the greatest attempted theft ever".

Murder on the Union Castle ship

But the most lucrative ship that I personally encountered was another regular mailship to Britain from which an errant blonde had been thrown overboard by the crew into Durban Bay.

The resulting murder inquiry provided a colleague and me with columns of good copy to sell to Fleet Street, especially to the old, still nearly respectable British *News of the World* in that era when that Sunday paper focused almost entirely on straight court reports for its salacious true romances and scandals. (The long established *News of the World* was known to millions then as the Prostitutes' or Scoutmasters' Gazette, and served an important social as well as a harmlessly salacious interest in its precisely accurate, explicit but subdued, column-length court reports, often naming and shaming abusers of women or children.)

Union Castle mail ship entering Durban Harbour.

In this case, the court was told that members of the British ship's crew had smuggled a drunk prostitute on board, but when she became too unruly, they first pushed the woman into a sleeping officer's cabin, and when she unexpectedly re-appeared, they tried to keep her quiet and at the same time take her up on deck where she "disappeared".

Did she fall or was she pushed?

That was the perennial legal enigma.

I wasn't sufficiently interested then to remember the answer now. But I do remember a marvellous quote from the sleeping ship's officer.

"It was after midnight," he told the court. "I was awakened by a noise and opened my eyes to see a naked lady sitting next to my bed, smoking and making some attempt to sing."

It sounded like the caption to a cartoon drawn by James Thurber.

But our jobs weren't all play and no work. There was an occasion once, when I and two of my colleagues nearly worked ourselves to death in the unexplored reaches of Durban Bay. This is how I remember it:

Misled by the Moon

At mid-20th-century, Durban Bay offered space for romantic, elegant flying boats, splashing down more smoothly than pelicans, after flights down the Nile and stopovers on the lakes of Africa's Great Rift Valley. A final destination for these large, graceful aircraft was the bay, where they "landed" against a backdrop of still unspoilt mangrove swamps and islands and beaches, and yachts nestled in their inner harbour safely protected from the Indian Ocean.

Durban Bay looked so beautiful from the palm-fringed Esplanade that three of us decided to take our girlfriends (our future wives) on a romantic moonlit picnic on one of the remaining uninhabited and unvisited islets. The three were Rex Gibson, in later years editor of the *Sunday Express,* then *Rand Daily Mail* newspapers which brought down a Prime Minister; Laurie Bloomfield whose photographs of the Cato Manor Zulu uprising went round the world and became an icon of "Oppression", used globally for three decades, and me.

We callow suitors set off from the yacht basin in a hired rowboat on the flood tide, late in the afternoon. It was a hard pull for the three men, interrupted only by constant complaints about the other two not rowing in unison, not rowing hard enough; or splashing us, instead of the girls, with our ill-timed oar-strokes. Yet we managed to row in a roughly straight line across the widest stretch of the bay and into the mangrove swamps to the islet of our last-minute choice.

We were forced to beach quite far from shore, but apart from repeated remarks about the mud and having to clamber over thick mangrove roots in the water, no one complained, much. We settled in a sheltered patch of damp sea-grass, hidden from the lights of the city and its moored ships; watching the great face of the moon ascending. It was only as we broached our beer and clinked our champagne glasses, that the girls started to complain loudly.

"There's a tick on me," said one.

"There are two ticks on me. Look at my leg!" said another.

We examined her leg in the moonlight, grabbed more beer, and poured soothing wine. Then I began to think of the pepper-ticks "back on the farm". They sprinkle themselves all over you, countless numbers, each one the size of a grain of pepper. They dig into your flesh and hide under your skin, especially in your crotch or any warm crevice, and drive you mad with itching. One of the only known reliefs, it is said, is to fill their burrows in your flesh with petrol and set them alight.

In three ticks we were all suddenly standing up.

Then one of the girls screamed.

When our feet came back to grass-level we could see she was pointing at the shoreline a few yards away. Gradually we discerned in the moonlight crabs on newly-exposed sand, crawling towards us with their claws held skywards, gleaming in the bright moonlight. They were looking friendly and waving their claws as if in welcome. But the girls didn't think so. They insisted that we immediately carry everything – including them – through the crabs and back to the boat.

Given no time to remonstrate, we carried out their unreasonable wishes with a remarkable show of male efficiency. But once safely deposited in the boat, our slightly agitated partners were forced to get out again. We stared in astonishment at newly exposed sand which seemed in the moonlight to stretch as far as we could see in every direction. We shipped the oars and pulled and dragged the boat until we at last reached distant, ankle-deep water. Then we pushed the unloaded boat, trying to make it skim, while the girls splashed behind; their feet only momentarily touching the sand below. We gallant rescuers managed to clamber aboard only twice – to row across the deep shipping lanes of the bay and to float, exhausted, into the yacht basin.

Next day we tried to get half our money back on the hired rowboat, on the grounds that it was grounded for nearly all of its return voyage.

"Surely you checked the tide tables before you went? Even if you didn't, you must have known it was spring tide. Didn't you notice the moon's tidal message?"

Trades people appear to know little about moonlit romance.

But it wasn't the first time that good men and true had found themselves beached in Durban Bay. For instance, on 23 May 1842, only 110 years before our mishap, Captain Thomas Smith of the 27th Regiment Royal Artillery, stationed in the fort made of sods near The Point, mounted a night attack on the Boer laager further down the lagoon at Congella. (The Voortrekkers, under Andries Pretorius, had recently defeated Dingane's massed Zulu regiments at Blood River, and believed they now owned the place.)

"But with extraordinary stupidity, Captain Tom Smith hadn't considered the tides or the state of the moon, which was full, and his troops were caught on a bare beach in bright moonlight."[1]

And back in 1854, when the Brits built their Durban Club on the bay side, they too misjudged the tidal rules. They were too busy creating civilisation by declaring their club rules of precedence and club procedure and exclusive upper-white membership. History records that they planned to create a golf course within the bay, and to play only when the tide was out. How stupid could they get? Sanity returned decades later when they built their golf course in the marshy flatlands where horses were raced.

Today they can play golf inside the racetrack while tens of thousands of madly cheering punters are urging on the winner of the July Handicap. The original problem in the 1850s was that the place which was to become Royal Durban Golf Club was riddled with cursed ticks.[2]

The lesson we learned from all this is: Before you embark on anything, study its history. □

1. *The Zulu Kings* by Penny Howcroft. ISBN 978-0-620-48405-1.

2. *Senior Moments, The Story of Seniors' Golf in South Africa* by Talbot Cox.
   ISBN 978-0-620-454117.

25.
Murder and hangings.

Twenty-three of them,
all condemned on the same day.
And all executed on 21 March the following year ...
Nuremberg could have had nothing on this scale,
not even with the spectre and spectacle of Von
Ribbentrop twitching and turning on the rope for more
than a quarter of an hour as a result of
the incompetence of the Executioner ....

Chris Marnewick, in his book *Shepherds and Butchers*.[1]

n the "Dragon Mountains" above KwaZulu, I encountered two cases of violence in the mid-20th century that for the first time altered my comfortable views of the norms of social behaviour.

The horrors committed there by disparate interests brought home the enormity of the ignorance, and the depths of the divisions that cause so much misunderstanding between South Africa's gloriously different cultures.

The first event involved a peace-loving, strictly moral Indian family living down on the coast near Stanger, a place where Mahatma Gandhi once stayed, where he was revered, and where his gentle ideas are appreciated. It was a place of rural peace and calm in the mid-1950s.

None of us could believe, therefore, the report we received from a local correspondent in that area one morning. A team was rushed to the scene, only an hour's drive from Durban. I was in no way involved in reporting the tragedy, for I was regrettably promoted to political and parliamentary correspondent for the *Daily News* and *Sunday Tribune* and the details of an extraordinary death scene in rural Natal escape me … yet the image of it has been etched deeply in my mind for nearly sixty years.

The news team returned with photos confirming the report – but they brought back no explanations. The photos were of five young girls (perhaps there were more! But my memory fails to visualise it). Five slim, pretty sisters, aged from pre-teen to about 19 years, swaying in the morning breeze from ropes around their necks and tied to branches in a tree. All were clothed in what appeared to be similar nightdresses reaching to their ankles which floated on the air. All of them newly dead, with necks awry, where nooses on five different rope lengths suspended them above the ground. The image of children's corpses, swaying in the wind, was beyond any words of anger, sorrow, shock or – for us in the white community – any explanation.

The reporting team had been asked not to interview the parents or the extended family, and the shocked journalists, like others who witnessed the scene, had no wish to contest that request. The police seemed equally bewildered, but came to the conclusion it was a mass suicide. There had been several inexplicable suicides of young innocents in the same community in recent times.

Among the questions for which nobody seemed to have answers were: What was the Indian maidens' motivation? Did the eldest help the others to die before committing suicide herself? Why was the youngest included in so grim a ritual of death? Did they jump simultaneously? Why did any one of them wish to die, unless prompted by some fanatical elder? Why? Why? Why?

The tragic deaths were followed by a joint inquest, at a time when I was in faraway Cape Town. A finding of "suicide" was recorded, but I heard of no adequate explanation. Perhaps, I thought, if there had been Indian women reporters; or Indian women police officers and Indian magistrates in that era; perhaps if the entire community of various races and ethnic groups had cared enough for each other, the mystery, and the great emotional – and cultural – barriers might have been penetrated. Instead, the Indian community's view turned inward and the rest of the public gaze quickly moved to more mundane topics such as gunshot and assegai murders.

Police patrol hunted down and speared to death

My phone rang late at night on 21 February 1956 in my semi-rural home in New Germany near Durban. I'd had an hour's sleep, so this was going to be a long night for an afternoon newspaper reporter. The news editor said he'd had a tip-off about raids in the Drakensberg mountains – a police raid and a Zulu impi counter-raid, and it was said a battle on the slopes of the Great Escarpment, in which there were a number of deaths.

"A driver is fetching a photographer and will pick you up in thirty minutes. Get to Bergville as fast as you can."

It was a tough, winding drive in those days; even on the national road that wound along the crinkled edge of the Valley of a Thousand Hills and took us, hours later, to a turnoff to the mountains. At dawn, in the rain, we reached the then picturesque little village of Bergville and went to the police station to establish the basic facts. The men on duty were mainly in the dark – literally, for it was before dawn. They had no confirmed information, but they'd heard that "a whole lot of policemen have been hunted down, one by one, high in the mountains, and murdered by Zulu tribesmen".

How many dead? They had no official figures, they said.

We searched for the local mortuary. There wasn't one, but we found a room, cleared of furniture, with covered bodies lying on the floorboards. Only their feet stuck out from beneath their shrouds. I counted ten muddy boots, while studying the scene very carefully. Just to be sure, I counted the boots three times. ("It is said" of journalists that they have *three* failings. "One is they can't, extemporaniously *(sic)*, spell. And they can't count.")

We had no other information, certainly no official permission to be there, let alone the right to examine the wounds. I checked the notes on the labels attached to boots. No full names or ages were listed. Our confirmed facts at this stage were: Five men dead. Two white sergeants and three black constables. The only survivor would be one white constable. I telephoned the little information I had to the news editor on his instructions "always to keep in touch". It was before dawn, so the inadequate phone-lines were not busy and he could not, at that inconclusive hour, have much to say.

Dawn broke as we drove as fast as possible for an hour through mud and slush up a mountain track to the farm nearest the scene beneath the looming Drakensberg. The farmer, Carl Zunckel, and his wife were outside their front-garden gate. So were a couple of senior police and a few silently watching Zulu men and women. In the homestead was a farm telephone which was working. A blessing, I incorrectly assumed, for it suggested that we would be able to relay our stories before deadline and seek information from senior police and other sources if we could identify them. The farm phone was ringing its communal, farm-line "Zunckel tone" as our vehicle, covered in mud, braked to a standstill outside the homestead.

"It's for you," said the farmer before we had time to introduce ourselves.

On the party line was our news editor!

"What's the story?" he asked.

"Ronnie, we arrived forty seconds ago. It's still eight hours to first deadline and ..."

"Phone back as soon as you have some facts," he said. The call itself would take an hour to get through from so remote an outpost at the far edge of a thin web of shared party lines.

Despite the automatic ban on journalists, and on witnesses, and a police instruction that we could speak only to the highest police authority, I somehow managed to get the facts by keeping a low profile and talking quietly with everyone willing to have a conversation. The most relevant information was that the one policeman, who had escaped with wounds, was already in hospital some 50 miles away. He would be the "I-was-there" witness, if I could get around stifling police regulations.

Meanwhile, after collecting and dispatching all the local and official information and phoning it through before first deadline, I persuaded one of the Zulus in the farmyard to take me closer to Chief Mdungunga Hlongwane's kraal to talk to some tribesmen. They were frightened, and angry. And they were voluble.

But though the tribe's case was simple, it took a long time to be articulated. They trusted nobody now. The facts emerged finally in this form:

The tribesmen were on their own land, farming their own crops when the police came ... not for the first time. The police destroyed their crops, systematically, over a few days. It was outrageous, tribesmen felt. Beyond reason. The tribe, who once lived (more than a hundred years previously) on all the land now occupied by white farmers, had been pushed off the fertile soil and forced to live in the mountains where cattle could not thrive and few crops would grow. They had managed to survive. But then the police came ... not for the first-time ... and destroyed their only livelihood. An impi of about 40 fighting sticks went out to stop the police destroyers, who used guns.

That was one side of the story. I would have the official version soon enough, concerning drug-running and armed criminal gangs and the rest.

The Zulu marijuana farmers – "dagga" suppliers in South African parlance – said they could no longer bear "persecution". They were defending themselves and their crops. They said that not to do so would mean slow death in any case. So the tribe had risen up. The impi, about half of them with the family name of Mdluli or Hlongwane, armed with sticks, spears, stones, and a panga or two, had gone in search of six rifle-armed police. The policemen, hard at work, were scattered over the vast mountainside. Each ran for cover. All, except one, were hunted down. They were dealt with in "the traditional way" of tribal war. (Faction fights among Zulu impis were a regular occurrence in those days. Almost as

'FRONT PAGE LEAD' on the second successive day of reporting on the murders in the highest, furthest away mountains of South Africa.

common as top rugby matches in Durban today. So prevalent were the "Sunday stick fights" that when stories filtered down to the towns that two or ten – sometimes even 12 or 20 – young, unidentified men had been injured or killed, the information merited only sporadic paragraphs in the urban press.)

A Zulu impi attack on a police patrol was, however, no traditional ritual. It was not even what news copy tasters might call "a normal mass murder". It was an obvious front-page lead; an international news story, and much more than that. But it unfolded in the normal way of all news dramas.

By the time I had painstakingly filed my report over a constantly interrupted country telephone line, other journalists and some of the foreign press corps were beginning to arrive from far away Johannesburg and Pretoria as well as Durban. Soon a South African Press Association correspondent and seven other journalists were trying to use Mr Carl Zunckel's farmline. I decided to move on.

By retiring to the sleepy village in the foothills below, I was able to get a second scoop (*ugh*) by striding into the local hospital and insisting on seeing Theunis Kruger. This was the name of the broad-shouldered, athletic, 23-year-old Constable Kruger, the lone survivor of the

Drakensberg massacre. Now, despite all police and hospital "regulations", he welcomed my therapeutic invitation to tell his story – in Afrikaans. Here is a shortened version of what filled front pages across the country the next day:

For three hours I was running, jumping and even crawling to get away from the shouting tribesmen close behind me. For six hours I lay doubled up in a hole beneath a waterfall ... praying ... sometimes crying ... I could not think clearly. Horror, yes, terror, jumbled up my thoughts.

Years later I was still trying to "feel" the horror and fear in a man's mind as he lies terrified in a hole behind a veil of water on a cruel mountain; the only survivor, waiting for the assegai group hunting him down.

Trite clichés hardly touch it. He continued his story in his home language:

My real, living nightmare began at 2pm when we had finished the dagga raid, dried our rain-soaked clothes in front of a fire, and were walking back towards camp. We were in the valley when suddenly about 40 tribesmen streamed down the mountain towards us.

They were chanting, and shouting: "Wah! Wah! Waa!" like that.

When they were about 20 yards from us, two native constables turned and ran.

Knobkerries came flying through the air and the two constables went down ....

We raised our hands above our heads and Sergeant de Lange spoke to the impi in Zulu. The tribesmen never even checked their stride. The three of us white men stood with our backs against an eight-foot bank, our revolvers drawn. The tribesmen were in a half-circle around us. Moments later our men were being battered. I think it was at this moment I fired a shot.

I saw one raise his knobkerrie and I fired. The kerrie crashed into my face and both the attacker and I fell to the ground. I think I killed him. Sergeant de Lange and Sergeant Koorts never even had time to shoot.

As I fell I rolled away, jumped to my feet and dashed up a less steep part of the river bank. I heard shouts, looked back and saw nothing but tribesmen raining blows.

Suddenly a panting black police constable appeared beside me, and about 20 shouting tribesmen on the left and right of us came over the bank and chased us. I asked the constable what they were shouting. The constable just kept saying: "Hulle kom. Hulle kom." ("They're coming. They're coming.")

We reached a mealie field, where one of my shoes came off in the ploughed soil. After a few moments I threw away the other shoe and ran in my socks. By now I was stumbling, falling, sometimes crawling along.

The constable and I reached a hilltop. We saw two tribesmen running along the ridge trying to cut us off. There was a cluster of trees in the kloof (ravine) below, and I made for these. I plunged down into the thick, tangled bush in the kloof. The native constable – I do not know who he was – ran off. I do not know what happened to him. [The African policeman was bludgeoned and stabbed to death.]

I heard water falling, crawled towards it and then spied a hole gouged out by past floods, behind a curtain of falling water. The waterfall was only about four feet high. I waded shin-deep into the water and squeezed into the hole.

Minutes later I heard tribesmen talking just above me. I do not know what they said, but suddenly boulders crashed over the waterfall. Then there was silence. I lay absolutely still. Ten minutes later, more talking, and more boulders. Then silence again.

For the next six hours I lay there, moving only inches to ease my legs. My eye, damaged by the knobkerrie, began to bleed.

After dark, I crept out of the hole and waded about 200 yards down the stream. There I climbed under a rock and fell asleep.

I woke up about an hour later. I crept towards a ridge, peered around to make sure no one was there, then went on to the next ridge where I did the same thing. I was going along in this way when suddenly I saw the lights of a car over one ridge. I thought it was Zulus looking for dagga, for I heard Zulus talking.

Later I learned this was a police van. When the car disappeared, I ran towards the camp about three miles away ….

Constable Kruger's doctors stated that he was suffering from a fractured cheekbone and bruises. He was suffering more from emotional shock than physical injury.

THIS WAS NOT THE END of the story of "murder and drug busts in the Drakensberg". The violent deaths of five policemen, each cut off from his unit and hunted down and massacred by "drug peddlers" with sticks, stones, and assegais ... the persecution of innocent tribesmen and the cruel destruction of their crops ... these were merely two opposite quarters that opened the drama.

There is more, which provides the reason for describing at length the incident more than half a century later.

On the one hand, drug-smuggling from this remote region was a constant, national problem. Some idea of the magnitude of this traffic is revealed by the quantity of dagga confiscated and destroyed by the police during the previous two years, namely, 2515563 lbs and 2757965 lbs respectively [each well over a million kilograms].

The deputy commissioner of police in Pietermaritzburg reported:

The police dagga squad recovered, in the Bergville area, nine tons of dagga from twenty-nine fields. This resulted in wholesale destruction of further dagga by the local African inhabitants to avoid trouble. The police were doing their best to eradicate it. On this occasion, it necessitated burning vast quantities of illegally grown dagga and a search for smugglers.

The search sparked a battle and a massacre of police. The massacre led to a manhunt, using helicopters, police in long lines combing the mountain sides, and sniffer dogs rooting in the dark ravines, the dongas and bushes. Most of the male members of the tribe, or more accurately, the clan, were detained. About 40 of them were questioned. More than 20 men were arrested, taken away in manacles, and charged with murder.

Twenty-five men hanged on one day

On judgement day, 23 men were found guilty of killing five policemen in the *dagga* (cannabis) raid in the district of Bergville. There was an appeal in which one of the accused was acquitted. The other 22 – plus three other men sentenced to death on other unrelated cases – were hanged on

21 March 1957. It was short justice. And by any standard, it was brutal.

Three years later, the same date, 21 March, entered world history when police – some say through fear – shot and killed 69 people at Sharpeville where thousands of people were attempting to hand back their compulsory passes as a protest against their harassment and restriction of movement.

But let us not confuse or conflate these historical dates. The Bergville murders carried elements of brutality, pathos, and injustice all of their own. So stark and tragic were they that I thought I might follow it to its roots and write a book on the subject, but abandoned the idea when others, much closer to the tribesmen, though, it transpired, with political motives, announced such intentions. Soon there were songs, and scripts. Yet it was not until nearly 40 years later that I came upon any actual portrayal of the event – when Duma Ndlovu produced a theatre drama, under the title "Bergville Stories".

"My aunt had told me about the incident, and it has stayed in my mind and haunted me ever since," says Ndlovu. "I just could not fathom how a civilised government could hang an entire community in one morning."

A current website describes Ndlovu's play, written more than 40years after the incident:

"Prisoners re-enact the day in 1956 when 23 (sic) Zulu men were hanged in a Pretoria prison for the slayings of five South African policemen. At the scene's climax, each of the actors steps into the spotlight at centre stage of the John Jay College Theatre (in America) to meet death. Their arms outstretched, they shout greetings to their ancestors; one emits a muffled shriek. And the final quartet performs a high-stepping warrior dance in defiance of the hangman.

"The Sowetans, unhappy about the presence of these interlopers from Bergville in Zululand, who are in essence their competitors for the few menial jobs available, surround the hostel, spoiling for a fight.

"Inside the hostel, the confined labourers, played by actors so exuberant they seem to have been propelled onstage by giant slingshots, pass the days and weeks reminiscing about when their lives had a natural order, before poverty compelled them into the Diaspora. They share the story of the 1956 hangings, a cataclysmic event from Zulu history that becomes, in the telling, a tableau of all the injustices inflicted on them by the outside world."

I was unable to see or trace Duma Ndlovu's play, but I trust it was better than the lengthy American review.

The case remained filled to the brim with suspicions, prejudices and injustices. It deserved accurate recall and replacing on the record by someone from a much younger generation than mine. I was soon reporting on Parliament, and unable to attend the "Drakensberg Dagga Murders" trial, but its story still haunts me and perhaps a million others.

Indeed the story of the Bergville dagga murders is ongoing. People are murdered in that area at a rate per population probably higher than anywhere else in the world except in Mexico and South America's "drug triangle". The local courts deal constantly with dagga smuggling cases, gang violence, and many murders, including those of innocent local farmers, black and white.

On the day of the murders back in February 1956, Captain P Dillon summed up that case: "Six policemen were on a routine 'dagga patrol'. They must have stumbled on more dagga than any policeman has ever seen before. We've confiscated a whole storeroom-full, but we'll now send in men to burn the dagga fields. It would take a convoy of lorries to carry the stuff out."

History keeps repeating itself in the mist-shrouded ravines of the Dragon Mountains. Great and small dagga tragedies have re-occurred every year for more than half a century since the drama I've just described. Here is a report that hardly made news outside of the circulation of the *The Witness* in Pietermaritzburg, Natal, in March 2008, which was 14 years after South Africa boasted full democracy with justice for all:

Five more Bergville murders

More weapons, livestock, a stolen vehicle, and bags of dagga were recovered in Bergville, following the boundary dispute that has led to the murders of five people in the area.

Police spokesman Senior Superintendent Jay Naicker said that police launched an operation to disarm the local people:

It became clear that it was important to disarm groups running amok in the area to ensure peace and stability and a climate suitable for negotiation. By yesterday, police officials had recovered a total of 35 firearms and arrested 21 suspects for various offences. The recovered firearms were four AK-47 rifles, one shotgun, three .303 rifles, one .22 rifle, nine 38 revolvers and 18 .9mm pistols. Four

By outlawing cannabis the apartheid government fostered a thriving underworld (photo DRUM Magazine).

suspects were charged with murder and 19 were charged for being in possession of unlicensed firearms. All suspects were expected to appear in court yesterday.

Three helicopters were used to deploy police officials to these areas. More arrests and recoveries are expected as the operation continues.

And the truth is ...

The truth of the matter is ... what?

The truth is that the justice system failed horribly in the "Dagga Murders", as it did under a number of political appointments to the Bench throughout the apartheid era. For instance, I was found guilty – after my retirement – for having published this criticism of racism on the Bench concerning a specific judge in a quite different context.

But I believe it to be true, and that the dagga trial also failed abysmally to take into account the circumstances, the way-of-life, traditions, and the culture of the tribesmen – and sent all of the accused to death in an inordinate hurry.

The truth is also that tribesmen, far from being poor as well as "dispossessed" were – and still are – farming one of the richest crops on the planet ... so rich that it has corrupted many people in the local area and spawned city gangs of extreme violence and with international connections.

The truth is that the herb, once an African traditional medicine (in a true sense of the word medicine) has become a costly, potent drug for users in all cultures and communities in the country – through being declared illegal nearly 100 years ago. Some say that "Justice" (meaning Parliament), in deciding what is legal, and what is not, has failed in this matter too. The execution, in a single day after an unusually brief murder trial, of 22 farmers who grew dagga illegally in the remote kloofs of southern Africa's highest mountains, is likely to be remembered by Zulus as a "cruel injustice" for generations to come.

The truth is that the "hanging until dead" of these 22 men (plus three other condemned prisoners), on the same day in Pretoria's "Maximum Prison" was the biggest mass execution in the 86-year history of the South African capital punishment system.

However, death by hanging occurred on an increasing annual scale for the next quarter century, and in 1987 it reached its highest rate: 163 condemned to death in a single year.

Three shivering people were conducted or half-carried – each by two young, strained, and shaken prison warders – up the gallows' steep stairs every week. Each condemned person was supported as he or she wailed or collapsed on the waiting gallows' trapdoor. Then each bound body was left swinging and kicking; bleeding and soiling the dark pit below.

You need to read Chris Marnewick's chilling, brilliant book[1] to gain an inkling of how brutal modern institutional hanging has been, as men and women were shepherded up the 54 steps to the gallows and dropped, bound and blindfolded, writhing on the rope. The author, who lived through apartheid in an Afrikaans community, and as a lawyer taught litigation here and abroad, describes in cold legal terms the act of killing seven shrouded prisoners at a time, and the psychological effects it has on the community involved in carrying out such justice.

Only once in 400 pages does the author allow emotional comment to explode. He allows a Senior Counsel to say:

... Twenty-three of them, all condemned by Judge Kennedy in Pietermaritzburg on the same day, 9th August 1956. And all executed on 21 March the following year – all except Mandlakayise Nzimande, whose appeal succeeded and who was released four months later on 3 August 1957.

I tried to imagine the scene. The place must have been like an abattoir. The logistical arrangements must have approached those of a small military operation. If, for seven "condemned", the chapel was considered crammed I couldn't see how twenty-two coffins and all the relatives, two per prisoner, could have fitted into the chapel for the traditional funeral service.

Nuremberg could have had nothing on this scale, not even with the spectre and spectacle of Von Ribbentrop twitching and turning on the rope for more than a quarter of an hour as a result of the incompetence of the Executioner.

So ended an episode of murder and justice's revenge; a South African tragedy which I still believe was as socially and politically significant as Sharpeville or Soweto '76. Yet few today remember that doubly tragic and doubly brutal event.

The multiple hangings in Pretoria's jail in the 1950s, were a curse that affected the jailers as well as the families of the men who were hanged while gagged on the gallows, kicking on the scaffolds until dead. This South African experience of the death sentence (still sanctioned in several parts of the world) became the subject of a film released to the world in 2016.

The worst mass hanging in South African history was described by Chris Marnovich in his book Shepherds & Butchers. The scene is accurately depicted in the dramatic film of the same name.

Shepherds and Butchers is a powerful, devastating story – not about police and dagga murders, but about ordinary, decent, lowly educated folk who find employment as prison warders. They come in all forms, from bullies to snitches, but the more conscientious, vulnerable youngsters, it seems, used to get the least wanted jobs: shepherding condemned prisoners from their cells to their deaths.

At Pretoria Central Maximum Prison the young warders, without training or advice, before or after, would report before dawn at the condemned cells to escort – and often provide physical support – to trembling or struggling prisoners all the way up those narrow flights of stairs to the gallows platform; blindfold the victims ... then watch them drop, kicking wildly as they soiled the chasm below them during their death pangs.

Chris Marnewick, a lawyer who practised among the communities from which prison warders were drawn, took the infinite trouble required to visit the scene at "Pretoria Central Max" and wrote a novel drawn precisely from life.

He and I discussed the details of his "fiction" – including the greatest mass-hanging in the South African nation's history, when those 22 tribesmen guilty of killing six policemen in the Drakensberg dagga murders tragedy were joined by one other prisoner in the condemned cells, and all 23 hanged on a single day.

Shepherds and Butchers does not reach into this excess. The "normality" of judiciously killing, three times a week, a young or middle-aged man (sometimes a woman) was more than enough to cope with in any precise telling. Even the drama of a murder crime begins to fade in the face of the killer's cold blooded, long anticipated, judicious strangling on a rope.

How then did such capital punishment affect the young men who witnessed it? How did they cope with going home in the evening to their own wives and children and bedtime stories?

The author visualises one such warder losing control and going wild in a gun-spree ... and accused of multiple murders ... so inexplicably awful that no lawyer wishes to defend him.

The drama is played out against this background.

The film based on Chris Marnewick's book launched in 2016, and Chris is living in lively, law-abiding New Zealand now. But his stomach-wrenching descriptions, relayed in film, need to be seen by anyone debating the death penalty.

The experience raises just three questions:

"How can we tolerate 164 deaths-by-hanging in a single year?"

"How can these young, unsupported warders live through it?"

"How can you ask a man to be a shepherd and butcher at the same time?"

After seeing this film, I assume we shall never again ask the fourth question:

"Shouldn't we bring back the death penalty?" ☐

1 *Shepherds and Butchers*, by Chris Marnewick (Umuzi, Random House, 2008).

26.
Some beautiful people.

You are a bright star in a dark chamber, where lights of liberty of what is left, are going out one by one.

A tribute to a white woman, made by
Chief Albert Luthuli (died 1967).

Between the simultaneous suicide-by-hanging of several Indian maidens; the massacre of a police patrol in February 1956, and the judicial murder-by-hanging of 22 Zulu warriors in a single morning in March 1957, came some inspiring moments any journalist might be happy to treasure all of his or her life.

For me an experience of this warmth involved three Beautiful People.

As a newly appointed "political correspondent", I chose to attend a meeting in a small, packed hall in central Durban. Outside the front of the building stood ranks of armed police, about 50 paces away from the only entrance and exit to the street. All of central Durban seemed empty, for everyone else had escaped to the beaches or to the hills to enjoy a public holiday. It was one of those politicised public holidays, rather in the way of current public holidays, which have been moved and turned politically upside down.

In the tropical humidity that day, Zulus were gathering for a meeting and for some planned, coolly controlled protests. It needed to be "cool", because the Nationalist regime was reaching the height of its power, with police in full control and no prospect of the government being challenged legally, or unseated by other means. The world outside was uninterested. It was a very different time, those years "Before Sharpeville 1960".

Hold those cheers

So the meeting began, confined strictly to those who could squeeze into a small hall somewhere between Somtseu Road and that symbol of colonialism, the Durban railway station. (Durban station was an ornate Edwardian-style brick structure, with a giant, glass-dome spreading over the main platforms; creating a canopy designed to withstand the pressure of several feet of snow! The design was colonisation at work, for it had been taken straight from a railway station built, shortly before, in freezing Canada.)

Durban ANC delegates defied the appalling heat in the name of dignity. Men in their best suits and ties and women in copious dresses – some even had shawls – packed tightly together below the platform in the ill-ventilated little hall where numerous speeches were about to be delivered.

I was squeezed in a corner immediately below and beside the platform, with Terry Wilks of the *Mercury*. We were the only white (albeit anti-apartheid) faces in the place. When the hall rocked with noise, we conducted our strict ritual of demonstrative neutrality; neither cheering, nor clapping, nor smiling. We did not even stand for the official opening during an unforgettable and still unfamiliar rendering of the hymn, later the national anthem, *Sikelel' iAfrika*.

This recognised etiquette of "unbiased neutrality" often had Natal newspaper reporters sitting on their hands – and in trouble. They also found it hard not to cheer at times, especially to support the Torch Commando, and its underground successor, filled with middle-aging ex-servicemen in the 1950s, which went under the James Bond-style disguise of "Natal Horticultural Society".

As happened at every all-white political meeting in those days (most especially at Nationalist rallies in northern Natal) this all-Zulu audience also grew hostile to the press. Here the front row of the rowdy audience was in touching distance, and demonstrated their displeasure at our perceived lack of enthusiasm for the fine speeches and the exciting occasion.

The stoic press, in turn, regardless of their undemonstrated sympathies, had to suffer the normal hostility and unending speeches from the ANC representatives. It was just like all the endless white pro- and anti-government party political meetings, except for the congestion and the heat.

The addresses of welcome; the praises; the thank-yous; and the oratory in English and Zulu droned on ... until the leader of the ANC Youth League clambered up onto the stage.

Within minutes he had the crowd up on their feet and cheering. Soon they were shouting and stamping. He spoke – he raged – in Zulu, which, unfortunately, Terry from *The Mercury* and I from *The Daily News* could not follow well. But we could certainly follow his drift, and we could easily judge the mood he was creating among the increasingly angry, dressed-to-the nines audience.

Injustice. Oppression – and Freedom! The concepts bounced off the walls and were clutched in fists raised ceiling-wards. People started standing on chairs, to make room for others to chant and dance.

The Youth League leader, shirt sleeves and fists raised to heaven, was screaming *Mayibuye iAfrika!* and stamping his elegantly clad foot as he added powerful war chants.

He was adrift of his allotted task of appealing to the delegates to put money in the collection boxes that had ceased to circulate. Men at the back were gesturing at the doors behind them and calling to the crowd to come out of the packed assembly so that they could demonstrate more enthusiastically in the street.

But everyone knew that there was a ring of police outside, ready to enforce the court order that stated clearly the meeting had to be indoors only. Everyone knew that an act of defiance was being generated – right in our laps below the platform. The consequences of storming off to confront the heavily armed police waiting outside were far greater than the tensions building up here indoors.

Mob frenzy

I have seen all kinds of riots erupting at meetings: decent voters, overcome by anger, storming platforms and mauling the speakers with their chairs; white mobs rushing through the streets smashing windows and beating up an occasional bystander; a convoy of "Natal Horticultural Society" ex-servicemen travelling to the platteland to break up an astonished National Party open-air rally, or Nationalist supporters at a dorp meeting attacking the press as we leapt for the open window under which we always tried to station ourselves in those interesting times.

Crowd moods are as hard to gauge as they are to describe or control, so all I can say is that this Zulu audience in Durban was becoming a mob. Its attitude was growing increasingly illogical, tempestuous, and ugly.

The programme was now thoroughly interrupted, and Fiery Youth had already taken over when the senior ANC leader stood up, walked to the front of the platform, and shouted. The chief had never been known to shout.

Those near the front who heard him, paused.

He began to speak. He spoke evenly and quietly. People began to sit down (so did the press– too far from the closed windows to escape). He spoke in Zulu, and he said things the press did not understand, and things that the ruffled, sweating delegates obviously did not want to hear.

There was shouting, but he did not raise his voice in reply. He talked quietly, with miraculous effect. People returned to their seats, almost shamefacedly and began "shushing" other people. He made them all smile. And then he asked them to sing. And I think my colleague and I went against all "newspaper ethics" by standing up to "honour the singing". No one could help smiling. Not even the press. But a man nearby, who had been barracking us, smiled most of all.

The chief, looking cool in his old, carefully pressed grey suit, said: "And now, ladies and gentlemen, the youth leaders – these fine young warriors in our midst– are going to get you to donate to our cause, and I ask you to give as generously as you are able ... but not more than you can afford."

Something like that. And I think it was then that I first heard him exhorting his audience: "Freedom will come. *Mayibuye iAfrika!* We shall have freedom in our lifetime!"

The way he said it, people became calm. Later, when the meeting came to a purposeful close, they walked out confidently through the ranks of watching police who stood cradling their rifles.

"Mayibuye iAfrika!" Freedom in our lifetime!

The Zulu men and women were repeating what their leader had said. His own words were: "We have reason to hope for freedom in our time. But you and you alone can turn this hope into a glorious reality."

The Zulu chief and Leader of the ANC was soon banned. He could be seen only occasionally and only in private, even after he had won the Nobel Peace Prize.

Freedom did not come in his lifetime.

However, in 2005, the South African Mint Company (Pty) Ltd launched the Protea coin series depicting "**Chief Albert John Mvumbi Luthuli**", 1898–1967.

He was an honest, sincere gentleman with a great smile. Despite his dignity, you wanted to throw your arms about the man. In private, he was a courteous listener who encouraged debate. There are very few such leaders in history.

I keep reminding myself it was a rare lifetime privilege to witness any leader stand up and instantly talk his wildly excited supporters into being civilised, thoughtful human beings again. Forty years later, when watching Nelson Mandela's leadership, I sometimes found it hard to believe that it was not Chief Albert Luthuli visiting us from the grave.

Note: The description above is based on an article written a number of years ago; sometime before the death of Helen Suzman. It was requested later for use by the Luthuli Memorial Trust. It is relevant again because of the relationship between the Chief, and the heroic fighter for freedom and justice, Helen Suzman.

CHIEF LUTHULI created powerful links between himself and Helen Suzman and Mandela, whom she visited during his long years in jail; links between three extraordinary, beautiful people.

While history is being rewritten with the intention of embellishing current political power and belittling the truths of the past, the process needs to be firmly corrected.

One way of doing so is simply to present incontrovertible evidence.

Helen Suzman did just this in 2007, decades after Chief Luthuli's death, when her achievements (and Luthuli's great role) were being presented in a racial and prejudicial light by the SABC and several pro-ANC writers.

Here is a copy of the letter Luthuli wrote to her during the heat of the struggle against apartheid back in 1963. (He did not use the *h* in his correct tribal name):

ALBERT JOHN LUTULI. Groutville Mission, P/Bag, PO Groutville.
6th May, 1963
Dear Mrs Suzman
I take this opportunity to express my deep appreciation and

admiration for your heroic and lone stand against a most reactionary Parliament, the Parliament of the Republic of the Union of South Africa. I most heartily congratulate you for your untiring efforts in a situation that would frustrate and benumb many.

In moments of creeping frustration and tiredness, please pick courage and strength in the fact that thousands of South Africans, especially among the oppressed section, thank God for producing Helen, for her manly stand against injustice, regardless of consequences.

For ever remember, you are a bright Star in a dark Chamber, where lights of liberty of what is left, are going out one by one.

This appreciation covers your contribution since you entered Parliament as member of the Progressive Party. This meritorious record has been climaxed by your fittingly uncompromising stand in the rape of democracy by Parliament in the debate that made it law, which was one of the most diabolic bills ever to come before Parliament.

Not only ourselves —your contemporaries —but also posterity will hold you in high esteem.

Yours very truly

(signed) AJ LUTULI

Locally rewritten history has continued to belittle Helen Suzman's role – just as the white Nationalists did. But the outside world saw otherwise, and close observers such as I saw her, after Chief Luthuli's death, as a greater individual force than any, except the embodiment of the ANC, Nelson Mandela himself.

It was for this reason that I put in words for the first time my considered view of her lifetime role. She had suffered a bad fall shortly before her 90th birthday. I wrote:

23rd June, 2006

Dearest Helen,

You are a fighter; a long enduring champion of our age, so we are able to hope that you will overcome the fall and go on towards your century. It is important that you do so.

By then, I believe, two more generations of South Africans will finally come to understand what you have done for them in your lifetime. Even many of our own generation do not yet fully appreciate your role.

There are very few of us left who actually witnessed your battles in those ugly years of the 1950s and 1960s when you were often alone, sometimes a lonely figure standing up to racism and those massed ranks of apartheid bullies. It seemed sometimes that we were watching from the Press Gallery a real, living version of the somewhat mythical Jeanne d'Arc. That's how dramatic it was. One had to be there, feel the hostility and hate amid the grudging respect, to understand. One had to be there to appreciate fully how much was at stake.

What the country has yet to realise is that you were fighting for the values to which the world's politicians merely pay token homage. Your fight helped keep alive the conscience that prevented totalitarianism and counter-revolution, and led South Africans to reform peacefully.

People often ask, "Who is your model?" One is tempted to respond: "I do not wish to emulate anyone." But if it were possible to emulate anyone, Helen Suzman should be everyone's top model – especially for her values and her valour.

Arlene and I (and my daughter Helen and all our family) wish you many more comfortable, painless, rewarding and serene years, while the world catches up with your lifetime's goals.

I hope to see you in Johannesburg in October. Get well. We love you very much.

She died not long after her 90th birthday, but her values, her constant fight for justice for all, live on among those who continue her never-ending quest in her name.

In that era of oppression from 1948 to 1990, there were many other heroes who – for the good of all – should be remembered today, but who are invariably forgotten. Their deeds are dismissed for failing to support unconditionally the new victors in the political scrambles for power.

The most unjustly treated by modern history – especially by the apartheid government and today's long-occupying Zuma – has been the early leader of the ANC.

Despite being deliberately "forgotten" for long-gone political reasons, his place in history needs to be restored. His life, times, beliefs, and actions raise many questions, some of which are answered in the next chapter. □

27.
"If X, Y, Z?"

Curiosity is one of the most permanent and certain characteristics of a vigorous intellect.

Dr Samuel Johnson, 1760s.

Dr X was indeed a vigorous intellect, and he poses questions for South African leaders today. So my query, if X,Y, Z? is neither a trick question nor part of a Maths equation. It is a socio-political and philosophical one concerning **Dr Alfred Xuma**, (X as in Xhosa) who linked the founding fathers of the ANC in 1914 to the leaders of The Struggle and thus to everyone in the post-revolutionary movement, including President Zuma (Z as in Zulu).

If Dr X could build a functioning, nationwide African National Congress (ANC) on the political philosophies embraced by the founders, and upheld later by Luthuli, Mandela, Tambo, and Sisulu – why should Zuma devalue those principles?

Dr Xuma preceded Zulu Chief Luthuli as President-General of the ANC. With broad vision, idealism, and hard work Xuma built and modernised the African National Congress in the 1940s; carried it through the WWII years and beyond the fall of his prime enemy, the Smuts Government; then into direct conflict with the first apartheid regime.

Xuma built from its early foundation an ANC dedicated to a just and honest society.

It is in stark contrast to the Zuma government's corruption and lack of vision. Is this merely a matter of aging and inevitable decadence?

Far from it, I believe. You only have to look back to see why. Xuma's history is directly significant to the ANC and to events in 2016. Xuma's written statements and his vision of the future also anticipated the intellectual basis of the Black Conscious Movement, long before Steve Biko's birth.

Dr Xuma preceded Chief Luthuli as President-General of the ANC. Then with broad vision, idealism and hard work, Xuma rebuilt and modernized the African National Congress in the 1940s; carried it through the Second World War years and beyond the fall of his prime enemy, the Smuts Government, then into direct conflict with the first apartheid regime.

Xuma's rebuilding of an ANC dedicated to a just and honest society is in stark contrast to the Zuma government's corruption and lack of vision. Xuma quietly resuscitated the ANC in the 1930s by firing those office bearers who were incompetent or peddling their own interests and seeking out and personally recruiting black intellectuals – although he knew they might rival him for leadership.

It was under his leadership that the ANC Youth League and the party's Women's League were formed, at the same time as he was – mainly in private correspondence – challenging the government of "General" Smuts at home, and the venture abroad of "Field Marshal" Smuts.

Few whites (and only a very small minority of blacks) heard Xuma express his simple, but deep concepts concerning Africa's future as he synthesized the ANC's policies and modernized its structure. For a politician he was remarkably silent. Yet his private correspondence reveals his character and the way he dealt with big issues and small. His written protests of injustice to Africans were sent directly to his targets: including the UN and SA premier Jan Smuts.

What a privilege it would have been as a political reporter to have discussed Dr Xuma's favourite issues with him – and to have repeated his remarks to General Smuts and to have observed his reactions to Xuma's barbs! But it could not happen.

It was different in 1946 when Smuts was still in power, and Xuma saw him for the first time at the United Nations headquarters in New York. In a protest to the UN Xuma wrote:

"I have had to fly 10000 miles to meet my Prime Minister. He talks about us, but he won't talk to us."

And he informed the United Nations that Field Marshal Smuts, less than a year after signing the UN charter on fundamental rights, had allowed the introduction at home of an Asiatic Land Tenure Act which was appalling in its racial discrimination.

"There is something that seems to lift the Prime Minister's spirits abroad and depresses them at home," Xuma wrote.

He offered other barbs which contributed to a widespread South African view that Smuts had left SA to govern itself while he concerned himself with "lesser" (ie international) issues.

IN 2012 XUMA'S AUTOBIOGRAPHY and selected works (edited by Peter Limb of Michigan State University, USA, author of a number of works on recent South African history) were published by the Van Riebeeck Society.[1] These tell us a great deal about the remarkable Dr Alfred Xuma.

He completed his teacher training at Clarkebury Institute (which Mandela later attended) at a time when several qualified African barristers were returning from studies in America – as well as ANC founders Pixley ka IsakaSeme and the Reverend John Dube, and Charlotte Maxeke (first African women graduate in South Africa and pioneer leader in women's rights).

"They stimulated me into action," wrote Xuma, and set off to better himself in the outside world.

Auspiciously, he left from the Cape Town home of Walter Rubasana, who had just become the first African Provincial Councillor ever elected in South Africa. Xuma departed in 1911 for the United States with very little, and returned to Rubansa's home in 1927 as a doctor of medicine with added qualifications in obstetrics, gynaecology and surgery gained at the Mayo Clinic and other institutions in the USA and at Edinburgh, Glasgow and Budapest.

He set up his practice in central Johannesburg, right opposite the Magistrates' Courts. He settled in Sophiatown (only to be forcibly removed years later, under apartheid rules, and re-settled in Dube, Soweto.)

He quickly became a successful figure; a cosmopolitan who (like Mandela, later) had once been a herdboy, and a victim of apartheid. Yet Xuma transcended all local politics and the fighting within the African political movements. In the 1930s he refused to join the ANC as he considered it passive and ineffectual, and became vice-president of the All Africa Convention instead.

Finally he assumed leadership of the ANC and re-built the almost moribund organisation from scratch into a significant democratic movement in which he emphasised the roles of women, youth, and civic society outside of mainstream tribal law.

He led the ANC for a decade until – ironically – he was snubbed in 1949 for being "too conciliatory". He resigned as president of the ANC because he refused to entertain violence as a political policy.

His basic, unchanging, uncompromising philosophy had gone far beyond the ideas of the founders of the movement. This was clear in 1945, three years before apartheid was introduced, when Xuma wrote an article for Cabinet Minister J H Hofmeyr's *Forum* giving his vision of a future, post-war South Africa. It reads, quite astonishingly, like a summary of the SA Constitution that was triumphantly (but painfully) negotiated half a century later.

Yet he had earlier named all its principles – with one addition: "(It must be) a South Africa in which all the people will be prepared for full and useful citizenship through *a sound system* (my italics) of compulsory State education."

"Education above all else," he wrote in another declaration on what South Africa needed.

Mandela, who towered physically over tiny Xuma, said of him years later: "He has an air of superciliousness ... (This said perhaps with Xuma's reference once to Mandela in the Youth League as one of my "kindergarten boys").But Mandela also rejected Xuma's outdated regard for "British fair play" in a different world.

"Everything was done in the English manner, his idea being that despite our disagreements we were all gentlemen," said Mandela, adding that, though devoted to the ANC, "Xuma's medical practice took precedence."

Oliver Tambo (like Mandela) believed that Xuma had encouraged them in their political careers and thus prepared them for The Struggle. Walter Sisulu and Chief Luthuli praised Xuma for pulling the ANC together. But Luthuli thought that by the time DF Malan came to power in South Africa, the situation could be summed up as: "Congress was urgent, Xuma cautious."

Sadly, Dr Xuma had become – like gentle men everywhere – an anachronism in politics. (Chief Luthuli was ousted as head of the ANC for the same reason.)

Xuma was not an orator. But he was a powerful and constant writer addressing every issue to its source in unequivocal terms. Thank goodness, therefore, that some of his wide-ranging and prolific writing has been assembled and immaculately published.

It tells us what all of us ought to know about him and his role in South Africa's history. It constantly keeps prompting that question: "If X, why Z?"

If Xuma could resuscitate and clarify the idealism of ANC founders such as lawyer Pixley Seme, journalist Solomon Plaatje, and the great teacher Rev John Dube; if Luthuli, Mandela, Tambo and Mbeki (despite his odd notions on the 21st century challenge of HIV/Aids) could foster the ideal of a democracy of equal opportunity, justice and freedom of the press – why should Zuma's stewardship collapse so quickly into chaotic non-delivery and corruption?

Corruption spread, under Zuma, at an astonishing rate, even for a government whose power had ruled unchallenged for two decades.

The Black Press

There is something else to treasure in Dr Xuma's writings. It is his links and constant support of black journalists; together with his links and constant jousting with some superb representatives of liberalism in a highly conservative society.

The press people with whom he was in contact included Betty Radford, a *Cape Times* journalist from Britain who founded the left-wing *Guardian* in 1937. Ruth First was one of its contributors. Both joined the South African Communist Party (SACP) and used the *Guardian* to publish the SACP's views without it becoming the communists' official organ. The *Guardian* also supported the ANC, through the war years, though ANC President-General Xuma was explicitly wary of undemocratic as well as Stalinist communism. The communist *Guardian* was often banned in the 1950s and it closed down in 1963. Xuma meanwhile, supported black journalism and was admired by black journalists such as Henry Msimang, co-founder of the Industrial and Commercial Workers' Union (ICU); by Bloke Modisane of Jim Bailey's *Drum* magazine, where all journalists showed their support of Xuma; and by Richard Thema, the intellectually-inclined editor of the white-owned *Bantu World* for 20 years.

(*The World*, totally subsidised by the Argus Company when I was editing *The Star*, was finally forced to closed by government decree in 1977. But it re-appeared in precisely the same form with the same editor and proprietor within a year, when a formally registered title of a small "community paper" *The Sowetan*, was unearthed for the African newspaper to continue under apartheid "law".)

The liberals

Dr Xuma's relationships and his correspondence with many of South Africa's active liberals is of considerable interest to historians because – while he deeply respected democratic and liberal concepts – he strongly disagreed with his liberal acquaintances because he perceived a primary need to emphasise "Africanness".

His now published letters are a reminder of the fundamental role active liberals played in South Africa in mid-20th century; people with dedicated purpose and cultured minds such as Margaret Ballinger, first President of the Liberal Party, JH Hofmeyr, and others whom we might have forgotten without some help from Xuma and the American Peter Limb, who has researched his life. The few of Xuma's liberal contacts that I happened to know in the late 1940s and early 1950s were all exceptional, idealistic yet singularly dedicated people. They included: Prof RFA Hoernle of the SA Institute of Race Relations; HP Junod, the white-maned Swiss missionary who came to Pretoria to wage an indefatigable fight for prison reform in South Africa; Prof ZK Mathews of Fort Hare, a fine leader who might not have wanted to be seen as "a liberal" or representing any political movement; and Senator Edgar Brookes of the Liberal Party, later professor of politics and history at Natal University in Pietermaritzburg, where he was on an anonymous panel of leaderwriters for the *Natal Witness* ... a conjunction we young professional journalists disapproved of in principle ... though the issue of outsiders writing anonymous editorial "leaders" under a newspaper's title doesn't seem to bother me as much today as it did in those tense times.

Parliament's official opposition, the Progressive Federal Party (PFP), lost tens of thousands of its voters in the referendum, then dramatically lost its leader (Van Zyl Slabbert) — and finally its status when, after the 1987 elections, the rightwing Conservative Party became the official opposition.

entering areas of unrest. It said the very presence of the media encouraged demonstrations. The riots grew worse.

There were more than 100 pieces of legislation hampering the flow of news. Tyson instructed his reporters: "You can only try to tell it like it is". ("Telling it like it is" became the paper's motto.)

English-language newspapers contested

several other newspapers began to consistently break the emergency regulations in order to publish vital information. Pik Botha said, plaintively: "Nowhere in the world are newspapers allowed to write so much against the Government."

In 1987, F W de Klerk's brother, Wimpie de Klerk, resigned as editor of the Nationalist-supporting newspaper, Rapport,

Another of Dr Xuma's correspondents, with whom he seemed constantly at odds, was the Secretary for Native Affairs, Dr Douglas Smit, whom Xuma accused of habitual racial discrimination ... unlike his wartime United Party predecessor in Parliament, Deneys Reitz, Minister of Lands, who had complimented Xuma years before on his "damning indictment of the white man's policy in Africa".

But if Dr Smit was conservative, he was a lamb and a liberal compared with Dr de Wet Nel, the naïve apartheid Minister of Bantu Affairs. Smit was being called upon to help implement the recommendations of the previous government's Fagan Commission in expectation of Smuts's return to power. The first aim was to house the millions of black people who flocked to towns and cities during urgent urbanization and industrialization during five years of war. Vast slums were a WW2 phenomenon that suddenly pertained, not only to Johannesburg and Durban, but to post-war Rome and Naples and other cities around the world.

Urbanisation and workers' housing required particularly urgent attention in SA, but the United Party had been slow in the years immediately after the war to provide it; almost as slow as their contemplation of even a qualified vote for Africans.

To give prime minister Verwoerd his due, at least he had a plan – an impossible, mad plan of racially dividing the nation in the manner in which post-war India was divided, and he also "solved" the slum clearance and housing problem by swiftly and efficiently providing sub-economic housing of a quality in excess of that produced even 60 years later. But he did so while simultaneously banning all free movement of people and removing tens of thousands from towns and cities. His motivation was repugnantly racial, in almost everything he said and did.

When politicians don't listen

Dr Smit, representing the defeated United Party in Parliament, and Dr de Wet Nel, representing the new apartheid government, clashed in Parliament regularly when I was in the Press Gallery in the 1950s. Each was always in the House of Assembly, ready for battle, as the other spoke.

Both elderly spokesmen, however were very deaf.

When the Minister of Bantu Affairs rose in the government benches to speak, the ex-Secretary-General for Native Affairs, would ostentatiously take off the huge pair of earphones he needed to hear properly in that non-technical age. Then he would ostentatiously rest his head on his desk in feigned – or possibly sudden, deep – slumber.

Next day, it was the turn of Dr Smit to deliver on behalf of the Opposition his crushing response to apartheid policy (he would obviously have read the parliamentary Hansard transcript of the minister's speech by then). The Minister of Bantu Affairs would pick up a similar giant pair of headphones, listen for a moment, then clatter them down with theatrical disgust and start studying his bill.

In my parliamentary gallery reports in the late 1950s I dubbed this amusing, but repetitiously childish exchange as "the silent war of the old brigade".

But I wonder what Dr Xuma would have called it?

Other names from SA's past

Looking back today, I deeply regret not being aware in my youth of Xuma's role – and not seeking him out during my younger days when he was in silent retirement in a distant Province of SA.

The South African Native National Congress delegation to England, 1914. L to R: Thomas Mapike, Rev Walter Rubusana, Rev John Dube, Saul Msane, Sol Plaatje.

Steve Biko, pioneer of Black Consciousness, and Donald Woods, editor of the Daily Dispatch in East London. Their friendship was part-cause of their persecution by the local Security Police. Biko was murdered while in police custody and Woods — once a fun-loving, light-hearted political correspondent and friend of this author —had to flee at night to become a refugee in England where he died without hope of return to his homeland.

He was the living link between the ANC's remarkable founders, such as journalist Sol Plaatje, and the freedom fighters more than half a century later.

Xuma might have banished much of my ignorance and my (white) generation's probable misunderstanding of black politics. We were too young to be aware of him as he quietly resuscitated the ANC by firing those office bearers who were incompetent or peddling their own interests, and by seeking out and personally and purposefully recruiting black intellectuals strong enough to rival him for leadership.

What a contrast to the lack of principle today!

We were schoolboys, or youngsters serving in WWII, when the ANC Youth League and the party's Women's League were created under Xuma's leadership, and when he was privately challenging "General" Smuts's government at home, and "Field Marshal" Smuts's ventures abroad.

Few non-politicised whites (and only a small minority of blacks) in my early days heard Xuma express his simple, but deep concepts concerning Africa's future while he was synthesising the ANC's policies and modernizing its structure.

At the same time, even though he embodied the ANC, he was an early fount of the intellectual basis of the Black Consciousness Movement, long before **Steve Biko**'s birth.

By the time whites of my generation were ready to understand all this, and some of us were ready to report on black politics, Xuma had disappeared from the scene, **Luthuli** was about to be banned and **Mandela** was soon forced to disappear in a disguise.

Many of the most articulate leaders of the African movements were fleeing to the US and London, Lusaka and Moscow. They had gone underground, or were being hunted, banned, imprisoned, or prosecuted in political trials that often lasted years.

So, by the 1970s, it was a weakness of mine and probably all other white newspaper editors that our personal experience of black politics was limited, even for Xhosa-speaking **Donald Woods**, editor of the faraway little East London *Daily Dispatch* and a friend and voice for Steve Biko.

My own contacts were limited to black businessmen; members of the Soweto Committee of Ten, such as compassionate spokesmen **Dr Nthato Motlana** (temporarily jailed with my black colleagues and who spoke at a memorial for Steve Biko); **Murphy Morobe** (an earnest, honest free-thinker, despite becoming later a spokesman for President Mbeki); and others like my courageous Sowetan editorial colleagues – and close friends as well as most other jailed African journalists listed elsewhere and in another book, all of whom were the targets of white racial violence despite being committed to non-violence, as the late Dr Xuma had been long before them.

What we independent journalists did understand, better than most whites, was apartheid and the horrifying injustice of it.

For me the principles of justice and freedom naturally took precedence over dispassion and even-handedness in political reporting. Even so, I blush at the memory of my role as a political correspondent reporting parliamentary elections within "English Colonial Natal" where English racial fury at Afrikaner racial nationalism was at its height, and my negative reporting of Nationalist candidates verged on propaganda. Our one-sided campaign to reject a proposed nationalist Republic outside of the Commonwealth illustrated two things for me: first, that propaganda doesn't work on *a literate and aware* electorate; second, that no amount of newspaper editorialising will change a newspaper reader's mind.

Propaganda is a feeble weapon in an educated society, as well as being an unethical one. I soon learned that taking sides, even with the byline of "political reporter", ethically demanded accurate reporting of both sides of any news story.

However, one of the great obstacles to publishing "without fear or favour" and in defending justice and equality was the ANC's partial embrace of communism; a creed which in practice denied freedom and justice, fervently supported tyranny, and encouraged violence and terrorism (outside its own disciplined ranks).

The apartheid government thrived on the "bogey" of communism. It banned even mere discussion of it in SA and created crude rules of censorship we had to fight off for 30 years ... until the fall of the Berlin Wall.

In that single symbolic move, Russia went on to accept a somewhat chaotic form of democracy; numbers of new nations grabbed independence and joined the UN – and the National Party lost its last thin justification for its foul existence. ☐

1. *AB Xuma. Autobiography and Selected Works* edited by Peter Limb, published by the Van Riebeeck Society of South Africa in its Second Series no 43.

28.
Cabinet minister admits his ignorance.

*His knowledge of life and ordinary human beings
is so hazy, he really deserves some sort of decoration:
a medal inscribed "For Vaguery" in the Field.*

Look Back in Anger, John Osborne, 1956.

This chapter's headline – a confession of a minister's ignorance of his portfolio, and of the contentious and outrageous law he proposes – is perhaps unique in all politics, I believe. But newspaper ethics prevented me at the time from reporting this rarest admission ever.

It happened during the Parliamentary Session way back in 1957 or possibly 1958 that I had my second breakthrough in communication with the Cabinet. I had come to Parliament as a correspondent believing that the National Party – having finally secured total power by hook and by crook; having also eliminated the little representation there was for "non-whites" in Parliament; having banned the ANC and PAC and legislated against almost all forms of extra-parliamentary opposition through its Suppression of Communism Act, and having turned national education into a political weapon through its special "Bantu Education Act" – surely now had completed its ethnic and racial putsch, and would try in future to render itself more amicable to the races it had excluded from a common and mutual society.

Fort Hare University.

However … on our desks fell the papers for the First Reading of a new Public Health Amendment Bill. Or perhaps it might have been heralded by a report leaked to the pro-government Nationalist Press … today my memory fails to pinpoint the source. Whatever the original report was, it seemed too incredible to be true.

Surely the Government did not intend to close down more than sixty hospitals and more than 200 medical clinics operating in exclusively African territories in the country – just because they were run by independent Christian missions?

They represented the greatest force for sound education as well as healing throughout black Africa … the only efficient source at that time, in fact. To close mission hospitals – followed possibly by the closing of schools like Healdtown and seats of learning such as Fort Hare University – would be an act of madness as well as barbarity.

No one from the Department of Health or any other source would confirm our suspicions. It was essential to get an accurate account of it as soon as possible. I was desperate enough on such a silent and possibly huge issue, to try the near-impossible task of bearding the minister – the facially hirsute and grey, yet sensationalist, Dr Albert Hertzog himself.

Dr Hertzog was an ultra-conservative racist, and proud of it. He spoke very gently, and very quietly, but as soon as he was given a public platform to address his supporters outside of Parliament he would rave; uttering sensational ideas that made even his fellow-cabinet ministers blanch. And his colleagues were already purposefully ultra-white.

He was the one who, years later, rejected belated moves to introduce television into South Africa.

He vetoed it so forcefully that South Africa remained perhaps the only "civilised" nation in the world not to witness the broadcast of man's landing on the moon in 1969. Unless we managed to enter one of the less-developed nations to the north, we were unable to see TV until 1976.

Hertzog was mocked and condemned mercilessly for his "flat-earth" outlook, but he remained adamant and unperturbed. (Looking back half a century later, one might be excused now for thinking he had a sound point about TV. Sometimes, when I see all those sub-normal advertisements and all that rubbish being screened on TV, I think … almost, but not quite … nostalgically of Dr Hertzog.)

In hindsight, Dr Hertzog's character and his words and deeds deserve study, for they are in most cases contradictory and often unique.

His political rantings came strangely from a man of such intelligence and sound education. He was possibly the most polite of all the politicians I've ever met. As an ardent Afrikaner segregationist who hated the "English", his use of the English language was impeccable – though his marriage to an English woman may have accounted for some of this.

His angry political reputation was on my mind when I finally managed "to beard him" in the Lobby. Of necessity the interview had to be sharp, clear and very brief.

I must have said something like: "Dr Hertzog, I am from the *Natal Daily News* and our readers, and perhaps the world, need to know – before ignorance causes harm – whether you intend to close down the mission hospitals in the Transkei, or not."

I wasn't going to wait for the expected brush off. I planned to keep asking questions and provoking the worst scenarios of breakdown in national public health, until he gave me some sort of response. I was ready to reject small talk, and was anticipating from him several forms of evasion or insult.

Instead, I had no way of dealing with his unexpected and frank response, in words similar to these:

"My boy, you will have to forgive me. I must tell you, off the record, that I cannot say anything about this matter because I simply don't know anything about it."

"But ... but ... but ... but you have been in charge all this parliamentary session and ..."

"Yes I am the Minister of Health, but as you will know, not long enough to get to all the good people there, or to discuss the proposed legislation. My regrets. You'll understand, I'm sure ..."

He smiled, shook hands, and asked to be excused.

As he walked away I could see the message in the headlines beginning to form in my head:

MINISTER OF HEALTH ADMITS KNOWING NOTHING

ABOUT HIS DEPARTMENT'S POLICY

And a straphead, perhaps: "Will I close down Mission Hospitals? Who knows? Not I," says Dr Hertzog.

But of course there could be no headlines, even if the peculiar and ineffable doctor was unaware of the convention of "off the record".

It usually goes beyond "I tell you in confidence", for confidences can be broken where public interest demands it.

And my potential personal scoop of a possibly a never-before-published headline meant nothing.

The usual furtively euphemistic legislation ("Advancement of Bantu Health Bill" or some such title) would be passionately debated in Parliament and inevitably passed before we saw the loudly predicted and tragic results unfold.

Mission schools were already closing down. Mission hospitals were already starting to shrink. Now all 60 of them would go. Hundreds of clinics were being forced to shut their doors in poverty-stricken areas, with nothing to replace them except words and empty promises.

I thought this might be Parliament's darkest hour. But, while press communication rapidly improved, and "Bantu Homeland infrastructure" continued to collapse, worse things were to happen to Parliament's frail, partly gagged, and tortured forms of freedom and justice.

And a worse fate was about to threaten the life of Parliament itself.

Extraordinary march and a kiss of death

Behind the railings enclosing the House of Assembly in Cape Town, policemen placed automatic weapons carefully on gun tripods before lying prone, like marksmen at war. I was upstairs in my office in the House of Assembly in Cape Town, on the phone to the editor of the Natal *Daily News*.

"I cannot hear you," he said.

"There's a helicopter hovering right outside my window," I shouted. There was a pause as the helicopter, close-by at eye-level, swung away and the noise subsided.

"We live in interesting times," said the editor a thousand miles away.

We were witnessing, days after the Sharpeville massacre in 1960, the nearest thing so far to civil war in South Africa since General Smuts bombed white miners at their barricades in Johannesburg in 1922. We were looking at the nearest point to revolution, so far, in the history of South African protest movements.

The residents of the two black townships outside Cape Town were marching on Parliament. It was a spontaneous uprising and a strange one, although its origins were easy to see.

The Pan Africanist Congress (PAC), which had organised the pass law protest at Sharpeville, was especially strong in the Cape townships, where anger at the Sharpeville massacre was quick to rise. In Langa township the anger led to riots, police raids, arson, looting, and murder. But first the people of Langa and Nyanga joined in their silent, peaceful march on the "Mother City".

It took even PAC officialdom by surprise, and Philip Kgosana, its young, natural-born Cape Town leader, had to dress hurriedly to catch up with the procession. By lunchtime on 30 March, between 20 000 and 30 000 demonstrators were approaching the city centre, blocking the freeway that skirted Table Mountain.

At the same time shop workers, office secretaries in their summer dresses, and clerks in their shirtsleeves poured into the city streets. To their surprise they found armoured cars and some tense, gun-toting policemen guarding a line stretching from Parliament to police headquarters on the eastern side of the city centre.

The lunchtime crowds sensed no crisis. Girls clambered up onto an armoured car and peered through its sighting slits and down its gun barrel. Others started ambling eastwards in the hope of witnessing whatever event was about to occur.

The steel cordon thrown around Parliament made itself almost invisible. I walked through it and was heading towards the distant freeway exit when I managed to get a ride with an American in an open convertible.

Up the road, where the freeway skirts Devil's Peak before pouring into the city at the top of Roeland Street, we suddenly came upon the marchers. There was only one other car partly visible on the entire stretch of double highway. University student Kgosana, in a pair of shorts, was standing on the back of it, leading; conducting; orchestrating the crowd. He did so in utter silence. And the crowd, stretching out of sight up the foothills of Devil's Peak, responded with waves or silent smiles.

The freeways, and the grass on the open park on the right, were invisible under a mass of shoulder-to-shoulder black figures. The silence should have been eerie. Or imminently dangerous. But somehow it was a peaceful silence. Our open tourer drove slowly towards the advancing noiseless mass of marching protesters.

"My God," said the American. "What do I do now?"

It was impossible to turn round as masses of pedestrians filtered down the narrowing street towards the walls of the Roeland Street jail. "Drive very slowly," I breathed. "Don't bump anyone."

The bank of silent figures miraculously parted. Without an option, we moved slowly forward in first gear into the mass; our heads in the open car no higher than the chests of men clutching their kerries.

From among the marchers, men and women took it upon themselves to step out of the crush and signal the crowd to open a path.

There were no sounds, except the purr of his sleek car in low-gear (in those days when automatic drive was rare).We drove slowly, and very carefully, through a silent sea. No one banged anything against the sides of the car. No one even touched it.

Some people actually smiled as we brushed by. It was a strange, almost warm, certainly an adrenalin-pumping experience ... "like Moses parting the ocean", I nearly said to the stranger at the wheel of his convertible.

When we finally reached the other side of the massed multitude, I tentatively suggested that we might drive back to the leaders of the crowd so that I might interview them. He drove straight on. I was still wondering how I could return to the crisis point when he suddenly came upon a place to swing into the empty incoming traffic lanes, and head back into the silent, seemingly serene, close-packed mob that had been marching in the hot sun for seven hours since dawn.

Kgosana, it appeared, was intending to lead the masses to Parliament, but he learned that it was surrounded by armed police and troops, so he swung right and marched on police headquarters – where Patrick Duncan of the extra-parliamentary Liberal Party had, only a week previously, negotiated with Colonel "Terry" Terblanche, not only to release Kgosana and another PAC leader without bail, but also to suspend the pass laws for a month.

Two or three thousand pass demonstrators had carried Kgosana away shoulder high on that occasion. But the colonel's promise had been countermanded by the minister. Now a multitude ten times that size was descending on the ill-prepared city.

At the same time, lunch-hour crowds consisting mainly of white office-workers swarmed into the city-centre streets below. They did not see the huge, silent, marching ranks on the highway above them on the slopes of Devil's Peak. Instead, the townspeople photographed or surrounded the unfamiliar armoured cars parked among the city blocks.

The marching multitude, thirsty, frustrated, and tired at this stage, still seemed inexplicably peaceful, almost cheerful, as the colonel and the

Liberal leader negotiated once more, then addressed the leaders of the march, promising them that if they went home peacefully now, Philip Kgosana – instantly recognisable as the only man in the city wearing incongruous, navy shorts – could later speak directly to the minister.

Kgosana and his assistants listened, they talked, they warned the colonel that this was the last time they would accept his word and his pleas for calm. They turned and they followed their massed demonstrators who were singing to keep up their energy, and impatiently going home ...

Later the Cabinet minister's broken word and the detention of Philip Kgosana became the sparks which created a conflagration of major riots in Cape Town.

On this critical first day, I joined other journalists in writing our reports of the drama, recounting my unique experience of strange peace in the midst of the march – meeting my main deadlines upcountry with full coverage that filled the front page later that afternoon. Then we retired to a nearby (whites-only) tavern to analyse the retrospect.

I noticed one of the regulars at the bar pick up a copy of Cape Town's *Argus*. He glanced at the huge front-page headline and at the side-panel announcing the declaration of a national emergency .... One sniff, then he turned to the sports pages, which fully absorbed his attention until his departure.

More than 30 years later I met the PAC president of the 1990s, Clarence Makwetu, by then a tall, greying figure rather like Mandela. He had been one of the young leaders of that march, and his eyes lit up at the memory of it.

"One of the great days in my life," he said. "After that, we had to turn to violence to be heard."

The hero of that day, Philip Kgosana of the Pan Africanist Congress (PAC) had to flee soon afterwards to London, where my colleague John Jordi sardonically witnessed the treatment he was given by jealous ANC cadres. They arranged, especially for the local hero at his moment of triumph, a national press conference in London ... on a sleepy Sunday afternoon.

"The political kiss of death," Jordi reported. ☐

29.
Liars, and a snake in the grass.

All political parties die at last of swallowing their own lies.

John Arbuthnot 1667–1735.

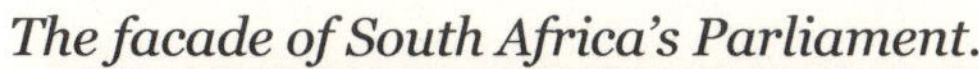

olitics, and the humbug of a Parliament that changes the laws in order to stay in unquestionable power too long, are the last things I ever wished to witness day-in and day-out as a reporter.

Unfortunately South Africa has, in its short life, experienced two such Parliaments; the first emerging in the 1950s and the second, in the 21st century, after Zuma became president.

Experience over centuries has taught us that rot sets in with governments the moment they are no longer challenged and accountable, or if the same clique of rulers or parliamentarians have been in power too long.

I arrived to observe Cape Town's Parliament in the 1950s when this political and moral decrepitude was ingrained in an all-white government representing a minority within a minority. Seven parliamentary sessions of it finally drove me – momentarily – right out of journalism. Yet, among the bad memories, I recall occasions of hilarity, of bravery and of irony.

The facade of South Africa's Parliament.

Perhaps the most astonishing personal experience was the one described in the previous chapter, of witnessing a cabinet minister admitting his ignorance of his portfolio. That admission came as a result of a long process in communication. The process began elsewhere, with Senator Jan de Klerk, Snr, (father of 'FW', the Nobel prizewinner, who was the last and final, prime minister of South Africa, and the last president during the apartheid years).

The elder Senator was a large man with a large cigar, who brushed me aside on the Senate staircase where I waited to intercept him in my first bitter days of reporting politics in the 1950s.

Anger overcame my reluctance, my lack of interest, and my shyness as a "new boy" to Parliament – knowing already that Nationalist MPs, let alone cabinet ministers such as this Senator, would not even say "good day" to *vreemde, Englese pers* political correspondents.

"Senator!" I shouted, as he continued up the stairs, waving his cigar and muttering *"Nee! Nee!"*

"Senator, you will really want to react to this," I called, catching him up and pushing under his nose a press telex message that had been delivered to me in the slim hope of somehow getting his confirmation or response.

He paused on the top step, looked hard at me, then read it. The telexed news report in my hand was possibly outrageous. A misquote of the Senator very probably, because it flatly contradicted his own portfolio's policy. That's why my newspaper wanted his reaction. But its content wasn't important as far as I was concerned, and I cannot even recall its portent. I remember only the precedent it set.

Here was the first Nationalist cabinet minister I'd met who could be persuaded to be seen discussing government policy with the opposition press in the precincts of Parliament. His response was predictable – he denied the veracity of the report and gave me his version of what he had said. But on this particular occasion a politician's version of fact seemed convincing and the original report palpably incorrect. He was surprised by the chance to correct it. He even said thank you!

This was one of the few occasions I spoke to the elderly Senator, but I was to befriend one of his sons – **Prof "Wimpie" de Klerk**, an Afrikaans newspaper editor on a Nationalist newspaper who demonstrated as much courage as any man in the long history of opposing the evils of apartheid.

And I was aware of a younger son, "FW" who was little more than 12 years old when "the Nats" came to power on that fatal election night in 1948 ... the night we *Engelse* journalists were pushed by Nationalist supporters into Pretoria's Church Square fountain as taxi-rank hooters celebrated the announcement of General Smuts's fall from power.

Young Frederik was fast asleep at that moment, eyes closed beside a radio where his father had stationed him to keep tabs on the late-night election results, in the hopes of some announcements of his party winning more seats and bringing the Nat Party closer to power.

FW's eyes must have been only partly open when, near the end of his political career, he took leadership of the most conservative section of his government in the Transvaal, and when he attempted to censor, or at least curb, the opposition independent press in the latter days of apartheid rule. But that was years away – as was FW's sudden and brave acceptance in 1990 of non-racial democracy.

Back in the 1950s the government, and nearly all of its opposition, in Parliament and out, were not speaking to each other ... not after the effrontery of the National Party's "fraud" in subverting the Constitution, the Courts and Parliament itself in order to maintain white domination.

It was a scandal that might almost prompt war.

I REMEMBER AN ANGRY, strange night, after a traditional annual dinner – a tradition harking back to beginnings of a South African Parliament, and perhaps even to the early Cape British administration at which the Cabinet hosted the press. During this particularly subdued and wary occasion at which communication was attempted, the Minister of Health, Dr Carel de Wet, accused my colleague, Bob Steyn, of being a *veraaier* – a traitor to his people.

Bob was a soft-spoken Afrikaner of deep conviction who, as political correspondent of the *Cape Argus*, shared a parliamentary office with me. He left the dinner early, to avoid trading insults with the minister. But four of us, two pressmen and two Opposition MPs, waited outside the venue, in the ancient Greenmarket Square in Cape Town. When the minister appeared, we grabbed him, each by an arm or leg, and like schoolboys, bounced his dinner-jacketed body up and down on the cobblestones. The wine of that night, and his ruffled dignity, prevented him from taking public action against us.

My favourite parliamentarian (other than Helen Suzman of course) was not involved in our shenanigans, for he was an elder who had served in Smuts's War Cabinet and been seriously injured years before in a physical scuffle against wartime pro-Nazi "Nats".

Harry Lawrence was always "an officer and gentleman" who cared and lived to serve others. I seldom spoke to him – but deeply admired his courage, his style, and his provocative wit.

Having given up his spacious Cabinet quarters a decade previously, and resigned on principle from the all-white United Party Opposition quite recently, he now occupied a tiny office below street level in the parliamentary building; the least deserved place for a man of his rank, stature, and experience. He accepted it without a qualm. He was more accessible there to his Cape constituents, he said.

One busy day he invited me down to his cubicle during the lunch break. A parliamentary waiter, in grand uniform arrived simultaneously, bearing a tray with the meal the ex-minister had ordered earlier. His lunch consisted of: A bottle of wine. A bunch of grapes. A cigar standing in an empty wine glass.

"Enough here to share," he said – provided you don't smoke cigars."

At about this time I had the privilege of being one of the few late-night witnesses to Harry Lawrence springing his best-known baited trap in the House of Assembly. He was about to skewer his enemy, a biased "Mr Speaker", yet again. He also wished to make squirm a particularly nasty member across the floor. The tale is still told in parliaments around the world.

It can be summed up thus:

Lawrence, rising to his feet: "Mr Speaker, I wish to say to the Honourable Member from 'Platberg' that he is," ... pause "... *a snake in the grass* ...."

"Order! Order!! Order!!!" shouted the Speaker, thumping his gavel to gratify the astonished gasps across the government benches, and to subdue the shouts and the opposing laughter across the Assembly.

"Withdraw! Withdraw that instantly!"

Lawrence, waiting a while for the tension to rise, and anticipating just in time an order from the Chair to leave the House. "I shall reluctantly withdraw those words, Mr Speaker, but I shall say this to the Honourable Mamba ..."

It was a rare moment to witness first-hand, as was a small side-incident when a disturbed elderly white man and would-be assassin shot Prime Minister HF Verwoerd in his seat in the grandstand at the Johannesburg Rand Easter Show. A worried foreign TV journalist told us in the Parliamentary Gallery, that he was being questioned by the police about a cable he sent to his TV station in the US saying that he had "missed Verwoerd at Parliament" some days ago, but promised to "shoot him at the upcountry Agricultural Show".

BY 1957 THE NATIONAL PARTY had re-altered parliamentary constituencies, mobilised, and transferred dependent civil servants to key voting areas in an election that gave it a politically invincible all-white parliament. But even that manipulation did not reduce its members' fears or raise their confidence. Not only the world, but also countless moderate Afrikaners were against the Nat Party's brutality. Yet it continued to rule by causing fear and encouraging hatred. This produced small yet deep divisions within the party itself.

This was also why no Nationalist in the early days could afford to be seen talking to the opposition press ... with one exception. From the beginning, it was essential that the Minister of Foreign Affairs, the loquacious and vain Eric Louw, should converse with the outside world. And this he did, loudly and sometimes effectively.

Thus, I had met the Minister of Foreign Affairs in the Lobby of the House very early on in my stint of seemingly endless sessions of Parliament. Spotting a new face in the Assembly Press Gallery, he had approached me in the Lobby and said in English: "Ask me this question and you will get an interesting reply." I took out my notebook and said: "Consider your question asked," and, whatever it was, recorded his brief answer in shorthand.

But this dubious relationship could not last. Eric Louw was a reminder – in stature and technique – of Goebbels, the Nazi propagandist of the previous decade. Very soon he had a brush with my senior colleague, Newman Robinson, political correspondent of *The Star.*

Newman was a quiet, friendly fellow, a convinced pacifist, non-combatant who had gone to Hitler's war as an ambulance man, and therefore had seen more blood and encountered more danger than most combatants in the No Man's Land of El Alamein and the North African Western Desert.

In all our years together I saw Newman in a rage only once.

He entered our office in Parliament and, without greeting, he said: "Come with me. I need a witness."

He was too angry to explain his mission as we marched across the street to the Foreign Minister's headquarters. Newman, a man possessed, for he never acted like this before or since, stormed into the Private Secretary's office, and said: "Where is he? Tell him I need to speak to him right now. He can't hide."

Wide-eyed, the man said, "Mr Robinson, I'm afraid he is not in ..."

"And I'm afraid I have cause not to believe you," said Newman, and pushed past the protesting secretary; opened the minister's door, and strode in. The minister was not there.

Newman turned to the minister's secretary and said: "Tell him, from me, that he is a bloody liar," said Newman.

And we left. It was the first, and last time, I'd seen my senior colleague be anything but a very quiet "gentleman".

I wondered why he should be surprised or upset at a politician lying.

That happened very early in nearly five years and seven sessions of watching a politically corrupt, undemocratic government in action. I finally escaped from reporting in the Assembly, but the experience helped prompt me to leave journalism for a while.

Politics was obviously getting on our nerves. That mass protest march on Cape Town following the Sharpeville massacre in 1960 was the only real news story – as opposed to political analysis and parliamentary reporting and squabbling – that I had done in years. Fortunately the decade that followed was, for me, a disruptive roller-coaster ride filled with extraordinary experiences and memories. But they hardly belong to the story of journalism and can best be left till near-last in this book.

Other conversations with the enemy

It occurs to me now that I subconsciously re-enacted Newman Robinson's scene at Parliament more than 20 years later in a different theatre of life.

The public stage was a reception – a party really – arranged by my old friend, former journalist Aubrey Sussens. Everyone from "Mr Jo'burg" to "Miss South Africa", "Mr Rugby" and all of Transvaal's newspaper editors were there. It meant I might bump into "Johnny" Johnson, the editor of *The Citizen,* which had been exposed by the *Rand Daily Mail* as a government secretly-funded propaganda organ. Johnson at this time was continually publishing false allegations about *The Star*.

Approaching the entrance to the party's venue I told myself I would be perfectly calm and dismiss him with an icy stare. As I went up in the lift, I even practised a cold stare, just to reinforce my determination not to argue or even exchange words with him. Unfortunately, while I was about to be introduced to the beautiful Miss South Africa by my host at the door, I saw the editor of The Citizen across the room.

"Johnson! You bloody liar!" I shouted.

It caused a hush to fall upon the scene. It resulted in a taut and interestingly vibrant party. But I don't suppose it impressed Miss South Africa. ☐

30.
The daily 'rush' – hitched to a star.

Adhere to independent, honest and responsible standards of journalism that do not pander to personal or sectional interests but are concerned solely with the public interest.

The brief of *The Star's* editor.

As a new decade began for the 1970s, so began a new life for me as I stepped in trepidation into the new, glass-walled, double-storey foyer of *The Star* and, avoiding the queues waiting at the banks of lifts, walked up four flights of marble stairs to the editorial offices.

This building was a far cry from the one I had entered from another street in the same block as a would-be cadet nearly a quarter-of-a-century earlier. Its modernity seemed uncomfortably more imposing than the old newspaper building I knew of here in Johannesburg as well as in New York's Times Square, or the new utilitarian London Times building Murdoch was soon to build in Canary Wharf.

I had been warned in advance of *The Star*'s new image by the reserved, staccato, John Jordi, its "editor elect", when I had accepted his offer of becoming his deputy.

The editorial staff occupied the second floor of the entire frontage of the building. And in the factory at the back the newspaper was preparing to accommodate the roar of global state-of-the-art presses printing five sections in four or five successive daily editions.

It was becoming, by international standards, a surprisingly large newspaper.

Jordi, a lean, tall, sardonic man, had been a wartime volunteer who served in the Royal Navy, and then worked his way up from a senior reporter on the *Pretoria News* to the foreign desk in London and bureau chief in New York.

He'd said, when flying down to Cape Town to offer me a job as his deputy: "*The Star* will demand all we've got. It's becoming a bloody great tanker, which when you signal a change, nothing happens. And only when you think you've lost control does it begin to change course. By that time it may be too late, or irrelevant."

The Star's editorial floor was an extraordinary place at that time; for me at least. No one would ever again act as a frantic "copy boy" grabbing a story from a reporter's typewriter while he was still typing. Instead copy whizzed across the building with a bang and a whine, up and down several storeys on metal wires and in pneumatically-powered tubes.

Edited copy paper from the Subs Room was dispatched through tunnelled walls, and down to "The Works", where linotype operators transformed the typed text into columns of lead for dispatch to the proofreaders and back to the Newsroom for checking. Meanwhile, the lead "formes" of early pages were already being assembled on "The Stone", checked again, and rushed to the Machine Room for bolting on the presses.

Ah, the proofreaders! All of them seemed to be humble literary giants in those days. Their corrections of "copy", at the height of hysteria on an afternoon paper deadline, remained erudite and immaculate. They worked on streams of text at such speed in a big afternoon deadline paper that they had to gather in far greater numbers than on morning papers, and concentrate with the intensity of flights of fighter pilots hurrying into battle. They could not prevent misprints further down the line, however, because corrections were rushed through, and in themselves, unchecked corrections carried the risk of fallibility, either on "The Stone", where the lead type was assembled, or in the Press Room as the pages were manhandled.

The extraordinary thing was that the heavy, clumsy system seemed – to us, later – to be quicker than computerisation. The production staff was far greater, of course, before computers came, and the standby, normally half-empty "Stop Press" column could carry late news "on the run", well beyond the going-to-press deadline.

As early as "pre-war days" afternoon editions had been selling on the far ends of the 100-kilometre "Gold Reef" before 4pm, carrying fresh reports on the same afternoon's stock exchange prices ... when in later years news vans failed to reach those same traffic-clogged destinations in time. But obviously the old mechanical way could not be compared with the silent efficiency of flickering digits. When the ceiling of *The Star* Newsroom was changed to accept early computer wiring, some old, once urgent, missing news copy was finally traced to where the stories had fallen off the aerial tube tracks on the "pneumatic wire" months before.

And the best anecdotes of "balls-ups in the works" could no longer be told, such as these:

Of the time, the fastest stonehand in town had locked up the leaded page one and pushed away its trolley, with a grand gesture, in the direction of the pressroom – only to see it topple over some fallen lead and spill the front page ... delaying, beyond resuscitation, the first edition.

Or of the time an assistant editor rushed to the Press Room with an urgent message, shouting dramatically, "Hold the Presses!" and fell down the metal stairs, doing himself some damage. The presses, each set bigger than two steam locomotives, ground slowly to a halt ... as they were to do several times more during the next few weeks when machine crew recalled the incident for newcomers and repeated the shout, unfortunately, for dramatic effect, "Hold the Presses!" in imitation of the assistant editor's action .... The presses, again and once again, ground to a halt.

IT MUST BE A DISTURBING experience for a stranger to visit such a large newsroom in the hopes of seeing how it works.

In recent years in the computerised world, the visitor to a large metropolitan afternoon paper near deadline would see banks of reporters staring anxiously at their screens to make out what they had written, or worse, staring at what they had *not* written on an unwinking, semi-blank screen. As the seconds ticked by, there would be odd shouts, which made the relative silence and inaction more acute.

Nothing seemed to be able to distract a journalist at that moment – except those old "newfangled damn computers". For a sensitive observer, however, nothing could be more excruciating, surely, than watching a writer desperately trying to think, while acutely aware that his time was up. I remember when computers were first introduced in the 1980s that – in the laboured silence pierced by curses of "my fucking cursor's frozen!!" – reporters of both sexes wished momentarily to return to the bad habits of their all-male forebears of the 1940s: grab a cigarette and head for the pub.

But they are so much more disciplined than we were. Our first computers, even when they froze, insisted on it. They did so even when each computer in the early 1980s was as big as a restaurant refrigerator, but isolated among the long rows behind double-doors in a silent air-conditioned arena on a different floor.

Today, computerisation of all forms of communication moves so fast that a formal newsroom may soon be redundant.

Hard times ahead

Computerised printing was not even on the horizon in 1974 when John Jordi, in his mid-50s, dropped dead at the editor's desk, literally.

I was at home that morning when it happened, about to leave on holiday for the coast. Thrice he had asked me for a contact address, but I was hoping to disappear completely for a much needed two-week break. My car was packed and I was heading for my front door when a frantic telephone call summoned me back to that desk. I had to move into his office while his body was still being attended to in the building.

John was a great and relatively young editor who did not survive long enough in the chair to make his presence and his vision fully felt. Intellectually, he was a born rebel. Some of his political views were Left of the Liberal Party (which was too Left to win any seat in an all-white parliament).

Yet as an editor, he gave every political party an equal hearing – going so far as to suggest to readers of *The Star* that white voters should support the least dishonest, most efficient, and least racist candidates –

"even if they are Nationalists". As his deputy I did not always agree with him, but he didn't mind. It was his custom to argue more with his friends than his enemies, whom he scorned. A fine man with a head immune to the disengaging effects of alcohol, which was a challenge for me, his drinking companion.

And suddenly he was gone.

I arrived at the office without time to unload any of my packed holiday luggage. I remained, as deputy in his office for seeming unending months, running *The Star* precisely in the way he would have run it.

My view was, and is, that newly appointed editors – and worse, aspirant editors – too often introduce change merely to make their mark, in the way of would-be alpha-male dogs. Change, at least in a highly successful paper, should be long considered and then dropped, or very cautiously applied.

My worst mistake was to drop a long-running comic strip from one of the back pages … the beloved Andy Capp, whose single joke illustrating his wily, henpecked, male chauvinism seemed to have long ago run out of steam. I replaced him with Hägar the Horrible, who offered a genuine quip each day. Reader reaction to this change was the most prolific and angry that I ever experienced. Even *The Star*'s production staff was threatening, half seriously, to stop reading the paper.

The vociferous public accepted Hägar only after Andy was returned to the same page, and Modesty Blaise – a second-generation version of the old wartime pinup Jane – was given equal space in which to shed her clothing. However that comic mistake of mine was made only after I had been in the editor's chair for several years; had somewhat bigger issues and changes to deal with, and stupidly thought I knew what I was doing.

A deputy editor left in charge of the bridge of a big paper is a stand-in whose job it is to keep all its passengers safe and the ship steadily on course. Nonetheless, as the man temporarily on watch, I dreaded handing it over to a new "captain", whoever it might be. Even when it turned out to be me, I retained a subtle scent of personal dread for nearly a year. In the end, however, as famous author Herman Charles Bosman might have said after a year in the Death Cell: "In the end, you can be comfortable and relaxed anywhere."

René de Villiers, the first Afrikaans-speaking editor in the history of *The Star,* had retired as John Jordi took command. Now De Villiers visited the editor's office, which he had so discreetly avoided doing after being elected a Member of the Opposition's non-racial Progressive Party in Parliament in his retirement.

He gave me the most helpful advice I ever received: "Harvey, there's no need to worry about any crisis because, on *The Star*, there's always a worse crisis coming along in 15 minutes."

When big is beautiful

Shortly after I took over, I was blessed with a succession of general managers who saw, as clearly as John Jordi and I had done, the need to make changes without allowing change to offend our long-standing readership or to alter the paper's apparent imperturbable personality. Within a decade, however, I had conspired with them in instigating changes none of us had dreamed of. Circumstances, technology, and the need for growth, survival – and therefore strength – forced us to adjust swiftly.

By the mid-1980s, when we faced the worst of threats, I found myself to be editor-in-chief of *The Star*'s fully computerised multi-publications, including our new daily Morning Star (working title only); our new separately created *Saturday Star* and later-launched *Sunday Star* (replaced by the *Sunday Independent*). It also included of course the main, traditional multi-edition, five-section afternoon daily *Star*, as well as the Friday *Star International Weekly*. We also launched the world's first 24-page daily newspaper colour TV supplement, *Tonight!* Only then did I feel our freedom was fairly safe, for I fully appreciated how essential it was for *The Star* to be big enough to face down its political enemies and would-be censors.

In a few years we grew into one of the three biggest newspapers in the world.

This is an extremely modest claim, because we are talking only of the daily newspaper's physical bulk. In those days the dubious honour of publishing the world's thickest daily broadsheet was competed for each year by the *Los Angeles Times*, the *Sydney Morning Herald* and *The Star*, Johannesburg's afternoon daily. These three newspapers possessed the three biggest Classified Advertising sections in the world, and *The Star*'s was believed to be the first in the world to be fully computerised.

Still, no one wants to be known as "the thickest", and none of our bulk and prosperity had anything do with the quality of our journalism, although we prided ourselves on the newspaper's international, "upmarket", conservatively written, finely edited and displayed content. It was the "Smalls" section that made us extra big – the births, deaths, marriages, car sales, job vacancies and other activities that thrived with the increasing population, sophistication and wealth of our metropolitan readers. The unofficial and insignificant title of "Biggest in the World" rotated across the globe following the economic status of our competing cities on three continents and the skill of our vast, efficient advertising sales staff.

Obviously, considering the literacy rate in South Africa, we could not compete with the Western world in circulation figures, but we could – and did – communicate across the cultural divides and soon boast of more black readers than the entire "black" press in the Transvaal; more Afrikaans readers than both of the Afrikaans Nationalist government-supporting papers; more sales than any two other daily newspapers in the country ... and rising.

For these and very significant political reasons, size is important. And pm deadlines are significant, because the presses don't simply thunder through the long night or weekend as they do in most of the world. In *The Star*'s basements they had to print, collate, insert and dispatch a newspaper of up to a regular five-separate-sections, 120 broadsheet pages – not in the normal way through the long night, but at nearly 50000 copies each hour; sometimes a thousand a minute and a print order of a quarter of a million copies of a five-section newspaper every day. Now that was worth watching; for a minute at least.

South Africa's biggest newspaper grew to the point where, if you were able to cut its pages to fit the size of a book, your daily read would be as thick as Dickens' *Bleak House*. Too big to read all of it properly in a day. It was indeed, by any standards, an astonishingly big daily paper, and probably the biggest same-day paper ever published anywhere.

In those worst of political times, *The Star* grew in size and profitability, which meant that "Aunty Argus", despite her "grey" *Times*-like presentations, attracted the most readers and advertisers and could continue to support the largest "foreign" newspaper office in Fleet Street. It covered an entire floor of Reuters London headquarters with highly qualified journalists numbering more than the staff of an average small daily. The reason for this was that Britain's 19th-century practice of laying undersea cables across the world made London an international clearing-house for news. For instance Africa's nations – and the world – kept in touch with Africa through lines to London.

Our company could afford to buy copyright and lifting rights from about 20 of the English-speaking world's top news publications, and half a dozen big and small local and international news agencies.

History had bequeathed us with *total and exclusive* lifting rights in Africa to all content ranging from news and sport and finance to features and arts and analysis in *The Guardian, The Observer, Sunday Times, Daily Mail,* and *The Times* in Britain, as well as from the *New York Times, Washington Post, Los Angeles Times* and others in America and elsewhere. Argus newspapers probably owned the richest lifting rights in a world where most big papers had only two or three exclusive "lifters".

The Star subeditors copytasted a million words of our combined news services before breakfast every morning. (This often made subeditors smile ruefully at the layman's view that mainstream newspapers strive to fill their columns.)

One wonders whether any *digital* newspaper will ever attain such riches of news content or the means of publishing it in one piece ... and the means of helping its community to help itself through the paper's publicised messages of their effort and charity.

The vital role of 'bridging'

A source of great pride was the way *The Star* had always, in its hundred years, helped the needy and those hit by tragedies and disasters. And now the paper's main concern centred on the victims of racial discrimination. The newspaper encouraged its readers to be aware of these matters, and it tried to help the helpless where possible.

We were by no means the first in charitable newspaper campaigning, and I kept particular note of *La Prensa* in Buenos Aires, which had been surviving a ruthless dictatorship mainly because the people – even those who hated the newspaper's democratic, liberal views – wanted it so. The editors of *La Prensa* knew that its strength lay in the newspaper's reputation as an independent journal fighting for freedom. But for more than 50 years it also offered free medical and free legal services to the poor.

At one time more than 30 doctors did voluntary work in a clinic within the *La Prensa* building, and queues filled the ground-floor passages, including some of the 30 000 people who annually made use of the paper's own "public" library. *La Prensa* also created a "flying literacy unit" which travelled the country, teaching peasants to read.

All this, sadly, did not save some of its editors from being murdered by secret police. Yet it survived ... though it is unlikely to survive the digital age.

The Star had lesser, but wider challenges relating to its readership. Its "Action Line" consumer service rapidly turned into a service for queues of black people seeking help with their "pass" documents; security of their homes and other basic legal problems ... a response so overwhelming we had to call in the aid of the all-women white voters protest movement, the Black Sash.

The newspaper also built on one of its upper floors a super-kitchen and auditorium for cooking lessons and meal planning. Like many newspapers, it encouraged its readers to support dozens of "Star" charities, ranging from funds for winter blankets to literacy courses.

For 50 years the *The Star Seaside Fund* had sent needy children on holiday to the coast to be cared for and to see the sea for the first time. It still does so. The newspaper launched, under James Clarke, one of the first environmental newspaper campaigns in the world, when "green" was simply a colour.

But best of all our many social and editorial stand-alone projects, were our various "newspaper-in-education (NIE)" initiatives, and especially the TEACH Fund, exhorting big business and all the paper's readers to help build classrooms for children without schools. "Teach Every African Child", a title created by Manager (ex-journalist) Jolyon Nuttall, raised sufficient money over a ten-year period to build many whole schools, as well as added classrooms and ensure an education, for an estimated quarter of a million children who might have missed education altogether!

This communal contribution I counted as one of the newspaper's greatest achievements in a hundred years of service.

Active partnership with its readers and all its community – Left and Right, white and black, brown and foreign, speaking more than a dozen languages including Greek and Portuguese – is I believe the mark of a true mainstream newspaper. Our policy was *to reason* with all our readers rather than lecture or hector them ... apart from those who propagated nationalist racialism. Moderation was our traditional stance, but not often possible in so extreme a political climate.

The constant adherence to the declared policy of Argus newspapers of championing the interests of ALL sections of society, and of course all races, and seeking *bridges of understanding* between all sections of our readership, was an example of, and small part of the reason why, we believed it was possible for the "miracle" to be achieved by Nelson Mandela and FW de Klerk after 1990.

The power of the written words of all the apartheid-opposing press for nearly half a century, led by active reformers of every race in every culture, formed the chemistry that led to democracy. The "Rainbow Nation" lived shortly in that miracle, except among the tribally illiterate where, sadly, the killing fields flourished briefly, even after freedom came.

Such "miracles" might be possible again in today's ultra-communication systems. But, looking back, one is forced to ask oneself: Will all the global electronic news services and commentaries; the publicly organised community bonding, the legal defence resources, and other services offered by a newspaper like *The Star* in its heyday a few decades back, be available to any local independent digital news organisation in decades to come?

An answer to this will hopefully be considered later in "Book II. *End of the Deadline*", about the future of the press, which will complement this one. □

31.

June '76 Soweto protests get world attention.

In the case of news, we should always wait for the sacrament of confirmation.

Voltaire 1694–1778.

T*elling it like it is*," was the slogan we agreed on for our newspaper in the 1970s. The decision was not easy, for I worried about the phrase's mauled grammar. Sure enough, we received in the next fortnight unprecedented numbers of protesting letters – most of them from schoolroom classes written at the suggestion of English teachers. (They objected proprietarily with forthright confidence because many schools of all races used our paper as an educational tool in class.)

We knew then we had "a winner", despite having to explain, hundreds of times, the difference between a slogan and a statement.

We used our popular slogan until Emergency Regulation censorship made our commitment impossible and we protested this by publicly withdrawing our "*telling it like it is*" slogan in the late 1980s.

Yet in the most significant, most explosive, uprising in apartheid's history (more politically-charged than the death of 69 protesters at Sharpeville 16 years previously) we think we fulfilled our promise to the slogan's 17th letter. During "Soweto 1976" the protesters were unarmed children, mostly. The police were relatively few, as was the death toll.

The uprising was never intended as a violent one. It was spontaneously carried out by "learners" ... yet it proved to be an iconic moment in African history because of a basic and priceless right that was being denied to those children and because the tragedy arising out of their protests gained instant international publicity.

What made the event unique in a world already weary of sporadic uprisings, was not only that it was a "children's revolution", and recorded not belatedly by a flood of incoming foreign correspondents, but instead by reporters and citizens and parents who lived in the great township. They were people who were familiar with every nuance of the issues and the politically imposed education which their children were defying.

White citizens (especially white journalists) were prevented from entering the exclusively black township without a written permit. It was a rule that every good journalist disobeyed … but for most of them movement was necessarily secretive and restricted.

In a year when State television was just beginning to be tested and introduced (radio content was strictly controlled by the State, and digital communication systems were unheard of), it was only the efforts of Johannesburg's newspapers that made "Soweto '76" world news and African history.

I repeat here the newspaper experience of the Soweto riots because I believe it encapsulates most of the key decisions with which the accountable free press across the world is required to deal. Far more is required than, say, a single narrator's running commentary, or one eyewitness account of some events.

There are demanding questions that editors need to ask themselves while any major story is breaking exclusively in their territory on deadline. They include the obvious, such as:

- How to ensure, in the heat of chaotic times, that the vital news has sufficient detail to judge its accuracy and weight?
- As the minutes tick by and the violence escalates, what is sure enough, rather than safe enough, to publish in the interests of all readers, and at what particular moment in the escalating public crisis?
- After the first edition the questions are: Have we published too little of the impossible-to-check information from numbers of reporters? Or too much that could prove dubious and possibly highly damaging to the paper and to society generally?
- Is the published collation of dozens of reports good enough to keep and update, or has the scene changed so far that a total revision is required in the next 15 minutes?
- What vital information is not yet available to readers near the violence, or those preparing to commute home or take other action?

There is huge pressure on deadline in a newspaper. Many times higher on an afternoon paper. And, oddly enough, I found after having worked on all forms of newspapers over the years, that the bigger and more authorative the newspaper, the higher still the pressure. Furthermore, the space to manoeuvre grows tighter.

In my own case, as an instinctive hands-on reporter, I found it particularly difficult when world news broke on our doorstep. My job in a crisis was to stay at the editor's desk beside which my predecessor, friend and former foreign correspondent John Jordi had collapsed and died only 20 hectic months previously.

The seemingly unwieldy, multi-layered *Star* worked with a smooth, historically drilled hierarchal structure, modelled on ships at sea and designed to discount failure in a crisis. These moments emphasised the role of an editor as responsible for "everything", like a sea captain. (In the newspaper's case, as I have noted in other contexts, this means responsibility for every word published in the editor's newspaper – including the advertisements which an editor seldom sees in advance nor reads in print after publication. It is a practical as well as a legal requirement. The editor is responsible, even in his or her absence.)

On Friday 16 June 1976, I was probably the least experienced editor of a daily newspaper in South Africa – and happened to be the youngest editor in the hundred-year history of *The Star*. So I had to force myself to sit at my desk and simply wait for the crises to be reported.

This is what happened:

At midday, 140 minutes before the first deadline, editorial comments on the crisis are already written; the manager's teatime talk is abandoned, and I have no answer yet to a side issue that worries us both: what is the fate of our "*Star* high schools" in all this student destruction? (*The Star* and tens of thousands of its readers who had volunteered funds to the newspaper's TEACH Fund were directly involved in trying to ameliorate the educational issue that was the cause of the riots.)

Towards first deadline I am informed of only three things:

Several schoolchildren have been shot or wounded by the police.

"How many?"

"We have no idea of numbers yet."

"Let me know when you have some balanced and checked facts."

We have a second report that other protesters are armed with sticks and stones and are marching on a nearby town on the West Rand. There's a huge pall of smoke over the West Rand.

"Source?"

"A traffic cop, but from a neighbouring area."

"Any confirmation of fires as well as smoke?"

"Can't get through, but the cop has reported the sighting to the fire station ... it's a helluva story if the demo has moved right into town!"

(We're on deadline for the only edition that covers the West Rand.)

"No. The report has too many consequences to use without a proper cross-check and some details to assess its size ... hold the story."

"But we do know that fire brigades have reacted. They just haven't got through to where buildings are reported to be burning yet."

"Print that with a qualifier about no confirmation of rioting there, and little else is known at going to press."

We're getting great copy from our reporters and their car drivers in Soweto itself. The World *is passing on eyewitness accounts by their staff for use tomorrow a.m. Shall we use today?*

"Yes. With bylines."

On the first major deadline a deputation comes into my office with a selection of photographs. It is a deputation because the photos are filled with emotion and impact – and the best is not ours. The photographer is Sam Nzima from our ("black") sister paper, *The Sowetan*.

The photo is handed to me. It's a picture that will go round the world many times. It's a photo of a sturdy, weeping youth, Mbuyisa Makhubo, with the body of 13-year-old Hector Pieterson in his arms and another pupil, Antoinette Sithole, palpably in shock as they walk down a typical Soweto street. In the first moment in that electrified ambience, shorn of all future political exploitation, the close-up human picture is heart-stopping.

"Any other pictures?"

The entire deputation appears shocked. They're thinking of clearing most of the front page to give the Hector Pieterson photo the sensational over-size coverage it deserves. Through my mind flashes a picture, taken in the Cato Manor Riots more than 25 years previously. It is of a police baton poised above the swirling dust of a riot as the Zulu policeman's "knobkerrie" hovers high above the crouching head of a Zulu woman. "Put that on page two," the editor had said.

It took me years to understand, and inwardly to "forgive" him. He was one of the few editors in our company that I had admired as a young reporter. The fact that the picture appeared on the front page that day of every other afternoon newspaper across the nation, didn't make it easier. Nor did the reminders of its constant re-publishing across the world for years to come.

The Cato Manor Riots had raged intermittently for many days

(Source: Sam Nzima).

with many Zulu and Indian residents losing their lives. The riots had been sparked by a youngster being slapped for stealing an apple from an Indian shopkeeper. How many more lives might have been lost through incitement in the heat of that day, if that brilliant, shocking picture had appeared *upfront and on site* in the heat of the continued battle?

I come to appreciate now the wisdom (and courage) of that editor defying our professional contempt and our instant journalistic judgements. I give inward thanks to his memory as I tell *The Star*'s delegation:

"Print that as a close-up vertical on Page One, next to this smaller horizontal one."

The second is a static photo: the body a white social welfare worker lying beside his vehicle. The prostrate body is partly visible beside some stones used by passing rioters to kill him in Soweto before he could flee. It transpires that half of Soweto later mourns the well-known social worker's murder.

The balanced, sobering juxtaposition of the large upright and smaller horizontal photos are the result of the only two instant decisions with which I am immediately at peace. The day rolls on, with more frantic, sensational news, and rumours and exaggerations.

315

Students voice their protests. It is easily forgotten that tens of thousands of white citizens, English and Afrikaans, objected to Apartheid and to institutionalised racism. A few joined the United Democratic Front (UDF) and similar organisations, but most avoided illegality as well as radicalism, even when their sons were sent, under protest, to join the national army. Parents and conscripts protested, even though they were supposed to be benefitting from Apartheid. But nearly all baulked at open defiance of the law.

We kill the stories which lack detail and confirmation, and print what we can as the deadline for each edition arrives. Our news stories and all the news photos are sent to our other afternoon papers and to the world outside.

As the day wears down to the deadline of the Late Final Edition, we know we have a newspaper with almost all that has happened so far, and all of it checked and printed.

(The biggest, the most sensational story of the smoke seen rising, and a mob said to be marching on a sleepy neighbouring West Rand town, finally turns out to be a false alarm. It is fortunate therefore that we have withheld this headline "news", despite the observations of a municipal traffic cop who is our "official" source. The discipline of print is suddenly stark ... unlike running commentary on airwaves whose broadcast announcements disappear and alter in minutes.)

Sophie Tema, a great reporter whom we had seconded to *The World* newsroom deep in Soweto, fills the centre of our page one with an eyewitness account from the middle of the riot. Her report gives the coverage of events the direct, human touch and the full understanding it requires. Our own group of African reporters has stepped in where whites are forbidden entry without an apartheid pass, and has not only sent us highly professional copy, but gone to the assistance of the injured after filing their copy. We are about to relax and celebrate when more news comes in.

Across Johannesburg, on the opposite, north-eastern side, peaceful demonstrations have suddenly turned into riots on the border of the Alexandra black freehold township. Pedestrians are being stoned, awnings and windows being smashed. Looting has broken out. Shops are being attacked, and barricades are being erected across the main highway to Pretoria. There are reports of tyres burning in the streets. All reporters still in the newsroom leap to their phones, making random calls to the north-eastern area. In ten minutes we realise that much of what the tip-offs claim are true, but just as many tip-offs are exaggeration or entirely false rumour.

The Late Final edition begins to roll, only minutes late, and carrying all the checked and double-checked extra information required by commuters who are about to exit their city offices. They can buy a newspaper on the street corner and learn which routes to avoid, and which streets they can safely use. The people of Alexandra can learn that the rumours of violence are exaggerated. Workers can return to all suburbs and to the freehold township along certain routes without fear of attack from any quarter. All our readers now have many shocking facts to absorb; and editorial opinion on cause and consequence to ponder, support or reject.

With no television whatever, and only censored State radio broadcasts, it is the first and only reliable news available to anyone in the metropolitan area, or the world outside. Next day we learn that "a miracle" is unfolding and that, despite the destruction overnight and in coming days of beer halls, government offices and many schools, the Star Schools are being *protected* by rioting students. Not a single windowpane is broken. We also learn, soon after our last deadline that among the mounting casualties is a lone, unarmed (African) policeman, stoned to death by children.

The photographer's role.

Sam Nzima's emotion-draining image of children confronting death in Soweto that day helped spark the first successful mass uprising against apartheid. His picture, first published and despatched to the world within hours by *The Star* in Johannesburg, also turned the "Soweto Riots '76" into an internationally recognized turning point in history. The event offered many lessons to society. Yet the celebrations of its 40th anniversary in 2016 demonstrated that few of those lessons have been noticed, let alone learnt.

For instance, within months of the 40th anniversary of Soweto '76, similar riots with similar causes and effects, broke out in our democracy a few hundred kilometres from Soweto – and very few recognized the close resemblance.

The 2016 mass protests occurred in what was once Vendaland in the north-east corner of South Africa. Residents were, perhaps consciously, copying the past by attacking and burning schools and government buildings. Their reason for doing so – objection to administrative and municipal boundaries – in no way seemed to justify their nihilistic and self-damaging actions. Populist reactions from all quarters of the rest of South Africa were puzzlement and condemnation of the reported violence. The current government reaction was: "The culprits will be arrested, by force if necessary."

However, like Soweto '76, the protestors had been unable to articulate their *basic* frustration and anger. In both cases the basic cause of their deep-seated anger; their burning of property and even schools, was that they felt they were the victims of *discrimination and injustice*. How quickly do governments – and their supporters, black as well as white – continue to forget about the rights of minorities.

Role of African reporters

Another lesson from Soweto '76 may be seen in the myths that arose even though most participants were still its living witnesses. One example is the recent, oft-recorded view that African reporters reached parity that day with the journalistic standards of the rest of the world. That does not accord with reality as journalists saw it in those days. Our belief, partly in our newsrooms and totally in the senior editorial positions in those days, was that African men and women journalists were equal to their counterparts of any other colour – and often superior in that they usually wrote in a second language. Equality of black and white skills applied to editors (such as my colleagues Percy Qoboza and Aggrey Klaaste) – and to photographers.

Present black writers have no cause to belittle their predecessors. Sam Nzima, for instance, demonstrated not only the art, but also the instinctive skills of a press cameraman, including the skill of outwitting the police and meeting his deadlines.

His feat helped preserve not just the heroism of the school children's revolt, but of the icons and reputations that were created by it.

Another lesson

One final example of the lessons still to be learned from Soweto '76: As I write, thousands of *newspaper* journalists around the world are being taught the skills of *video* photography. Meanwhile *television* news coverage of intricate topics such as *Brexit* and the strangely trumpeted US elections have shown that television – not newspapers or the web — are *best* at covering major news ... especially almost constantly running news of major terrorist attacks and mass assassinations. Other media should not forget their specialist roles.

Rapidly evolving technology is likely to make video-takes ubiquitous and constantly available. We need then to remember the lesson regarding the emotional impact of visuals. It seems to me that a *still* photograph, whether depicting war, peace, human suffering, or human dignity, far outweighs the impact of video coverage of the same topic. Will the world remember, and take into account that lesson? Will the "critical, emotional, frozen moment in time" be recorded in the future? Or will it merely be a moment extracted from the ubiquitous video? I fear that I shall never know. □

32.
The other side of the story.

Between the conception and the creation
Between the emotion and the response
Falls the Shadow.

T S Elliot, 1888–1965.

The credo "tell both sides of the story" prompts me to give you a different view of *The Star* newspapers, which I have just described with so much admiration and affection during the 20 years I was its deputy editor, editor and editor-in-chief. Here is a view directly opposite to my own experiences and prejudices.

It came from one of *The Star*'s best writers, Jon Qwelane, who became, regrettably in my view, the most opinionated and prejudiced of reporters during those last and worst days of censorship and political oppression. When it was all over, and he was seeking support from Archbishop Desmond Tutu and Reverend Alex Boraine's Truth and Reconciliation Commission (TRC),for his personal views, Qwelane wrote: "It is not only the manner in which our bosses failed us as journalists which must be probed and finally exposed, but also the hopelessly indefensible treatment which they gave the news."

His protest was never taken seriously by the TRC, but it sounded to me that this fine writer, whose career had required special favouritism and protection at one stage, was now mouthing the ravings of apartheid's minister of information.

Qwelane went further, calling the opposition press "fellow conspirators" of apartheid ... and he meant that literally. He wrote:

"Perhaps the most indefensible part of collaboration with the apartheid regime by media bosses was the secret pact they sealed with PW Botha ... it was agreed by all concerned that there was a 'communist-inspired total onslaught' against South Africa and it required a 'total strategy' to counter it .... Yet it is totally because of the 'total strategy' to which they were an active party that we had severe censorship: nearly every story had to be vetted prior to publication, photographs showing army or the police could not be published, and the only truth we could print without fear was the monumental lie dredged out daily by Botha's Bureau of Information."

321

That may have been his personal view from his corner of the reporter's room, but he went on:

> *"It is anybody's guess how many years the 'total strategy' pact delayed our political freedom, and it is also anybody's guess how many lives might have been spared had there been no 'total strategy' madness to give Botha's soldiers and police licence to murder and destroy at will, in full knowledge that all their actions would go unpunished."*

Had I not been so shocked – gob-smacked – by this viewpoint, expressed publicly a few years after my retirement, I might have enjoyed the irony of seeing Jon's extraordinary, wildly false, tirade in *The Saturday Star*. The irony was he was using the extra weekly newspaper I had helped create, and his byline was below an "Undercurrent Affairs" logo which Jordi and I had used over 17 years to criticise censorship, racism, and every other vestige of apartheid ... including its crimes of violence *and* its "total strategy" propaganda.

If he had mentioned to me *just once* his concern about the "silent conspiracy" he raged about – instead of doing so only years later in the easy post-apartheid era – I could have put him right on a single, but fundamental fact: There was NO pact of any kind with PW Botha. There never could be. If it were possible *The Star,* under my watch or anyone else's would have rejected such *toenadering* (approaching closer) in front-page headlines.

Many years ago, before Qwelane joined the newspaper probably, the head of the SA Police had appealed to editors to "tone down" their reports in the interests of national security, and to "avoid civic violence". If we co-operated, there would be no need to introduce direct censorship, the police chief told a formal meeting he requested with editors. I went deliberately on record in public and to the police and press, in the only joint meeting held in our times at Police Headquarters, to state categorically: "Whatever your appeal – or threat – may be, my newspaper cannot and will not 'tone down' its reports, as you request."

But later there had been an incident challenging this common precept. Without any editor's knowledge, the National Press Union (NPU), a trade body representing the owners of all mainstream newspapers, including government-supporting Afrikaans newspapers as well as anti-apartheid English-language newspapers, had foolishly tried to reason with the president about the severity and illogicality of the increasing censorship laws. They should have known that nobody could reason with PW Botha.

He simply told them – and apparently they passively accepted "for the sake of argument" – that he was fighting a total onslaught against South Africa. When Botha announced this "agreement" publicly, I remember phoning in anger to tell the Argus Company's senior National Press Union representative that he had been trapped, and that I would never accept Botha's propaganda, or tone down our reports.

"I never expected you would," he replied. That was the sum total of it, among all opposition newspapers.

It is still impossible for me to understand how Jon, even from his seat in the reporters' room, could not see that the real reason for 40 years of attempted censorship, and three years of "State of Emergency" blackout attempted by the government, was *because* the press refused to "tone down" voluntarily its reporting of events.

Jon himself did some great reporting for *The Star*. His stories got the favourable treatment they deserved. It seems inexplicable that anyone could have such contradictory views on this area of journalism.

There is another issue, of course, on which most white journalists sharply disagreed with a number of leading black journalists. Sadly it involved those of the racially-exclusive black journalists' caucus who believed that journalism was there not only to serve their inarguably deserving cause, but that the cause should take total precedence over even-handed, honest journalism itself. They managed not to use the word propaganda, but that is what they were clearly advocating ... to "balance" no doubt, the government's propaganda.

One of the most able of them was among the most ardently in favour of ideological-style reporting; the kind of slanted, one-dimensional propaganda furiously rejected by all moderate independent newspapers and already "old news" for unquestioning converts. He also joined other politicised voices in believing that the efforts of our newspapers to provide *regional editions* for our readers were the true mark of an "apartheid press". One could ignore his insult while still failing to understand his logic.

His view was illustrated when we provided extra regional editions, as is done across the world to cater for the needs and interests of readers. It is a valued newspaper service, not a racist put-down, or propaganda tool. *The Star* Africa Edition, to which some black journalists were dedicated, had to be sold in a ridiculous and unnecessarily costly manner because of the political bias of a handful of fellow journalists. Because of the politicised, internal complaints, we resorted to distributing similar piles of copies of the "City Late" and the "Africa Edition" at Soweto bus and train depots so that every reader could make a choice. The Africa Edition copies quickly sold out; the City Late option, focusing heavily on financial news, had to be returned from working class areas – and pulped.

However, we could not afford to indulge the black-caucus demand for too long. Despite its protests, we continued to meet the demand in Soweto for soccer news, not rugby news, and for more Soweto and other township news. We refused to allow any ideological pressure group to prevent *The Star* from dropping several daily pages of stock-market statistics and replacing them in the special edition with vital educational material (expertly collated at considerable editorial cost) and desperately sought by parents and children in every black community.

We did accede to political sensitivities and changed the name *The Star* Africa Edition, but years later, in 2012, *The Star* proudly launched the Africa Edition again, to meet a demand no longer challenged by ideological journalism.

However, back in the 1980s, there was one real and bitter grievance against the anti-apartheid press which was to the disgrace of *The Star* and all our newspapers: We imposed racial discrimination on ourselves, even to the point sometimes of allowing signs that read: "Whites Only", or worse: "Bantu Only", to appear in some parts of the premises. I don't remember ever seeing such a sign in our offices – our staff rightly and immediately tore them down in Editorial, but I knew the policy was in place in some parts of our factory area under our same seven-storey roof.

It was the fault of crazy "Factory Apartheid". If your factory employed people of different, officially designated "ethnic groups", the Separate Amenities Act required that you provided separate entrances, restrooms and every other possible division between the different races.

My brother, manager of a factory in Durban, once pointed out to inspectors that he would have to provide *five* entrances to the factory; *four* back-door exits, *five* separate canteens, and *ten* lots of toilets for less than 50 people.

"Why ten?" he was asked.

"Maybe more," he said, "because we accommodate Indians mainly, but also Africans and 'coloured' people as well as whites of two language groups and our visiting Japanese company directors ... And all groups happen to consist of women as well as men. Will they have to have separate staircases as well?"

He was gambling on his threat to close down his factory rather than comply ... as well as on the inspector being sane. It worked.

For a newspaper like ours that railed against apartheid, enforced segregation was believed to be untenable, But shutting down was totally untenable. Logic and reason would not work in the case of saving *The Star's* giant printing plants. So we operated on a split decision. In all editorial departments we simply ignored the ridiculous racial division of restrooms and every other discrimination in other departments – but we were unable to do so at all times, and never if visiting the printing shop's canteens and toilets. Some clerk, some receptionist, or some printer would object to de-segregation, or would secretly complain to a government inspector only too happy to enforce the Separate Amenities Act's grotesque rules, knowing that constant defiance in the printing factory area might force our entire newspaper operation to close down. It was the same in every print-shop in the nation.

Fortunately, all isolated, naked hatred within our city block was quickly doused, but the distrust remained. Political differences, more than racial tension within our own ranks was inevitable. There was the bitter suspicion about spies – government informers – who seemed always at work among our ranks of reporters. Black reporters quite logically suspected they were being betrayed to the Secret Police by white staff. Most white (English-home-language) staff believed quite logically that the spies could not come from the obvious source which was the talented (and often fiercely liberal) Afrikaans-speaking journalists on our staff, but would come from the least suspected "group" – someone among the outspoken Africanists.

That was the theory. But one of the biggest spies turned out to be one of the most obvious and easily suspected: an Afrikaner in an English newspaper subeditors' room who professed conservative and radically rightwing opinions. All his colleagues reluctantly suspected him, but withheld judgement on him. He was revealed as a spy only when he left the paper to give evidence in court for the police against some of his trusting colleagues. In *The Star,* it was sometimes suspected without any proof, but confirmed only many years too late, that the main informer had been a top crime reporter – paid by us, but also paid by some intelligence unit in the police.

A search for a key spy in the *Rand Daily Mail* got nowhere near the source until it was discovered that the Secret Police informant was the editor's private secretary.

In the great game of trying to distinguish fact from gossip in a world of treachery, the editor of the *Sunday Times,* Tertius Myburgh was in 2015 "proven" and "revealed" – 25 years after his death – to be a spy. He had oft been looked at askance simply because of his loyalty to his Afrikaans church and his family and friends. And more particularly because some leaders of the National Party, when asked, confided that he *was* their spy.

But professional truth-twisters such as government spokesman Eschel Rhoodie and spymaster General Hendrik van den Bergh would say such things, wouldn't they? And pass it on to their own gullible Cabinet ministers. Press gossip was one of the security-conscious regime's sharp weapons.

However, gossip and biased accusations, published as a "proof" decades after his death, of being a spy and a traitor to his fellow journalists, form a separate ugly issue. The allegation appears to be a different and dangerous counter-form of disloyalty and treachery.

Back in those final years of plots, spies and secrecy under apartheid law, *The Star* had to sweep its conference rooms constantly for 'bugs'. And our meetings with investigative journalists were held in small rooms near the centre of the building as rumours flew like poisoned arrows.

I was also a victim of the 'spy fever', it seems. It happened I suppose when Ken Owen who, after my retirement from newspapers, became editor of the *Sunday Times.* I heard he spread his office with gossip of me "being in the pocket of Dr Eschel Rhoodie", the arch propagandist of apartheid!

Owen's astonishing assumption was that I had censored all his news reports on Rhoodie which he had once wired to us under his official "Own Correspondent, New York " title. His assumption is contradicted by our vociferous coverage of Rhoodie's 'Image' conference (See Chapter 8) and many newspaper cuttings and editorials in the 1980s.

The truth is that several of his reports *were* 'spiked'. But these concerned different issues and entirely different circumstances. His unsourced news stories – quite apart from the Rhoodie affair – brought strong and credible protests from the US Embassy and several senior officials in Washington. When he failed to provide corrections or explanations, we asked about his sources. He would not tell Our Foreign Editor, even off the record.

Finally he wrote to me apologising, and explaining some personal and domestic problems had made working very difficult. I suggested he apply for temporary special leave. I did not pass to other Argus newpapers his private letter of apology ... but I did file it, in case of further outburst.

Owen has died, and I mention the issue only because his strange canard, invented *thirty years* previously, was repeated in mid-2017 in his former newspaper!

Who could believe that rumour- arrows could fly so far?

Being bombed, and worse

Suspicion, induced by the poison of disloyalty, was bad enough in *The Star* while under physical and political pressure. Distrust among staffers at several levels was worse. Betrayal and jail were worst of all. My memories are haunted by all three stages. They were peripheral to our aims and our daily efforts, but constantly demanded attention.

For instance black reporters, who were a relatively new minority in the vast newsroom, naturally congregated together – despite pleas and even orders to change their desks. A black news editor or his deputy would experience great difficulty in exercising his authority, not over whites who offered untypical respect, but over black journalists. Communication at every level on a hectic 24-hour edition seven-days-a-week editorial floor was always inadequate; sometimes with tragic consequences. I recall once, in the very early years of my editorship, having to stand between a black journalist, unaware of the threat at a Christmas party of a drunken printer's apprentice who said he intended "shooting that black bastard who wasn't invited to our 'wayzgoose'" (the traditional, over-exuberant annual celebration of printers). As the rumour spread I moved with some fellow-drinking volunteers to stand between the "gunman" and our visiting contingent. We discovered later that the agitated printing apprentice *did* have a gun which he had bought that day. However, it was the head of our journalists' trade union editorial chapel, a guest – as all of us in editorial were – at the printers' party, who almost caused a tragedy. Not because he was a racist, but because of his hysteria when he was quietly informed of the gun crisis. The fuss was unnecessary as the gun was unloaded, but the incident taught us that racism and mistrust was high among some staff in some departments. It remained embedded for years.

Indeed, the tragedy of mistrust among loyal journalists had reached comic proportions when I received a deputation one day protesting the presence of a new (white) photographer on our staff.

"It's obvious. He's a spy," a deputation from the newsroom protested.

"What evidence do you have?"

"You can see it."

Indeed, I could. Our new cameraman wore a trench coat that winter, with deep pockets for some of his equipment. He dressed like a bad movie double agent. He proved a great, and loyal, staffer, one of the few wrongly accused suspects able to emerge unscarred from the clouds of poisonous suspicion that spread in those last few years of tension.

We had other troubles, more blunt, from anonymous bombers from outside who physically attacked *The Star* building. Several explosions occurred, mainly at ground level and at the factory side entrances. There was some damage, but no human casualties from these amateurish attacks. Instead of creating fear, the explosions created some mental comfort. We were pleased to learn that the suspect arsonists or would-be killers appeared to belong mainly in the ranks of crazies of the Far Left and Far Right, who seemed inept. Their behaviour was a sign that the paper was on its intended course.

However, towards the end, the nature of the threats changed, and increased. There were far fewer threats from angry Portuguese (white) immigrants who had suffered the collapse of the Portuguese colonies. And weird letters threatening murder were drying up – but the letters and phone calls warning of bombs in the building were increasing. Only a few went off, causing fires, quickly extinguished, near two of our side exits. But the anonymous bomb warnings increased to a point where we had to devise a "five-point alarm system" to avoid evacuating too many departments too often.

An occurrence I recall of the Editorial Department and the Front Ground Floor being ordered to evacuate immediately, led to some of us wisely staying behind to finish our work. Next day we received a bulletin from our own security staff stating that in future we should NOT jeopardise our lives by leaving the building (as ordered) and waiting across the street for a bomb to explode. The huge glass façade of the building – which had so impressed me when I entered the new building 20 years previously – might shatter and kill or mutilate colleagues and bystanders on both sides of the street.

The ultimate fear

Bomb threats and bitter suspicions were less feared than the police powers enabling them to jail any journalist for questioning, without charge or any form of access to the courts.

One day three police marched into our first-floor newsroom and marched out with one of our most reliable, most senior reporters, Harry Mashabela. The newsroom quickly emptied as reporters followed the procession downstairs and onto the street. I was notified, and ran down to intervene.

Outside in Sauer Street – a main thoroughfare for city traffic – a crowd was gathering to watch journalists preventing the police car from leaving until I arrived. Harry was sitting in the back seat beside a cop; two more were in front looking grim. The usual discussion occurred about their rights to enter our building and apprehend our staff.

Twisted legality, but not justice, was on the side of the police. They had every right. We had none.

I leaned into the police car to nod to Harry and say to the police: "The newspaper and its editor are responsible for all information available in this building. You cannot arrest individual staff members. You will need to discuss this, not with him, but with me and our lawyers."

"It has nothing to do with the newspaper," said the senior cop. "We have reason to believe this man knows something, arising," he stressed, "out of his private affairs. It may be helpful. We are not arresting him. We are taking him in for questioning."

They were taking him to John Vorster Square, about five blocks away, where one detainee held for "questioning" had once been thrown from a sixth-floor window ("jumped" said the police) and another had died from assault. ("He slipped on some soap," they averred!)

The remembrance of those notorious cases must have been in all our minds.

So was the obvious threat of major action by the "Riot Squad" against our staff who were seen to be publicly creating a crowd and forcibly preventing the police from "doing their duty".

It occurred to me that suddenly we were – in terms of normal legality, not just apartheid law – in the wrong. There could be flamboyant mass arrests and a propaganda coup for the State.

"All right, you can go," I told the police in the car. "But we are sending our top lawyers down to your headquarters immediately. Be warned, if anything happens to Mr Mashabela you will be in big trouble."

While I was alerting our lawyers and arranging an immediate and urgent deputation to John Vorster Square, with threats of action in the highest courts and in Parliament, Harry was already arriving at his dreaded destination.

He was instantly assaulted.

The irony was that the natural, justified, and loyal behaviour of our staff was the cause of this "alleged" assault. It transpired that an unidentified senior police officer, apparently controlling the operation by radio and, infuriated by the public humiliation of his police squad, allegedly hit Harry in the face as he was led into police headquarters, breaking his glasses and injuring his neck. The only witnesses, of course, were police.

The deeper tragedy was that Harry was not aware of the cause of the instant assault nor – much more important – was he aware of the future protection of our lawyers, even though they arrived too late. He was released days later without further "allegations" occurring, but he could not be aware of that protection at any stage of his incarceration. His experience during his unlawful (but legal) solitary imprisonment and inquisition was the lowest time of his life.

I was not to know until I retired about a decade later that he blamed me for failure to protect him. After quarter of a century that knowledge still haunts me. It remains the lowest point in my life too.

Other perceived 'lows'

My contemporaries in journalism might differ with my opinion and choose other events as my lowest experience.

Many editors, both those within our organisation and rival newspapers, would say that *The Star* editor's worst moments came when he published material about an illicit love affair conducted in a five-star hotel by the President of the World Alliance of "Reformed" Churches (found guilty, later, of misusing church trust funds). Many newspapers were sitting on this evidence, but didn't want to publish it as he was a politically active anti-apartheid spokesman. And US Senator Ted Kennedy was in South Africa and scheduled to meet him.

Most newspapers seemed unconcerned about the source of this material (illicit sound-tape and video recordings made by the "Secret Police"). My colleagues seemed concerned only about this popular public figure's role as an anti-apartheid supporter and his right to prominence and privacy.

However, I believed no honest newsman had any choice but to publicise this case. What if the Pope or the chief *dominee* of the local Dutch Reformed Church were involved in such behaviour? I asked myself. Would the free press not publish the reported behaviour? Would the newspapers give in to the plea that privacy over-rode the public good?

Far more important: did all my critics wish to ignore what I saw as the *real* issue in this sordid case? It became the main lead in our newspaper and was significant enough to stay on page one for many days. I believed that it was our cardinal duty to expose the source of the "dirty tricks" which involved secretly taped hotel-bedroom evidence being mysteriously planted in newsrooms around the country – by senior police!

The story is a long one, including a detailed and dangerous investigation by reporter Chris Steyn, and the longest, most expensive Press Council inquiry in history, with a judge and four assessors called upon to hear Press Council evidence in public. (When the police failed to act against *The Star* for accusing them of disgusting, illegal dirty tricks, I had challenged them publicly to seek redress in the Press Council. The resulting inquiry found *The Star* justified in publishing its accusations that top police at John Vorster Square headquarters were guilty of smear tactics. The police were not fired, but protected by the State, as are top officials in President Zuma's government as I write. At least, in our apartheid-period case, the top police who had been exposed in our daily repeated headlines were quietly and quickly removed from their posts.

The story, with all its issues and challenges, is fully told in "Chapter 11, Dirty Tricks", published in *Editors Under Fire*, (Random House 1993), and in a later book, *Publish and be Damned,* by the brave reporter on the case, Chris Steyn-Barlow.[1] At the time of the national controversy, only our chief rival, the *Rand Daily Mail,* did not criticise our paper for exposing the eminent clergyman. Instead, the RDM's ombudsman wrote a long column commenting on criticism of *The Star* by many rival newspapers across the nation. He strongly disagreed with all *The Star's* critics.

He wrote: "Newspapers that initially ignored the reports ... were in my opinion wrong. Self-censorship is no more justifiable than other forms of censorship. And it is damaging to the reputation of the press."

Our campaign, though had not been aimed at the infamous churchman, but at the notorious senior police indulging in illegal smears of public figures. For *The Star* to have turned a blind eye, was a dishonourable choice, I believed. It was an option with which it could never comfortably live.

'Don't Vote'

Another disagreement with all other "white" newspapers in the country, ranging from those supporting PW Botha's "Reform Referendum" to those opposing it from the Left and the Far Right in 1987, led to me being mocked – and even abused by some of my colleagues. They found agreement on just one thing: *The Star* was wrong in proposing that voters should abstain from Botha's "Reform" referendum, which I described as a "con trick" against the black majority which was denied a vote. The referendum was no more than a typical Botha trick, designed to isolate the Far Right voters and simultaneously damage the Progressive Party voters on his Left. In this he spectacularly succeeded.

In any case, it would be quite wrong, I believed, for whites to vote in a referendum to decide on the future of all other races when the "non-electorate" were denied any say whatever in a matter directly concerning them. In any sane society or democracy such a procedure would seem illogical and verging on idiotic. Especially as the result – white support of PW Botha's quaint, but unstated, ideas – was, under the rules created by him, a foregone conclusion.

Yet even the sanest of liberal journalists, a young man who would one day be a sound professor of journalism, attacked me viciously. Tyson verged on "madness" he wrote – and I regret I never became aware of his personal insults until many years after the event. Instead I had to accept at the time the ridicule of nearly all other editors of every persuasion (except black) as well as from most of my own staff.

Yes, that was a low moment, but alleviated by independent academic analyses of the polling, and by the historical justification of hindsight, and by reminders that the *Sowetan* had demonstrated its support of my decision by putting out its own ironic poster for its mainly black readership reading: "DON'T VOTE."

B-i-ig Mistake

Finally, I must record yet again, my very worst mistake, which has already been described, paid for and apologised for many times. My mistake was to allow one of our weekend editions to publish a late-night report emanating from an unusual source, suggesting that Ruth First, a genuine patriot and one of South Africa's greatest martyrs, was killed by a parcel bomb sent, not by apartheid's secret agents, but by her own communist colleagues.

I'd been asked why we would **not** publish this claim, when we usually published all claims and counter-claims from all parties.

My off-guard response to staff as I left the building was stupid from every perspective: "All right. Use it down-page, but point out strongly that it is a dubious claim from a suspicious source and is unlikely."

The claim was libellous. Publishing a dubious claim, even beside a credible denial, remains libellous.

I knew this, but my thoughts were on exposing yet another "dirty trick" of the Secret Police – *not* on the feelings of Ruth First's family. The pain from such an assassination being portrayed as an internally organised betrayal added hugely to the pain of the murder itself. Our report, instead of focusing on the "Secret Police", diverted some attention from them.

As some of Ruth First's family and the London-based ANC itself were banned and living outside South Africa, they were unable to collect any damages. Instead I persuaded our company voluntarily to pay out, unasked, a sum greater than any of our newspaper group had ever paid in a libel action before. It could never be enough, I believed, but my regret was eased when peace came and I was eventually able to apologise in person.

Looking back on these and all my other mistakes, I still believe my all-time career "low" remains the low-profile case of Harry Mashabela. If only I had known that our plan could go wrong! If only I had harried our lawyers. Or got into the police car. Or even caused a street riot. Anything

– short of placing the newspaper itself in jeopardy – to protect a fine, innocent always-upright colleague like Harry Mashabela who enjoyed no civil rights and no justice. □

1. *Publish and be Damned* by Chris Steyn-Barlow (Galago 2006).

5

Bad times, good times.

1987 – 2017

33.
Security Police and memories to haunt us all.

*Why, I wonder, do they need to put manacles on my
legs. And cuff me to a pole in the room.
Now the interrogation begins. So that's Section Six.
In teams of two every four hours the same questions,
the same aggression and hostility.*

Quraysh Patel, former journalist of The Daily News, Durban.

General Johan Coetzee liked to play both "good cop" and "bad cop". He was polite, efficient, dedicated and informed.

Very well informed.

He was also intelligent and communicative. We communicated mainly in writing. He wrote terse threats, politely. I replied with protestations that were meant to be polite but which sometimes ended up in anger.

Not cool.

In my early days as Editor of *The Star* in the 1970s we had some "interesting" jousts. For instance General Johan Coetzee, when he was still a brigadier as head of the Security Police, phoned one day: "Mr Tyson, I need to see your reporter, Leggatt." (Hugh Leggatt, back in 1974, was a political reporter who survived police harassment but left later to join a newspaper in Vancouver.)

The "good" cop's request could be summed up as: "Your reporter's story on that incident last week suggests he knows something about some terrorists. We'd like his co-operation."

"Are you wanting to question him?"

"Not necessarily. But we need his information."

"Are you threatening us?" I asked, referring to an unpredictable habit the police had, of putting uncooperative reporters in dreaded solitary confinement indefinitely, or until they "cracked".

General Coetzee

Star caricature by "Andy" who also ended up in Canada.

"We need to talk to him. Tell him to bring his toothbrush," said the bad cop.

I assumed he was taunting us — because he would know that I had no option, in any case, but to warn the reporter in advance of the possibility of being locked up. There was no way we would want a reporter to meet the Security Police alone, and in this case I felt instinctively that the general would never arrest a journalist in the presence of an independent witness, in his own office, in the centre of the capital city.

We drove to Pretoria, reviewing the story we had published, its implications and the options. What was it that Coetzee knew that we didn't? The news report we had published was so "normal" I hadn't even briefed our lawyers.

The "good cop" greeted us with civility and a show of concern. The reporter professed no knowledge of any possible "terrorism", or the identity or whereabouts of any terrorist. It was a procedure journalists were forced to cultivate during the next 15 years.

The "bad cop" raved on about this for long enough for us to know that we were safe. Then he transformed into the "weird cop". In all earnestness he delivered a long briefing on the ubiquity and danger of innocent-looking terrorists. They might be mowing your lawn, he said. They might be in your office reading files or planting a bomb. It was our duty to report anyone and anything that was suspicious. Something on those lines. I remember only the fascinating picture of "terrorists" mowing my lawn.

"What was that all about?" asked a relieved reporter as we set off on our way back to Johannesburg. His suitcase for a possible "jail journey" was still in the boot of the car. His question was difficult to answer. I hadn't applied the theory of surrealism at that stage, but later, my answer would be: "Try to forget it. It is senseless. It is surreal."

That theory proved wrong. Locking up, and sometimes torturing (usually black) journalists was soon to become very real indeed. Later, when "terrorists" were being locked up all over the place, my newspaper — on the sure grounds that one man's terrorist is another man's freedom fighter —dropped the term, using it only when quoting the authorities. It angered many of our more vociferous readers.

So who is a terrorist?
By coincidence, while I was recalling the incidents above, I came upon

a file I'd forgotten ever existed. It is a 20000-word monograph I wrote during a sabbatical enjoyed while still editing *The Star* in the late 1980s.

Obviously the question, "Who is a terrorist?" was much on my mind at the time. My file quotes half a hundred "authorities" on the subject.

I shall not bore you with a hundred pages of perhaps all the definitions and the precise deeds that might qualify as terrorism, but I shall repeat one of our many dilemmas within this subject:

Sometimes the word terrorist slips into the newspaper without the required quotation marks (for the authorities have insisted, with some logic, that if we quote a police or army spokesman who has used the word terrorist, we cannot put phrases such as "township residents", "insurgents", "freedom fighters", or anything else in the officer's mouth).

But with every Cabinet minister and white Nationalist politician using the word "terrorist" indiscriminately – and with every South African TV news announcer using those quotes without adding the word "so-called" to indicate quotation marks, the word "terrorist" takes on a new meaning.

This wider description gains currency, and is accepted over a broad spectrum of South African society. The term is not only inaccurate, it helps to legitimise and broaden the support of real terrorism.

The wider usage of the word terrorism is not only deliberate propaganda for the State; it is also unwitting propaganda of considerable benefit to real terrorists who murder innocent citizens merely to make a point.

HOWEVER, THAT DAY, so early in my editorship, signalled for me the gradual increase of the bleak, cruel system of imprisoning reporters without any charge or trial, merely for refusing to reveal the name of an innocent confidential source. Soon this became a constant and dangerous battle of wits. The government introduced its notorious "Clause 205" which made it easier to lock up journalists and their witnesses, "forever if necessary", than it was to detain political activists under legislation that specified 30 or 60 or 90 days without trial.

The case more than a decade later of the young men of Duduza African township where three were killed and three wounded during a police raid on the night of 26 June 1985 illustrates the nightmare which township residents, reporters, and editors had to face throughout that time.

The extraordinary example, which we thought of as "the mystery of the flying hand grenades" and its consequences was reported in our newspaper in great detail over several years and I shall give here only the nub of it. It revolved around the question: who threw the hand grenades?

The police said the dead youths accidentally killed themselves (and blew off their own hands) when their grenades exploded prematurely during a "coordinated terrorist attack".

All three? Accidental?

It sounded hardly credible.

Very soon *The Star* found itself reporting in successive editions a similar attack at that time, bringing the casualty list to eight dead and seven seriously wounded – and no less than four versions of one dramatic incident involving bands of anti-apartheid students, armoured police trucks, armed police, and unidentified black civilians with grenades. None of the explanations – except the logical presumption – seemed credible.

The various versions came from as far apart as the usually silent Police HQ in Pretoria, and the ANC in Lusaka, Zambia. The Lusaka version outlined a classic spy conspiracy in which police provocateurs provided grenades booby-trapped to go off instantly in the hands of innocent protesters.

When we published all versions and all counter-claims, General Johan Coetzee accused *The Star* of deliberately publishing falsified reports in order to besmirch the good name of the police. He began searching for the best means of gagging us.

(This may be an injustice to General Coetzee. It happens that, to my part-regret at being deprived of an official news source, *The Star* was publicly boycotted at some stage by every police commissioner whom I dealt with over 20 years, usually through my personal dispute with each commander over facts and fiction. My regret was that every boycott by all police deprived our readers of possible news. And we were boycotted so often over so many years that I cannot now be sure if it was General Coetzee or a successor who was involved in the case I am now describing.)

Fortunately our reporters dug deep until they identified two witnesses at the extraordinary midnight scene. They had no objection whatever to having their names published and they swore that the issue was quite simple: police agents threw the bombs.

While the "unrest" in Duduza was increasing alarmingly, the Commissioner of Police called me to say that his investigating officers had located our two witnesses. Contrary to our version, they had volunteered and signed affidavits which proved that the incident involved "terrorists" with bombs who had killed themselves while attacking the police.

"What the hell's going on?" I asked the news editor. "What's happened to your reporters' sources?"

Fortunately again, the reporters traced the young witnesses and confronted them at the funeral of some of the Duduza victims.

Reporter Rich Mkhondo, with three more reporters as witnesses, listened to one of the young men explaining that he was detained for a day and had been warned that he could be locked up without trial under Section 29 of the Internal Security Act.

"So was the witness threatened?"

"Yes."

"And he changed his story the same day, as quickly as that?"

"Well, he was in chains, and he complains that someone put a gun in his ear."

I sent a message to the Police Commissioner stating that his police subordinates had let him down. He should not rely on a witness with a gun in his ear. If we found any evidence of a witness being harassed, we'd go to court.

We now had a standoff. But more important than our conflicting beliefs was the safety of the two witnesses on whom we both relied. I suggested we should both ensure that, whatever the developments were, the witnesses should not be harmed or interfered with in any way. I pointed out that any harm to them would create "terrible headlines".

That was not the end of the story. The astonishing conclusion was reached years later, during the hearings of the Truth and Reconciliation Commission, when 13 men, the police and security agents involved, sought pardon for their sins. They confessed that they were involved in a plan to rig the timing of the grenades to zero seconds, and that they convinced protestors to throw the weapons *simultaneously* at midnight as a symbolic gesture of defying apartheid. It was a gesture that persuaded them to kill themselves!

The Security Police and their agents involved were granted pardon on the grounds of having no option but to carry out orders approved by the top police and their Cabinet minister, Louis le Grange.

It was a diabolical trick that twisted the event into something too weird to portray even in a fictional spy story. What we did strongly believe – with previous evidence to support it – was that we might during some future police crime find another witness with a gun in his ear.

THE FULL EFFECT OF SECTION SIX of the Terrorism Act was one of the most terrifying experiences of apartheid, even when it didn't involve systematic physical torture in jail. Certainly the uncertainty of not knowing when you might be released from solitary confinement in prison, or when "interrogation" might end, was one of the so-called law's true horrors.

As a journalist, your indefinite detention would depend on your resolve not to betray the source you had promised never to reveal. Or it would depend on your source coming forward to protest his innocence. Or it could depend on a shift towards legality by the authorities themselves.

You had to hope that the possibility of you betraying, under "interrogation", some informant would never arise. But if it did, the possibility that either your informant or the police might take pity on your innocent plight, seemed beyond hope.

And yet hope is what everyone needs most when secretly locked in solitary by guards without accountability. Hope and courage are his or her only counters to despair and contemplation of possible death.

The innocent, uninvolved prisoner aches for some kind of communication with the outside world, or any kind of company; even if it be a cockroach or a bird that can be seen each day – possibly "forever" – through a cell window.

Quraysh Patel, ex-reporter without political intensity, whose quotation is used at the head of this chapter, also spoke of the dreaded loneliness of indefinite solitary confinement ... when I finally persuaded him years ago to recall his "Section Six" experience:

"Forget about loneliness. (Think of it as) a refuge from the interrogators .... Use soap to make dice .... Use soap and bread crusts to make chess pieces. Play chess. The days pass unnoticed."

Not much comfort, really.

All through those years, the "Section Six" fate which some reporters faced was also the nightmare which I and legal adviser Peter Reynolds and some of his team of specialist lawyers lived with during countless days and nights. We sought desperately to print the news, yet avoid it endangering our staff as well as their sources. Every reporter involved in reporting protest was a candidate for the trap I have described.

Often we published without quoting any source — but always having Sherlock Holmes-style physical proof such as spent cartridge cases — to produce to the Security Police when their inevitable call came.

Thoughts of the experience of those who defied time while living through "Solitary" still come occasionally to bother me, even a quarter of a century later. □

34.
Apartheid's curse.

Despotism tempered by assassination,
that is our Magna Carta.

A critic within Soviet Russia.

When apartheid was abolished by the stroke of a pen, the suffering of some of its protesting victims were finally described in emotional detail to the Truth and Reconciliation Commission (TRC). The evidence provides memories of horror that cannot be erased by anyone who has heard it. They encapsulated the deepest experience of decades of apartheid: its hate, fear, prejudice and increasing destruction of law and justice. The TRC hearings were the nearest to capture the experience of humanity in several million souls across the previous government's barricaded colour lines.

The Truth and Reconciliation Commission was not the first of its kind in the world, but it was the first to bring together, face to face, and

But only suffering and satire can provide a picture of what the extremes of South African apartheid were like.

The Casspir was a familiar but dreaded sight in African townships in South Africa as the civil war against apartheid reached its climax. The Casspir was designed by the SAP (Police) in partnership with CSIR (Council for Scientific and Industrial Research) in the late 1970 as a 4-wheel drive armoured vehicle capable of withstanding direct hits from two landmines simultanesouly. It was used at home and in cross-border warfare. When peace came, the Casspir was used as an Armoured Protection Vehicle in many riot-torn countries. (Photo: Greg Marinovich).

without a judicial trial the torturers and their victims. It was drama too powerful and too real to be captured adequately in theatre. What everyone heard there still rattles in our skulls. Antjie Krog, a poet and writer who was a radio reporter covering the TRC hearings, captured those anguished voices in her broadcasts, and repeated them in her moving book on the subject.[1]

"They held me ... they said: 'Please don't go in there ....' I just skipped through their legs and went in .... I found Bheki .... He was in pieces .... He was hanging in pieces .... He was all over .... pieces of him and brain was scattered all around .... That was the end of Bheki."

"AT CALEDON SQUARE I heard a loud sound. Policemen were celebrating. They said: 'We've got Looksmart!' I was in my cell when I saw Looksmart being dragged up a flight of stairs by two policemen. They were beating him as he went up the stairs. I noticed that his beard had been pulled out ... one by one ... on one side of his face. He was bleeding heavily from the mouth. Two days later they took him again – his hands handcuffed behind his back. That was the last time I saw Looksmart Ngudle."

"THIS WHITE MAN with the red scarf, he shot into the outside bathroom where Sonnyboy was hiding .... I was standing in the kitchen .... I saw him dragging my child. Sonnyboy was already dead. He was holding him by his legs like a dog. I saw him digging a hole, scraping Sonnyboy's brains into that hole and closing it with his boot. The sun was bright ... but it went dark when I saw him lying there. It's an everlasting pain. It will stop never in my heart. It always comes back. It eats me apart. Sonnyboy, rest well, my child. I've translated you from the dead."

"I ASKED THEM: 'Show me the mark on his chin, then I will know it's my son.' They showed me the mark on his chin, and I said: 'It's not my son.'"

"WHEN FUZILE didn't come home that night I went to look for him. Now this makes me mad really. My son was shot and nobody told me. I looked everywhere and nobody told me my son was in the mortuary .... They later gave me his clothes. His t-shirt looked as if it had been eaten by rats."

"THAT MORNING I did something I had never done before. My husband was still at his desk busy with the accounts of our business. I went up to him and stood behind his chair. I put my hands under his arms and tickled him .... He looked surprised and unexpectedly happy.

"'And now?' he asked.

"'I am going to make tea,' I said.

"While I poured water on the tea bags, I heard this devastating noise. Six men stormed into our study and blew his head off. My five-year-old daughter was present .... That Christmas I found a letter on his desk: 'Dear Father Christmas, please bring me a soft teddy bear with friendly eyes .... My daddy is dead. If he is here I would not have bothered you.' I put her in a boarding school. The morning we drove there we had a flat tyre. 'You see,' she said, 'Daddy does not want me to go there …. He wants me to stay with you …. I have watched him die. He wants to be there when you die ….'

"She is now a teenager and has tried twice to commit suicide."

ARCHBISHOP DESMOND TUTU (presiding at that the end of the very first day of testimony offered in East London) speaks into silence as he says: "We should all feel deeply humbled by what we've heard, but we've got to finish quickly, and really turn our backs on this awful past and say: 'Life is for living.'"

After reading, and hearing mainly second-hand, the Truth and Reconciliation evidence, I realised how little I had known; how small were our own frustrations and fears under apartheid. After learning of those remote horrors which were recalled so vividly, I believed that life would still be worth living if we remembered three things:

We needed to recognise the qualities of forgiveness, caring and understanding that exist in every individual we meet.

We needed to be aware that fear, hate, cruelty and other throwbacks to barbarism still exist in all of us.

We – especially those of us blunted by decades of trying to report the rising horror and sworn to report both sides of all issues – need to apologise for not doing a great deal more to obviate the pain of torture of many unnamed prisoners at the time; and the pain of all human beings deprived of dignity and respect under apartheid. I, for one, failed to find out enough, or to do enough in this half-hidden struggle. Is it sufficient to know this now? If not, how does one, as a privileged, independent journalist, belatedly apologise to anyone without sounding like an insufferable hypocrite?

When repetition blunts reality

Reporting on apartheid was an angry, repetitive, sad and seemingly hopeless job that dominated our days for nearly 50 years. The tarnished injustice of it was barnacled with greed and guilt, and rendered boring by its constantly repeated malpractice.

After the first 20 years, however, its basic evils were so self-evident it became difficult to cover oft-repeated items of it as "news".

After about 30 years, fresh and eager foreign correspondents

The notorious official notice 'slegs blankes' that suddenly appeared on beaches and benches were a source of anger, embarrassment or discomfort for a majority of white South Africans. Yet few broke the law in protest, and small children defied their parents by treating apartheid benches as playthings. But open defiance of unjust, racial law was a rare act among law-abiding anti-apartment voters.

would arrive from overseas; use our newspaper library files and our facilities to report their sensational findings, and exclaim: "But don't you see the shocking injustice of it all!"

We would simply point these surprisingly naive foreign correspondents or earnest writers to our library "morgue", and to press cuttings stacked behind the current files that recorded even more sensational and shocking human tragedies, cruelties, racist discriminations and other crimes described in our headlines. The evils were publicly highlighted in our editorials, in letters, in court case evidence, in parliamentary debates and in prison-death postmortems occurring year after year.

Yet the only readers who seemed to be really moved by the "shock-horror" headlines were those readers who were moved right out of town for not being white.

The endless suffering and stupidity of apartheid began with the land grabbing of the racially ideological Group Areas Act, and reached its ideological worst in the strange social engineering devised by the Population Registration Act.

"Population registration" was in fact racial registration, requiring labelling the race of every man, woman, and child. It led to "a million" personal tragedies personified in a thousandth case which the newspapers never let their readers forget.

The case of Sandra Laing was revealed to the world through local press reports. Its inhuman circumstances were refreshed, and the message reinforced, over and over again over the years. Her lifetime of personal tragedies seem beyond belief – a parody of Kafka and our ridiculous State.

Let me remind you – now a generation or two later – of the cold facts: Sandra Laing was seen as a "black" girl. But she was born to two white Afrikaner parents, who quite naturally treated her as white, for they were unaware of any black ancestry in their family histories ... a common ignorance in South Africa. She was brought up as a (privileged) white, but when she went to a white school she was taunted, challenged, and then reclassified by the authorities as "coloured". Her humiliation led to her going to a boarding school a thousand kilometres away. Then the law was amended slightly so that the bewildered teenager could be re-classified as "white".

"I feel confused," she told the press, which had followed the story over the years. At only 16, to the unspeakable horror of her parents (supporters of the apartheid government!), she ran away with an African. Her African "husband" refused to let his privileged "white" wife reclassify as an underprivileged "coloured" which she wanted to do in order to get her children into school. So her children – and her second family with another black husband – lived unrecognised by the law and the South African administration. Her situation deeply wounded her, her children, the children's father, as well as Sandra's racist parents, who had forsaken her after her first runaway marriage. Sandra, through immense press publicity, became the bitter icon of apartheid.

Icons were brutally effective in combating apartheid. For instance, the press constantly highlighted a report of one bureaucrat who denied any general confusion in race classification and boasted that he used "the pencil test". It entailed placing a pencil in a child's curls, and if it stayed there, the tight curly hair "proved" that any dark-complexioned person must be "coloured".

This was the second international icon of apartheid, created purely by angry press publicity. Many more – such as the bus conductor who, it was said, was fired for ejecting from his bus a "non-exempt" Chinese male sitting in the "white" section who turned out to be an "exempt" Japanese person bringing business to the country.

It is sad to remember how people in their political prejudices were so cruel and uncaring ... as were the press, sometimes in some ways, in their sardonic anti-apartheid campaigning.

IN AN ATTEMPT once to define the meaning of apartheid, I managed to describe it, inadequately, in 400 words. About 1600 books have also failed to capture its essence. But as a "one-liner" I might define it as "inequality and xenophobia codified to prosecute the oppressed majority".(Instead, today's 20-year-old "new" SA government exploits less blatant law, and uses blatant words such as "racism", to cover corruption and to silence many of its critics.)

However, to combat apartheid, words were never enough. Even constant exposure of its evil consequences and criticism of senseless arrogance failed to sway its more ardent supporters. What hurt them though was satire, and revelations about apartheid's gross stupidity.

The 'funny side' of apartheid

As mentioned earlier reporting on apartheid dominated our days for nearly 50 years – the entire working lifetime of some of us alive today. The shining injustice of apartheid was corroded with greed and guilt, and dulled with repeated exposure.

Yet there was always humour both bright and bitter to illuminate the years. History has shown, from Poland to North Korea, that humour is an unbreakable weapon for oppressed people to use against tyranny. As Archbishop Tutu wrote in his foreword to *Laugh the Beloved Country:*[2]

I discovered a long time ago that humour is a serious business. It certainly helped many of us to survive the idiocies and the humiliations of our unlamented former apartheid dispensation – a dispensation which, extraordinarily, continued for decades despite the fact that nobody (as far as I can tell today) ever supported it.

The English-language press went out of its way to highlight apartheid's cruel absurdities – and government denials – decade after decade. In *Laugh the Beloved Country's* collection of South African humour through the ages there are samples of press cuttings from SA newspapers that were published by Ben Maclennan of the South African Press Association (Sapa).[3]

Here are a few of those samples, re-arranged in subject matter, without attribution to any single newspaper as papers across the nation shared their reports:

Four Gestures to Humanity

Ambulances in the Cape Peninsula are not run (like most in the country) on an apartheid basis. When a single ambulance must serve people of different races, the patients are asked – if they are conscious – whether they mind travelling together in the same vehicle.

After repeated representations by non-white actors, the De Aar Town Council has decided to allow non-white groups to give performances in the Town Hall on condition they are attended by white audiences only.

Beaufort west would be only too pleased to allow the Japanese to use our municipal (strictly segregated, whites-only) swimming pool .... Besides, this is a big wool-growing area, and the Japanese are very interested in our wool.

The Department of Community Development granted special permission for coloured players to use the "whites only" golf course, provided they did not use the toilets and stayed 50 metres from the clubhouse. But when the amateur Kingsgate Football Club signed up three white players, two Indian policemen warned the chairman that the Indian club had broken the law by letting whites play on a field in an Indian area.

Apartheid in God's House

A *predikant* has instructed a congregation of illiterate farm labourers to pray – not to *Our* Father Who art in Heaven – but to *The* Father. Since Jesus was a "white", only white men could say "*Our* Father", said the preacher.

Where in Holy Scripture is there a single suggestion or any evidence that Christ was coloured or black? On the contrary, it is clearly shown that he was white, for he was of the house of David, and we have it on record that King David was a white man. "When the Philistine … saw David, he disdained him: for he was but a youth, and ruddy and of a fair complexion." (1.Sam 17.42) – JA Wannenburg, *Was Christ Coloured?* 1955.

The General Synod of the Nederduitse Gereformeerde Kerk decided yesterday that mixed marriages (skin colour) were physically possible because of the uniformity of the human race. Nevertheless they were undesirable in the eyes of the Church.

Political Wisdom

"We do not want chaos in South Africa." – Prime Minister P W Botha explaining why cinemas would not be opened to all races.

"In making the highest sacrifice for peace and stability, the members of the Venda (tribal) Defence Force are gaining valuable operational experience." – Defence Minister General Magnus Malan.

"Contact across the colour line is welcome so long as the motive for this contact is the greater separation of the races." – Minister of Health Dr Carel de Wet.

Sex Across the Line

There was a great danger that African girls were trying to get whites in trouble, said the magistrate in the Regional Court yesterday in acquitting a church elder and a Sunday-school teacher (his partner in two "crimes" under the Immorality Act) of having sex across the colour line.

A Constantia housewife told the magistrate that for three hours she watched three Coloured men and a European women commit an offence under the Immorality Act in a field near her home on January 22. She said she did not wish to interfere, but after three hours, it was "too much". □

1. *Country of My Skull,* by Antjie Krog (Jonathan Cape, 1998). She generously allowed me to use here any quotes I chose.

2. *Laugh the Beloved Country,* A compendium of South African humour, compiled by James Clark and Harvey Tyson (Double Storey, 2003).

3. The examples quoted here were among hundreds collected from the files of newspapers by SA Press Agency reporter Ben Maclennan (*Apartheid, the Lighter Side,* Chameleon Press 1990).

35.
The 'miraculous' nineties.

Since wars began in the minds of men,
it is in the minds of men that the defences
of peace must be constructed.

UNESCO Constitution.

The 1990s nearly brought peace and democracy to South Africa.

The murders and public violence; the plotting, pretences and crises inflicted on us from all sides by extremists and isolated, fearful groups, are momentarily forgotten as if they were a bad dream.

We remembered only the goodwill – and the joy of sharing in long queues on a long day, the act of democracy that brought us together at the polling booths in 1994.

"Not a single racist was seen at the heavily supported polls," someone recalls.

However, "the miracle" didn't "just happen".

In fact the long-awaited first democratic general election wasn't a miracle. It was the result of the courage, the statesmanship, the patience and far-sightedness of the active leaders of two bitterly divided, undefeated groups. And it happened because one single individual ensured that the election would happen – offering a trusted service beyond the influence of any politician or political demonstration.

Nor was there a single incident worth public challenge when millions of people queued to mark an X in a polling booth for the first time in their lives. Organisation of this event was beyond the capabilities of any government that had yet existed in South Africa. It required input and action from volunteers in every section of society.

The years 1987 to 1990 had been blackened by suspension of law and the introduction of increasingly dictatorial "Emergency Regulations". I remember it as a bleak, testing period when I finally gave up all illusions and said publicly that the time had come for *The Star* to defy openly the emergency laws we had been circumventing by various means – such as printing blank spaces on our front pages, signalling censorship we were not allowed to name; outwitting the censors; and dodging constantly renewed regulations trying to stop us doing so.

But suddenly in 1990 – four long years before South Africa finally voted for democracy, I witnessed the secret end to apartheid authoritarianism. Contacts with the ANC in London, Lusaka, and elsewhere had already occurred on separate occasions in the late 1980s with top government officials, businessmen, and a few of us pressmen.

Real reform, though in secret, thrust itself to the top of the agenda the moment FW de Klerk wrested the presidency from PW Botha who, like all despots, was unwilling to give up power. Botha had to be pushed out by an inner circle of Nationalist leaders.

I now had the good fortune – on the eve of my last and seventeenth year of editing SA's largest daily newspaper, to meet in Lusaka, Oliver Tambo, the patient, peace-seeking, banned president of the ANC, as well as ebullient, pipe-smoking Govan Mbeki. It was all very productive – and very secret.

Later I met the 54-year-old President Frederik Willem de Klerk on civil terms. I was one of many who had clashed with him often since his days as Minister of Internal Affairs when he was seeking to curb the press and threatening to increase censorship. But now as PM he proposed a private, one-on-one discussion.

We met alone for lunch in secret in the aptly named "Mole Cottage" in the private grounds of a "country club" in Johannesburg's environs. At the outset, and to forestall his presumed purpose, I told him my newspaper would not support his campaign for election as president. He shrugged.

That was a foregone conclusion, he said. What he sought was opposition support for his proposed reforms. I said that if his reforms were real and non-racial he could obviously expect support.

They were. But they were not enough. Nonetheless most of us in the anti-apartheid press did publish the government's first steps with cautious approval.

At the start of the new year of 1990, however, President de Klerk's actions reached beyond all our expectations. At his Tuynhuys office in Cape Town he told me (and two colleagues I'd request permission to bring to the meeting) that he was about to announce the end of apartheid – and then release Nelson Mandela.

We were stunned.

"Have you cleared it with your caucus?" I asked, being only too well aware of how conservative and all-powerful it could be. He was not going to comment on caucus business. Instead he smiled faintly. "I've warned members to fasten their seatbelts," he said.

Our reaction was: "You've gone beyond everyone's expectations – further even than any parliamentary opposition party would have dared!

"When will you release Nelson Mandela?"

"That I cannot tell you. There is no guarantee what he will do ... or how the nation will react."

The nation, at this stage, did not even know what Mandela looked like at this moment in his life. His picture had been banned for 27 years.

On the following Sunday, Mandela, the world's icon of freedom, walked free.

We could savour press freedom again, after being baulked for more than 40 years by government laws and threats. For me it was an especially delicious moment for I was on the eve of my retirement from fulltime journalism. I tried to explain this joy in an interview requested by the South African Press Association:

"The unbanning of the ANC and at least 35 other organisations means they can now speak – and we can report them!

"In fact we have been breaking the regulations all over the place in recent times, but obviously we could not report those unuttered views which were being censored at source. Now – until and unless we are *forced* to do otherwise – we intend to publish as freely as the newspapers of America and Europe."

After half a working life of interference and harassment, it was a life's dream come true.

The full, behind-the-scenes story may never be told from every angle, but the headlines (from *The Star* during my last year, and during the times of the next two exceptional editors, Richard Steyn and Peter Sullivan, who followed my retirement in late 1990) are a guide. Those "history in headlines", listed in Chapter 8, mirror especially well the few frantic years of creating a democracy as the millennium ended, and define the exciting new future that was born in the 1990s.

The 21st century would bring very different priorities ... and disappointing standards of journalism due to reckless cost cutting. But that is a story for *End of the Deadline* to tell. □

36.
Memories and cherries.

Life can only be understood backwards;
But it must be lived forwards.

Soren Kierkegaard died aged 42 in 1855.

There comes a moment when it may just be permissible to look back to the good times and the bad times in each of our lives in order to ask: Was there a purpose to life? Or did it just happen? Or did you determine most of it yourself?

The latter two, combined, I prefer to think.

Luck was a constant ally; self-choice was my subconscious habit … so my mistakes were my own, and they were many.

Is life worth living?

I am reminded of yet another morsel of wisdom. It came from Oliver Wendell Holmes in the 19th century: "Life is an end in itself, and the only question as to whether it is worth living is whether you have had enough of it."

Enough said.

Whatever it was, I wish to share with you a few good times, never to be forgotten amid all the stress and drama that South Africa offered under apartheid.

In search of 'a better way'

I once decided to interrupt a chosen career in the mistaken belief that real gold might be worth more than journalism's poor monetary rewards.

The Sharpeville Massacre and the reaction it caused in our all-white Parliament prompted the question: Is there a worse newspaper job than reporting the vile results, year after year, of a pretence "democratic" parliament, dominated by one undemocratic party? What is one doing here? Why be a journalist? Or why be a dogs body at the end of a metro paper's Mahogany Row? It's certainly not for the money.

"Money is the secret to a better life," I told myself, and left newspapers.

I was wrong, and was taught a sound lesson about real value.

There were of course other reasons for leaving newspapers.

Boredom was one, for having asked to be relieved of political reporting I found myself in a backroom glass cubicle in the Natal *Daily News,* trying to do editorial "admin" work. To make matters even gloomier, I had also clashed with the Argus Company's head honcho who had flown to Durban to castigate me for refusing to accept the position of deputy editor of the newly launched *Sunday Chronicle.* It was during the closing stages of the Company's longest period in which the newspapers were badly dominated by money-counting Management.

I was raising three toddlers in the beautifully isolated hills above a sub-tropical ocean. I was doing much additional writing for several upmarket publications in Britain, Holland, and for South Africa's *Financial Mail.* I was being offered a pittance to move to Johannesburg, a city I never wished to see again.

The managing director was angry at my explanation for turning down his offer. Perhaps I was, for once, too succinct.

"I believe the style and launch of the *Sunday Chronicle* was misconceived. I believe it will fold within a few months." (With mixed feelings I watched my prediction come true, on schedule.)

"Tyson, if you're afraid to take chances you're not going to get very far in this company," he huffed.

Around that psychological moment, I was approached by two of my colleagues – both former senior political correspondents – and invited to become an "Assistant Public Relations Adviser to the Transvaal Chamber of Mines".

I knew that Laurence Gandar, editor of the *Rand Daily Mail,* had left newspapers at one stage to join the mining industry, in the hopes I think, of improving black employment systems. In my lowly case, working with other senior journalists who were close to the heart of gold seemed a very good idea. It wasn't about "selling soap", they said. It was *not* "PR", they added with the disdain that seems to burden journalists.

My new job was the very opposite of selling soap, I soon discovered. Instead of seeking publicity and communication, the most important things we "advised" on, turned out to be wrapped in mysteries of High Finance and labelled "Top Secret".

These vital issues were discussed by management of the Big Seven mining houses, from Anglo American to Union Corporation. The members of the exclusive and active Gold Committee used to gather in a discreet boardroom behind a carved wooden sign representing *Under the Oaks.*

The name celebrated the Chamber's tradition of *al fresco* and informal lunches once held by leaders of the Big Seven. They gathered, in strictest confidence, under the giant old oak tree spreading its branches over a vast circle of tables at the Johannesburg Country Club. There was another famous oak in the middle of the club's quaint, rolling cricket field within sight of where they sat in perfect Highveld lunchtime weather – cool shade in summer, dappled sunlight in winter, without evidence of wind or cloud. And not an eavesdropper, nor political, nor industrial spy in sight.

These were no ordinary businessmen. Most were consulting engineers, patrons of the arts, of music and literature, with a wide spectrum of academic as well as engineering degrees, usually from Oxford or Cambridge. (An exception was one genial corporation head, elected President of the Chamber after my time whom my colleague there described as "both a Trial, and an Error".)

Mining in South Africa has always been an enclave within industry operating between space-age technology and mass cheap labour. For more than a century its relationships with the Transvaal and apartheid governments were even more hostile than those of the opposition press with the National Party. In today's environment the mining industry is in some relatively threatening straits. It remains distant and seems still out of touch with national needs and issues. Its eyes are fixed on world prices and world demand.

When I first arrived at the Chamber's headquarters opposite Johannesburg's old Stock Exchange, the chief public relations adviser had already been promoted to Uranium Adviser, uranium being the hottest issue in the world at that time. I won't tell you his name, not only because I may have forgotten it, but because he dwelt in an ultra-secret world. He dressed in silk, monogrammed shirts and Saville Row suits. He flitted around the world as an expert traveller in the early era of jet planes, and he lived like James Bond, returning only to brief the Big Seven in the tightly-shut Chamber of Mines boardroom which was declared to be temporarily "Under the Oaks".

His stories quickly reached us in our expansive offices across the passage, and they prompted speculative dialogues: "Did you hear that he was holed up in his bedroom in the George V Hotel in Paris, this time with four representatives of the French government? Or were they agents of the UK or USA?"

"In his bedroom? *Four* against one? Did the opposition include their legal experts?"

"Yes, but by dawn he'd told them: 'Gentlemen, my principles (or maybe he said principals) cannot budge. Those are the terms. Take them or leave them.' And they signed at double the price offered last time."

How we assistant advisers envied Hugh's highlife! He flew even higher than the uranium "yellow cake" was designed to do ... though it was still scattered and stacked in barrels lying casually in the open air in a fenced-off uranium depot on the outskirts of Johannesburg.

The rest of us dealt in more mundane things, like gold. Gold sold at a fixed price of $35 an ounce in those days, and the Chamber had calculated that if it could advance the inevitable doubling of that price by just a single day – it would be worth several million dollars. Therefore the industry was spending money on assistant advisers to hasten the day. But the job was a real slog.

It required getting beyond the world's "gold bugs" – who were over-committed to the cause – and composing persuasive messages and information for the world's unconverted financial movers-and-shakers. Sometimes it involved lavish entertainment, or inviting some of the world's top economists and internationally-known financial writers to share a campfire in one of SA's best game reserves. The anti-fixed-gold-price campaign took years. Then, overnight, the gold price was unleashed and went mad.

We "Assistants to the Industry" had additional, less high-flown duties than altering the gold price and selling uranium, however. We used to keep a check on the fleet of passenger prop-planes that ferried "I–*must*-go-down-a-goldmine" international tourists to the great new mines suddenly opening up on the furthest reefs, where the sightseers would least affect production. It was a hugely costly operation. Just sending them down in skips to 3000 feet underground cost, in lost time and inconvenience, hundreds of rands for the cage-drop that was counted in seconds. Each of countless tourists also received a free return flight to the mine, free lunch, free protective clothing to wear underground, and free drinks.

It wasn't always worth the effort. After a seven-hour day, climaxing in the usual dramatic gold-pour of molten metal, I once heard an American woman ask in a penetrating voice: "Is this a diamond mine, or what?"

And once, when a young woman began to scream as she rode down an incline shaft of an old mine, the female guide accompanying the tour had to slap the tourist out of her hysteria.

"It was a rat! A rat fell off the rock roof and down my blouse," she claimed.

"Nonsense," said the no-nonsense woman in charge of tourist visits, defensively to the mine manager at lunch. "It could only have been a little titmouse."

Regularly through the year I escaped the humdrum routine of conducting around the mining industry financial journalists from across the capitalist world, or writing endless articles comparing Man taking one step on the Moon, with Man pioneering another step deep into the Earth. (The environments that had to be pioneered 13000 foot underground were as hostile and as dangerous to man as those in Space, requiring new, unique technologies and engineering that had to be developed locally on site ... there were no other world experts.)

The illusionary gift of gold

Fortunately I shed office-wear and goldmine-issue boots to settle occasionally in the Chamber of Mines' luxurious new apartment and presidential suite overlooking the ocean in faraway Cape Town. This was the time when goldmines, which had been up to their necks in ultra-deep levels of borrowed investment funds, suddenly reached a moment of dizzying prosperity never attained before or since.

The market for uranium exploded – and now, as the control of the price of gold was on the eve of being unleashed and soon would be moving rapidly from $35 to $40, $50, $60, then $70 an ounce, mines watched their thin margins of profit double overnight; then re-double and continue re-doubling until they were confident enough once again to bet multi-millions on exploring for minerals more deeply and more widely. No longer was it necessary to rely on by-products such as silver, or "sidelines" such as coal to survive.

South African gold, especially with the by-product of uranium, was undisputed king of world mining, and the Chamber of Mines (at the urging of our James Bond man, Hugh the Uranium Adviser), changed its lowly bureaucratic style and established a luxury office near Parliament and presidential suites on the Atlantic shoreline. Three PR people were needed to take turns to run it. This was a job suited to my abilities. It did require some boring stuff, like keeping a watch on labour relations and industrial legislation and foreign affairs policies and other political trends and relaying the industry's views to the antagonistic Minister of Mines at Parliament.

However, my main task, it seemed to me, was to keep two people happy: the butler and the cook who serviced the Chamber's new parliamentary "penthouse". Actually it was on the third floor, but the Austrian butler, of minor nobility and with his austere, looming bulk and magnificent white mane, used to overawe visitors merely by answering their knock at the door. The French cook was excitedly divine with her luscious dishes. Both were too perfectly cast to last.

Soon he was replaced by a less overpowering, more solicitous English butler who had been a violin player in a London orchestra and trained in "house service" in the Counties. The new cook was his homely wife whose to-die-for dishes surpassed those of her predecessor. (And the French wine cellar in the apartment not only improved, it no longer "leaked".)

Her *piece de resistance* was to serve a full, garnished seafood meal for 12 within the confines of the shells of 12 and more giant, fresh lobster. I loved the French dry-whites that William served with it. However, my attempt to impress my *former* boss, now the editor of Cape Town's largest circulation paper, with my new living arrangements, failed. It turned out he couldn't eat fish, and he wouldn't drink wine. Other than that, he was too irritated by the smell of money and the presence of the butler to say anything except demand yet another tot of 20-year-old whisky.

It is true that William the Butler could be irritating. One weekend I asked him to pack a sandwich for me to take up Table Mountain. When, at midday, I opened my rucksack on a comfortable ledge above the Atlantic, I was suddenly the target of the mockery of my mountaineering friends. They were amused by the first item I discovered in my backpack, carefully wrapped in crushed paper. It was a silver flask of consommé and sherry, followed by a silver dish with a silver lid containing delicate cucumber sandwiches and cocktail snacks.

Nonetheless, these were minor sins in a butler. During all the hardships and constant activity I had to cope with, he became a stalwart supporter. My routine was daunting. It contained an average of twenty, yes twenty hours of daily activity and less than four hours sleep. The schedule was this: Up early for a giant breakfast on the veranda above the Atlantic waves. Rush to deal with the enquiries, the messages, and all the issues raised by the Chamber's Legal Department, Labour Department, Health and PR Departments, Research labs and others – not to mention the idle thoughts of the President or the Gold Committee.

By 11.30am I would be exhausted by the pressure, and had to be resuscitated by Cook's irresistible morning tea in all its glorious presentation. Then off in the Chamber's august automobile to lunch somewhere, in town or along the Cape coastline, discussing matters with "contacts" or checking on the daily events with members of the Parliamentary Press Gallery.

Lunches with amiable "contacts" seldom ended before 4 or 5pm .... Hurry back to prepare for the arduous nightly events. Dinner at seven. Just time for a quick nap, to catch up with the previous night and to be woken after an hour by William, offering some miraculous beverage to restore and maintain an overworked man's health.

"Is it dinner here or Bishopscourt, William?"

"Not here, sir. You mentioned earlier the Mount Nelson."

Fast shower while William sorts suitable wear from my old suitcase or items he has unpacked into a cupboard, then off to dinner and a party – or worse, dinner and show, with pre- and post-parties. Back as early as 3am but certainly before Cook's special breakfast.

On the last night of my month-long watch on political affairs, I staggered home exhausted at mid-afternoon.

"Tell Cook no dinner tonight, thanks William. And no drinks. I need to sleep. Or to stare at the wall."

"Rather stare at the sea, sir, while reclining on the veranda. The sunset will cheer you."

Two hours later William was back, his presence signalled by the proverbial cough. "No dinner sir, as you wished," he said apologetically. "But 'cook' is certain that if you partake of a little of this. It will do wonders."

I finished the whole lot of course. What else can you do with two dozen oysters, a smidgeon of smoked salmon with caviar, and clinking bottles of strength-giving Guinness stout?

That's how I vaguely remember it all. It was too good to last. As was the inflated profitability of the mining industry in a world where oil cost less than $2 a barrel.

And, definitely, the financial highlife was too good for my body to last. (The short, profligate era of active gold and uranium marketing by the Chamber could not last long either. Its Cape Town office returned to a drab "normal"; never to reach such heights again.)

Before that happened, I received a call from Aubrey Sussens, a colourful, bigger-than-life, journalist who took to PR and made so much money he decided to retire to London – taking his Rolls Royce and African valet with him. Both became disillusioned and both soon returned to Africa where Aubrey, among many things, represented the Nieman Fellows of Harvard University in the US.

"Harvey! What the hell are you doing with the Chamber of Mines in Cape Town? You're supposed to be heading for Harvard University in Cambridge, Boston. You were nominated and accepted as a Nieman Fellow months ago."

"Would you believe it! I'll drop everything and try to get there right away."

"You can't now. You're a bloody capitalist, not a journalist anymore."

That certainly gave me pause, as they say. Deep, introspective pause. No point in reminding him that he was "a bloody capitalist" too … but rich.

It was soon after this that I was approached by George Palmer, the brilliant editor of the *Financial Mail,* for which I had been his freelance Natal correspondent. He had succeeded the first editor of the publication, and was now moving to America. Would I like to take over the editorship? Writing and editing articles about Finance? About Money? I knew as little, and now cared less, about both than I did about deep-sea fishing. And fishing, I remembered, had just made me nauseous only three nautical miles out of Hout Bay the previous night.

It was then I learned a new and vital newspaper technique from George – a man who knew nothing about newspapers, a man who had moved to the *Financial Mail* directly from the Stock Exchange or thereabouts. The job he was offering me was easy, he said.

George had discovered perfect weekly journalism by himself, or from his staff. "When you want relevant information from any financial enterprise or businessman, get his most direct competitor to provide the questions," he said.

George's offering was tempting, but I knew I didn't have the right qualifications or interest. I did not wish to work under drawn-out weekly deadlines, or be restricted to one specialised subject. I yearned once more for the daily "sixty-minute countdown", for the hurly-burly of action in news production, instant debate, planning investigations, exposing the unrighteous and beating the censors, chasing frantically those deadly afternoon deadlines. In a word, I was homesick.

Swallowing my pride, I knocked on the door of the Managing Director of the Argus Company. The occupant was now Layton Slater, a newspaperman *par excellence* – though never a journalist. It was easy to see, without him ever suggesting such a thing, that his life was dedicated to truth, honesty, protecting journalists and enjoying cricket, horse-racing, and fighting for a free flow of news unstained and unstopped by politicians, advertisers, businessmen, or dictators and robber barons.

"I can't give you back the job you left," he said. "And I can't pay the ridiculous salary you're earning. I cannot even place you at the same level as those who have advanced since you left us. But I'm sure I can find an editor of a daily who will give you the chance to catch up."

So there I was, after only a couple of years, back in Cape Town of all places, on pitiful pay with a wife and three children to feed. My title was Assistant *to* the Editor. My job consisted of all the Editor's minor tasks that he hated – including dealing with complaints and the constant arguments and accusations of the Zionists and the Islamists in the community, accusing each other of criminality and lying, and accusing the newspaper of favouring their enemy and never reporting their side of the case.

That was 50 years ago, and I have the feeling that the current Israeli-Palestinian conflict in the Middle East broke out right inside my cubbyhole in *The Argus* building, within shouting distance of the Finance Editor's office.

I was suffering at the time from too much religious bickering; too many petty Letters-to-the-Editor and too little salary. But at least I had accepted that, in choosing a life, money wasn't worth much, and never is. □

37.
Dreams of Academe in the cherry fields.

*When I hear somebody sigh, "Life is hard,"
I am tempted to ask: 'Compared to what?'*

Sydney Harris, New Yorker cartoonist.

After missing out on a priceless year at Harvard University, my mind turned increasingly to the thought of a life of pure research in the tranquil fields of academe. I knew there was no chance of that ... until, by pure chance, I found myself there for a while.

In the year that Dr Verwoerd was removing South Africa from the increasingly antagonistic Commonwealth, I was chosen (I know not how nor why) to be my country's last Newspaper Commonwealth Fellow.

Each year a top senior journalist was selected in Australia and Pakistan; India and New Zealand; West Africa and southern Africa; or Canada and elsewhere in the Commonwealth to study Britain's press, parliament, industry, and universities. We worked on different British newspapers for several months, but came together as a group to study at Oxford.

My dream came true in the "digs" I was allotted. They consisted of a spotlessly clean attic studio with a pointed ceiling which temporarily housed my Oxford living quarters-and-study. The well-appointed attic overlooked a cricket field bordering on the tree-lined Thames where we Commonwealth "flannelled fools" might play against other Oxford pick-up sides. We would spend Sundays at a favourite pub on the opposite river bank. The other six days a week we would study, debate, and write papers on the socio-political and economic consequences of creating a European common economic zone, proposed but not yet named, let alone accepted in principle. Studies at all sorts of levels were being held all over Europe.

The best part of each working day occurred when we joined the college dons and academic staff for sherry in their common room. The common-room debates among professors of widely differing disciplines were cut-and-thrust duels that were rapier-sharp and fascinating, and highly entertaining for outsiders ... though some ripostes were almost cruel enough to draw blood. We observed in academic society both insecurity and arrogance as well as much skill – and much deep-seated frustration.

The most revealing moment in the staff common room came one evening when my best friend among the Commonwealth group, deputy editor of a Nigerian newspaper, whose skin colour was blacker than mine was pale white, suddenly put down his sherry and pointed at the door where a stranger to us had entered. My friend's face contorted with ironic anger as he shouted: "Ibo man!"

In the silence that followed, I whispered: "So you know that man?"

"No, I don't. But in my country there's no mistaking an Ibo."

Such racism seemed inexplicable in a colleague so good-humoured and erudite, whose father was a well-known Nigerian diplomat. It was a racist remark I was never able to forget. What I did soon forget was my hankering for a serene life in academe.

The Cost of Good Living

It is true that money cannot buy the best things in life. Often money cannot even buy the little things the rich might enjoy on their day off ... things that many journalists get without ever being asked to pay.

Journalists rely on variety and luck in place of money. I made very little money in all my years in the game, and hardly cared until retirement – when I finally went into orthodox work as an over-paid "consultant" to international investors.

Earning money, I then discovered, was easier than I had believed ... but I also learned that money bought very few of life's "cherries", certainly not the kind I had accidentally enjoyed. Such as:

Hailing the Chief

This "cherry" appears again in another context in a travel book which, given enough months of semi-clarity, may follow ...a warm memory in the cold, snow-covered wastes above Moose Jaw, Saskatchewan, where I met a real "Indian" Chief (today carefully and colourlessly described as a "First Person" of "First People", or a "First North American', or some such). He lived in a cabin on stilts above the snow, and he ruled his fellow tribesmen in a Reserve where every individual received generous government grants. I asked him what he did with this lifestyle out there in the wilderness.

He replied: "We eat people who come here and ask stupid questions."

He hated his state grant and confined lands. I took to him instantly. Also to my guide, his beautiful daughter, who yearned for the past and its First People's values, and the physical and spiritual tests to which tribal "braves" once subjected themselves. Though ostensibly a delicate, nubile female, she yearned to test herself as a "brave"; pitting herself against old tribal warrior lore and its direly painful physical trials of endurance.

A dry cherry

Searching for two thirsty days for a beer – and finding it through the good grace and hard work of my teetotal host – at a restaurant above Salt Lake City. But only one beer.

He wanted me to meet the head of the Mormon Church. "I'd have to stay another day", I objected (thinking of their Prohibition). "Is he important?"

My sophisticated host looked shocked. "Next to the Pope or Christ returning, he is the most important man on Earth."

This startling perception was a reminder to my host of his duties and liquor did not pass my lips for another two cocktail hours and dinners.

A Double Take

Witnessing the launch of the world's first vertical takeoff fighter aircraft at Farnborough Air Show. This was significant for me because it taught me something about perspective and context in photography. It also taught me the lesson that rarely do the arts of photography meld with the preoccupations of a reporter.

I was allowed onto the tarmac for a close view, and to capture some of the early public images of the first vertical-takeoff aircraft as it reached 30 feet from the ground. Then I waited at the landing spot, beyond the picket-fenced crowds, to get another precious shot of the pioneering hovercraft returning to Earth.

The lesson I learned: maintain perspective; don't waste so much time. Without being able to capture movement, photostills that illustrate vertical hovercraft taking off and landing are impossible to tell apart ... *Duh.*

Farming it Out

After a long night in Munich's *um-pah-pah* beer halls, another touring journalist and I were hauled from our beds by a guide taking us to interview the Bavarian Minister of Agriculture. The interview began in desperate silence. Then I triumphantly summoned sufficient wit to say: "Mr Minister, I know nothing of agriculture. But my friend here is from a great agrarian country, and if you will permit, he will ask all the questions today."

Champagne at the Ritz

Interviewing the manager of "our" hotel in London: "Delighted to be your guest. Can you tell us why – apart from the orchestra, the cake forks, the cucumber sandwiches – this event, "Tea at the Ritz", is so famous across the world? …. Is that so? …. But you don't normally serve this champagne at these soirées do you? Never knew that the Ritz had its own Ritz-labelled champers …. Better than Dom Perignon, you think?"

Preferable to the Ritz, and the Savoy, and even the laid-back Athenaeum hotel, was this editor's privilege of reciprocity with several famous West End clubs. I remember being in the library of one of the most exclusive of them one day when members were raising their voices beyond the permissible whisper and saying things like:

"Well, he may be a decent fellow, but he's not one of us."

"Communist or not, he shouldn't come here. Rules are rules."

I knew they weren't talking about me because I could see they were debating *The Times'* report that the leader of all Russia, Gorbachev, would be staying in these august premises during a visit to London.

"The club will be crawling with bodyguards and spies and whatnot," pointed out one member.

"There'll be gawkers crowding up the street and newshounds baying at our door. It's not right," said another.

"Either the committee must resign, or I shall," said a senior member.

I felt I was listening to an extract from a PG Wodehouse satire.

My own favourite "gentleman's club" was tucked behind Buckingham Palace; the delightfully simple, comfortable Caledonian. It was not the least stuffy. Even back in my time they allowed members' wives to stay there. Of course women had to use a separate side entrance in order to avoid the bar area and library. They had to reach the breakfast and dining area from the opposite entrance to the members. And they had to keep their voices down. It was all very quiet and civilized – until wives departed (through the side door) and loudly uttered their thoughts.

Having now named the club in writing, I suppose I shall not be able to return there.

Hunting the Quark

Good fortune allowed me to wander only briefly into the world of gold and uranium mining, then to live long enough – another 50 years – to see the Higgs Boson finally found. In linking those two events I was thrilled to discover that I have had the rare privilege of actually witnessing mankind's hunt for the Quark!

And not only the shy, lonely Quark, but also the Neutrino and the Proton and the latest, rarest of particles that are the seeds of the existence of the Universe, now slightly better understood by mankind.

Back in the 1960s I understood nothing of this. The Quark and the Neutrino would not be discovered until the next decade ... but scientists were already looking for the first signs of the little beasts. All I could make out when visiting East Rand Proprietary Mines (ERPM), the world's deepest mine at the time, was that men were going down into the dark to look for something so small that it had no weight and could not be seen. The Quark would be lighter than light, according to one miner watching the hunt.

"So? How are they going to find it?" I asked him.

"Dunno. There's no one there at the moment, but I've been told to take you down so you can see – or, rather, not see – for yourself".

We were both already dressed for the descent. ERPM's deepest human-access level was several shafts and nearly four kilometres down in increasingly hot rock. The visit to the "Quark trap" required a long, apprehensive walk along an ill-lit, deserted tunnel. No one normally came here. Hot rock was the least of the problems. This was deepest – and oldest – of all giant goldmines in the world. Its problem was the weight it had to support in its depths. I'd already trained myself in visits to other deep mines not to think about the weight above your head when walking towards, or crawling into, a stope, and not to worry about rockfalls. But this was different.

The whole point was the depth of this non-workplace underground. It had to be so deep that only a little Quark or one of God's other little particles could slip unseen through miles of solid rock and become isolated enough for its presence to be detected, perhaps. So deep, I unfortunately knew, that the amount of pressure not only increased the likelihood of rock falls, but of rock bursts from *below*. It was easy to imagine how one might be squashed, as flat as a fly between bricks, as the floor exploded and hit a too-heavy falling ceiling.

Why didn't the miner accompanying me – or the absent scientists – think of this? No imagination, I imagined. Yet, when I saw the "Quark trap", I realised you needed more imagination than I could dredge up. We were staring into a caged recess in the passageway where a dark tank of water stood. Nothing moved, least of all the measuring instruments one thought one could faintly discern. We stared in long eerie silence, then turned and hurried away.

"Satisfied?" asked the miner,

"Nothing to see," I confirmed. "What do they expect to find?"

"Dunno," said the miner, pausing only to adjust his headlamp and tie up one of his protective leggings. "If there's nothing to weigh, I suppose they hope to trace movement that will show up as tiny, separated streaks in the dark. That's what I hear."

Well, it was more than we could see … until the next century, on 12 July 2012, when the serious overseas newspapers, God bless 'em, carried carefully prepared coloured diagrams of the entire linkup from Atom and Electrons to Neutrinos and Protons to the Photons and Bosons and the "final" Higgs Boson which completed the theory of "force carriers" that gives mass to matter, creating gravity and reining in the exploding universe.

Now, as I write this, more than 50 years after the Quark was found (but not seen), the hunt for a tinier *Pentaquark* (an anticipated one-fifth the Quark's "size") has ended at last. The little non-particle, according to today's reports, has been identified, but of course remains permanently invisible.

Life's discoveries, you'll agree, remain a constant and fascinating marvel.

In the matter of mining, I count it a privilege to have been in at "below-ground floor" so to speak. Also, to have made several other visits to ERPM and to greater mines such as Western Deep Levels … an enterprise costing multi-billions in today's terms, and a huge financial risk only one man, Ernest Oppenheimer, would be prepared to take.

Acting on incomplete evidence and an apparent "balance of probabilities" he created a monster mine, requiring technologies still being developed in the manner space-travel technology was simultaneously being pioneered in the 1950s.By 1984, Western Deep had produced ten times more gold than he had hoped. Sadly he died before the very first ounce of it was brought to the surface.

Don't look for happiness

It was Stendhal who wrote that those who have known "the feeling, or sensation, or joy" of happiness four or five times in their lives should feel gratified.

Only five times?

Yet Stendhal led a full life, nearly sixty years. Marched under Napoleon to Russia (and back, lucky boy). Served as a diplomat in sunny Italy. Wrote famous books under the pseudonym Stendhal, and was both a famous and notorious womanizer nearly all his days and nights. Died on the eve of his 60th birthday. Cause of death: venereal diseases. Obviously strove too indiscriminately for gratification.

However, I believe that self-gratification of any kind is a small, often dubious reward in life. Even when it results from adventure, novelty, risk, and discomfort. Better to count ourselves lucky when we recognise and enjoy unexpected, challenging, or novel experiences that result in warm encounters and happy memories. There should be – not five – but thousands of them. Here's one:

Cherry on the Top

One of the sweetest cherries in my life came after a rugby match in 1995; the one which President Mandela attended and which, within a decade, had become a political cliché.

I had retired from *The Star* and from the board of the Argus Newspapers Company when it sold to Independent Newspapers. A kind colleague, Peter Sullivan, knowing that the new asset-stripping owners of our newspapers would not welcome me to *The Star's* executive suite at the Rugby World Cup Final in Jo'burg in 1995, arranged for me to have "the best seat in the house".

It was an open seat at ground-level on the halfway line, just behind coach Morné du Plessis and the Springbok reserves waiting to replace the weary and the wounded in the greatest sporting event yet encountered in a brand-new democratic South Africa.

The first novelty occurred on the sideline near my seat. Zulu tribal dancers gyrated and waved their weapons as the New Zealand All Blacks confronted the 'Boks with a Maori war dance. White rugby fans sang an old Zulu song. A giant Boeing in South African colours slid over the stadium rooftops like a metal lid, momentarily cutting out the sunlight and momentarily freezing out all other sound and movement.

The All Blacks all-time giant wing, Jonah Lomu, was soon tearing down the touchline trailing clinging tacklers behind him. At the last moment, flyhalf Joel Stransky sent the ball steeply upwards above the desperately outflung arms of jumping forwards. The ball seemed to reach the height of the long-gone Boeing before dropping between the goalposts and crowning his country "world champions".

And there at the prizegiving was broadly smiling Nelson Mandela, in Springbok cap and No 6 jersey, throwing up his arms in pure joy.

But the sweetest moment of this memory came afterwards, as the crowds left the arena in shuttle buses. We drove in convoys for about 10km, through Jo'burg's inner suburbs, skirted the city centre via Hillbrow's crest, then into the western suburbs beyond the universities and showgrounds where our cars were parked. Our progress was impeded the entire length of the route as the "white" suburbs erupted in black faces. Multi-hued suburbanite crowds took to the streets to join in shouting, waving, singing, and impromptu dancing.

In that moment an entire nation of people with 11 official languages, plus half-a-dozen more home-language tongues from India and Malawi to Portugal, were suddenly fused in an expression of inexplicably shared joy. We were, for one day, One Nation. The moment of sharing was unforgettable for everyone who witnessed it, better – if that can be imagined – even better than exercising freedom and equality on election day 1994.

When is so ecstatic a celebration by all in South Africa to be repeated?

The *Vrot* Ones

Journalism has granted me three thousand, two hundred and four such cherries. There's no money that can buy this stuff.

Admittedly, there are many *vrot* cherries as well. Really *vrot* ... an expressive word that translates into English as "rot" or "rotten", but with much wider connotations than the English term, ranging from slightly slushy overripe to seriously, stinkingly decomposed. I'd like to advise my grandchildren that these *vrot* ones need to be buried as soon as possible, in order to make room for more fresh ones, which of course are available in all our lives.

Early on I was lucky enough to discover that if you want the beautiful fresh ones, you have to go out on a few limbs and shake the branches. Then the cherries simply fall into your lap.

Money can't buy them, but I learned that you need to recognise them instantly and value them immediately for what they are, despite the *vrot* ones. Enjoy them, and record them. Because when you get really old, your memory will refuse to recall them properly.

On the other hand ... while cherries help balance our lives, seeking them as a concentrated diet is as delusional as eating Marie Antoinette's cake before the French Revolution. We need to remember, for instance, that our fathers who lived – and died – in the 20th century witnessed wars and civil and economic disruption for 50 years. And South Africans, black and white had the misfortune of living in a land for most of the next 50 years filled with prejudice and hate; guilt and anger; racialism and despotism; deprivation or indignity at home or abroad.

They lived – as we still do – in a land of inequality and lacking education.

So what are we to do?

Perhaps the first thing we might do is to remember and hold up as our national heroes all those – of all colours and cultures in South Africa – who struggled constantly for justice and peace. Those precious few of all colours and prejudices who, like President Nelson Mandela, devoted lives to self-sacrifice for the sake of friends and enemies and in the cause of justice and democracy.

Mandela demonstrated that there are and have been such people in deed and purpose, and that they need to be held up as a new nation's heroes. Let me now offer a few samples. □

38.

A pantheon –
to honour the past
and alert the future.

Hero worship is strongest where there is least regard for human freedom.

Herbert Spencer 1820–1903.

Heroes in battle and militant leaders of struggle for a national, ethnic or ideological cause are easily recognised and remembered by history. But vital peacemakers are often ignored even though they are more numerous – and often more enduring and courageous – than national heroes.

Nelson Mandela belongs to both categories of course, and for this reason became the world's foremost hero and more especially the champion of peace and reconciliation.

William Schreiner (centre, seated) with South African Party leaders, and activists, including John Tengo Jabavu, Walter Rubusana and Abdurahman in the delegation which lobbied the London Convention on Union for the multi-racial franchise. INSERT: **Pixley Ka-Isaka Seme**, *Lawyer, journalist, author and founder of ANC.*

But who should be remembered as the practical peacemakers?

There could be many nominees.

However, I believe there is a need for the names of all those who deserve remembrance to be gathered in a single, abiding and distinguished pantheon. It is their work that ought to be displayed as a reminder to younger generations – and as a shield against future race hatred.

A proposed pantheon of such public-spirited people seeking peace will require, at the very least, an independent, Wikipedia-style website to which all have access and ability to motivate, (and challenge) the nomination of potential candidates.

Over the years, going back to the creation of South Africa, it is easy to create a list – far too long to detail – of South Africa's courageous peacemakers; those who devoted their lives to peace and justice for all.

I believe a hundred or more might qualify for proper or renewed public recognition and, sometimes, a place in SA's history.

A digital pantheon recording the ideas, deeds and energy of those who struggled for peace, justice and reconciliation might resemble, in different ways, the Helen Suzman Foundation that works today for those precise values. It would be a popular South African pantheon which all school history teachers might visit and register online.

The pantheon would exist mainly for one reason, best described by Alfred North Whitehead, the economist-philosopher who said after World War 2: *"The deliberate aim of peace very easily passes into its bastard substitute, Anaesthesia."*

Honoured in that "Pantheon of Reconciliation" might be former famous figures such as **Mahatma Gandhi**. The memory of his work as young man in South Africa is already fading and already insufficiently remembered today. Despite his preoccupation only with the plight of the Indian community, he is a good example because he stood for reconciliation and peace in all his world-recognised struggles against oppression.

Alfred Xuma (commonly called AB), the leader who resurrected the ANC in the 1930s, is another. As an earlier chapter here records, he not only built up the ANC into a relevant force, adding the Youth League and Women's League, but he sought top candidates to rival him for his position in re-aiming the ANC's policies in positive fashion. All his life he argued, organised, and advocated peace and equality for all ... decades before Mandela.

Prof Jan Hofmeyr, university vice-chancellor then Minister of Finance in Smuts's government in the 1940s is a third sample. I know this from personal observation, for I was reporting some of Jan Hofmeyr's speeches in the late 1940s, and writing about him since the 1950s when Alan Paton published Hofmeyr's biography. In it **Alan Paton** (sufficiently well-known in the history of SA literature) praises Hofmeyr's championship of equality and non-racism when it was still just a vague idea in white South African politics.

Hofmeyr said three or four generations ago: "Colour and colour alone should not be the yardstick by which people are judged ... (in) the political and economic life of our country."

In practical political terms, this was radical, even subversive, coming from a white South African back then. He was half a century ahead of his time when he uttered the optimistically prophetic words: "One day South Africa will be governed by our principles because there is no other way it can be governed."

His view was promoted by the active leaders of the much maligned, threatened and banned members of South Africa's Liberal Party at the time. These are the ideas and values that animate the SA Constitution's vision – that are the central thread of the open, opportunity society for all.

It is important to remind ourselves that they were not given life by the Freedom Charter or the founding of the Progressive Party in 1959. They go much further back. In fact they stretch back almost 200 years and belong to a political tradition twice as old as that of the ANC, which was also seeking the same ideals in the 1910s.

The basic ideas of justice for all was rooted in South Africa by the likes of **Dr John Philip,** who championed racial equality at the Cape in the 1820s. Also the heroic and unsung Cape Attorney-General and constitution-maker, **William Porter.** And **Andries Stockenstrom**, who campaigned for representative government at the Cape in the 1850s and lobbied for *a non-racial franchise* which was granted in the Cape in 1853.

Adam Tas, John Fairbairn, and **Thomas Pringle** fought for a free press and an end to slavery. Their legacy lives on, though less robustly, in the second decade of the 21st century.

The founders and modern leaders of the ANC are already – and justly – ensconced in our popular history, but not all, and not all the black newspapermen, such as **John Tengo Jabavu** and **Sol Plaatje** and their contemporary African activists who were ready to listen and negotiate for the sake of peaceful political progress at every stage.

Going back – perhaps too far – one might consider **Chief Moshoeshoe** who met the "mighty king of the Zulus" and Faku, Paramount Chief of the Pondos, and Sekhukhune, a leader in the Northern Transvaal. He also sent envoys to the chiefs of Bechuanaland and other areas urging them all to "unite, and not fight" with the educated leaders of their people, outside of tribal rule. Moshoeshoe, regrettably did not accomplish his dream of equality of rights among the tribes and others across all of southern Africa, but his fight in favour of that vision remains relevant and still needs recognition today.

Pixley Seme, among those who founded the ANC seems underrated in the public consciousness today. It was he who opened the "Native National Congress" meeting with the words: "Chiefs of royal blood and gentlemen of our race," and warned that it would be difficult to reach agreement when this was "the first time that so many elements representing different tongues and tribes ever attempted to co-operate … in one great house". Seme identified their common cause as creating African unity "for the purpose of defending our rights and privileges" against whites who had "formed what is known as the Union of South Africa – a union in which we have no voice in the making of laws and no part in their administration".

It was the above-named group of journalists and activists who drafted a visionary constitution, calling for "co-operation between the Government and the aBantu Races" and for better understanding between the white and black inhabitants of South Africa. A call which, for very different reasons, is still relevant today.

Also to be recognised now should be the leaders among the teachers and preachers who sought – peacefully and with infinite patience – justice and equality before a South African nation was even mooted.

There are many other obvious candidates down the years whose deeds and ideas should be honoured in our society for the sake of peace and constant reconciliation in the future.

I am tempted to name a short-list of 20 people, brown, black, and white – unbiased, non-violent men and women who fought for justice and the rights of all whom I watched closely in action during the four decades of apartheid rule. They include peacemakers of all religious, non-religious and political persuasions – among the bravest being those who opposed the prejudices of *their own* people, churches, and parties, such as those under Verwoerd. A number of Afrikaners, beyond just the martyrs, could play a role in any pantheon. Their contribution is all the greater because of their courage in stepping outside of their own passionate culture. Frederik van Zyl Slabbert comes to mind instantly … a leader who resigned as head of the Parliamentary Opposition to seek a more positive way for change and by reaching out to the banned black nationalists. There are other white Afrikaans politicians and preachers, rivalling the numbers of "heroes" of other cultures, who sacrificed their own heritage to help others. As would other successive leaders, or those acting in other organizations such as the Five Freedoms Forum, the non-violently active leaders of the Mass Democratic Movement, the United Democratic Front, and the Black Sash.

A history of African journalism in SA

The story of African journalism in southern Africa is already being rewritten to rid it of its colonial myopia according to a new study group. This should be welcomed – even if it is biased to match earlier bias by "European" historians.

Better still, would be a history written by journalists dedicated to truth, rather than an academic exercise in "giving confidence to black people", as suggested in a radio interview by the project's organizers recently. The history of African journalism in South Africa, from its beginnings at the founding of the nation a hundred years ago to the disappointing disaster of President Zuma today, is a huge and inspiring one. It features enough talent, drama, courage, victimization and triumph to fill a thick book … without any need for reassuring propaganda.

I was unable to trace the early history I sought, but there are several African editors and commentators who could write it. After much research I published some extracts about early black journalism in a semi-fictional form in order to popularize the bigger story of the creation of the 100-year-old nation of South Africa *(Blood on the Path)*.[1] The factual heroes of that historical novel need to be considered in any formal list of South African journalists, as well as candidates for naming in any roll-call of national heroes. There is motivation aplenty in *Blood on the Path,* and the names include, in no particular order: John Tengo Jabavu; already mentioned journalist freelancer Solomon Plaatje; writers and activists of that time including AK Sogo and (The Rev) John Dube, communicating with paramount chiefs such as Dinizulu and Sigau.

And now let me name just three great peacemakers who are not required in any list of national heroes, but who are nevertheless due for more recognition than they have received in the ranks of journalism.

Leading, disadvantaged and brave journalists, well-known within their profession and never forgetting true moderates risking their lives – not for war, but for peace – such as **Percy Qoboza** and **Aggrey Klaaste.** Good, amiable friends of mine, making no claims to heroism, despite their dogged defence of truth.

If I am going to name friends I must also refer you to the silent white newspaper editor who sacrificed his career to protest, on principle, his newspaper proprietor's move to destroy editorial independence: **Richard Steyn,** editor-in-chief of *The Star* in 1991. His heroic stand on the principle of *editorial* independence is scheduled for another book of mine on the media and their future. Returning to a search for emblematic national figureheads, let me single out a little-known, politically-discredited leader who deserves true national recognition.

A Zulu working between Zulu enemies

Dr Oscar Dhlomo is my most likeable yet unlikely candidate for nomination as a national peacemaker. He was bent on reconciliation to end hate and violence, and to benefit his enemies as well as his supporters.

He is an unlikely candidate because he was the deputy of Chief Mangosuthu Buthulezi's Inkatha organisation, which fought the ANC for power before the first democratic election. The battles went on in "the killing fields" of KwaZulu-Natal, and in the streets of Johannesburg where peace was the last thing on the minds of the kerrie-wielding warriors.

Deeper research into the life of the late Oscar Dhlomo is required from those who would judge him, but my experience of him suggests that he was an extraordinary model worth following. Oscar, when I learned of him, was conducting *"the only peace-making game in town"*, I wrote in the late 1980s, when secrecy in tentative negotiations with the ANC abroad were dominated by assassinations, murders, and mass killings at home.

There wasn't another peacemaker in sight.

Oscar had been elected the chairman of a think-tank to which all parties, including ANC representatives "in disguise" were invited to discuss, over just two or three days, the possibility of peace in the zone then known as Natal and the "homeland" of Zululand.

The Nationalists representing President FW Botha's apartheid government were highly conservative Natal people. All the other delegates – young and old, rich, poor, left-wing and rightwing – represented interests in conflict with all the others. But Chairman Oscar Dhlomo simply kept them making their speeches until they at last began actually talking to each other.

The conference went on for a week. Then another week. And another. The delegates complained to their supporters, to each other, and to the press. Finally they were all either seduced by Dr Dhlomo's patience, or became addicted to the reconciliation business.

Either way, after *six* weeks of constant daily, formal debate and after-hours discourse, they came up with a miraculous plan. It was an offer of peace and even prosperity to all Zulus and "Natalians" – black, white, brown, and Indian; rich and poor; academics and the millions unable to read.

The plan was to "free up" the "black", "white", and Indian areas officially demarcated in Natal and in the Zulu homeland, by becoming an integrated independent federal province. It would declare Durban a "Free Port". It would impose its own taxes and create its own (non-apartheid) laws. It was a rich, radical dream that even the "racist" government's delegates eventually wanted.

President PW Botha rejected it instantly.

I expect Inkatha and the ANC also repudiated their delegates' decisions, because their own warring factions wanted to do it *their* way.

Oscar, I felt at the time, deserved something much bigger than an "Oscar" for his patient reconciling and peacemaking. When his plan was rejected by all the main black and white party leaders, he turned his considerable talents to improving education in Zululand. But again he was let down.

The hidden heroes of South Africa's greatest moment in history

One of the men involved in a key moment in SA history already has a famous record in several parts of the world for his legal abilities, his role as a reconciler, and his extraordinary mastery of administration.

Yet most people are unaware – as I was – of his abilities when he was called upon to manage, hands on, the first-ever democratic election in South Africa. Despite those ongoing "killing fields" in the streets of Johannesburg and in "Zululand"; despite rumblings among the Pan-Africanist Congress and the Afrikaner Far-Right, the 1994 general election in South Africa became probably, the first unchallenged, efficient and fair national election run in all Africa and much of the world.

The view that a prophet is seldom recognised in his own country applies ominously to **Mr Justice Johan Kriegler**, the man who ensured South Africa's peaceful transfer of power in 1994. His legal knowledge, his organisational skills, his experience, and his principled judgements have been sought and praised only internationally.

He has been asked for advice from troubled or emerging nations across the world – from Afghanistan to Zimbabwe; from Angola to East Timor; from Sierra Leon to Iraq. He has been there, and to many other troubled states – to help them in their searches for democratically lawful and hopefully lasting peace.

He is known as an enemy of undemocratic leaders and a champion of justice. He has crossed swords with dictators like Mugabe and far less evil semi-dictators such as President Mangope of Bophutatswana ... yet he is not officially welcome at home.

The serious matter, though, is that he is the most formidable individual challenger of autocratic government anyone is likely to meet. He is more than that. I don't know him well, but I watched him daily at close quarters as he and Judge Dikgang Moseneke, one of the drafters of the Constitution,performed the miracle of creating, controlling then launching South Africa's first democratic election two decades ago – a feat perhaps in several ways unparalleled anywhere.

"A miracle" they called it the day after that unforgettable election. A miracle that brought cheers from the whole world and tears of joy at home, with little recognition for the man who ensured it would actually work.

The amount of effort required to organise simultaneous voting across a modern, industrialised Third World country that was still threatened by violent rebellion from right and left, and from separate groups of black and white extremists, has never been properly acknowledged. Nor has anyone remembered the reluctance of the threatened "all-white" civil service at the time … the people who would be responsible for orderly voting.

On his side Johan Kriegler confronted, then accepted, the cooperation he was offered by everyone and every interest group including the ANC and the National Party and perhaps the most influential of all at that moment on that issue: "Big Business", which was ready to pour in millions of rands and thousands of staff and untold resources and skills from the communications industry to create awareness and to calm the populace. It turned out to be a key role. The campaign was – and it remains – the biggest bipartisan political operation in the sub-continent's history.

The sloganeering was about *"Participation, Goodwill, Prosperity,"* and the campaign involved any volunteers who could devote considerable time and skills, as well as private funds.

Judge Kriegler, heading up the work of the Independent Electoral Commission of 1994, came to the weekly meetings of organised Business's seconded helpers known as the National Election Executive Committee. As an independent volunteer who also served on that committee, I was amused to see how top businessmen reacted to the judge's dictatorial no-nonsense style.

He offered orders more than gratitude to very generous Big Business. And he worked fast. He came to the meetings to ensure there was political neutrality in the movement, and to make clear the urgency of the task.

Millions of first-time and often-illiterate voters had to be taught where and how to vote. Thousands of electoral officers and their helpers had to be trained. Transport to the polls of millions of people in distant areas had to be ensured.

All of us, even the willing but discomforted Big Business leaders, grew to admire Judge Kriegler's sense of judgement and his dedication to excellence, justice, and equality, if not his abrupt, often world-weary, paternal manner.

The results still speak for themselves.

Judge Kriegler, who had been appointed to the Bench by the apartheid government he palpably opposed, found his personal mission in political transformation. He is one of the small band of figures that should be considered as the "main man" in a true pantheon of the women and men who ensured the founding of "the New South Africa".

Without the calming spirit and inclusive embrace of all South Africans by Mandela and without his leadership and that of "the resident president", de Klerk, there could be no election. And without the belief and judicious efficiency of Johan Kriegler, the election might never have been an overwhelming, peaceful and undisputed one.

However, without a third hero, the democracy which all South Africa voted for might have stuttered and failed after little more than a decade.

It is the wisdom, the courage, the leadership, but mainly the principles upheld in every circumstance by mainly two men that protected democracy during the reformation of SA and the early corruptive years of President Zuma.

Africa's champion of Justice

The man who shared Judge Kriegler's responsibility in bringing SA to an unchallenged and peaceful day of voting for democracy is former **Deputy Chief Justice Dikgang Moseneke.** Whatever the future may hold, history has ensured that Judge Moseneke already has an astounding and unique place in it. This was acknowledged by all sides in South Africa from the day of his retirement from the Bench in mid-2016. I remember in the last century, before he took his place on the Constitutional Court saying to him: "You are going to be Chief Justice one day; you will hold the fate of our country in your hands."

I was wrong, because not once, but twice, he was bypassed by the ANC Government – for fear of his independence. Despite this, Dikgang Moseneke as Deputy Chief for much of his 15 years in office, became the acknowledged champion of justice, and not only in South Africa. He also brought awareness of true jurisprudence to a number of other nations on this continent.

All this from a boy who went to jail at the age of 15, accused of terrorism! A youth who gained, from Nelson Mandela and other fine minds in prison, an education that led to Dikgang learning Latin and several other languages and gaining a BA degree in English and later an LLB before leaving prison on Robben Island.

The rest, as they say, is history; already attested and on the record for all to see. But I believe there is more to come from this astounding man. In 2017 he was already occupied in an official role dealing with South Africa's cardinal problem of the past – and of the future: the quality of education under dubious government administrations.

Developing situations within the democratic state may prove that Moseneke's name and the names of the **current Chief Justice of South Africa** and several outstanding members of the Bench and Bar will need to be considered for any mooted "Pantheon of Peace". ☐

1. *Blood on the Path* by Harvey Tyson (Springbok Press 2009).

39.

Choosing champions to stand beside Mandela.

There is only one thing here worth minding
and that is to be able to be true and just,
and to show charity, even to the untrue
and the unjust.

Marcus Aurelius. Bk6,47.8 b.121 d.180.

I t is not for want of quotes that I repeat from Chapter 7, the Marcus Aurelius statement above. It is the theme of this memoir, which suggests that, for any community of many hues, it is essential to foster the thoughts that unite them; forgive the hurts which, if cherished, are inclined to damage their personalities. We need also to embrace the same symbols, and I am suggesting – even if it is only as a pastime at first – that we should search history to identify our true and greatest common heroes. Who would you put at the top of your list? (Don't say "Trump". This is serious.)

For the sake of South Africa's constitution, its peaceful progress, its search for an ideal "Rainbow Nation", and for the sake of every individual, I believe South Africans should focus very sharply on a common culture and history even before we manage to throw off the blanket of blind racism that is being offered in many quarters, including some of the media that encourage hysteria over racial incidents that are bound to continue. We need to reduce the issues that divide us and focus on the values that bring us together ... something much more than the lists canvassed tentatively in the previous chapter.

We might create, for instance, an Olympian-style **"Winners' National Gallery"**, led by the figure of Nelson Mandela of course, and joined on the lower platforms by three or four more champions ... real heroes, acceptable as the defenders of a common culture embracing all sections of the nation; all ages and genders and seeking support for the poor and disabled ... those kind of heroes.

Is it possible to find such icons who are acceptable to all, and without reservation from any meaningful group? These "winners" would not be our easily recognised popular idols, those that fight power in a single act on behalf of justice, or those of admirable courage who are instant heroes. Such bravery is a shifting gift, spent sometimes in a spontaneous act in which he – or she – risks her career or freedom.

Helen Suzman

Sol T Plaatje

John L Dube

Ahmed Kathrada

Archbishop Desmond Tutu
(Source: Benny Gool)

Nelson Mandela

Popular heroes plunge into flames or raging torrent to save life. The hero, more than a heroine mindful of family, does so instantly, at risk of death to save the life of another human being; possibly a stranger of little worth. It is the spontaneous physical act that is admired; deservedly. It is the mark of brave humanity.

A true leader of the top order on the other hand, may have to test his inner mind; combat doubts and fears in solitude for years; wrestling with conscience; considering options; weighing consequences. Even a natural-born leader, adopting the role with ease; grabbing the reins and leading many followers loudly and joyfully, may fall into an ego-pit of his or her own making. True leaders, it seems, instinctively avoid those pitfalls. They exercise patience and test their judgements. They seldom think of themselves. They are constantly aware of others needing help.

In short, it seems to me that true leadership is not a matter of personal courage and passion, but of moral courage and compassion. True leaders forge social, not military history and nowhere is this better illustrated than in the very brief recorded history of South Africa where people of countless cultures of Africa, Asia, and Europe, speaking many more than the 11 official languages of the country, have all struggled, conquered and/or suffered. Those true leaders who have stood the test of time have all bridged – not defended – the interests of race, wealth, or power. Some of their names appear in the previous chapter, and you will immediately think of course of many others, beginning with those masters of compassion, **Mandela** and **Gandhi**; then of lesser brave mortals such as **Archbishop Tutu** or the martyr to vicious violence, **Steve Biko**, founder of the Black Consciousness Movement, **Sol Plaatje** or **John Dube**, two of the founders of the ANC or one of your own personal favourites whom you believe is a top national hero. Only since the 20th century have women been able to display leadership across the board, and I have in mind two modern women, one named **Helen Joseph** (the other heroic Helen is featured in an earlier chapter and of course I would wish to see **Helen Suzman** deservedly placed as a No3 in a democratic South Africa's iconic roll of honour).

However the individual whom topicality favours is **Ahmed Kathrada,** who walked the long walk to freedom in Nelson Mandela's shadow and whose entire life was devoted to the ideal of non-racism. He is a strong contender for second place among, say, four who might stand below the nation's existing icon. There are dozens more whose lives were an inspiration and who deserve consideration for a place on a representative platform of champions of the multicultural nation.

To start the difficult choices, let me begin by focussing on just one possible candidate who is totally unknown to the vast majority of people today. He was a single, small, fragile poet, whose compassion was greater than his considerable courage. His moral aims and achievements remain as great as those of any celebrated "hero" in the world, though his early concerns focussed on his family dependants and on the nameless poor, such as this lost, lonely child with his pet springbok:

THE BECHUANA BOY

"Poor boy," I said, "thy native home
Lies far beyond the Stormberg blue
Why hast thou left it, boy! to roam
This desolate Karoo?"

The boy describes how the *"Bergenaar"* tribal robbers came in the night, burning down the huts and slaughtering every man in the village, then carrying away those women and children still alive. After driving their captives across the "roaring dark, the broad Gariep" river – and drowning some – they sold the rest to

"The White Men gathered round;
And there, like cattle from the fold
By Christians we were bought and sold,
Midst laughter loud and looks of scorn –
And roughly from each other torn.

"My Mother's scream so long and shrill
My little Sister's wailing cry,
(In dreams I often hear them still)
Rose wildly to the sky."

After further verses about bitter hardships, suffered alone in slavery under a white sheep farmer, the Bechuana boy says:

"While friendless thus, my master's flocks
I tended in the upland waste.
It chanced this fawn leapt from the rocks,
By wolfish wild-dogs chased;
I rescued it, though wounded sore
And dabbled in its mother's gore;
And nursed it in a cavern wild,
Until it loved me like a child.

"... When suddenly, with haughty look
And taunting word, that tyrant took
My playmate for his pampered boy,
Who envied me my only joy."

The child runs away again, with his springbokkie.
Sooner rather than later, he meets the narrator, and explains:

"For I am in the world alone."
Such was Marossi's touching tale.
Our breasts they were not made of stone:
His words, his winning looks prevail –
We took him for "our own".
And one, with woman's gentle art,
Unlocked the fountains of his heart;
And love gushed forth – till he became
Her child, in every thing (sic) but name.

"One" was the poet's second woman, presumably, who "adopted" the boy
and the springbok fawn. (She was the companion of the poet and his wife
and travelled across southern Africa with them.) The poet is at pains to
show that he has not, in any guise, become a slave-owner.

The poetry is not quoted by me for its worth as art, for I disagree
with many critics who praise his verse without reserving such praise
for a few of his lesser-known sonnets. The "ballads" being quoted here,
however, emphasise the author's *empathy* as leader of a vulnerable family
group facing hostility in a wild and empty land. His interest encompassed
all those he believed to be unjustly treated.

THE SAN (my title)

Let the proud White Man boast his flocks.
And fields of foodful grain;
My home is 'mid the mountain rocks,
The Desert my domain ...
The crested adder honoureth me,
And yields at my command
His poison-bag, like the honey-bee,
When I seize him on the sand.
Yea, even the wasting locusts' swarm,
Which mighty nations dread,
To me nor terror brings nor harm –
For I make of them my bread.

Thus I am lord of the Desert Land,
And I will not leave my bounds,
To crouch beneath the Christian's hand,
And kennel with his hounds:
To be a hound and watch the flocks,
For the cruel White Man's gain –
No! The brown Serpent of the Rocks
His den doth yet retain;
And none who there his sting provokes,
Shall find its poison vain!

Optimism overtakes empathy here, as it does when the poet discovers a Xhosa warrior's heart:

THE KOSA (sic)

... Bright gleams the fire: its ruddy blaze
On many a dusky visage plays.
On forked twigs the game is drest;
The neighbours share the simple feast:
The honey-mead, the millet ale,
Flow round – and flow the jest and tale;
Wild legends of the ancient day,

Of hunting feat, of warlike fray;
And now come smiles, and now come sighs,
As mirth and grief alternate rise.
Or should a sterner strain awake,
Like sudden flame in summer brake,
Bursts fiercely forth in battle song
The tale of Amakosa's wrong;
Throbs every warrior bosom high,
With lightning flashes every eye,
And, in wild cadence, rings the sound
Of barbed javelins clashing round.

But lo, like a broad shield on high,
The moon gleams in the midnight sky.
... 'Tis time to rest: The mat is spread,
the hardy hunter's simple bed:
His wife her dreaming infant hushes
On the low cabin's couch of rushes ...

The poet has been there, has he not, filled with awareness and sympathy. Yet his poetry continues to burst forth in every direction. He rhymes the feelings, for instance of a white widow, fearing each hour the attack of some Khoisan or some black warrior. He goes on a thrilling hunt by summoning friends "with musket and spear" to join them hurriedly "when lion is near".

Call Arend and Ekhard and Groepe to the spoor;
Call Muller and Coetzer and Lucas Van Vuur.
Side up Eildon-Clough, and blow loudly the bugle:
Call Slinger and Allie and Dikkop and Dugal;
And George with the elephant-gun on his shoulder –
In a perilous pinch none is better or bolder.

The wounded lion nearly proves a match for all of them. One of the hunters, Bezuidenhout, sprawls and falls under its paw ... but the other hunters suddenly focus coldly. *Together* they fire unerringly at the killer to save their clumsy friend.

> *... Now, boys, let us dine,*
> *And talk of our deeds o'er a flask of old wine.*

Warm, comradely escapades for the poet among Boer and Brit and brown and black hunting friends, as well as servants.

But such empathy is superficial. There are deeper, darker shades where the boundaries lie – or where the lines imposed on leadership are deliberately crossed:

> *He bids me call you forth,*
> *bold sons of Kahabee,**
> *To sweep the White Men from the earth,*
> *And drive them to the sea:*
> *The sea, which heaved them up at first,*
> *For Amakosa's curse and bane,*
> *Howls for the progeny she nurst*
> *To swallow them again.*
>
> *... Then come, ye Chieftains bold,*
> *With war-plumes waving high;*
> *Come, every warrior, young and old,*
> *With club and assegai.*
> *Remember how the spoiler's host*
> *Did through our land like locusts range!*
> *Your herds, your wives, your comrades lost –*
> *Remember – and revenge ...*

*Kahabee or Kahabiis considered the patriarch of all the Xhosa border clans.

Perhaps our poet meant to write "avenge", but no matter, for this was unpublished verse; portrayed in the *style* of Shakespeare's stirring exhortation by King Henry of England leading his troops to war. In comparison with the "Immortal Bard" our poet here is a pigmy when describing a relatively modern scene: the African warrior summoning his troops to battle. However it memorably demonstrates again the poet's empathy, and he would have known, being South Africa's first independent journalist, that it was but a shadow of reality. In reality, in his

British colonial world, a call of that nature was incitement to violence; not tolerated by any state anywhere. The poem was nonetheless a significant demonstration of his capacity to see *both sides* of a violent issue.

It also foreshadowed his absolute determination never to brook censorship or curtailment of free speech, so prevalent and generally acceptable in real life in his era.

Man of many colours

The poet stood on one leg; his other life-long shrivelled leg dangling; his hand-carved crutch pointing ahead as he surveyed the *poort,* the formidable mountain pass, at the entry to his new home in a forbidding, empty valley long ago abandoned by temporary human occupants. Tom Pringle's party, after *six months* of travelling in small ships, wagons and on foot, was reaching the approaches to a patch of land promised them beyond the legendary Baviaanspoort – "Baboons' Pass', he called it. He saw the baboons watching them from perches hundreds of feet up the cliffs soaring above the astonished settler party as it inched its way over the boulders of the riverbed in hired wagons precariously over-filled with life possessions. It took the wagons *five days* to struggle up the few miles of the neck of the pass.

Fortunately neither he nor his brothers and cousins and wives and children knew that they would be forced to live in crude tents for another six months. Every member of the extended family was intent on what Pringle later described:

> *"... the mountains, again converging, left only a narrow defile, just broad enough for the stream to find a passage; while precipices of naked rock rose abruptly, like the walls of a rampart, to the height of many hundred feet, and in some places appeared absolutely to overhang the savage looking pass or poort, through which our wagons struggled below, our only path being occasionally the rocky bed of the shallow river itself, encumbered with huge blocks of stone which had fallen from the cliffs, or worn smooth as a marble pavement by the sweep of the torrent floods."*

The driftwood, hanging high on the rocky walls and in the branches of willow trees told an eloquent tale of its dangerous, obliterating floods. Later, while settling in the valley beyond, Pringle had another eloquent tale: The rains came, so heavily it was difficult to keep the watch fires burning. At midnight the silence was suddenly shattered by the roaring of a lion close to the tents.

It was so loud and tremendous, that for a moment I actually thought a thunderstorm had burst upon us. But the peculiar expression of the sound – the voice of fury as well as of power – instantly undeceived me ....

It was quite unlike the sound of a roaring lion in some Zoological garden, he explained. It was a "voice in a state of freedom and uncontrolled power".

As partyleader, he must have felt an exaggerated weight of personal responsibility for having persuaded his Scottish clan to follow him to a new life in "a strange, barbaric land". However he only hints at his own disabilities, struggling over rough terrain, trying to help farm virgin land while carrying one or both of his crutches to support a leg, withered since babyhood when his nurse dropped him by accident, and didn't admit to his fall until it was too late to treat the damaged limb.

And this is just the start of Thomas Pringle's story

He decides his party is better off in terms of governance, than are the rest of the settlers nearer the coast. After several years of intense pioneering and learning to adapt to conditions of sowing wheat and Scottish seed in Africa, he finally leaves his Pringle-family party of a dozen men and a dozen wives and children, and sets off for Cape Town to take up, as a life-long cripple, his promised job in Cape Town.

In getting there he furnishes another reminder of Africa two centuries ago, by travelling by wagon across the Great Karoo, instead of returning by sea to Cape Town. Beyond Beaufort, he and his wife and travelling companion were soon delayed in desolate Karoo country, where on one day they counted "32 skeletons of oxen, picked clean by hyenas, and where no human habitation was seen for four successive days".

(This last quote is not directly from Thomas Pringle's *Narrative*, but from letters quoted in Jane Meiring's *Thomas Pringle, His Life and Times*, published by AA Balkema 1968.)

The slight, crippled figure of Thomas Pringle directly spurning not only the insults but the cajoling of Lord Charles Somerset, autocratic descendant of the Plantagenet kings, is the climax to a great event in African history – lonely defiance of the colonial ruler Lord Somerset in a campaign to launch a free press in Africa.

The full passion of press freedom is also directly verbalized by this poet in words every 21st century independently-minded journalist might use today. The words can be found in various published versions of his "Narrative".

Yet he is hardly known to South Africans of the 21st century ... despite his heroic eloquence; despite his figure as a slight, crippled man determined to go angling, hunting, farming – and even climbing mountains, with or without his crutch ... and despite his detailed observation of people who happen to be "Hottentots", "Bushmen", "Caffers", "Boers", and even Englishmen, all of whose features and actions this ardent Scotsman describes without any awareness or word of racism.

His story is not only relevant for today's world, but is also filled with colour. His courage is tested far more in the safe haven of colonial Cape Town than in South Africa's wildest territories. This is because he takes up a job as a public servant – a government librarian – vouched for him because of his physical handicap, as it was accepted before he left England that he would not be able to work on the land with his family. But librarian was too small a job for him. He dreamed of publishing a newspaper and starting an education centre.

The opportunity arises when his friend from Edinburgh University, John Fairbairn, finally joins him in Cape Town as once promised. They meet the Reverend Dr Abraham Faure of Cape Town's *Groote Kerk,* who is also interested in an education centre. Then Pringle launches what may be the continent of Africa's first newspaper, the *South African Journal* and Dominee Faure launches a similar title in Dutch, *De Zuid-Afrikaansch Tijdschrift*. But, despite all efforts not to cross swords with Lord Charles Somerset, ruler of the Cape, the inevitable clash soon occurs. Lord Somerset will tolerate a "tame" publication only because the Earl of Bathurst in London has decreed it. Pringle will tolerate only the truth in his paper.

A face-to-face clash is inevitable. Pringle records the meeting, adding: "But this attempt to cajole, when he found he could not bully me, disgusted me even more than his insolence. I saw the motive, and despised it: I saw the peril too, and feared it ... I resolutely declined therefore, his repeated invitations (to recommence publishing) unless *legal protection* were granted the press."

The struggle to report real news continues, until Pringle not only sees his and Fairbairn's publication summarily closed down by Lord

Somerset, but also their source of funding – the popular Educational Centre – also shut down by government order. Finally Lord Somerset, as Cape Governor attempting despotic rule, banishes Thomas Pringle. The story of course cannot end there either. Pringle's partner, Fairbairn, is finally able to re-open their press and Lord Somerset is recalled to London. Pringle, meanwhile, has moved to another calling as secretary of the anti-slavery movement in Britain. He lives only just long enough to see his most cherished life-wish attained: the legal banning, throughout the British-influenced world and empire, of slave labour.

Fortunately Pringle happens to be one of the best-chronicled figures in South Africa's early recorded history. There are at least two contemporaneous "Narratives" on his life-work. Among government papers there are many records of his fight with Lord Charles Somerset. There are also several modern versions of his work, one of them by Randolph Vigne, founder in the 1960s of the African Resistance Movement.

Another source is *Thomas Pringle in South Africa* by Professor John Robert Wahl, of Cape Town, Oxford, Yale and Orange Free State Universities, who spent the last 20 years of his life researching the deeds of Thomas Pringle. Prof Wahl focuses entirely on rendering accessible Pringle's final "Narrative" ... which unfortunately lacks the exuberance and colour that Janet Meiring brings to the subject by using Pringle's contemporaneous letters and more than 60 other references. There is also the biography John Fairbairn by HC Botha, published by the Historical Publication Society 1984.

History correctly records that it was his more pragmatic friend John Fairbairn who technically and in practical, inoffensive terms established the right of freedom of expression for the English, the Dutch, and the isiXhosa readers in the British Colony of the Cape nearly 90 years before South Africa was founded. But it was Pringle who fought – and won – the battle.

Freedom of expression and freedom of information have been under threat ever since, even under our state-of-the-art democracy. Journalists of all cultures of the South African Broadcasting Company were risking their careers in opposing censorship even in late 2016.

In the light of all this, the anti-slave hero, the anti-race campaigner; the founder of press freedom more than two centuries ago, must surely be considered among the heroes – the finest leaders – recorded on this African continent. It is the lessons in empathy that he demonstrated which should be remembered by all today. It is the lengths he was prepared to fight for truth and for *two* universal basic freedoms which need to be preserved.

And it was his empathy with humanity – unqualified concern for every individual on Earth – which surely makes his name deserving of great honour in a democracy claiming to represent equality and non-racism. ☐

Acknowledgements

SO MANY PEOPLE have provided support that it is not possible to list them, even if I exclude those already acknowledged in these pages. However several people must be mentioned, for without them you and I might never have seen *The Other Side*.

First is Arlene my wife who has encouraged me and protected me from interruptions throughout my constant writing in general during 8 to 14 hours each working-day for many thousand days.

And Vanessa Swanepoel, talented website designer and manager, who has led me, inch by inch, through a maze of misunderstood digital instructions into a wwworld (*sic*) where thoughts and memories can be held safely in a wild and enigmatic computer. Together we disciplined some of my disorganised digital procedures by trying not to take our project too seriously, or assume it could launch perfectly as a new publication should. Our assumptions were correct. I had far too much to learn too quickly about simultaneous self-publishing and online publishing. So here we are again, thanks to the added efforts and high-quality standards of Robin Stuart-Clark's book designing and printing and to Helen Holyoake's expertise on reaching out to readers.

Gratitude is again owed directly to my wise and argumentative old colleagues, fellow explorers and companions for 60-years: Rex Gibson, former editor of *The Rand Daily Mail* and of the *Sunday Express,* and James Clarke, author and newspaper columnist who happened, long ago with *the Star's* support, to publish two full books of headlines in history.

My family and others who have read and endured many of my writings in the past deserve medals for bravery as well as loyalty. Where, however, do I stop in listing those whom I owe?

Yet stop I must, for now.

H W T